1990

University of St. Francis
GEN 821.1 K39
Kerby-Fulton Kathryn
P

S0-BRF-619
3 0301 00088837 6

Reformist Apocalypticism and Piers Plowman

This is the first scholarly book to pay attention to alternative non-Augustinian views of eschatology and their implications for the study of *Piers Plowman*. Kathryn Kerby-Fulton discusses the major prophets and visionaries of alternative traditions of apocalyptic thought, which are characterized by the denunciation of clerical abuses, the urging of religious reform and an ultimate historical optimism. Her book offers an original proposal for the importance of such traditions, particularly as represented in the writings of Hildegard of Bingen, to the understanding of Langland's visionary mode and reformist ideology. Dr. Kerby-Fulton also explores the relevance of the prophetic mentality fostered by Joachite thought, and the reactionary response it triggered in anti-mendicant eschatology. Above all, this book provides a stimulating challenge to recent assumptions that Langland's views of the course and end of history are wholly conventional, or easily explained by Augustinian eschatology. The outcome of this fresh study of contexts for *Piers Plowman* suggests that Langland's position in relation to different apocalyptic traditions was at once more sophisticated and more original than scholars have hitherto realized.

CAMBRIDGE STUDIES IN MEDIEVAL LITERATURE

General Editor: Professor Alastair Minnis, Professor of Medieval Literature, University of York

Editorial Board
Professor Piero Boitani (Professor of English, Rome)
Professor Patrick Boyde, FBA (Serena Professor of Italian, Cambridge)
Professor John Burrow, FBA (Winterstoke Professor of English, Bristol)
Professor Peter Dronke, FBA (Professor of Medieval Latin Literature
Cambridge)
Tony Hunt (Reader in French, St Andrews)
Dr Nigel Palmer (Lecturer in Medieval German, Oxford)
Professor Winthrop Wetherbee (Professor of English, Cornell)

This series of critical books seeks to cover the whole area of literature written in the major medieval languages – the main European vernaculars, and Medieval Latin and Greek – during the period *c.* 1100–*c.* 1500. Its chief aim is to publish and stimulate fresh scholarship and criticism on medieval literature, special emphasis being placed on understanding major works of poetry, prose and drama in relation to the contemporary culture and learning which fostered them.

Titles published
Dante's Inferno: *Difficulty and Dead Poetry*, by Robin Kirkpatrick
Dante and Difference: *Writing in the* Commedia, by Jeremy Tambling
Troubadours and Irony, by Simon Gaunt
Piers Plowman *and the New Anticlericalism*, by Wendy Scase
The Cantar de mio Cid: *Poetic creation in its economic and social contexts*, by
Joseph Duggan
The Medieval Greek Romance, by Roderick Beaton
Reformist Apocalypticism and Piers Plowman, by Kathryn Kerby-Fulton

Other titles in preparation
The Genesis of Piers Plowman, by Charlotte Brewer
The Book of Memory: A study of memory in medieval culture, by Mary Carruthers
*Rhetoric, Hermeneutics and Translation in the Middle Ages: Academic traditions and
vernacular texts*, by Rita Copeland
Medieval Dutch Literature in its European Context, edited by W.P. Gerritsen,
E.S. Kooper and F.P. Oostrom
Literary Theory in the German Middle Ages, by Walter Haug (translated from
the German)
Chrétien de Troyes and Arthurian Romance: Once and future fictions, by Donald
Maddox
Women and Literature in Britain, 1150–1500, edited by Carol Meale
Dante and the Medieval Other World, by Alison Morgan
*The Early History of Greed: The sin of avarice in early medieval thought and
literature*, by Richard Newhauser
Chaucer and the Tradition of the Roman Antique, by Barbara Nolan
The Theatre of Medieval Europe: New research in early drama, edited by Eckehard
Simon
Richard Rolle and the Invention of Authority, by Nicholas Watson

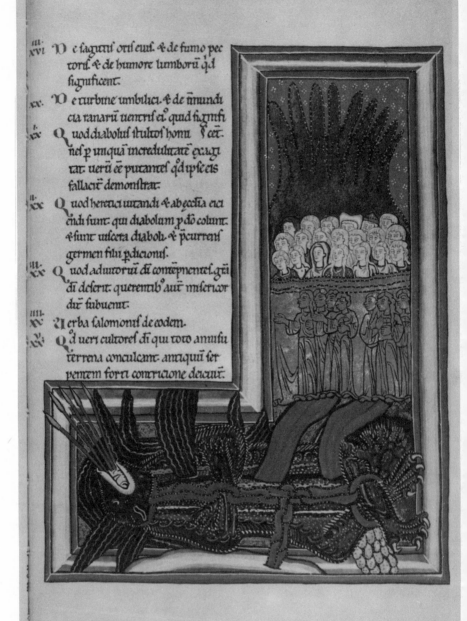

Hildegard of Bingen's vision of the faithful triumphant and
Satan bound (*Scivias* II, 7, from the Eibingen manuscript).

Reformist Apocalypticism and
Piers Plowman

KATHRYN KERBY-FULTON
University of Victoria

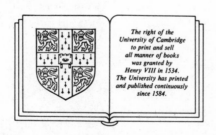

The right of the
University of Cambridge
to print and sell
all manner of books
was granted by
Henry VIII in 1534.
The University has printed
and published continuously
since 1584.

CAMBRIDGE UNIVERSITY PRESS

Cambridge

New York   Port Chester   Melbourne   Sydney

LIBRARY
College of St. Francis
JOLIET, ILLINOIS

Published by the Press Syndicate of the University of Cambridge
The Pitt Building, Trumpington Street, Cambridge CB2 1RP
40 West 20th Street, New York, NY 10011, USA
10 Stamford Road, Oakleigh, Melbourne 3166, Australia

© Cambridge University Press 1990

First published 1990

Printed in Great Britain at the University Press, Cambridge

British Library cataloguing in publication data

Kerby-Fulton, Kathryn
Reformist apocalypticism and Piers Plowman. –
(Cambridge studies in medieval literature; 7)
1. Poetry in English. Langland, William. Piers
Plowman – Critical studies
I. Title
821'.1

Library of Congress cataloguing in publication data

Kerby-Fulton, Kathryn.
Reformist apocalypticism and Piers Plowman/Kathryn Kerby-Fulton.
p.   cm. – (Cambridge studies in medieval literature; 7)
Originally presented as the author's thesis (doctoral–York)
Includes index.
ISBN 0-521-34298-8
1. Langland, William, 1330?–1400? Piers the Plowman.
2. Apocalyptic literature – History and criticism.   3. Langland,
William, 1330?–1400? – Religion.   4. Reformation – Early movements.
I Title.   II. Series.
PR2017.A65K4   1990
821'.1 – dc20   89–9807   CIP

ISBN 0 521 34298 8

821.1
K39

To Gordon

139, 216

Contents

Contents

Acknowledgments

Among the many people to whom I owe a debt of gratitude, I would like to mention the following individuals especially. To Charles Czarski, who so kindly responded to a letter from a total stranger by sending a copy of his entire thesis on the prophecy of Hildegard of Bingen, I owe a special debt. It was Charles' careful and illuminating study which clearly established for me the relation between Hildegard's earlier and later prophecies and I can only hope that it will soon be published so that others can benefit from his work as I have. I would also like to thank Jim Binns of the Centre for Medieval Studies, University of York, for his help with various points of Latin. Also, Dr. Marjorie Reeves very generously read the Joachite section of this study and Dr. E. Randolph Daniel has spent several hours of his time patiently answering my barrage of questions about Joachism; the thoughtful advice of two such historians of apocalypticism makes me feel much more confident about the ideas presented here. I owe a greater debt than I can express to Celia Sisam of St. Hilda's College, Oxford, who, together with Anne Elliott and Karina Williamson, supported me (morally as well as academically) when my interest in Langland's apocalypticism came under attack at Oxford. I would also like to mention here the late John Brückmann, who first introduced me to medieval religious intellectual thought and whose death was a great loss to all medievalists, as is the recent death of Professor Morton Bloomfield, who was a most gracious and generous external examiner of this study at the doctoral thesis stage, now "too little and too lately known." Finally, I would like to thank two very special teachers, Penelope Doob, who first introduced me to Langland and who has provided support and inspiration over the years in innumerable ways, and Derek Pearsall, to whom I owe my greatest academic debt. His tolerance, kindness and scholarly discretion, as well as his great love of *Piers Plowman*, provided just the right atmosphere for the kind of intellectual questioning to which so many supervisors and institutions pay lip service but do not really want in their graduate students.

I would like to thank the Royal Society of Canada, the Canada Council and, initially, my father, for their financial support of my doctoral work, and both June Belton and Colleen Donnelly for their cheerful and meticulous work at the typewriter. I am also grateful to Maureen Street for her patience and care in copy-editing the manuscript. Finally, my greatest personal debt is to my husband, Gordon, who has never failed to provide practical help and moral support through the years that we have both lived with this study. Poor payment though it may be, this book is dedicated to him.

Abbreviations

AFH	*Archivum Franciscanum historicum*
EETS	Early English Text Society
Ep.	Epistle number (in *Patrologia Latina* 197)
MGH SS	*Monumenta Germaniae historica: scriptores*
PG	*Patrologia Graeca*
PL	*Patrologia Latina*
RTAM	*Recherches de théologie ancienne et médiévale*

Introduction

The Prophets Isaiah and Ezekiel dined with me, and I asked them how they dared so roundly to assert that God spake to them; and whether they did not think at the time that they would be misunderstood, & so be the cause of imposition.
Isaiah answer'd: "I saw no God, nor heard any, in a finite organical perception; but my senses discover'd the infinite in every thing, and as I was then perswaded, & remain confirm'd, that the voice of honest indignation is the voice of God, I cared not for the consequences but wrote."[1]

William Blake's perceptive characterization of the prophetic impetus as the "voice of honest indignation" is perhaps the most apt definition one could find for this peculiar form of religious inspiration. All the medieval prophets and visionaries considered in this study were persuaded that the voice of their own honest indignation was the voice of God and that divine indignation would soon spill over into apocalyptic wrath if this voice continued to be ignored. A comparison between such writers and Langland is not invalidated, I believe, by the fact that Langland was less explicit and perhaps a little more uncertain about his prophetic vocation than they were. That all such prophets were plagued by self-doubt at some point is obvious (it is not by chance that even William Blake, the most bold-spirited prophetic writer in the canon of English literature, placed himself as the questioner in the above exchange: "and I asked them how they dared so roundly to assert that God spake to them . . ."). Langland portrays instances in which his right to speak out must be affirmed (xII. 23–38)[2] and in which the worth of his poetic activity is challenged (B. xII. 16–29), but the fact that *Piers Plowman* is as it stands today suggests that such indignation usually prevails and that what is felt to be the truth will out in the end. Although Langland is more a poet than a self-proclaimed visionary or prophet like the other writers discussed here, there is a voice of indignation in certain passages of *Piers Plowman* that cannot easily be explained in other terms. What follows, therefore, is an attempt to study the influence of medieval reformist apocalypticism, and its related traditions, on this prophetic voice in *Piers Plowman*, in the hope that the self-proclaimed prophets and visionaries of the later Middle Ages can illuminate for us some aspects of this less self-proclaimed but equally indignant seer of visions.

We are fortunate to have, to compare with *Piers Plowman*, the explicitly prophetic visions and prophecies of a group of medieval writers who, like Langland, spoke out against injustice and abuse, and envisioned reform. Such writers most often focused their indignation upon the clergy: as the spiritual leaven of all men, a faltering clergy imperilled the entire community; thus the concentration of these prophetic writers on clerical chastisement and reform can be understood as a more central concern than at first it might seem. Among the prophetic traditions explored here as relevant to *Piers Plowman*, then, we will be most concerned with the influence of reformist apocalypticism, with its emphasis on prophecy of clerical chastisement and renewal.

I will argue here that, of the types of prophetic and apocalyptic literature available to Langland, Latin religious prophecy answers the greatest number of questions which the prophetic elements in *Piers Plowman* raise for us, although, of course, it does not answer them all. Langland seems to show little interest in the political prophecy of his day[3] and in spite of the detailed studies of recent scholars, the popular Antichrist lore is of little assistance in understanding either his treatment of Antichrist or his apocalypticism.[4] Langland makes use of biblical prophecy but must go beyond it in order to deal specifically with the issues that concern him most in his prophetic passages, notably clerical reform and the renewal of the *vita apostolica*, first of all in the clergy but also in all men according to their spiritual capacities. The type of prophetic writing which could best meet this need is an alternative tradition of apocalypticism in which a number of apocalyptic events (sometimes even the coming of Antichrist) is projected forward into a period long before the End of the World. This type of apocalypticism usually stems from either exegetical (for example, Joachite) or visionary (for example, Hildegardian) sources; it is clerical in origin and focuses primarily on the state of the Church. This book argues that it is to this type of writing that Langland turned in his sense of current clerical crisis.

However, it was not just ideological material that he found in Latin religious prophecy; he also found long-established literary conventions for the presentation of prophetic, and especially visionary, experience. Any analysis of the medieval religious visionary tradition must take into account the influences of biblical and apocryphal apocalypses on this tradition. Chapter 3 of this study deals with two such apocalypses, those of Esdras and Hermas, and then proceeds to an analysis of two medieval visionary-reformist writers, Robert of Uzès and Bridget of Sweden. The aim of this chapter is to illuminate the conventions of medieval visionary literature, and Langland's use of them.

There is, then, no single type of religious prophecy which illuminates *Piers Plowman*, but rather there are four, and these are reflected in the structure of this study. It begins with an analysis of the Hildegardian visionary tradition, and the related apocalyptic and religious vision literature (in chapters 2 and 3), and then proceeds to a discussion of anti-mendicant "apocalypticism," which is actually a pseudo-reformist tradition (in chapter 4). It then finishes with a study of Joachite prophecy, the most optimistic brand of reformist apocalypticism (in chapter 5). Although the reader will see something of the development of apocalyptic thought in the later Middle Ages, and will learn to recognize recurring patterns and mentalities relevant to Langland, a unified account of the history of medieval reformist apocalypticism is simply not possible here for reasons of the limitations

Introduction

imposed by lack of space and by the current state of scholarship. If the present study is somewhat eclectic, it is because I believe Langland was, and I dare not impose any more unity on these distinctive types of prophecy than the case will bear.

Some definition of terms would be helpful at this point. My sense of the word "apocalyptic" is well summarized in this quotation from a recent article by Marjorie Reeves: "Following the original sense of the word, I take 'apocalyptic' to mean here the disclosure of hidden divine purpose in history, to which common usage has added the dimension of imminent crisis" ("Development," p. 40). "Eschatology" properly refers to the science of the four last things: death, judgment, Heaven and Hell, or, more generally, to the events of the end of history. An apocalyptic thinker is someone who gives evidence of insight into the meaning and course of events which is not apparent to others. When this insight involves a superior knowledge of the last things – and in the Middle Ages this is frequently the case – apocalypticism acquires an eschatological orientation.[5] Finally, "millenarianism" or "chiliasm," derived from the Latin and Greek words for "one thousand" respectively, refer literally to the period of bliss prophesied in Apocalypse 20:1–6, during which Satan is chained in the abyss. More generally, the terms refer to a belief in future blessedness attainable here on earth before the end of history.[6]

Two words in common (and, often, imprecise) use in literary criticism should also be mentioned here.[7] A "prophet," in the popular modern sense of "one who predicts future events," captures only part of the meaning which is conveyed by original use of the term. The older sense of "one who speaks on behalf of God," that is, one who puts God's point of view to a particular (usually straying) people, gives a better understanding of the role and stance of such a figure, especially in biblical literature. For some of the major apocalyptic thinkers of the period, like Joachim of Fiore for example, prophecy took the form of a special insight into the meaning of the Scriptures and into Salvation History itself. Finally, a visionary is "one who has visions; one to whom unknown or future things are revealed"; the term is used in this study with a special emphasis on receiving the communication in a visual way.

"Reformist" apocalypticism is my own term to denote the medieval "school" of alternative apocalypticism which is concerned primarily with clerical reform. This is usually to be accomplished by imminent chastisement, and followed by spiritual renewal. Broadly speaking, almost all these writers are *meliorist* as well as reformist in the sense that they believe in a coming age of spiritual growth during which the recently chastened clergy will shine forth as never before. But within this group two distinct philosophies of renewal can be seen: one, with its emphasis on simple reform, is slightly different from the other, which is more progressivist. A good example of the latter is a writer like Joachim of Fiore, who envisioned the new age not so much as a return to pristine glories (that is, a reform), but rather as the spiritual zenith of all history (that is to say, progress). Although it is important to bear this distinction in mind, the term "reformist apocalypticism" in this study usually denotes a sense of the optimism of renewal as well, because even the

3

apocalyptic reformists who speak most avidly of a return to first principles will also speak as if the future reformed clergy will represent the pinnacle of spiritual achievement for all time. Let us turn now to a more detailed look at this type of apocalypticism before proceeding with the question of its relation to *Piers Plowman*.

THE NEW APOCALYPTIC THEORY OF THE LATER MIDDLE AGES

St. Augustine bequeathed to the Middle Ages the decisive view that the zenith of history had already been achieved in the coming of Christ.[8] As Marjorie Reeves explains, "Others, following St. Augustine, saw the time process as positively decaying, a world grown old whose only significance lay in the miracle of new growth in Christ happening in its moribund carcase" (*Prophetic Future*, p. 2). St. Augustine's juxtaposition of decay and renewal epitomizes the conflict in the minds of Christian preachers and reformers of all ages: how can one reform a world that one must despise and hope, soon, to be freed from? Does the hope for reform clash with a divine plan for the eventual destruction of this imperfect creation? How should one interpret the dark and mysterious references to the End Time in the Bible? Can contemporary prophets and visionaries legitimately add to one's knowledge of biblical eschatology? And finally, perhaps most importantly, is it within the power of mankind to sustain renewal once it has been achieved?

There is a cynicism in the Judeo-Christian tradition about such things and for over a millennium the view that Christians could not hope for much in this aging and torn world held sway. During the twelfth century, however, this began to change. There developed an alternative to, though not a widely accepted replacement for, the old eschatology, the old pessimistic view of a world worsening toward the appearance of Antichrist. The alternative was really more than an eschatology: it was a full-blown apocalypticism. Fueled by urgent desire for Church reform and a desperate need to know the fate of the Christian Church in the divine plan, apocalyptic zealots ransacked every available source for clues that would help them fill in the part of Salvation History which the old eschatology had left blank, that is, the gap between their own time and the coming of Antichrist.

The new apocalypticism, even in all its bewildering variety, is thus consistently characterized by an attempt to understand history in terms of its eventual end by prophesying a complex pattern of events which will occur before – often long before – the End of the World.[9] Perhaps the most obvious characteristic of a "new" apocalyptic thinker is the tendency to create these patterns or systems, which historians of apocalyptic thought tend to call "programs." The motivating factor for each prophet will nearly always be an overwhelming concern with Church reform and the question of renewal: can there be a renewal of the Christian Church or is it already too late? Some found positive answers to this question in new readings of biblical texts or earlier writers, or in visions and revelations, or in inspired interpretations of current history. Some found hope in the new orders of the Church, some found Antichrist himself in them, but the state of the Church's religious orders or of one particular order or heretical group is nearly always at the heart of the apocalypticist's concern.

4

Introduction

Other characteristics that distinguish the new apocalyptic thinkers from their pre-twelfth-century counterparts are related to this obsession with the future of the Church: all feel that there has been a crisis of leadership, especially in religious affairs, and that leaders from the Pope down to the parish priest have failed the Church. Many feel that it is time to return to the basic principles of the early Church, and hold Christ and the disciples as the perfect, if not the only, models for clerical imitation. Apostolic poverty and simplicity of life and belief become ideological tenets as apocalyptic reformers yearn to rid the future Church of the excess baggage of worldly wealth, on the one hand, and what they see as overweening intellectualism on the other. But though this anti-materialism and anti-intellectualism fuel a sense of despair about the present time, the prophet's zeal for reform always betrays itself in the conviction that there will be at least one period of the future when these evils will be eliminated and the Church will once more enter a Golden Age of spiritual vitality. The most powerful attraction of the new apocalyptic world view was that it gave each writer a chance to write a history of the future. As Beryl Smalley has said of Joachim of Fiore, "Joachim warms the heart of the student of historiography. He stimulated men to speculate on the course of history, to differentiate their own time from others. He provided a canvas on which each could paint his *Weltanschauung.*"[10]

A final characteristic shared by apocalyptic reformers of the later Middle Ages is that, in spite of sweeping visions of the future and extremes of ideology, many were both very realistic and, in certain ways, very reactionary in their treatment of the present time. Whatever new-found optimism they may have held for the future, pessimism regarding the present was widespread and no doubt accounts for the ruthlessly realistic terms in which they handed down judgments on contemporaries, envisioned Church reform by brute force and reacted indignantly to current political, social, and religious events. This odd combination of grim pessimism and tenacious optimism, reactionary indignation and unflagging hope for large-scale renewal is found in some measure in all the reformist apocalyptic writings studied here and accounts for some of the tensions one finds. These thinkers were constantly evaluating both the secular and religious institutions of their day and the mixed results they had from these evaluations brought mixed feelings: the desire to adhere to the time-honored ways was often at odds with the perception that these practices had allowed for current abuses. But even writers like Hildegard, who began as a conservative reformer, were usually driven to admit that, in the last analysis, any practice which contributed toward corruption had to go. One of the most surprising aspects of medieval apocalypticism, despite its associations with the fantastic, is the realism that it often displays, a realism usually based on a profound insight into human nature, politics, and institutions.[11] In spite of the tendency toward dualism in early apocalyptic writings, thoughtful medieval writers do not seem to turn to apocalyptic ideology, finally, in order to place the blame for human problems on huge, supranatural, anonymous forces of Evil.[12] Even when they resort to the rhetoric of dualism, their writings actually show evil as coming from within individuals and human institutions. The apocalyptic crisis you will suffer, they warn the reader, is self-instigated.

In this sense, the apocalypticism is chosen by writers not as a form of escapism

5

from present realities, but as a way of projecting the faults of the present onto a screen large enough for people to realize the implications involved. The choice is dramatic, fantastic, even presumptuous, but the motive is quite practical. Medieval apocalyptic writing, with its belief in a divinely predetermined pattern of chastisement and renewal, acted as a reassurance to the troubled and a warning to the wayward. In this type of writing the future becomes one large exemplum, revealing the implications of present behavior and urging repentance. All the symbolism and systemization are subservient to this end.

Traditionally, the apocalyptic mentality has always differed from the prophetic mentality in that the former is deterministic. As Bernard McGinn writes, "In contrast to the prophetic view in which Nineveh's repentance might stay God's hand, the apocalyptic author saw all real decisions as already made. The Lord might choose to reveal all or part of his plan regarding history's fate, but he does not change his mind" ("Early Apocalypticism," p. 10). However, as McGinn goes on to explain, "World-historical determinism . . . is not individual determinism." Later medieval apocalypticism shares with its earlier Jewish counterpart the call to the individual to make a choice between good and evil, but the extent of its world-historical determinism – or its *interest* in its determinism – is perhaps open to question. Reformist apocalypticism, above all else, urges action, and suggests that any individual in the audience could make a difference to the outcome of events. For where divine chastisement is a certainty, hope and reassurance follow closely behind. This feature links such apocalypticism very closely to Old Testament prophecy while distinguishing it somewhat from both early Christian apocalyptic and the popular medieval eschatology of its day. Roger Bacon, who was one of a disparate group of medieval English thinkers to have been touched by the new apocalypticism, captured this sense of urgency in a letter to the pope written about 1267, in which he urged the study of prophecies

against the comeing of Antichrist . . . if the Church would do all it can, I believe that God would give a fuller revelation . . . For not all prophecies are irrevocable and many things are said in the prophets about the coming of Antichrist which will come to pass only through the negligence of Christians. They would be changed if Christians would strenuously enquire when he will come, and seek all the knowledge which he will use when he comes.[13]

Reformist prophets seem to choose the future, just as Dickens did in *A Christmas Carol*, as a way of confronting the present. For this reason, most medieval apocalyptic theorists are not much interested in the actual End of the World – another feature which is at first surprising. All their calculations and schemes are directed at finding out how much time is necessary for salvaging the Church from the present corruption which engulfs it. This may be, of course, an over-simplification, but it is true to say that, beginning in the twelfth century, the new apocalypticism sprang up as the handmaiden of religious reform polemics, and the goal of reform is always transformation, not annihilation. This, I will argue, is Langland's use of apocalypticism, as a servant to reform aspirations.

Medieval apocalyptic writers, then, brought to their subject some paradoxical

Introduction

features: a sense of realism about current affairs, a desire for activism in meeting the needs of the events and problems to come, and an optimism about the future and pessimism about the present that characterize reforming zeal. One thing which will become clear from the parallels drawn between Langland and the reformist prophets of this study is that this type of apocalypticism is hardly the form of imaginative escapism which some literary critics have assumed it to be.[14]

Whereas the old eschatology, embroidered in legendary fashion around the figure of Antichrist,[15] had been rather abstract and emblematic in nature, in the twelfth century there was a new impulse toward historical realism and immediacy which altered the whole character of apocalyptic expectation in reformist circles. The traditional eschatology, an unlikely mixture of Augustinian pessimism and Sibylline fantasy,[16] had solidified into a well-known pattern, a pattern which became popular even in vernacular texts, and will be familiar to readers of Middle English texts such as the *Cursor mundi* or *The Pricke of Conscience*.[17] At the appointed time, Christendom will be overrun by the sons of Ishmael or by Gog and Magog but will be saved by a great conquering king who will subdue the invading hordes and preside over a limited period of peace and prosperity, which is usually described in materialistic terms. This king will then lay down his crown and be taken up into Heaven. The reign of Antichrist will be a period of unmitigated cruelty with the deception of many Christians and the persecution of the faithful. Elijah and Enoch will return to counter Antichrist and the Jews will be converted before the two witnesses are put to death by Antichrist. They will, however, be resurrected (usually after three days) and Antichrist will himself be struck down by St. Michael or Christ. The Day of Judgment will follow soon thereafter, usually preceded by a version of the fifteen signs before Doomsday. There were, of course, variations of detail within this basic pattern, but the pattern itself was remarkably constant. A great deal of fantastic material became attached to the figure of Antichrist, but the whole effect of the scheme was rather static. There was not a great deal here for those who wished to read the "signs of the times" or work out the historical implications of events around them. Above all there was no special role for the Church other than trying to prepare people for the worst, and no one knew how close or how far away that might be.

It is not surprising, then, that at some point a desire to shift the emphasis of the old eschatology and to bring apocalyptic speculation closer to the present time should have surfaced. Historians have speculated about why this should have happened in the twelfth century, and especially in twelfth-century Germany, where the new apocalyptic thought first appears.[18] Some have cited the development of heretical movements as an important factor. The heretical groups, frequently the product of frustrated reforming zeal themselves, were often seen by the laity as representing everything in the way of good living and spirituality which the orthodox clergy preached but did not practice. The strength and tenacity of the heretical groups proved an embarrassment to the Church and in some areas gave it strong opposition. The existence of the heretics focused attention on the need for reform and triggered a stream of apocalyptic rhetoric as the authority of the Church was seen to be threatened.[19] At the same time the Crusades brought

7

Christians into contact with non-Christian peoples who similarly threatened the universality and even, in places, the existence of the Church. Non-believers had always had a role in traditional eschatology and the new threat brought forth developments of that role. Finally, and perhaps most significantly, in the twelfth century Europe was feeling the effects of the Investiture Controversy and the conflicts between Church and state which it had raised. In the eyes of many, Henry IV had blocked the progress of Church reform and thus set himself up as an enemy of the Church – an Antichrist figure. From another standpoint, the higher profile of the papacy engendered by the reforms of the twelfth century brought another powerful player into the eschatological drama, heightening apocalyptic expectations, as any bid for universal authority (real or imaginary) always does (McGinn, *Visions*, p. 94).

Thinkers in twelfth-century Europe, under the strain of a peculiar set of political and religious pressures, not only turned to apocalyptic traditions but developed and expanded them. Basically, they began to elaborate upon and, in some cases, to challenge the Augustinian view of the seven ages of the world,[20] which is founded on a correlation between the seven days of creation, the six ages of man and the ages of the world:[21]

Day of creation	Age of history	Age of man
1	Adam–Noah	infancy
2	Noah–Abraham	childhood
3	Abraham–David	adolescence
4	David–Babylonian Captivity	youth
5	Babylonian Captivity–Christ	late manhood (*senioris aetas*)
6	Christ–End of World	old age
7	New Jerusalem	

The Augustinian view of world history placed the prime of man or zenith of human history during the reign of David and saw history as already running down by the time of Christ. From this perspective we can see how revolutionary the ideas of latter-day renewal of the twelfth-century apocalyptists were, and indeed, how revolutionary some of Langland's predictions were, for example his notion that there would be the reign of yet another David over a utopian kingdom (III. 440ff.).[22]

The sixth age was the age in which medieval Christians believed themselves to be living. It was to be followed by the End of the World and therefore became the focus of much apocalyptic speculation based on detailed mathematics or new readings of old symbolism. Christ had said that no man would know the day or the hour of His Coming (Matthew 24:36), but for some reason this never prevented eschatological speculation. Vincent of Beauvais, in his *Speculum historiale*, gives us a clue to medieval attitudes on this subject. It seems that, as with so many other rules, this one too had its loopholes: "Qvantum vero temporis ad finem saeculi & aduentum iudicis supersit, certum est neminem mortalem esse, qui nouerit; *nisi forsitan Dominus alicui speciali gratia reuelauerit*" (p. 1324, emphasis mine). Perhaps believing that recent developments in apocalyptic thought amounted to just such a special revelation, he went on to include both Joachite and Hildegardian speculations in his chronicle, thereby transmitting them to a larger late-medieval readership. Excitement about these new ideas is evident even in the cautious Vincent of Beauvais. As Töpfer (*Reich*, p. 47) has suggested, the bland, politically innocuous, wish-fulfillment dreams of earlier Sibylline-influenced eschatological traditions were transformed in the course of the twelfth century in response to the political, social, and religious needs of the time. Leaving behind some of the folklore of a fossilized eschatology, reformist apocalyptic theory developed its own typology which began to be used effectively in the worlds of political and religious polemics – a trend which would continue in the centuries to follow in disputes ranging from the anti-mendicant controversies through to those of the Protestant Reformation.

In summary, then, as later medieval apocalyptic thinkers tried to read the signs of the times and work out for themselves the historical implications of current events, each came to his or her own conclusions and the result is a group of writings as diverse and colorful as the individuals and contexts that produced them. They do, however, show these persistently common features: (1) an urgent desire for clerical reform and concern for the future of the Church, (2) an attempt to fit the present time and coming periods of time into a pre-eschatological pattern, (3) a concern with the state of the Church's religious orders and/or the role of one order or group in particular in the future of the Church, (4) a sense of a crisis of leadership in the present time, especially within the Church, and (5) a desire to return the clergy to the rigorous discipline of early monastic founders or of the early apostolic Church itself, with particular emphasis on poverty and simplicity of life, amounting, in some writers, to a full-scale progressivist renewal. Such writings are further characterized by a persistent mood of pessimism regarding the present (flanked by a marked optimism for some future period) and a sense of grim realism about what will be required in order to enforce reform in the present. Finally, all these writers exhibit a tendency toward conservatism with regard to religious and social institutions, except where these are seen to be corrupting forces and at this point tradition gives way to renewal. Imaginatively satisfying, polemically and ideologically useful, the new apocalypticism was too effective an instrument for certain writers and thinkers to ignore. A writer like Langland, who seems to have had a good eye for the imaginative and mind-stirring riches of many different areas of thought, could not resist it either. In the pages that follow I will show how a knowledge of this material can illuminate certain passages, images, and themes in *Piers Plowman*.

PROPHECY IN *PIERS PLOWMAN* AND THE CASE FOR REFORMIST
APOCALYPTICISM IN THE POEM

Previous scholarship on the question of Langland's apocalypticism has tended to revolve, in sporadic intervals, around a number of key issues: whether the prophecies in the poem are indebted to the political prophecy tradition,[23] or to the works of European religious prophets,[24] whether Langland was influenced by

9

monastic or Franciscan apocalypticism,[25] whether certain passages in the poem or the tripartite structure of the *Vita* itself reflect Joachite influence,[26] whether Langland's stance is prophetic or apocalyptic,[27] whether Langland is a radical or a revolutionary,[28] what the role of the friars is in the last passus of the poem, and, perhaps most important of all, whether the end of the poem portrays the actual End of the World, or an apocalyptic crisis which will be followed – as Conscience's pilgrimage suggests – by reform and renewal. Unfortunately, it is not possible here to give each issue the history and analysis it deserves, but several of these points will be raised at appropriate places throughout this study. However, the last-mentioned issues should be briefly considered here because they are so important to the topic under discussion in this section, and to the argument of this book as a whole.

Critics have been in considerable disagreement about the meaning of the coming of Antichrist and the onslaught of false clerics which Langland portrays at the conclusion of *Piers Plowman*. Criticism of this part of the poem falls generally into two camps. One group espouses the view that the end of the poem is essentially pessimistic and portrays the engulfing of the Church in the grip of Antichrist in preparation for the Last Judgment. In opposition to this group a number of critics espouse the view that the end of the poem holds out hope for a renewal of the Church through Conscience's search for Piers to destroy Pride and give the friars a "fyndynge" (xxii. 381–84). The problem with the former reading is that to assert that Langland is portraying the End of the World in the last passus one must disregard all the earlier apocalyptic passages in the poem and fall back upon the rather strained interpretation that Conscience is going out to seek Piers in the form of the Second Coming of Christ. Even then, one must face the question of why he should bother to give the friars a "fyndynge," which would not be of much use to them at the End of the World. Emmerson, who will serve as an example of one of the recent proponents of this view, asserts that the "conclusion has often been misunderstood because its description of Antichrist's attack has not been interpreted . . . as reflecting the popular medieval Antichrist tradition" (Emmerson, *Antichrist*, p. 193).[29] Unfortunately, critics have all too often shown ignorance of anything *but* the popular eschatology, which in any case does not solve the problems connected with the passage mentioned above – and these are not small problems. Emmerson dismisses Langland's earlier explicit prophecies of renewal with the following:

It is true that the *Visio* also includes a series of prophecies that envision the ultimate regeneration or reform of society (3: 284–30; C. 6: 180), perhaps by a good king or Last World Emperor, but none of these utopian societies are [*sic*] established. Significantly, the characters who predict the *renovatio mundi* in the *Visio* are spokesmen of natural reason and lack the greater perspective provided by the traditional Christian interpretation of history.

(*Antichrist*, p. 194)

He finishes his discussion of the conclusion by merely asserting, rather than proving, that Langland is portraying the coming of Antichrist just prior to the Last Judgment:

Introduction

Furthermore, the ending is pessimistic in that it does not suggest, as Morton Bloomfield and others have argued, that a regeneration of society will follow Antichrist's reign. *Piers Plowman* follows the conservative exegetical interpretations of Antichrist rather than the radical Joachimist expectation of a *renovatio mundi* after Antichrist's defeat . . . On the contrary, the fact that Do-Best is eschatological suggests that what follows "contemporary impiety and sin" is the Last Judgment and not the establishment of a millennial society.

(*Antichrist*, pp. 200–1)

Whether Langland expected Piers to usher in a millennial society such as he describes in Passus III we do not know, but at the very least we know that Conscience goes in search of Piers as an expected leader of clerical (especially fraternal) reform, something which would seem to preclude the Last Judgment's following upon the coming of this particular Antichrist. As we will see, Langland's sense of apocalyptic expectation is far more sophisticated than the popular Antichrist tradition which is the subject of Emmerson's book.

R. W. Frank long ago did a helpful analysis of the views of both the "optimistic" and "pessimistic" schools in his essay "The Conclusion of *Piers Plowman*" and he provides a good, though brief, assessment of the apocalyptic import of both the friars and Piers. Although his notion that Langland uses the term "Antichrist" simply as a polemical label of abuse is not entirely satisfactory, he recognizes that the critical obstacles to the "pessimistic" reading are greater than any which the "optimistic" school has to deal with, the main obstacle being that the "pessimistic" view leaves Conscience's pilgrimage without any meaningful purpose in the poem. He is also correct, I believe, in his assertion that Langland's expectations of reform need not necessarily be interpreted as naive utopianism or Golden Age millennialism. He writes,

Some critics, I have remarked, believe that at the end of his poem Langland despaired of mankind's salvation. The line about the friars, however, reminds us that Langland's despair grows in large part out of a specific evil, the work of the friars, and so his agony, though intense, is not complete despair. Some students find a note of hope and expectation. But the line shows that Langland has for the specific evil a specific remedy, a "fyndyng." So his hopes too are limited and do not require an age of perfection. This is not to deny that there may be chiliastic elements in Langland's poem. Langland did hope for reforms and a better age. But Langland's hopes are embodied largely in the figure of Piers, whom Burdach explains as a symbol of the semi-divine character of human nature. In *Dobest* Langland employs this current belief that man was a mixture of the divine with the human to express the hope that someone – most probably a good pope – can be found to reform the Church and administer properly the Church's power of forgiveness of sins. But beyond this his expectations do not go.

(Frank, "Conclusion," p. 315)

This study will explore the question of Langland's apocalyptic and reformist expectations by placing them against a background of such writings, particularly in chapters 2, 3 and 5. In chapter 4 I will discuss the role of the friars in anti-mendicant "prophecy," which is actually a kind of pseudo-reformist apocalypticism in that the friars' opponents adopted the form and style of truly reformist apocalypticism for their own polemical purposes. Langland's use of anti-mendicant elements, particularly in the final passus of the poem, is illuminated in such a context. I hope

11

that this discussion will be a contribution to the problematic question of Langland's anti-fraternalism, which previous scholarship has found difficult to reconcile with his apparent use of Franciscan ideology, and, more importantly, with his *genuine* concern for the reform of the friars. Such a concern is not part of the anti-mendicant mentality and, as such, it has been too often overlooked in *Piers Plowman* by scholars anxious to fit the poem into the anti-mendicant tradition.

Langland's apocalypticism raises literary as well as ideological questions, and these will be particularly explored in chapters 2 and 3. Previous scholarship has noted the unconventional aspects of the poet's use of the visionary tradition, particularly the ambivalence of the dreamer's self-image, the multifarious voices in the poem's narration, and the incohesiveness and uncertainty of the structure of Will's visions.[30] These questions all relate to Langland's use of the medieval conventions of visionary literature, but criticism has so far tended to concentrate mainly on the secular rather than the religious side of this tradition: that is, critics have been more likely to think of Langland's use of the dream vision in the context of their knowledge of Chaucer's love visions rather than in the context of religious visionary writings (as, for example, those of Langland's contemporary, St. Bridget of Sweden). Given the usual context of the study of Middle English literature within university English departments, this is entirely understandable, and I have no wish to imply here that the secular vision genre is *not* relevant to *Piers Plowman* but, rather, that Langland was aware of *other* models as well – models which may, in fact, have been more pertinent to *him* than they are to modern students of English literature. Apocalyptic writing has a distinctive style and follows some very distinctive literary conventions, among which are an apparent lack of surface cohesion, a particular brand of self-deprecating autobiographical visionary stance, and a shifting use of allegorical imagery. These and other features of apocalyptic writing have given trouble to critics of *Piers Plowman* in the past because they do not admit of exact parallels elsewhere in Middle English literature. It is hoped that some of the comparisons here will open up alternative interpretation to critics of the poem from the Latin visionary literature of the Middle Ages. Many critics have referred to the "visionary" qualities of the poem but there has been relatively little research on the question of what social, theological, and historical significance the concept had in Langland's own time. It is clear that in the Middle Ages a visionary, who was usually a recluse or a member of a monastic order, was someone with a specific role, a vocation in society. Visionaries like Hildegard of Bingen or Bridget of Sweden were asked to give word of God's pleasure or anger, to give leadership to the Church and society, and even to answer specific problems or solve biblical cruces. A visionary such as Hildegard of Bingen carried on a large correspondence, almost as a kind of counseling service which she offered the community. Looking at the life and writings of a visionary like Hildegard not only points up one of the apocalyptic traditions available to Langland, but also puts into context some of the other themes of *Piers Plowman*: the search for authoritative advice, for a reliable counselor or interpreter, and the thirst for interiorized spiritual knowledge. These themes, it is interesting to note, were ones which Langland's imitators were quick to pick up on in poems like *Mum and the Sothsegger* or *Pierce the Plowman's Crede*.

Introduction

Visionaries closer to Langland's own time, such as St. Bridget of Sweden (who was very popular in England in the later Middle Ages), were part of the same tradition. Thus we may take into account in reading *Piers Plowman* the fact that Langland had at his disposal well-established traditions for the recording of visual religious experience, both in contemporary prophetic writings and in early apocalypses, which were by definition visionary works. We need a better knowledge of such traditions before we can completely assess the implications they will have for the study of *Piers Plowman*. The present study is only a start to this process,[31] but suffice it to say at this point that I believe it is no longer good enough to understand the visionary aspect of the poem in the same way as we understand the conventions of the dream poetry of Chaucer. There is evidence that the religious visions exerted their own influence on the poem.

Much has been included in this study in order to illustrate certain similarities in ideology, patterns of thought, expression, and imagery between these writers and Langland, with the purpose of portraying the apocalyptic mentality they shared, rather than attempting to list sources and allusions. Furthermore, although I have tried to indicate the availability of all the works discussed in fourteenth-century England, this does not mean that I am arguing for the influence of any particular writer on Langland. Rather, the study should make clear the influence of certain *kinds* of prophetic and apocalyptic writing on *Piers Plowman*. Source-hunting is a notoriously impractical business in *Piers Plowman* studies, and in the area of religious prophecy scholarship has not yet reached a stage where it is in control of all of its own sources. Perhaps as research in this area develops we will be in a position to name specific sources, but that time has not yet come.

There are a surprising number of problems inherent in a study like the present one, not the least of which is the fact that there was no native tradition of this type of prophecy in fourteenth-century England; one therefore has to assume transmission from the Continent of virtually every prophecy or prophetic writer discussed here. Fortunately, even with the current haphazard state of our knowledge of the circulation of Latin religious prophecy in medieval England, the assumption can be supported by a certain amount of concrete evidence. It may well be that when our knowledge of apocalypticism in medieval England improves, other prophecies than those noted here will prove to have been important to Langland as well.

In this I find myself sympathizing with Morton Bloomfield, without whose work this study would hardly have been possible: "Much is still unknown . . . but if I have been able to direct the investigation of *Piers* towards the right questions, even if I have not provided all the answers, I feel that this work has not been in vain" (Bloomfield, *Apocalypse*, p. 154). Although the present study differs from Bloomfield's in attempting to relate Latin religious prophecy rather than the apocalyptic elements of monastic ideology to *Piers Plowman*, the problems in each case are similar and they are not yet entirely soluble.

There are a number of reasons why the problems inherent in the study of prophetic thought in *Piers Plowman* have not yet been solved, but the two most important are the difficulty in finding clues to Langland's sources within the poem and the chaos of scholarship outside it. Bernard McGinn, a scholar of long standing in the field of medieval apocalypticism, writes of the latter problem:

While several bibliographical and historiographical surveys devoted to Joachim of Fiore are in existence, there is almost nothing which attempts to deal with wider questions of apocalypticism *per se* in the medieval period . . . In terms of the availability of many texts only in manuscript form, the antiquity and inaccessibility of some printed editions, and complicated questions concerning the authenticity and ascription of various works, it is difficult for the scholar to gain the type of control over the sources which would allow him some security in evaluating the interpretations.[32]

The former problem, however, that of Langland's seeming vagueness about the sources of his ideas, is a problem with which all *Piers Plowman* scholars are familiar. And in one sense, it is rather unfair to expect the poem to provide us with clear statements of medieval doctrine, whether they be political, theological, philosophical, or anything else. However, there are a number of definite, albeit fragmentary, allusions in *Piers Plowman* to various prophetic and apocalyptic ideas, although Langland is maddeningly vague in his handling of many of these. About the reason for this vagueness we can only speculate. To me *Piers Plowman* reads like the work of a man whose exposure to books of various kinds was at one time wide, enthusiastic but unsatisfied, unfinished, and, at the time of writing the poem, perhaps not all those books were within reach. It may perhaps be fanciful to imagine his praise of life in the cloister as a wistful memory of a time when the freedom to browse in books was a reality for him and to invoke the metaphor of banishment from an Eden to which there could be no return. Fanciful perhaps, but Langland's use of academic and doctrinal ideas, though often impressively detailed, is sometimes not as directly bookish as one might expect. Working on the apocalyptic aspects of his thought has greatly increased my respect for his erudition, but *how* he used his sources remains something of a mystery.

Another possibility is that Langland gathered some of his ideas from discussions with others. It would be difficult to overestimate the importance of word-of-mouth for the transmission of apocalyptic ideas in the Middle Ages, even among the educated. For example, we have substantial evidence in Salimbene's chronicle of the verbal transmission of Joachite teachings among the friars,[33] and Gebeno of Eberbach similarly describes his first contact with Joachite thought as having occurred in deep discussions with a visitor to his monastery.[34] Furthermore, Holdsworth in his study of medieval visions suggests the importance of the "monastic grapevine" for the transmission of both written texts and oral tales ("Visions," p. 150). Finally, the fact that Langland seems to have made everything he touched his own by the time he had incorporated it into *Piers Plowman* is an important part of our problem with his sources, although this is perhaps a small price to pay for the originality of his poetry.

Still, in the face of all the things we cannot prove or clarify, there are some things about Langland's apocalypticism which we can say with certainty. First of all, Langland deliberately chose to incorporate into his poetry a range of apocalyptic notions which comparable English contemporary writers did not. A number of Middle English writers complained of clerical abuses, but Langland is almost alone

Introduction

in going so far as to prophesy clerical chastisement and reform.[35] Writers like FitzRalph, Chaucer and Wyclif knew and used ideas derived from anti-mendicant writings in a variety of ways, but they did not, as Langland did, draw explicitly upon the apocalyptic strands of the anti-mendicant school. Langland's apocalypticism is so hard to contextualize because most of his famous English contemporaries show little or no evidence of having been interested in it. We still know surprisingly little about the "users"[36] of religious reformist apocalyptic ideas, but we know enough to suggest that they tended to be reasonably well educated and that they almost always wrote in Latin. As we will see, there are only smatterings of evidence, outside of *Piers Plowman* itself and a reformist tract once attributed to Wyclif, that such material had filtered down to English vernacular writers. On the whole, vernacular works in medieval England usually make use of only the popular Antichrist lore and eschatology. Langland's sources had to be Latin, Continental, and clerical in origin and this suggests to me that Langland must have moved, at some point at least, in reasonably sophisticated circles.[37] It would also seem that, in comparison with his contemporaries, both Langland's apocalypticism and his reformist ideology were somewhat radical, though by no means unorthodox.

A study of the actual prophetic passages in *Piers Plowman* shows that Langland dabbled in more than one "school" of prophetic and apocalyptic thought, but only the religious-reformist brand seems to have captured his imagination or shaped his reformist ideology. Before looking at the main traditions or schools of prophetic thought which were current in Langland's time, it will help to outline briefly which elements in *Piers Plowman* might be called prophetic.[38] There are first of all the actual prophecies, among which the most important are Conscience's long millenarian prophecy, which ends in a riddling passage at the end of Passus III, the obscure warning prophecy at the end of Passus VIII (revised substantially from the B version) and the prophecy of religious reform in Passus V (lines 168–79). Alongside these straightforwardly prophetic passages in the poem, there are many related ones which are just as significant for assessing the apocalyptic character of *Piers Plowman*. There are passages of vague foreboding (such as Prol. 62–65), of doomwarning (such as Reason's sermon in Passus V), eschatological exhortation (such as IX. 334–54), and passages of mass devotion or repentance which are typical of (although not peculiar to) apocalyptic prophecy (such as VII. 152ff.).[39] There is Langland's adaptation of a motif found in vernacular prophecy of the folklore variety (based on the *impossibilia* topos) and spoken by Reason in defense of his lack of pity for Wrong, whom the king is about to relegate to irons:

> "Rede me nat," quod Resoun, "no reuthe to haue
> Til lordes and ladies louen alle treuthe . . ."   (IV. 108ff.)[40]

There follows a lengthy list of the social, ecclesiastical and monastic reforms which, if accomplished, would allow Reason to take pity on scoundrels; it is an interesting little piece partly because of its clarity in a genre in which obscurity is the norm, but also because it tells us that Langland's chiliasm (if this is representative) is entirely reformist, and heavily Church-oriented. There is the curious passage that links madness or imbecility to prophecy and the *vita apostolica* in Passus IX, which itself throws up a chain of related passages and poses the question of Langland's awareness of the Spiritual Franciscan and Joachite writings. In a different but equally prophetic vein there are several passages which make use of religious visionary conventions, as we shall see in chapter 3. Finally, there is the Antichrist section at the end of the poem, with its complex use of apocalyptic and eschatological traditions.

Leadership roles in the poem are often apocalyptically significant or suggestive, for example the various kingship roles of David (and Saul) in the prophecy at the end of Passus III, the "reformer king" prophecy in V, the "Last Emperor" role given to Piers in XXI. 426, or even Langland's treatment of Christ himself as knight, king, and conqueror in Passus XXI. The complex figure of Piers has a number of apocalyptic overtones, some quite obvious, like the plowing and harvesting symbolism (which Langland nevertheless understates), and some less obvious, such as Langland's post-Resurrection vision:

> Y ful eftesones aslepe and sodeynliche me mette
> That Peres þe plouhman was peynted al blody
> And cam in with a cros bifore þe comune peple
> And riht lyke in alle lymes to oure lord Iesu.   (XXI. 5–8)

This portrait ever so subtly calls up the apocalyptic associations of the reading for Wednesday of Holy Week from Isaias 63:[41]

Why then is thy apparal red, and thy garments like theirs that tread in the winepress? I have trodden the winepress alone . . . I have trampled on them in my indignation and have trodden them down in my wrath. And their blood is sprinkled upon my garments . . . For the day of vengeance is in my heart: the year of my redemption is come.

(Isaiah 63:1–4)

Langland's tendency to understate certain kinds of apocalyptic or eschatological elements is a point worth pausing over for a moment. There are several examples of this throughout the poem, for instance in the mere mention of Saturn in the prophecy at the end of Passus VIII:

> Ac y warne 3ow werkmen, wynneth whiles 3e mowe,
> For Hunger hiderwardes hasteth hym faste.
> He shal awake thorw water, wastors to chaste,
> And ar fewe 3eres be fulfeld famyne shal aryse,
> And so sayth Saturne and sente vs to warne.
> Thorw flodes and thorw foule wederes fruyttes shollen fayle;
> Pruyde and pestilences shal moche peple feche.   (VIII. 343–49)

Saturn figures in a number of such foreboding prophecies[42] and as Bloomfield pointed out (*Apocalypse*, p. 212) it was thought that Saturn would be in the ascendant on the Day of Judgment. Furthermore, Saturn has another eschatological connection in that he is often represented with a hook because he "repeþ down grene thyngis"[43] through his pestilences and misfortunes. In the image of the falling of the fruits from the Tree of Charity there is similarly an embedded

16

Introduction

eschatological motif of the cutting down of "grene thyngis" because in the Book of Revelation this image is used in the description of events following the opening of the sixth seal: "And the stars from heaven fell upon the earth, as the fig-tree casteth its green figs when it is shaken by a great wind" (Apocalypse 6:13). In fact, the vision of a tree itself is common to a number of apocalypses, and the motif of a violent wind is among the commonest of portents in apocalyptic prophecies,[44] a portent Langland uses in precisely this manner in Reason's sermon in Passus v. Such hints and suggestions of apocalypticism are scattered throughout certain passages, but Langland's use of this material is dignified by a definite restraint. Whether this restraint stems from uncertainty or an understandable dislike of the sensational side of apocalypticism it is difficult to tell.

Other reasons for Langland's apparent restraint and inexplicitness could range from a politic prudence – some apocalyptic material was, after all, extremely controversial and a number of prophetic writers landed themselves in prison for their efforts[45] – to his possible distance from written sources, mentioned above. However, there is another reason, I believe, and this is the internal tension he seems to have experienced (or, at least, the poem expresses) between eschatological despair and a prophetic optimism, a problem to which we will turn now.

Like so many reformers, Langland sees the state of the clergy as a barometer of apocalyptic pressure. In an awkward analogy (comparing valleys to laymen and hills to clergymen), the fourteenth-century preacher Thomas Wimbledon suggests this view in his comment that darkness even on the hilltops is a sign of the end of the day: "But whan þou seest prestes, þat beþ put on þe hiʒe coppe of spiritual dignites, þat schulde be as hilles aboue þe comune peple in parfit lyuynge, þat dirkenesse of synnes haþ take hem, who douteþ þat þe world nis at þe ende?" (*Wimbledon's Sermon*, pp. 112–13). The feeling that God has forsaken the world largely because of the corruption of the clergy is expressed throughout *Piers Plowman* in passages like XVII. 72–122 where it is used as an explanation for continual disaster and the inefficacy of prayer to abate it:

> Ac þe metal, þat is mannes soule, of many of this techares
> Is alayed with leccherye and oþer lustes of synn,
> That god coueyteth nat þe coyne þat Crist hymsulue printede
> And for þe synne of þe soule forsaketh his oune coyne . . .
> For what thorw werre and wrake and wikkede hefdes,
> May no preyere pees make in no place, hit semeth.
> Lewed men han no byleue and lettred men erren;
> Noþer see ne sond ne þe seed ʒeldeth
> As they ywoned were – in wham is defaute? (XVII. 78–81, 85–89)

Langland struggles between a desire to use the image of an utterly forsaken world given over to evil and the desire to urge reform by emphasizing that there is still hope. This passage describes a forsaken and inverted world, yet it ends, "Ac ʒif prestes doen here deuer wel we shal do þe bettre . . ." (XVII. 122). Langland's use of eschatological notions is thus often rather qualified or compromised by his concern for reformation, a dichotomy which one finds at the root of reformist apocalypticism itself. This is perhaps why such elements often remain subtly in the

17

background in some passages, or why Langland's emphasis is so often *not* on the End of the World, even when he uses eschatological symbols, as in this passage from Reason's sermon:

> Beches and brode okes were blowe to þe grounde
> And turned vpward here tayl in tokenynge of drede
> That dedly synne ar domesday shal fordon hem alle.   (v. 120–22)

The upturned trees are one of the signs that Doomsday is actually at hand,[46] but the emphasis is on the fear of "dedly synne *ar* domes day" (italics mine). The eschatological concern, instead of swallowing up concern for the present, serves to heighten it.

There is a tension in Langland's writing between the preaching of eschatology and the preaching of a less universal and ultimate form of retribution. This tension, which (as I have mentioned above) lies at the very heart of reformist apocalyptic thought, is, I believe, what attracted Langland to it. Here was an apocalypticism that expressed imminent cataclysm in the same terms as traditional eschatology had forecast for the End of the World, yet placed that crisis within the framework of history and followed it up with a vision of spiritual renewal. To a man with reformist interests, torn between the hope and despair which the poem expresses, this alternative prophetic world view would have looked very comforting indeed.

There are, then, a number of prophetic passages, images, and subtle allusions to the apocalyptic themes throughout the poem, but they form, at best, a series of fragments when isolated from the poem and listed as above.[47] The fact is that there is no consistent apocalyptic or prophetic thread in the poem connecting all these passages together – at least not in the narrow sense of these terms. If there is any cohesive ideology which connects and supports these fragmentary apocalyptic nodes within the poem it is the ideology of reform. Furthermore, any student of reformist apocalyptic thought will immediately see in *Piers Plowman* all the basically *non*-apocalyptic reformist issues which came to be associated with this brand of apocalypticism throughout the Middle Ages. Briefly, they are the issues of the mendicant controversies and the broader but related issues of clerical poverty and perfection, denunciation of clerical abuses, anti-intellectualism and the fervent hope for a coming age of spiritual renewal. None of these themes except perhaps the last would be automatically associated with apocalypticism by students of *Piers Plowman* not familiar with the history of Latin religious prophecy in the later Middle Ages and, indeed, all these themes and issues were widely discussed in non-apocalyptic terms as well. However, the fact remains that they were all extremely important issues in medieval apocalyptic thought: can it be simply coincidence, then, that Langland combines within his poem a perpetual concern with all these issues and a distinct, if fragmentary, apocalypticism? I think not. This is not to say, of course, that Langland would not have been concerned with the issues of, for example, the mendicant controversies if he had not dabbled in reformist apocalypticism, but rather that in this brand of apocalypticism he found an alternative way of understanding the mendicant problem within Salvation History.

Introduction

Among the issues of reformist apocalypticism which will be perpetually resurfacing in this study are the medieval concepts of "perfection," *vita apostolica*, and repristination,[48] that is, reforms which will return erring clergy to a pristine state of purity. "Perfection" is a concept with which students of *Piers Plowman* are already familiar in the work of Morton Bloomfield.[49] Reformist thinkers were repeatedly discussing the "fulfilling" (*perficiens*) of clerical duties (or perhaps it would be more accurate to say the lack thereof). The key word in discussions of this sort is often some form of the word *perficere*, usually translated (sometimes unhelpfully) by forms of the English verb "to perfect," when "to fulfill" or "accomplish" would be clearer. When Langland used this concept, as he so often did, he used the term "parfitnesse" (translating *perfectio*) or a form of it, and in so doing he was referring to precisely this problem of fulfillment of the individual's obligations in the Christian life, literally, of living up to the requirements of salvation in that vocation. Scholars of the poem have not always understood why Morton Bloomfield began writing a book on *Piers Plowman* as an apocalypse and ended up with a long discussion of medieval notions of perfection, but the connections are not fortuitous. Reformist apocalyptic thinkers and visionaries are often, like Langland, obsessively concerned with the requirements of the different paths to salvation.[50]

The ideal of apostolic poverty and the question of how literally clergy should live up to it were to become strongly associated with prophecy in the decades to follow (see Leff, *Heresy*, pt. 1), partly because of the Joachite tendencies of the radical wing of the Franciscan order – partly, but not entirely. Scholars have all too often neglected other sources of this ideology in apocalyptic writings, sources like Hildegard of Bingen, whose reputation matches that of Joachim in many respects. The problem certainly exercised Langland, both in his prophetic passages and outside of them. The question of *vita apostolica* was most hotly debated in connection with the Franciscans, but, as he tells us, Bloomfield realized in the course of his research that the question of apostolic poverty in the Middle Ages concerned many more than the one group who sensationalized it (*Apocalypse*, p. 95). In the later Middle Ages almost every order struggled with it in the apologist or polemical literature which it produced (hence Bloomfield's emphasis on "monastic philosophy"). By some sleight of hand a cunning apologist could prove that his order did in fact fulfill the ideals of apostolic poverty (and that his opponent's order did not). There can be no doubt that some of Langland's obsessive interest in apostolic poverty and apostolic way of life derives from apocalyptic sources, but the question is how much? In what follows I will attempt to answer this question, but more work needs to be done on the question of what literature of clerical reform, both apocalyptic and non-apocalyptic, was available to a fourteenth-century Englishman before it can be finally settled.

The problem of *vita apostolica* is, then, closely related to the question of perfection in the Christian life. The highest level of perfection, it was felt, was the imitation of the life of the apostles or of the early Church. Unfortunately, these concepts of *vita apostolica* were essentially derived from two not entirely compatible biblical texts, Acts 4:32 and Luke 10:1–12 (Chenu, *Nature, Man and Society*, p. 214).

Reformist apocalypticism and *Piers Plowman*

Up until the twelfth century the monastic orders saw themselves as living a true *vita apostolica*, but, as Chenu has shown, in order to do this they had to emphasize certain apostolic tenets, like holding all possessions in common (Acts 4:32), while virtually ignoring others, like itinerant preaching, poverty, and active ministry (Luke 10:1–12; Chenu, *Nature, Man and Society*, pp. 204–13). Traditional monasticism increasingly came under attack from the newer and more evangelical orders in the twelfth century. As the canonical movement established itself, placing more emphasis on the Luke model of the apostolic life (Chenu, *ibid.*, pp. 213ff.), and as the Cistercians took monasticism itself back to a very austere interpretation of the Benedictine rule, stressing poverty, anti-intellectualism and self-denial (Southern, *Western Society*, p. 252), the older orders became self-conscious about their apparent wealth and worldliness. Also, eremitism, yet another form of clerical life which stressed different "apostolic" qualities, was experiencing a revival which penetrated new orders like the Carthusians and the Vallombrosians (Chenu, *Nature, Man and Society*, p. 216). In spite of their many differences, what each group had in common was a desire to go back to "antiquity," back to the simplicity and austerity of the early Church, *ecclesia primitiva* (Southern, *Western Society*, p. 251).

In the midst of all this change, it is no wonder that the imaginations of reformist thinkers began to be stirred by apocalyptic notions of the return of all clergy to a state of apostolic rigor or pristine monasticism, "And be as Benet hem bad, Dominik and Frounceys" (IV. 177), as Reason says in *Piers Plowman*. But, aware that some of the ecclesiastical traditions had allowed for abuse, they were faced with the question of whether it would be better to change some aspects of the traditional institutions or whether the best possible reform would not simply be a return to the beginning. Some apocalyptic writers, like Hildegard of Bingen and Joachim of Fiore, in what is perhaps the most radical form of repristination, imagined a return to the eremitical life for the reformed clergy of the future.[51]

What the eremitical life, as it was idealized in legends of the Desert Fathers, had in common with the life of "apostolic poverty" was that, in both, one is dependent on Providence for the necessities of life. This is an important ideal for Langland which, in spite of the abuses of the false hermits and friars, he would dearly love to vindicate. Figures like St. Anthony and St. Paul the Hermit, always popular in reformist literature (Constable, "Renaissance," pp. 56–58), are similarly idealized in *Piers Plowman*. For example in Passus XVII *Liberum Arbitrium* reminds Will:

> Holy writ witnesseth þer were suche eremytes,
> Solitarie by hemsulue in here selles lyuede
> Withoute borwynge or beggynge bote of god one . . .
> Elles foules fedde hem in frythes þer they wonede,
> Bothe Antony and Arseny and oþer fol monye.
> Paul *primus heremita* . . .   (XVII. 6–13)

In this passage Langland clearly associates apostolic poverty with the traditions of the early Desert Fathers, in one of his many struggles with the question of what constitutes a "perfect" or "fulfilled" form of life. While for most reformers this type of dependence on Providence remains simply an ideal, as Constable has suggested, "Even if such rhetoric did not describe reality, however, it reflects the desire to return to the authenticity of the sources" ("Renaissance," p. 58). Even a writer like Bernard of Clairvaux, who was quick to condemn abuses of eremiticism, praises the itinerant preaching and poverty of St. Malachy with the comment that "This was the apostolic form . . . He who does such things is indeed the true heir to the apostles" (cited in Constable, "Renaissance," p. 56). Similarly, Hildegard condemned *vagatio* but exalted the itinerant hermit St. Disibodus in her poetry (*Prooemium vitae s. Disibodi*, Pitra, in *Analecta*, p. 453). As we shall see, this ideal, flagrantly abused as it was, remained an ideal for Langland. Much of his anger, I suspect, stemmed from the passion with which he cherished it. His charismatic portrait of "fools for Christ" (IX. 105–38), and its many echoes throughout the poem, are persistent reminders of his fascination with the extremes of apostolic perfection. Fools, hermits, Desert Fathers, apostles, beggars and friars jostle one another uncomfortably in the pages of *Piers Plowman* as Langland tries to sort out the false and the true apostles, and the various gradations of the ladder of perfection.

This is the type of "monastic philosophy" which Bloomfield saw at the heart of Langland's apocalyptic thought. But this type of literature had in many cases become associated with apocalyptic thought through the common bond of an interest in Church reform, as we see in writers like Joachim of Fiore, for example. By Langland's time there was a substantial literature encompassing all three of these themes and this same grouping of ideologies is certainly reflected in *Piers Plowman*.

What answers, then, to the problems of *Piers Plowman* can the religious prophetic traditions supply us with? To begin with, one strong indication that the study of religious prophecy might be a thrust in the right direction is that Langland's prophecy of a reforming king who will bring the regular clergy *ad pristinum statum* is manifestly written in this tradition. The *"ad pristinum statum"* theme was very popular with writers of reformist prophecy. The concept itself seems to have arisen during the period of canonical and monastic reform which the eleventh and twelfth centuries saw. As Bischoff says, "scholarship has been generally agreed in considering the maxim 'renewal through repristination' as the hallmark of the great canonical and monastic reform of the eleventh and twelfth centuries" ("Eschatology," p. 46). A number of Latin religious prophecies use the phrase *ad pristinum statum* (or a close version of it) in prophesying the outcome of future clerical chastisements, after which the clergy will be returned to a state of purity, usually by a king or reforming pope. There can be no doubt that this is the kind of prophecy which lies behind v. 168–79, because of the distinctively reformist-apocalyptic program which, as we shall see, Langland sets out in this prophecy.

In this study we will return again and again to the *ad pristinum statum* prophecy in Passus V because it embodies so succinctly a number of the very complex views of reformist apocalypticism. In this one passage Langland shows that he had grasped the essence of this type of prophecy and yet made it his own in his extraordinary vision of reform of the friars through provision for their needs. In chapters 4 and 5 of this study we will consider the apocalyptic function of the friars within the poem in the light of the various roles they played in the anti-mendicant eschatology of William of St. Amour and his school on the one hand, and that of the Franciscan Joachites on the other. The apocalyptic world view can be summed up in many ways as reflecting an awareness of the perpetual battle between the true prophets (or apostles) and the pseudo-prophets (or apostles). The stormy history of the friars in the later Middle Ages left an apocalyptic legacy in which they figure on *both* sides of this equation. This legacy is accurately reflected in *Piers Plowman*, where the fraternal problem lies at the heart of the poem, as it does in the history of medieval apocalyptic thought.

Perhaps the two most commonly read apocalyptic writers in fourteenth-century England, judging by the frequency with which their names occur in catalogues of manuscripts and contemporary writings, were Hildegard of Bingen and Joachim of Fiore. Hildegard's prophecies were read largely in the form of a collection of excerpts and, although pseudepigraphic prophecy circulated under her name, her original predictions were widely available in abbreviated form.[52] Joachim's ideas, however, were known in England largely through pseudo-Joachite writings and the works of prophets who had come under his influence. This study therefore deals directly (in chapter 2) with the genuine prophecies of Hildegard, and concentrates (in chapter 5) on the later and more widely read pseudo-Joachite material rather than on the major works of Joachim himself. Hildegard and Joachim represent the two types of apocalyptic prophecy which must have influenced *Piers Plowman* in some form: the visionary and the exegetical. As we shall see, there is evidence in *Piers Plowman* that Langland knew and used the conventions of visionary writing such as one finds in the works of Hildegard and other medieval visionaries (for example, the convention of receiving a vision during Mass, xxi. 4–5). Many of the themes of Hildegard's prophecies are common in *Piers Plowman*: the belief in a coming chastisement (including disendowment) and reform of the clergy, the view that the present time was one of crisis that would eventually lead to spiritual renewal and the belief that the pseudo-prophets, the Church's greatest trial, were to be men in humble attire who would seem to have rejected all worldly possessions. For Hildegard, these pseudo-prophets were to be heretics (although anti-mendicant writers would later use the prophecy for their own purposes); for Langland they were friars.

Turning briefly to the works, genuine and spurious, which make up the canon of Joachite material, together with the works of known disciples and those influenced by Joachim, we have a very wide range of literature. The possibility that Langland had come in contact with Joachite ideas from one of these sources is very good indeed. Previously, critics such as Bloomfield, Kaske and Frank have tried in various ways to suggest Joachite influence, particularly in the Trinitarian structure of the poem.[53] While these things remain a possibility, it seems to me that stronger evidence of Langland's contact with Joachite tradition (and I am using the adjective "Joachite" to include the broad range of Joachim's influence) is in the apocalyptic program he describes in his prophecies and in the last passus of the

22

poem. A careful reading of III. 436–81, v. 168–79 (and B.x. 322–35) and of certain parts of Passus XXII reveals that Langland imagined an age of peace and spiritual renewal *after* Antichrist, a belief which is most likely associated with reformist apocalypticism, probably (though not exclusively) with Joachism.

It will be helpful here to outline briefly some of the sources of Latin Continental religious prophecy in fourteenth-century England. What follows is intended only as a sketch of the different types of evidence we have that this kind of prophecy did in fact circulate in England, and should not be considered as a listing of all the available information – a project which itself deserves a book.

SOURCES OF APOCALYPTIC THOUGHT IN MEDIEVAL BRITAIN

There needs to be a study done of various manuscripts and other primary sources of apocalyptic material in circulation in England in the later Middle Ages. From the work of Marjorie Reeves,[54] Morton Bloomfield,[55] Robert Lerner,[56] and Jeanne Bignami-Odier,[57] and with the help of indices to catalogues of manuscript collections, I have been able to gather enough evidence to justify the presence of all the prophets or prophecies in this book; however, these results are fragmentary. Some of this evidence is given in notes or introductory sections about the various writers cited throughout this study, but much of it is too miscellaneous or inconclusive to admit of concise presentation. For example, a number of catalogues do not give incipits or any specific information which would help identify a prophecy or establish its provenance; the prophetic section of a manuscript is often described in terms like "some Latin prophecies" or in another non-specific manner. Until each manuscript can be studied in detail we will not know exactly what is still extant.

A study of such manuscripts could tell us not only which European prophecies were in circulation in England and when, but would also enlighten us about the readers and users of such prophecies:[58] of what social and educational classes were they? What interested them in these prophecies and how did they react to the more controversial passages within them? (Prophetic manuscripts and early printed prophetic texts provoked a good deal of marginalia.)[59]

The names of the major prophetic figures like Joachim, Hildegard or John of Rupescissa come up at least once or twice in most extant medieval catalogues of the larger libraries in Britain. For example, the medieval catalogue of St. Augustine's Abbey library in Canterbury[60] lists a book containing the "prophetia sancte hildegardis,"[61] after which the medieval cataloguer refers the reader to the "prophetia Abbatis Joachim supra in Bestiar' Henr' de Burgham,'" obviously assuming that a reader interested in the one would be interested in the other. The description of the Bestiary "supra" (p. 290) is typical of the type of book in which prophecies are often found in that it is a conglomerate of theological pieces, verses, histories, and miscellaneous curiosities, ranging from (the popular) verse of the Sibyl on the Day of Judgment to a piece on the *mirabilia* of India. Almost at the end of the list comes the Joachite item coupled with a *mirabilia* piece, "de Mirabilibus Anglie et / alia quedam prophetia paparum," the latter being a copy of the very

23

popular *Vaticinia de summis pontificibus*, attributed to Joachim (the manuscript is, in fact, still extant, now Oxford, Bodleian Library MS Douce 88). The association ("et alia") of these prophecies with "de Mirabilibus Anglie" is a good example of what seems (judging by medieval catalogue entries and lists of manuscript contents) to be a common medieval habit of associating "wonders" with "prophecies,"[62] which may suggest to readers of *Piers Plowman* that the "wonders" Will sets out to hear in the opening lines of the poem may indeed have been (or have included) prophecies. Another item in the St. Augustine's catalogue (p. 285) contains an unspecified "prophecia Abbatis Joachim" in the company of works by Roger Bacon, who had, as we have seen, a great interest in prophecy.

Among extant medieval English catalogues, the library of the Augustinian Friars in York should be singled out for special mention.[63] Even excluding the prophetic codices donated by John Erghome, which, one could argue, are something of a special case and likely not to be representative of the average cleric's literary tastes, the friary had a considerable collection of medieval apocalyptic works of its own, including "Joachim super apocalypsim" and "Joachim de concordancia testamentorum" (p. 36, no. 163) and an item called "prophecia hildegardis" coupled with a work of William of St. Amour (p. 44, no. 271),[64] as well as a good deal of miscellaneous unspecified prophecy. John Erghome owned copies of a number of the works discussed in this study, including the *De semine scripturarum*, the *De oneribus prophetarum*, and the prophecies of Robert of Uzès and John of Rupescissa.[65] The availability of so much Joachite material to an English friary suggests that English friars may not have been quite as immune to the prophetic enthusiasm of their fellows on the Continent as has sometimes been suggested.

Prophetic works in circulation in medieval England which are still extant are quite numerous: amid the perpetually popular prophecies pseudonymously attributed to Merlin or the Sibyl, a number of reformist apocalyptic works can be found. The most obvious place to look for prophetic works is in the type of miscellany described above, although the themes of these miscellanies can vary widely. Sometimes the focus of the miscellany will seem to be mainly on *mirabilia* literature, sometimes on historical writings,[66] sometimes on clerical ideology or on the literature of the mendicant controversies.[67] Some manuscripts carry a complement of anti-clerical, satirical or Goliardic material[68] along with their prophecies; others contain sermons and theological works,[69] while still others are concerned with astronomical texts.[70] This brief summary cannot do any justice to the question of the variety of manuscript contexts in which prophecies occur, but it is interesting to note that they most often occur in manuscripts to which a writer like Langland could have been drawn for completely different reasons such as, for example, collections on clerical ideology and the mendicant controversies, or collections of anti-clerical, satirical or Goliardic material, or the numerous manuscripts of theological and didactic works. If his comment at the end of the reformer-king prophecy may be taken literally: "Ac ar þat kyng come, as cronicles me tolde . . ." (v. 178), then it would seem that he had read prophecies in chronicles as well. In fact, *Piers Plowman* shows evidence of Langland's interest in all the types of writing which regularly occur with prophetic texts in medieval manuscripts, with the possible exception of astronomy. It is not unlikely that even a casual reader of one of these types of literature would come across prophecies from time to time – and Langland shows evidence of having been more than a casual reader in some of these areas (for example, his knowledge of the literature of the mendicant controversies is hard to overestimate).

A handful of English prophetic anthologies which carry predominantly reformist apocalyptic works are still extant, among which should be especially mentioned Cambridge, Corpus Christi College, MS 404, compiled by Langland's contemporary Henry of Kirkstede at Bury St. Edmunds. The manuscript contains nothing but prophecies of the Latin religious type, including Hildegardian, pseudo-Joachite, and other continental works. Numerous other manuscripts survive which are partially or even largely given over to such prophecy, but the Corpus manuscript is outstanding among English manuscripts in being entirely an anthology of current Latin European apocalyptic works of the religious type, obviously handpicked by Kirkstede himself.[71] It contains relatively little political prophecy and no genuine Joachite works and as such reflects the kind of current religious reformist interests which I suspect Langland himself had.[72]

An important source of prophetic material, as Langland himself tells us, was the medieval chronicle, and a number of English chronicles do indeed mention or quote from current apocalyptic texts.[73] Chronicles of the world-history type, such as Vincent of Beauvais's *Speculum historiale*, also played a role in the dissemination of the new apocalyptic thought. A final source of evidence for the diffusion of prophetic works in fourteenth-century England comes from uses of or allusions to apocalyptic sources by various English exegetes, scholars, astronomers, sermon writers, and poets.[74] The existing evidence is, once again, fragmentary, but there is enough to suggest that current Latin apocalyptic prophecy was available in one form or another to a moderately wide range of English readers and writers. As I hope this study will show, there is no reason, on the basis of existing evidence, to believe that Langland could not have been one of these.

137,216

LIBRARY
College of St. Francis
JOLIET, ILLINOIS

2

The visionary prophecy of Hildegard of Bingen in relation to *Piers Plowman*

INTRODUCTION: HILDEGARD OF BINGEN (1098–1179)[1] AND THE
DISSEMINATION OF HER PROPHECIES

The beginnings of later-medieval reformist apocalypticism go back to twelfth-century Germany, where the Great Reform had had its most profound repercussions; it produced religious prophetic thinkers like Rupert of Deutz, Gerhoh of Reichersberg, Anselm of Havelberg and Hildegard of Bingen, who each tried in his or her own way "to wrest meaning from the great revolution of their times."[2] The concerns of these German writers left their stamp on the religious prophecy of the later Middle Ages, but none more than Hildegard. Her influence as a prophetess was profound. Along with Joachim of Fiore, Hildegard is the most commonly cited authority in sermons, encyclopedias, chronicles and religious tracts in which authors and compilers chose to include current apocalyptic theory.[3] Chronicles of the period testify to the reputation which she and the younger visionary Elizabeth of Schönau (on whom Hildegard had a great influence) had acquired. In 1158 an annalist wrote: "In these days God made manifest his power through the frail sex, in the two handmaidens . . . whom he filled with a prophetic spirit, making many kinds of visions apparent to them through his messages, which are to be seen in writing."[4]

Hildegard carried on a prodigious correspondence with emperors, kings, popes, nobility and clergy all over Europe.[5] Her zeal for evangelism and reform seems to have been the motivation for much of her contact with the world beyond her abbey walls, although as her reputation as a prophetess grew people began to come to her for spiritual advice, reassurance and, one might say, "news" from above. Heads of religious houses wrote to find out whether God was in any way displeased with their houses or orders,[6] abbesses wrote to ask whether it was God's will that they continue in their positions or seek a quieter life,[7] clerics and scholars wrote to ask whether Hildegard could pronounce on theological points under dispute or clarify mystifying passages in the Bible.[8] At one point she was even asked to exorcize a demon from a possessed woman.[9] To read her correspondence is to gain an insight into many of the religious, spiritual and psychological problems which troubled twelfth-century society.

Although frail and prone to physical illness, Hildegard undertook preaching tours, everywhere urging reform and speaking her mind to all, respecting neither position nor social rank when she encountered flagrant abuse. At a certain point in

The visionary prophecy of Hildegard of Bingen

her life, her disillusionment with the clerical corruption she saw around her began to take its toll.[10] As Charles Czarski has shown in his illuminating study of Hildegard's prophetic works, "The Prophecies of St. Hildegard of Bingen," her apocalyptic ideology became more radical in the later years of her life and the most spectacular and virulent prophecies can all be dated to this time as a consequence. Hildegard has been described by the historian of apocalyptic thought, Bernard McGinn, as "one of the most strikingly original apocalyptic thinkers since the intertestamental period."[11] However, it must be said that this is the only area in which she received anything like the recognition she deserved as an author. She also wrote on cosmology, medicine, ethics, science and theology, as well as producing saints' lives, liturgical songs, poetry, a play and her three large, uncategorizable visionary treatises: *Scivias*, the *Liber vitae meritorum* and the *Liber divinorum operum simplicis hominis*. On top of this she conducted her vast correspondence, leaving a literary legacy which runs to volumes. And yet her works, aside from her prophetic writings, were all but ignored until the nineteenth century. Schrader ("Hildegarde," col. 519) has speculated that the domination of the scholastic and mystical movements in the later Middle Ages made her works seem difficult and strangely out of fashion to contemporary readers, a point which highlights the notion that, as a visionary, Hildegard can only with difficulty be classed among mystics.

If her works were obscure to contemporaries, they have not been made more lucid by the passing of eight centuries. Part of the reason for this may be the fact that she was recording the things which she believed she saw in her visions, and what was visually and imaginatively clear to Hildegard is often less than clear in the more laborious form of prose. The problems that she had in expressing her visions were no doubt augmented by the fact that she seems to have been very insecure about her competence in Latin and, despite scholarly studies of the problem, it is still unclear to what extent her secretaries contributed to the refinement of her work.[12]

Describing her mode of receiving visions in a letter written very late in her life, Hildegard says:

And as God wills, in this vision my spirit mounts upwards, into the height of the firmament and into changing air, and dilates itself among different nations, even though they are in far-off regions and places remote from me. And because I see these things in such a manner, for this reason I also behold them in changing forms of clouds and other created things. But I hear them not with my physical ears, nor with my heart's thoughts, nor do I perceive them by bringing any of my five senses to bear – but only in my soul, my physical eyes open, so that I never suffer their failing in loss of consciousness [*extasis*]; no, I see these things wakefully, day and night. And I am constantly oppressed by illnesses, and so enmeshed in intense pains that they threaten to bring on my death; but so far God has stayed me.

(trans. Dronke, *Women Writers*, p. 168 [Latin text, p. 252])

The interesting thing about this passage is that despite Hildegard's originality of self-expression and visionary perception, evident even in this brief excerpt, it is clear from this description that she was nevertheless influenced by visionary tradition. For example, even though she says she does not receive her visions in a

27

state of ecstasy, as most medieval seers did, she talks of her spirit mounting upwards into the height of the firmament, much like the kind of experience recorded in visionary texts well known to the Middle Ages like Cicero's *Somnium Scipionis* or II Corinthians 12:1–4, which records St. Paul's visionary experience.

Thus it is important to realize that even as a "real" visionary (that is, a practising visionary, as opposed to a dream-vision poet, like Langland), Hildegard can be seen to have been both influenced by and writing within the conventions of a strong literary tradition, a tradition which obviously *shaped* her experience to some extent. This tradition, and the literary conventions which characterize it, are part of the larger tradition upon which dream-vision poets like Langland, especially those interested in religious questions, were drawing. In this sense these two writers are both "literary" writers, and because convention is virtually inescapable in visionary writing, there is something to be gained in comparing these two seemingly different types of visionary. But Langland, too, may be seen as a "real" visionary in some senses. As A. C. Spearing has written of *Piers Plowman*:

The dreams have a genuinely dreamlike fluidity and fragmentariness, and the poem's turning points – scenes such as Piers's tearing of the pardon, and the vision in which he knocks down the fruit from the Tree of Charity and thereby sets off the Annunciation – have an authentically visionary effect. It is easy to believe that, rather than constructing allegories to express preconceived ideas, Langland really had visions which were not fully susceptible of rational analysis.[13]

Finally, if Judson Boyce Allen is correct, medieval poetry was written primarily with ethical goals in view, rather than with the artistic goals we assume today,[14] all of which brings the work of these two visionaries closer in purpose.

A second fact which forms the basis of this comparison is that even the most empirical study of Hildegard's and Langland's prophetic writings will reveal a good many shared attitudes and ideologies. Even more striking is the fact that they share many apocalyptic themes and motifs. All this does not add up to "proof" that Langland had read Hildegard specifically (although there is no reason to assume that he could not have, given the strength of her reputation and the relatively wide circulation of her prophetic works), but it does make her writings an important starting point for any study of the tradition of apocalyptic visionary writing before Langland.

Most of the studies of Hildegard to date (and the same applies to Joachim of Fiore) have focused, naturally enough, on establishing the canon of genuine works, possible sources, historical context, ideology and the like. However, both Hildegard and Joachim were better known by a general audience in the form of popularizations of their works: Hildegard was known during the Middle Ages and the Reformation primarily through the collection of extracts from her prophetic works made by Gebeno of Eberbach in 1220.[15] This study of Hildegard will use Gebeno's compilation as a basis for the discussion of her apocalyptic thought, largely because this is the form in which it was available to readers in the later Middle Ages. Popularizers like Gebeno were the people who created and sustained reputations and disseminated the ideas and ideologies of the major thinkers whose works were almost invariably too long, too cumbersome or too academic to have gathered a wide audience for themselves. For the purposes of establishing the apocalyptic tradition which may have influenced Langland's thought, one should study prophetic thinkers in the form in which they exerted whatever influence they had.

Gebeno of Eberbach compiled the *Speculum futurorum temporum sive Pentachronon* (hereafter *Pentachronon*) from various prophetic excerpts which he found in Hildegard's *Scivias, Liber divinorum operum* and correspondence.[16] He relied most heavily on material from the end of the *Liber divinorum operum* and from the letters, these being the main sources of her later and most fully developed apocalyptic thought, as Charles Czarski has shown ("Prophecies"). Had Gebeno not made the compilation, Hildegard's prophetic writings might have been doomed to obscurity;[17] as Gebeno himself notes (in Pitra, *Analecta*, p. 483), few could possess or read her books, not only because of their length, but because of her obscure style: "Libros S. Hildegardis plerique legere fastidiunt et abhorrent, pro eo quod obscure et inusitato stylo loquitur." However, taking this style itself as a sign of her prophetic authenticity ("hoc quoque argumentum est veri digiti Dei"), he accords to Hildegard's works the highest possible authority (*ibid.*, pp. 484–85). Gebeno opens by urging upon his readers a sense of Hildegard's importance, reminding them of her correspondence with popes, emperors, bishops, abbots and other dignitaries (*ibid.*, p. 483).

Later in the *Pentachronon*, Gebeno goes even further in his adulation of Hildegard and, in a curious passage in which he compares her to the eagle of Apocalypse 8:13 (who cries out "Woe, woe, woe to the inhabitants of the earth . . ."), he lists her among the great religious figures of the 1220s, among whom he includes St. Bernard, St. Thomas à Becket and "the abbot Joachim, founder of the monastery of Flora, who indeed is said to have had the spirit of prophecy" (*ibid.*, pp. 487–88 [my translation]). But, he continues, only Hildegard, to his knowledge, has predicted three future woes, and therefore only she can be fittingly compared to the eagle. According to Gebeno, the seven trumpets of Apocalypse 8 and 9 represent the seven ages of the Church since Christ, and the current time falls in the fourth of these ages. Taking the "Woe, woe, woe . . ." of the eagle's message literally to mean that three woes would come upon the world, he credits Hildegard above all the other holy ones of his time with having foreseen this. Gebeno goes so far as to compare her to St. John himself, who is traditionally symbolized by the eagle (*ibid.*, p. 488). As Charles Czarski has suggested, Gebeno went far beyond even the authors of Hildegard's *Vita* in his glorification of her prophetic powers (Czarski, "Prophecies," p. 219).

How much Gebeno's commentary added to posterity's understanding of Hildegard's apocalyptic thought is open to question. His greatest contribution was certainly his collecting and extracting of the scattered prophetic texts, because he offers little in the way of exegesis. There are, however, some things of unexpected interest to be gleaned from his meagre commentary. Most unexpected and most valuable from the standpoint of the history and transmission of apocalyptic thought is an extraordinary passage in which Gebeno gives his reasons for making the compilation:

De Antichristo nostris temporibus diversi diversa proponentes, frivola quaedom non per Dei Spiritum, sed de suo corde prophetarunt: aliis affirmantibus eum de proximo nasciturum, aliis jam conceptum, nonnullis vero dicentibus eumdem jam esse natum. Audivi, fateor, quam plures his curis occupatos. Infra triennium enim quidam abbas nomine Joannis, homo religiosus et in divina pagina satis eruditus, de Calabriae partibus veniens, in claustro nostro duabus hebdomadibus et eo amplius demoratus, mihi quasi familiari suo secretius retulit, Antichristum jam in proximo nasciturum. Cumque sollicite percunctarer hoc a quo percepisset: "Solitarius, inquit, magni nominis in partibus nostris Cardinali cuidam id aperuit, signoque manifesto comprobavit."   (in Pitra, *Analecta*, p. 484)

Clearly, he was motivated to compile the *Pentachronon* by the claims of various people, and especially those of a certain visiting abbot named John from Calabria, that the coming of Antichrist was imminent. Therefore, he writes, "ad confutandos et convincendos hujusmodi pseudo-prophetas, libellum hunc compilavi" (*ibid.*, p. 484). Obviously, he intended to set the record straight by publishing the version of events predicted by Hildegard, the most respected of Northern European prophets in his day.

Two points emerge from this passage: the first is Gebeno's evident irritation at these rumors of Antichrist's birth. One wonders if such irritation was not common, even among those who, like Gebeno, had an apocalyptic turn of mind. The second point is that this passage in the *Pentachronon* records the first encounter of Hildegard's apocalyptic thought with Joachim of Fiore's, because there is little doubt that the "solitary of great name in our parts" (that is, in Calabria) is Joachim himself.[18] Abbot John's simplistic representation of the views of Joachim on Antichrist would indeed strike someone familiar with Hildegard's prophecy as unsophisticated and sensationalized. Hildegard's predictions, as we shall see, give a detailed program of events which places Antichrist and the End many generations away; there can be little wonder that Gebeno preferred it to what he had heard of Joachim's. Ironically, in spite of Gebeno's efforts to "confute and convince the pseudo-prophets," over-simplified versions of both Joachim and Hildegard would later travel peacefully together in popular literature like Vincent of Beauvais's *Speculum historiale*. However, to give him his due, Gebeno at least succeeded in popularizing *genuine* excerpts from Hildegard in a way that no single short anthology ever did for Joachim's genuine writings.

Two final points should be made regarding Gebeno's comments in the *Pentachronon*. The first and perhaps most obvious is his overwhelming concern with what Hildegard had to say about clerical corruption and the future tribulation of the clergy. More than three-quarters of his extracts deal with this problem in some way. Even more striking is the fact that by far the largest number of extracts are worked into Book II, which deals with the "first time" of Hildegard's "five times" before the End, the "first time" being the current age, the age which Hildegard predicted would end in a massive chastisement of the clergy and consequent spiritual renewal. Gebeno seems to have taken this message to heart. Although the initial reason he gives for making the compilation is to "confute the pseudo-prophets" on the topic of the imminence of Antichrist, it soon becomes apparent that Antichrist is the least of his worries.[19] It is obvious that Gebeno had studied

Hildegard's prophecies for every clue concerning exactly what would happen to the clergy during and after the chastisement, a task which, as we shall see, is not as easy as it sounds. Hildegard was by no means consistent or overly detailed in her discussion of these points, but as a member of a regular order writing some fifty years after Hildegard, Gebeno obviously felt that time was running out for the clergy and that God's hand would not be turned away.

In this regard it is interesting to note that he gives prominence to Hildegard's letter to the *Colonienses* (in Pitra, *Analecta*, p. 487), which was to become the most popular extract, circulating in manuscripts independently and as commonly found in English manuscripts as the *Pentachronon* itself. The extract from this letter which became so popular contains one of Hildegard's most virulent denunciations of ecclesiastical abuse and most violent prophecies of clerical chastisement. In this prophecy she gives a role in the chastisement to the heretical groups which were on the rise in Germany in her time. By the later thirteenth and fourteenth centuries her description of the heretics seems to have been read as anti-mendicant literature, but at Gebeno's time the concern was still with the heretics, as can be judged by the prominence he gives to both the letter and the topic of the Cathars (in Pitra, *Analecta*, p. 487).

It is therefore possible to see even in these brief comments on Gebeno's compilation the direction he gave to later apocalyptic thought, with his emphasis on Hildegard's predictions of imminent clerical chastisement, his irritation with imminent-apocalypse prophets, his assurances that Antichrist and the End were still many ages and events away and his elevation of Hildegard to the highest possible prophetic status. For reasons which should now be evident, Gebeno's little book, with all its flaws, is the most important text we have for the study of the *Nachleben* of Hildegard's apocalyptic thought and in many ways one of the most influential apocalyptic works of the later Middle Ages.

HILDEGARD'S APOCALYPTICISM AND HER PROPHECY OF CLERICAL
REFORM: "VISIONARY DENUNCIATION OF ECCLESIASTICAL ABUSES"

As a general rule, the radicalism of an apocalyptic writer can be seen as a function of his or her growing disillusionment with the Church. As Charles Czarski has shown, many contemporary historical events and smaller incidents in Hildegard's own sphere of influence contributed toward her growing disgust with the ecclesiastical establishment.[20] Even though *Scivias* was finished before the heaviest disillusionment came upon her, it does show some of the despair and disgust of the later years. In one of the few *Scivias* passages extracted in the *Pentachronon*, she attacks the Doctors of the Church for not having proven themselves as teachers of the Gospel, and makes an impassioned plea for clergy to stick to the old ordinances and obligations of the Church's institutions (*Scivias* II, 5, 27:870–1023). This is the mildest and probably the earliest of the *Pentachronon* selections. Her concern in this passage with the fulfilling (*perficiens*) of clerical duties is characteristic of traditional reform literature, and forms the basis of her later apocalyptic discussions of this sort.

In fact, Hildegard's apocalyptic wrath, like Langland's, is usually directed at clergy who are not fulfilling or living up to what they have vowed.[21] Because these clerics follow their own "novel" ideas, they desert the paths of their founders and therefore, in Hildegard's view, the only right paths. By deserting these ordinances they create quarrels within their orders; they bear no fruit and, in the words of St. John, they are neither hot nor cold (Apocalypse 3:15, 16; *Scivias* II, 5, 27: 893ff.). She continues this lengthy diatribe against half-hearted clergy who prefer the vagaries of their own will to obedience to their vows by invoking the traditional monastic condemnation of *vagatio* as a metaphor for their instability of will, a metaphor which is common in reformist literature, and which Langland no doubt had in mind when he created his "wilful" clerkish dreamer.[22]

For Hildegard, disobedience to authority is not only morally wrong; it is unnatural. It is as if, she says, the angels were to raise themselves above the archangels. Hildegard's extreme conservatism shows up here; as with many medieval visionaries, capable of radicalism in other areas, the boundaries of her vision are decidedly those of her own age in the area of social conservatism (this, too, will be familiar to readers of *Piers Plowman*).[23] The force of God's message in this section of *Scivias*, neatly summarized in II, 5, 30, is that the faithful man should be content to suffer in humility those things which have been instituted to him by his predecessors.[24]

As Hildegard's apocalypticism develops, her criticisms become, increasingly, brutally frank. A striking sign of Hildegard's early disillusionment occurs in the well-known vision in *Scivias* of the five beasts,[25] followed by a graphic depiction of *Ecclesia* giving birth to Antichrist, all of which Gebeno extracted for the *Pentachronon*. Perhaps the most significant thing about this early apocalyptic vision is the horrible central image of the violent birth of Antichrist from *Ecclesia*'s battered body, a birth which is then blurred with an image of defecation:

In her vagina there appeared a monstrous and totally black head . . . From that head to the knees the image was white and red, bruised as with many a beating. From the knees to the two white transverse zones which crosswise seemed to touch the bottoms of the feet from above, the image appeared to be bloody. Lo, the monstrous head removed itself from its place with so great a crash that the entire image of the woman was shaken in all its members. Something like a great mass of much dung was joined to the head . . .

(III, 11:105–20; trans. McGinn, *Visions*, p. 101)

The blurring of images is typical of visionary style;[26] however, the interesting thing about this particular image is the powerful condemnation of the state of the Church that it entails. One would expect to find this type of image in a sectarian poem or pamphlet of the Reformation rather than in the pious, orthodox *Scivias*. Hildegard's anger about clerical abuse was to become more virulent as the years went by, but *Scivias* elsewhere shows little of the bitterness of the later works.[27] If anything in *Scivias* is really "prophetic" it is this image which anticipates the revulsion and bitterness of the later prophetic writings, the seeds of what, for Hildegard, would be a lifelong horror of ecclesiastical abuse.

Hildegard's vision of *Ecclesia* giving birth to Antichrist stands as an emblem of her apocalyptic thought in all its later manifestations, but most significantly for her very real sense that the Church would generate its own downfall. In the years after *Scivias* was published, Hildegard's apocalypticism became more militant, less abstract and more involved with current history.

These characteristics are nowhere more evident in the works of both Hildegard and, later, Langland, than they are in the prophecies of clerical chastisement, disendowment and reform that they envisioned. As we shall see, these prophecies spring out of a very sober, not to say cynical, sense of what it would require to reform the clergy. In both writers there is a strong sense of the mood fostered by twelfth-century apocalyptic thought which no longer advocated waiting passively for the degradation of the End, crippled by the knowledge of Antichrist's coming (Rauh, *Antichrist*, p. 511). Rather, reformers pressed for activism in the response of the Church Militant to the coming crisis, a mood often captured in discussions of the metaphorical "arming" of the faithful, as we see in *Piers Plowman* XXI.

Langland's second disendowment prophecy reflects this mounting militant spirit, as it moves from warning by exemplum:

> For couetyse of that croes clerkes of holi churche
> Sholle ouerturne as þe Templers dede, þe tyme approcheth faste . . .
> (XVII. 208–09)

to prophetic assertion:

> Riht so, 3e clerkes, 3oure coueytise, ar come auht longe,
> Shal dampne *dos ecclesie* and depose 3ow for 3oure pruyde.
> *Deposuit potentes de sede* . . .   (XVII. 214–215a)

to a conditional threat:

> 3if knyhthoed and kynde wit and þe comune and consience
> Togederes louyen lelelyche, leueth hit, bisshopes,
> The lordschipe of londes lese 3e shal for euer . . .   (XVII. 216–18)

and finally, after citing the ominous legend of the condemnation of Constantine's donation:

> An angel men herde an hye at Rome crye:
> "*Dos ecclesie* this day hath ydronke venym . . ."   (XVII. 222–23)

it ends in the militant cry:

> Taketh here londe, 3e lordes, and lat hem lyue by dymes
> Yf the kynges coueyte in Cristes pees to lyuene.
> For if possession be poysen and imparfit hem make,
> The heuedes of holy churche and tho that ben vnder hem,
> Hit were charite to deschargen hem for holy churche sake
> And purge hem of þe olde poysen ar more perel falle.
> (XVII. 227–32)

In its militant spirit the prophecy raises the same issues in much the same way as we will see in Hildegard's prophecies: concern with the "imperfection" of the clergy (line 229) and with the precise state of "perfection" to which the clergy should be reformed (line 219). Added to these concerns is the larger question of who should carry out disendowment (lines 216, 228ff.) and the general feeling that the corruption of the clergy accounts for the "perels" of the present time.

In Langland's first disendowment prophecy (v. 168–79) the promised coming of a king who will reform the possessioners has a messianic quality to it, but the threat of a hostile nobility was no fairytale:[28]

> Ac þer shal come a kyng and confesse зow alle
> And bete зow, as þe bible telleth, for brekynge of зoure reule
> And amende зow monkes, bothe moniales and chanons,
> And potte зowe to зoure penaunce, *Ad pristinum statum ire*,
> And barones and here barnes blame зow and repreue.
> *Hii in curribus et hii in equis; ipsi obligati sunt et ceciderunt*
> Freres in here fraytour shall fynde þat time
> Bred withouten beggynge to lyue by euere aftur
> And Constantyn shal be here cook and couerour of here churches.

(v. 168–75)

This prophecy, with its allegorical and visionary features, appears to be more otherworldly than the one in Passus XVII, but the tensions it registers are no less real. The promised redistribution of the wealth of the clergy (among the nobility and, even more radical, among the friars) is no less ominous for its allegorical coating:

> For þe abbot of Engelonde and the abbesse his nese
> Shal haue a knok vppon here crounes and incurable þe wounde . . .

(v. 176–77)

This prophecy gives us a window on Langland's apocalypticism. It links him with repristination reformers from the twelfth century onwards and, more specifically, with those who chose to express their desire for reform in prophetic terms. The passage also highlights Langland's sense that only a confiscation of their wealth could purge contemporary clergy of their corruptions, and, further, that this despoliation would have to be carried out forcibly and carried out by secular powers. Interestingly, however, the secular powers will be acting as agents of the Almighty, as the Latin quote *"Hii in curribus . . ."* stresses.[29] Finally, lines 173–75 outline Langland's program for the reform of the friars, a program which suggests that better use can be made of their monastic endowments than the monks are now making. The fact that Langland was willing to see such alterations made in ecclesiastical institutions in order to provide a "fyndynge" for the friars is surely a measure of the desperation with which this somewhat conservative poet viewed the state of the contemporary clergy. All of these ideas can be paralleled in the prophecies of Hildegard, including the prediction of a similar ecclesiastical upheaval.

In what follows we will look closely at her attitudes to the following issues of clerical reform as they are voiced in the *Pentachronon*: (1) disendowment and the problem of justifying such an extreme act, (2) the "pseudo-prophets" or "false brethren" and their role in the downfall of the Church and clergy, and (3) the search for the *vita apostolica* and the question of what kind of changes in religious life she foresaw after the chastisement.

The visionary prophecy of Hildegard of Bingen

We will begin with the question of clerical corruption and despoliation as she speaks of it in the opening of a long passage from the *Liber divinorum operum* extracted for the *Pentachronon* in which Hildegard sets out her fully developed apocalyptic program (*PL* 197, cols. 1006–38, excepting a few short passages). This passage is typical of Hildegard's penchant for allegory in her visions, both in fully developed scenarios and momentary metaphors; it is also typical of the bitterly graphic style she adopts on questions of corruption in the Church. She opens by calling the clergy "perversi mercenarii" (col. 1006D), who devour the goods of the people like wolves. The charge that the clergy had become mercenaries or merchants of spiritual goods is often echoed in prophetic contexts because of its popularity with reform writers. Langland, for example, uses this common motif in his ominous lines:

> Ac sith charite hath be chapman and chief to shryue lordes
> Mony ferlyes han falle in a fewe ȝeres,
> And but holi chirche and charite choppe adoun suche shryuars
> The moste meschief on molde mounteth vp faste. (Prol. 62–65)

And Gower, citing a pseudo-Joachite text as the authority for a prophecy on simony, uses the same image of clerical "chapmen."[30] Hildegard continues:

Sed perversi mercenarii propter avaritiam pecuniae parvulos meos in valles prosternunt, eosque ad colles et ad montes ascendere prohibent; ipsisque nobilitatem, haereditatem, praedia et divitias abstrahunt; et hoc ut lupi rapaces faciunt, qui vestigiis ovium insidiantes, oves quas rapiunt laniant, et quas laniare non possunt fugant; atque dolosa deceptione parvulos meos per majores judices, et per iniquos tyrannos devorant.

(*Liber divinorum*, cols. 1006D–1007A)

The most memorable image in the passage is not the commonplace wolf imagery, which had been used profusely by reformers at least from the time of the Investiture Controversy onwards to designate simoniacs (Rauh, *Antichrist*, p. 492), but the claim that the avarice of the clergy "prostrates" the little ones "in the valleys and prevents them from ascending to the hills and mountains," giving a strikingly visual form to an abstract concept. This brief allegorical image – not even complete as allegory – is typical of the seemingly unpremeditated visionary imagery one comes to expect from writers like Langland and Hildegard. These "momentary flowerings of allegorical visualization," as Derek Pearsall has called them,[31] can be picked up and abandoned with amazing agility and often involve a mixing of the literal or the non-imagistic and the allegorical. There is, for example, no allegorical connection between the *mercenarii* and the casting down of the little ones into the valleys, but, one senses, in visionary writing this is not so important. It is the ever-fluctuating wave of visual ideas which creates the visionary effect, as much an outlet for passion as a form of literary art for the indignant writer.

Hildegard's use of the wolf imagery is much harsher than Langland's in a comparable passage. For Hildegard the avaricious clergy are wolves who tear or put to flight the "little ones" of the flock; for Langland the clerics are negligent shepherds, sleeping Simons and "dumb dogs" who won't bark. He quotes the proverb:

Sub molli pastore lupus lanam cacat, et grex
In-custoditus dilaceratur eo.   (IX. 265–66)

In both cases the laity are "torn," but ecclesiastical complaint for a vernacular audience is, when orthodox, rarely as bold as that written for a clerical audience in Latin. (Conversely, the fact that Langland is sometimes bolder than most orthodox writers also betrays his Latin sources.) Hildegard, writing exclusively for clerical consumption, is at times brutally frank in an attempt to shock and reform.

Justitia, neglected and abused, now becomes a key allegorical figure in the *Liber divinorum operum* vision as Hildegard describes the falling away of ecclesiastical institutions from the pristine state in which the antique fathers founded them (col. 1012D). The scene becomes more apocalyptic as Hildegard envisions *Justitia* crying out over the mountains and her voice resounding[32] to heaven (col. 1013B). In a passage reminiscent of the laments of Boethius' Lady Philosophy, *Justitia* complains that her robe is covered with the filth of the sins of the clergy, who were joined to Christ "per imitationem circumcisionis" and the legal constitutions of the priesthood, but who now rise up as fornicators (Hildegard's style is sometimes explicitly sexual) (col. 1013D). The clergy are blind, deaf and mute, and neither teach nor judge according to justice. She cries out for judges who will vindicate her (col. 1014), but before the passage ends Hildegard pauses to insert an assurance to the faithful clergy, for whom she always had a great deal of concern: God sees the man who fights valiantly against the devil during these wicked times and will not give him over into darkness (cols. 1014D–1015A).

The message of assurance is not simply a conventional flourish. *Justitia*'s call for vindication is shortly answered in a spectacular clerical reform prophecy. The disendowment and chastisement of the clergy which Hildegard envisions is forcible, immediate, ruthless and total.[33] Just as the Old Testament prophets did, Hildegard promises that "a remnant will be saved" after the Day of Reckoning, but this hardly lessens the terror of the day itself. As this vision proceeds, those who suffer at the hands of the perverters of righteousness ("praevaricatores rectitudinis") are allowed to take up the complaint of *Justitia* and to carry out her vindication. It soon becomes clear that those who are victimized by the corrupt clergy are the laity, or to be more precise, the nobility (they, at least, are the spokesmen). They ask how long they are to go on tolerating these rapacious wolves, who ravish the churches and leave the laity poor and destitute (col. 1017D). They then argue, in what is for the abbess of a Benedictine convent clearly a "world-upside-down" topos, that they will take the judgment and purgation of the clergy upon themselves, and that in so doing they will act out of self-preservation ("et hoc etiam idcirco faciamus ne pereamus"). They propose that the clergy be told to choose between fulfilling their office "quemadmodum antiqui Patres illa constituerunt," or departing and relinquishing what they have. Hildegard pauses here to say that these and similar things will be aroused in the laity by divine judgment and then carries the dramatization further in a more strident vein:

Haec et his similia divino judicio excitati illis acriter proponent, atque super eos irruentes dicent: "Nolumus hos regnare super nos, cum praediis, et agris, et reliquis saecularibus rebus, super quas principes constituti sumus." Et quomodo decet ut tonsi cum stolis et casulis suis plures milites et plura arma quam nos habeant? Sed et num conveniens est, ut clericus miles sit, et miles clericus? Unde abstrahamus eis quod non recte sed injuste habent.

(*Liber divinorum operum*, col. 1018B–C)

Since it is the prerogative of secular, not religious, people to rule over estates and armies, the laity feel justified in taking away what the clergy have "non recte sed injuste" acquired. Bernard Töpfer has shown just how realistic this expectation was in terms of the contemporary tensions between ecclesiastical and secular powers brought on by the papal schism of 1159, which set Church against state (*Reich*, p. 35). What we are dealing with here, as in Langland's disendowment-reform prophecies, is perhaps better described by the term "expectations" (Töpfer uses the term "Erwartungen") than "prophecy." This type of apocalyptic expectation is not the product of the wish-fulfillment dreams of Cloud-cuckoo-land: it reflects very real tensions, expectations and political positions.[34]

Two further points should be made with regard to this passage. Hildegard has the laity complain that the clergy use their "power of speaking, binding and unbinding" to maintain a hold over them ("Sed quoniam potestatem loquendi, ligandi et solvendi habent, idcirco ut ferocissimae bestiae nos capiunt," col. 1018A). She obviously feels that the laity must resent the special privileges of the clergy (that is, their education and spiritual powers). We know from other passages that Hildegard had a great distrust of the *doctores* of the Church, preferring knowledge acquired by divine inspiration to that acquired by books, and frequently castigating them for their restrictive attitude toward spreading knowledge and their failure to preach the Gospel effectively.[35] The power of binding and unbinding, more specifically, was obviously being used, in Hildegard's view, simply as a means of oppression or coercion (as in the use of excommunication to make someone comply with demands). In any case, Hildegard seems to have felt no hesitation about speaking out even on such a sensitive point as this. Writing in Latin for a clerical audience, Hildegard is again able to be more strident than a vernacular writer like Langland, but the theme of the abuse of clerical power is evident in *Piers Plowman*, from the anti-clericalism of the pardon-tearing scene to the complaints of sophistry among friars and schoolmen.

One difficulty with this passage – and this is the type of difficulty we frequently meet in *Piers Plowman* – is the problem of determining to what extent the views placed in the mouths of certain characters are also the views of Hildegard. Although, as we shall see, Hildegard did not feel that the plunder of clerical wealth by secular powers was necessarily *just*, she did feel that it was *justified* to a certain extent and she saw it as a divinely permitted purgation of the Church through tribulation (*Liber divinorum operum*, col. 1017D). In the justifications given by the secular powers for their action and the reaction of the clergy as portrayed by Hildegard much depends on tone and this changes from excerpt to excerpt, but it would seem that Hildegard's sympathy usually lies more with the secular powers. She goes to great lengths in the next section of the *Liber divinorum operum* excerpt to give them elaborate justifications for their actions (cols. 1018C–1019A). Recognizing that in any disendowment of the monasteries the souls of those who gave the endowments are at stake, the laity advise discretion, "quoniam hoc rapina non est." Using a micro-allegory of the laity and religious as sons of a just father (that is, God), they explain that neither son should be allowed to oppress the other because it was never ordained that "both the tunic and the cloak be given to one son while the other remain naked," but rather that the laity should receive the cloak "because of the breadth of their concerns," and the religious the tunic, lest they be deficient in food or clothing, and lest they possess more than necessary ("et ne plus quam necesse sit possideant"). Wherever there is excess among the clergy, it is proposed, it will be given to the needy. This is the language, once again, of reformist thought, language which will be familiar to readers of Langland.

Hildegard was capable of irony and the arguments of the laity could be read as simply hypocritical rationalizations for greed, but there is too much here which falls in line with orthodox reform thinking and, more specifically, with Hildegard's own teachings (unequivocally stated elsewhere) to support such a reading. There is nothing that Hildegard wished more fervently in all her writings than that, as the secular powers say, the clergy should fulfil their duties "in the same way as the antique fathers constituted them" (col. 1018B). As Rauh has pointed out, Hildegard always measures the Church in relation to the timeless ideal of the apostolic "Urkirche" (*Antichrist*, p. 495).

Further proof that her sympathy lies with the secular powers can be found in her treatment of the clergy's reaction:

Sed cum tandem praesenserint quod nec potestate ligandi, nec solvendi, nec confirmatione oblationum suarum, nec strepitu armorum, nec blanditiis, nec minis, ipsis resistere potuerunt, divino judicio territi inanem superbamque fiduciam quam prius in semetipsis semper habuerant deponentes et in se reduentes, coram illis humiliabuntur, atque ululando clamabunt, et dicent: "Quia omnipotentem Deum in ordine officii nostri abjecimus, idcirco super nos confusio haec inducta est, videlicet ut ab illis opprimamur et humiliemur, quos opprimere et humiliare debueramus." (*Liber divinorum operum*, cols. 1018D–1019A)

This passage is rather remarkable for its political pragmatism. Hildegard was obviously under no illusions about the different strategies that the clergy would use, if threatened, to maintain their position. The power of binding and unbinding comes first on the list, which is arranged in order of ever-decreasing clerkly decorum. The characterization is by no means flattering: Hildegard refers to the "inane pride and faith which they had always had in themselves" and from there on the image of the clergy degenerates into the almost comic characterization which Hildegard usually reserves for her dramatization of demons.[36] The use of words like howling ("ululando") and the absurdly proud assertion that they are now oppressed and humiliated by those whom "to oppress and humiliate we ought" are markers of this type of treatment. It is clear that whatever guilt she might attach to the attack of the nobility, Hildegard had little sympathy for their victims. However, her conservatism, never content for very long with an upheaval of the social hierarchy, comes out at the end of the prophecy, where she promises that all will be righted and "famuli ad debitam servitutem subjectionis suae redeant" (col. 1019D). It is difficult as a twentieth-century reader to see this as the happy ending Hildegard intended it to be!

Although the despoliation prophecy we have just discussed from the *Liber divinorum operum* gained enough popularity to be circulated in manuscripts independently of its context in the *Liber divinorum operum* or *Pentachronon*, by far the most popular single Hildegard prophecy in circulation in the later Middle Ages was an extract from her letter to the clergy of Cologne (Ep. XLVIII, cols. 243–53). The extract, beginning in most manuscripts "O filia Sion, corona honoris capitis filiorum tuorum inclinabitur . . ." (or "De vivente luce iterum audivi vocem dicentem: O filia Sion," etc.), coincides with Gebeno's extract from this letter for the *Pentachronon* suggesting that it is the source for the independent piece.[37] The letter is one of two letters on the Cathar heretics known to have been written by Hildegard.[38] Extracts from both letters appear in the *Pentachronon* because for Hildegard the heretics had an apocalyptic significance and her discussions on the subject therefore turn into prophetic visions. She had visited Cologne and preached vigorously against the Cathars and the laxity of the clergy there (*Briefwechsel*, p. 168). For Hildegard, as for many reformers, the two issues were not unrelated: as the clergy became more corrupt, a confused and frustrated laity turned elsewhere for spiritual leadership. The heretical groups, whose clergy were often models of the ascetic life, gathered a large number of lay adherents and in some areas like Cologne were growing stronger as the orthodox Church grew weaker.

Hildegard prophesies in this letter that the heretics will play a part in encouraging the princes to rise up against the corrupt clergy and take away their property, persecuting and chastising them, until, as a result of their many tribulations, the clergy will arise renewed and purified. The prophecy is of interest to us not only because of its disendowment-reform theme, but because Hildegard's description of the heretics formed the basis of her later reputation as an anti-mendicant prophetess. As the pseudo-apostles of Hildegard's "apocalyptic grammar,"[39] the heretics can also be seen to play a role in her writings similar to the role that the friars play in *Piers Plowman*. For both writers these wayward spiritual guides are types of the pseudo-prophets of II Timothy 3, and as such signal not the End of the World, but the end of an era for the corrupt clergy. As symptoms of a disease that originated with the negligence of the clergy themselves, these pseudo-prophets will play an important role, for both writers, in the eventual downfall of the Church. The treatment of the pseudo-prophets by Langland and Hildegard is, obviously, not the same in every detail, but their symbolic function is exactly similar. Both writers chose to fill this symbolic slot in apocalyptic typology with the *bête noire* of their particular age.[40]

At the start of the *Pentachronon* extract, Hildegard hears a voice from the Living Light cry out: "O filia Sion, corona honoris capitis filiorum tuorum inclinabitur, et pallium dilatationis divitiarum eorum imminuetur" (col. 249A–B). The cloak, again symbolizing excessive riches, is soon to be diminished. Both the avarice and the shiftlessness of the clergy will bring God's wrath upon them in the form of despoliation and humiliation ("ad servos servorum computabimini") when they are judged by the laity ("et ipsi judices vestri erunt"). However, this will only be the first scourging ("flagella"): "alia autem et postea alia et pejora venient" (col. 249C). As Hildegard watches, the devil addresses the heretics, urging them to rise up and take their riches and honours from the clergy. Even though she acknowledges that the coming chastisement will be brought on by sham accusers (that is, the heretics), she stresses to her clerical audience that they "will not hide your works" ("opera vestra non celabit"), implying that the false accusers will only be returning evil for evil (col. 249D).

The description of the heretics or *populus errans* (as she calls them) which follows is, as we shall see in chapter 4, so much reminiscent of later anti-mendicant descriptions of the friars that it was readily picked up by polemicists (see Kerby-Fulton, "Antimendicant Propaganda"). Feigning holiness, poverty and chastity these imposters will incite the laity to despoil the clergy (cols. 249D–250A). In a delightful section Hildegard comically represents the devil gloating over these pseudo-apostles as his best scheme yet (col. 250B). Throughout this passage she exploits the satirical mode she reserves for "low-life" figures as, for example, when she has the heretics boast of their invincible chastity by saying that other men who strove for chastity before them had dried themselves out like baked fish (col. 250C). Hildegard's apocalyptic visions are not entirely solemn and show a good deal of vitality, with touches of graphic realism or homely imagery such as this one.

Fear of the heretics' power over the laity,[41] and especially over women (col. 251A–B) is a real concern for Hildegard, one which the anti-mendicant polemicists were not slow to pick up on. Hildegard, like Langland in v. 169, describes the despoliation as a beating, literally "with clubs and sticks, whence all the earth shall tremble" (cols. 250D–251A), but this threat is followed, as it always is in Hildegard, with an explanation of why such tribulations are necessary and how they fit into God's plan for Salvation History:

Nam oportet ut per tribulationes et contritiones prava hominum opera purgentur. Sed tamen multae aerumnae et illis accumulantur, qui aliis in impietate sua miserias inferunt. Infideles autem homines isti, et a diabolo seducti, scopa vestra erunt ad castigandum vos.

(col. 251C)

However, these deceivers, she says adamantly, will not be those who will come before the Last Day (that is, the pseudo-apostles of II Timothy 3), "sed praecurrens germen illorum sunt." And when it is discovered that they have indulged in the "perversities of Baal" (the idolatry of the priests of Baal being a standard allegorical image for simony in reform literature [Rauh, *Antichrist*, p. 490]), they will be hunted down just as rabid wolves, she promises. Then:

Nam prima aurora justitiae, in spiritali populo tunc surget, ut primitus cum parvo numero incoepit, nec ipsi multas facultates, nec multas divitias habere volunt, quae animas occidunt . . . Et sic postea in humilitate vivent, nec pravis operibus Deo rebellare cupient. Sed a multis erroribus purgati, deinceps in fortissima vi rectitudinis persistent.

(Ep. XLVIII, cols. 251D–252A)

Her assertion that the coming wave of spiritual seducers would not be heralds of the End, but only forerunners, and her exuberant belief in an age of renewal for the religious, a "first dawn of justice" which would follow upon the chastisement, were probably both factors in the popularity of her apocalyptic writings.[42] The pattern of renewal following upon tribulation gave her contemporaries both a way of understanding dark times and hope for the future beyond them. It is no wonder that Gebeno reached for his copy of Hildegard when confronted with rumors of the birth of Antichrist.

What Hildegard is describing in passages like the one above on the coming first dawn of justice is a drastically changed clergy, reduced to small numbers, humbled and poor. Her repristination visions were meant as both a return to earlier purity and also, in her later prophecies, a development of something even greater, a heightened level of spirituality new to history.[43]

The pattern of a clergy both institutionally and spiritually renewed by chastisement and despoliation can be seen in Langland's thinking as well. When he speaks of the awakening of Cain and his destruction by Dowell (B.x.333–34) at the end of the B-text version of the first disendowment prophecy, for example, or of the redistribution of clerical (mainly monastic) wealth so that the friars will no longer be corrupted by their needs, one sees the same kinds of concerns (now translated into fourteenth-century issues). The fact that Langland chose to end the poem on this theme suggests that it was of more than passing interest to him.

It is difficult for us as twentieth-century people to grasp the radical nature of such visions of drastic change for people like Langland and Hildegard. In Hildegard's day only the proponents of new orders, defending themselves against charges of "novelty," advocated changes in traditional monastic structure. The elaborate justifications which Hildegard places in the mouths of the laity suggest her nervousness about what she was advocating through her visions. Langland's prophetic policies, if realized, would have meant not only an end to a way of life for wealthy monasteries, but the setting aside of the *Rule of Francis*, a document which, in ideological if not in practical terms, Langland admired greatly. Change, whether in the twelfth or the fourteenth century, was regarded as more suspect than it is generally thought to be today; belief in change for the better, that is, chiliasm, and especially spiritual chiliasm, was relatively rare. In this sense Hildegard and the twelfth-century apocalyptic reformers are an important witness for Langland scholars.

Like many reformist thinkers, including Langland, Hildegard idealized the eremitism of the Desert Fathers.[44] With the flourishing of a multitude of new orders in the twelfth century, many of whom were stressing more austere models of the *vita apostolica* than traditional Benedictine monasticism had advocated, it is no wonder that alert individuals like Hildegard from comfortable clerical establishments began to foresee the necessity for imminent change, especially in the return of the clergy to a state of apostolic rigor. It is from the ideological ferment of the twelfth century that the notion that traditional monasticism would soon give way to newer institutions arises. Hildegard's contemporary, Rupert of Deutz, head of a Benedictine abbey, reformer, apocalyptic writer and monastic apologist, recorded his objection to the comment of a regular canon who had remarked that monastic orders would rise and fall just like ruling Kingdoms of Old

Testament history. Rupert retorted, to quote Chenu's colorful translation, "What an altogether wrong and insulting comparison between the monasteries of the Kingdom of God and those monstrous kingdoms destined to the fires of Hell" (Chenu, *Nature, Man and Society*, p. 215). This small incident, from Rupert's *Super quaedam capitula regulae divi Benedicti abbatis (PL* 170, cols. 535ff.), gives us some sense of the tone in which monastic changes were being discussed, and the apprehensions they raised. But Hildegard, unlike Rupert, was able to foresee the kind of change in established clerical institutions which could very well be compared to the fall and rise of dynasties.

In a very idealistic letter on monastic perfection and eremitism written to the Cistercians of Eberbach, Hildegard relies very heavily on parallels from biblical history for an understanding of the significance for the clerical institutions of the coming apocalyptic events. In the section extracted by Gebeno for the *Pentachronon* (Ep. LI, cols. 263D–264A, 264C–266A), she condemns those of the regular and secular clergy "who are called converted but are not"[45] because they love contrareity more than rectitude (col. 263D). Because they do so, they are similar to the pseudo-prophets (col. 264A). Hildegard's description of these pseudo-prophets, this time *within* the Church instead of outside it, is once again strongly reminiscent of the anti-mendicant literature of later years: these men are mild in speech but imprudent and perverse in example (col. 265A); what they have begun in humility and poverty they do not see through to the end (col. 265B); they are proud like the Pharisees and they take on riches, multiplying their worldly cares (col. 265C); they wish to have Heaven and earth at the same time (col. 265D); like asses, these men will eventually fall under the burden of a double load (col. 266A). Pleading with the Cistercians to purge themselves before the days of tribulation when they will be converted *perforce* to humility, poverty and servitude, she adds that God will carry out this purgation "quemadmodum etiam veterem legem Deus a consuetudine sua in spiritalem vitam mutavit, et ut unamquamque priorem institutionem ad utilora purgavit" (col. 264A). Hildegard daringly compares the coming changes in spiritual life with those effected in institutions under the Old Law with the coming of Christ. This bold use of the most significant shift in biblical history as a parallel to what is to come in clerical life is closest to Joachim of Fiore's prophecy of the coming dispensation of the Holy Spirit (see below, pp. 165–72). This expectation of clerical purgation and renewal, which she compares to God's purgation of institutions under the Old Law, seems to her so inherent in current events that she is willing to challenge the Augustinian view of Salvation History as declining after the Incarnation in order to accommodate it. As Guntram Bischoff has written of the twelfth-century apocalyptic reformist, the Premonstratensian Eberwin of Steinfeld (whom he believes to be the canon who provoked the remark made by Rupert of Deutz quoted above):

[His] exegesis amounted, in fact, to nothing less than an overthrow of the Augustinian tradition, and no matter how one might reason, the expectation that a future order would at last perfect the implementation of the true apostolic tradition could not be made to tally with the accustomed view of the already perfected corporate existence of the Church in a *mundus senescens*. ("Eschatology," p. 62)

The visionary prophecy of Hildegard of Bingen

This clash in medieval views of history is noteworthy for Hildegardian and for *Piers Plowman* specialists alike. The old Augustinian view of history is not an adequate guide to the understanding of any reformist thinker who, like Langland, shows such clear signs of having encountered the new apocalypticism. Langland, writing two hundreds years later, shows much the same desire as Hildegard in wishing to see "each single institution purged toward greater utility," with his forecast of wholesale and "incurable" (v. 177) institutional changes in the organization of the monastic and fraternal orders.

The last despoliation prophecy which we will consider comes from Hildegard's famous letter to Werner of Kircheim (Ep. LII, cols. 269–71) again, extracted by Gebeno for the *Pentachronon*. The letter gives yet another instance of Hildegard's daring parallels with biblical history in her discussion of the coming clerical chastisement; it also gives us some insight into the genesis of her prophetic visions through meditation on a particular biblical quotation which seems to have inspired the vision and which introduces new elements into her prophetic program. Variations from letter to letter also occur as she responds differently to different correspondents;[46] in general, she is harder on the secular clergy than on the regulars, as here. This letter was written in response to a letter from Werner and the society of priests of which he was Deacon (*Briefwechsel*, p. 174). Hildegard had spoken to this group on her last preaching tour (1170–71) and what she had to say was not flattering.

In this vision she sees the kings of the earth participating with princes in the takeover of clerical wealth, but with a difference: the kings will do so out of greed ("inhiabunt"), while the princes will "wish to show themselves obedient to God" ("et in hoc facto obsequium Deo se exhibuisse volunt"). The tone of this comment is, again, difficult to gauge; clearly Hildegard, once more, does not uphold the despoliation as *just* but as *justified*, or at least provoked (col. 270D). After detailing the sins of those who have neglected their priestly duties, she quotes Psalm 2:1, 2 ("Why have the nations raged and the people devised vain things? The kings of the earth stood up and the princes met together") and continues:

Nam permissione Dei, super vos in judiciis suis fremere incipient plurimae gentes, et multi populi de vobis meditabuntur inania, cum sacerdotale officium vestrum et consecrationem vestram pro nihilo computabunt. His assistent in eversione vestra reges terrae, et terrenis rebus inhiabunt, et principes qui vobis dominabuntur, convenient in hoc uno consilio, quatenus vos de terminis suis expellant, quoniam innocentem Agnum a vobis per pessima opera fugastis. (col. 271A)

The participation of the kings, which was not a factor in the other versions of the uprising, seems to have been suggested by the verse from the Psalms. As in the *Liber divinorum operum*, Hildegard warns that their priestly office will mean nothing at the time of the persecution. She seems to feel that while the people may be guilty of meditating "vain things," the clergy will have provoked the outburst "per pessima opera" (col. 271A).

This prophecy illustrates that Hildegard's concept of the prophet's role is partly exegetical. Like Langland she can use biblical verses as seals of authenticity, as funds of imagery or as kernels of wisdom which can inspire new visions or add new dimensions to old ones, as here. Prophets like Hildegard and Joachim of Fiore felt they had a special insight into the meaning of certain scriptural texts, and Langland, whatever he believed about his prophetic gift, shares with these writers some startling applications of biblical quotations to current or future events.

As the vision ends Hildegard, referring to herself as "paupercula feminea forma" (a formula which she often uses to affirm her utter helplessness as recipient [not creator] of her visions), sees an extended sword hanging in the air with one edge turned toward Heaven, the other toward earth: "Et gladius iste super spiritalem populum extendebatur . . . Et vidi quod gladius iste quaedam loca spiritalium hominum abscindebat, quemadmodum Jerusalem post passionem Domini abscissa est" (col. 271C). In making this bold biblical parallel between the destruction of Jerusalem after Christ's Passion and the imminent cutting down of the clergy, Hildegard is doing more than simply using a biblical allusion for dramatic effect. As she suggests in her letter to the Cistercians of Eberbach, she saw the coming clerical chastisement as a momentous event in Salvation History, one equal in importance to the events which closed the Old Testament era. Like Langland two centuries later she placed the issue of clerical reform at the centre of universal history. However, although this is one of her harsher letters, it, too, ends with the reassurance that the God-fearing, pure and simple priests will be saved, just as Elijah was promised that the Israelites who had not worshipped Baal would be saved (III Kings 19:18).[47]

Let us pause now to reflect on Langland's disendowment prophecies in the light of Hildegard's visions on the same theme. Langland's prophecies (v. 168–79 and XVII. 204–32) also suggest that the king and the nobility will carry out the takeover. The argument given in the Passus XVII prophecy is very close to the argument that Hildegard puts in the mouths of the nobility in the *Liber divinorum operum*.[48] Langland reinforces his argument by preceding it with the stories of the fall of the Templars and the legend of Constantine, but he obviously does not feel ambivalent about the essential rightness of committing such an act.[49] Hildegard, on the other hand, while believing that the purgation would be good for the clergy, feels she must disapprove to some extent of the act itself, as we saw in her letter to Werner of Kircheim. This difference probably reflects Langland's and Hildegard's personal situations. Hildegard was one of the possessioners herself, while Langland, as far as we know, was likely a member of the unbeneficed secular clergy. Another difference between the two lies in their attitudes toward kingship. While Langland, in the prophecy in Passus v, looks for a reformer-king, Hildegard distrusts kingship as an institution and places her faith in the nobility (no doubt because she was herself of noble birth).

However, despite their differences in historical and personal situation, Langland's and Hildegard's attitudes toward reform of the clergy are remarkably similar; both believed that the reform had to be forcible, that it had to be carried out by secular powers and that the clergy had no business in the management of properties, armies[50] or other secular affairs. Both felt that the children of the nobility were being robbed of their inheritance.[51] Both stress that poverty is the only temporal state conducive to spiritual life and that clerical "perfection" requires that clerics follow a certain, strictly defined manner of life. Both insist that a redistribution of the wealth amassed by the clergy is the only way to redress injustices. Both focus on a *populus errans* (for Hildegard, the heretics and for Langland, the friars) as the pseudo-prophets who signal that the rot has set into the clerical structure, but both recognize that these pseudo-prophets are only the symptoms and not the causes of the Church's problems: the Church itself has begotten the antichrist which plagues it. Both are prepared for sweeping institutional changes in the present clerical orders to bring them closer to the ideals of the true apostolic life and wholly reform the Church.

Langland struggles with these themes and concerns throughout *Piers Plowman*, and not just in the two disendowment prophecies, while Hildegard is similarly obsessed with the question of clerical goals, standards and ideals. For Hildegard it is clear that the state of the clergy and the vitality of spiritual commitment remain nothing less than the measuring-stick of the quality of life in all ages, past and still to come, and one suspects that these concerns are at the center of Langland's poem for the same reason.

CHRONICLING THE FUTURE: THE APOCALYPTIC PROGRAM

Hildegard saw everything in terms of the course of Salvation History. The glory of Adam, his closeness to God, his prophetic vision,[52] his perfection were all immensely important subjects in her work, set over against the Fall and God's laborious attempts to rebuild his revelation through Noah, Abraham, Moses, Christ and all the prophets and great leaders of history who had tried to regain something of what Adam had lost. This roll-call of Salvation History occurs often enough in Hildegard's prophetic passages that it becomes formulaic. She uses the series of Old Testament leaders before Christ, as Langland does his Abraham–Moses–Good Samaritan triad, to highlight the development of Salvation History.[53] Just as there had been forerunners of Christ's First Coming, so there would be forerunners of His Second, both good and evil, and Hildegard is similar to Langland, and other apocalyptic thinkers, in trying to read the signs of the current times to discover these. Hildegard says at one point in describing the decline into decadence of her own period of history that soon the "forerunning signs" of Doomsday which Christ foretold to his inquiring disciples will be seen, so that many will think that the Day of Judgment is imminent: "cum aliis quibusdam praecurrentibus signis, quae Filius Dei ante diem judicii discipulis suis perquirentibus ventura praedixerat in terra multoties fuerint, ut multi dicerent diem judicii imminere" (*Liber divinorum operum*, col. 1005D). Many would say that it was imminent but, by implication, Hildegard would not. The signs are, for her, a warning – a warning of the kind of cycle which has occurred many times on earth and is not occurring now for the last time.

There is no doubt, however, that in Hildegard's view her own time was apocalyptically significant. In the *Prooemium vitae s. Disibodi* (in Pitra, *Analecta*, pp. 352–57; *Pentachronon*, pp. 355–57), which is a kind of dedicatory letter to the monks of her former monastery at Disibodenberg, she reassures them that the time of the End is not yet come but describes her own time as the worst of all, by implication worse than the time of Antichrist (*Prooemium*, pp. 356–57). By the end of her life, when most of her important apocalyptic work was written, she regarded her own age with so much horror and disgust that for her it was like a second Fall of Adam. For Hildegard, the only way of grasping the horror of the present age was to place it in the context of all that had gone before – and then all that lay ahead. Liebeschütz (*Weltbild*, p. 143) notes that this typological framework is especially common in her correspondence. When a correspondent asks Hildegard about the sorrows of the present time, she places the whole situation within the context of Salvation History *sub specie aeternitatis* in order to try to provide an answer, an assurance that God has set some limits to the power of evil in their time, as He had done and would do in others (Russell, *Method*, p. 106).

Hildegard's disillusionment with her own times, and her unwavering belief that all previous ages were somehow more morally and spiritually inclined than her own, are such pervasive, if commonplace, ideas that they should be briefly noticed here. Much to the annoyance of modern women scholars, Hildegard characterized her own age as the "tempus muliebre," a time of debilitatingly feminine weakness in which spiritual strength was at its lowest point since the Fall (*Prooemium*, p. 355). This sense of the writer's own time being worse than any other and therefore especially historically significant, is very common among apocalyptic thinkers, as is the ability, which Langland also exhibits, to speak in glowing terms of past glories, uninhibited by any sense of historical realism.[54] At one point Langland introduces this notion in the midst of a discussion of clerical corruption in the present day. Nothing, he says, functions as well as it used to:

> For what thorw werre and wrake and wikkede hefdes,
> May no preyere pees make in no place, hit semeth.
> Lewed men han no byleue and lettred men erren;
> Noþer see ne sond ne þe seed ȝeldeth
> As they ywoned were – in wham is defaute?   (XVII. 85–89)

Such attitudes are not peculiar to apocalyptic writers by any means, but they do form part of the apocalyptic world view. Hildegard's periodization of her own age shows the ambivalence she felt about human capacity for reform, an ambivalence which creates the central apocalyptic tensions in *Piers Plowman* as well. Even when writing *Scivias*, she inexplicably altered the traditional Augustinian sequence of ages based on the seven days of creation and stated that now the sixth age was finished and the world was in the course of the seventh day of rest.[55] She looks back almost wistfully to the sixth age during which, she says, new miracles were manifested on earth, even as on the sixth day God created man. The sixth age, which had seen the Incarnation, the ministry of Christ and the apostles and the glory of the early Church, was now, for Hildegard, over. She is unwilling to associate this age with her own, so she shifts the present time into the seventh age. Her feelings about this time are definitely mixed. Being the seventh "day," it is a

46

time of rest, perhaps even of stagnation, but also a time when the seals of Scripture will be opened (an allusion to the opening of the seventh seal in Apocalypse, chapter 8) through, she suggests, a prophet figure like herself.[56] However, the implication is definitely that this "opening" will have to occur by divine intervention because the institutional Church has failed.

The concern of this type of writer is to fit every event into the larger plan of history. So keen is this perception of a plan of the whole of history that no apocalyptic writer works without one – whether it be sketched out explicitly, as with Hildegard, or alluded to implicitly, as with Langland, the plan becomes the key to analysis of present ills and to hope for the future. We will now turn to Hildegard's detailed and very explicitly laid out apocalyptic program as she describes it in the final visions of the *Liber divinorum operum* and then try to sketch in, as far as is possible, the program implicit in Langland's prophetic passages, having acquired a general sense of how such a pattern functions in apocalyptic thought.

Hildegard went back to her vision of the five beasts in *Scivias*, which signified five vaguely bad periods before the End, and refurbished it for the *Liber divinorum operum*, replete with extensive "historical" detail and a characterization of each age. Her own time, the time of the fiery dog, she characterized as the days of "torpid injustice" (col. 1017A). Hildegard explains that justice gradually grew among men from the time of the Flood, strengthened by the prophets and later by the apostles and Doctors of the Church, until the present time of feminine debility (col. 1017B). The decay of the present time, she writes, began with the coming of a "secular judge," whom she describes elsewhere as a tyrant and fornicator. Almost certainly this is Emperor Henry IV, who opposed the ecclesiastical reforms of Pope Gregory VII, and who was regarded as an Antichrist figure by contemporary reformers (McGinn, *Visions*, p. 94). She complains in the same passage of a "bearer of a spiritual name" who died by the judgment of God, probably, as Charles Czarski has argued ("Prophecies," p. 148), Pope Anastasius. Hildegard says that during the days of these leaders the "tempus muliebre" began to take hold, invoking the image of female weakness, as does Langland (B. VI. 328), to suggest crisis of leadership. "But," she adds, "the days of sorrow are not as yet come" (col. 1017C).[57]

In contrast, the approaching age, to be ushered in by the reform of the Church, Hildegard called the "tempus virile," which she associated in the *Liber divinorum operum* with the lion from the *Scivias* vision of the five beasts. During this time, Hildegard says, not only will the Church be reformed by violence, but there will be a parallel reform of society through violence, "quoniam Deus crudelitatem poenarum ad purgationem iniquitatum inimicis suis tunc concedet, sic etiam a principio mundi semper fecit" (*Liber*, col. 1020A). The time of peace which follows this will be characterized by spiritual strength and the conversion of the Jews, a time Hildegard compares typologically to the peaceful time before the birth of Christ (col. 1020D). Once again, the paralleling of a time so close to the End with the period of Christ's advent was a radical departure from Augustinian tradition. Hildegard gives a lavish account of the millenarian state of things to come: in line with man's changed behavior, the air will become sweeter, the earth more abundant and all the elements will work together in harmony (col. 1022A). Drawing on Isaiah's millenarian prophecy, as Langland does in a similar passage, Hildegard says that arms will be forbidden and only iron tools for cultivation will be retained; any man transgressing this law will be killed with his own weapon (col. 1022B). The Holy Spirit will pour out the dew of His grace in prophecy, wisdom and holiness. Hildegard here anticipates the Joachite *status* of the Holy Spirit (see pp. 165–72, below), especially in her emphasis (a constantly recurring feature of her prophecies) on a new prophetic spirituality. All religious orders will stand in righteousness at this time, having cast off pride and superfluity of riches (col. 1022C). So great will be the sanctity of men that angels will keep company with them, seeing the possibility of "new and holy conversations" in their presence (col. 1022D). However, a latent Augustinian world view is reflected in Hildegard's comment that there will be much rejoicing, but not full rejoicing, because of awareness of the future Judgment; men will be similar to pilgrims, she says, who strive toward their country, lacking full joy while still traveling (col. 1022D).

The transition into the next age (the age of the pale horse) comes with a wavering of justice and religion. Hildegard seems to be describing the kind of fluctuation which Langland portrays in the last passus of *Piers Plowman* as pestilence, famine and other disasters make for temporary periods of adherence to spiritual values, which then decline again as the memory of adversity fades (col. 1023C). But, she warns, a time of extreme sorrow will fall upon men when they forget to attribute their good fortune to God's grace; then sorrow will be heaped upon sorrow, as never before (cols. 1023D–1024A). In what is hardly a good advertisement for chiliastic pacifism, she asserts that the pagans will choose this time to invade the Christians because, as pacifists, they will be without arms or strength (col. 1024A). Many cities and regions will be destroyed and the Church's discipline will be polluted once again. When the pagans ("incredulae et horribiles gentes") attempt to attack, however, the Christian people, in penitence for their sins, will be protected by a miraculous dust cloud (col. 1025D). Hildegard then envisions one of those mass scenes of penitence and praise which are often featured in apocalyptic writing and which Langland portrays so movingly at certain points in *Piers Plowman* (such as VII. 152–57 or XXI. 207–12). The miracle brings about the conversion of the pagans and a renewal of faith among Christians.

With these last events, the pendulum begins to swing in a different direction and Hildegard describes a return to spirituality once again. In complete contradiction to older apocalyptic thought, she sees the deterioration of the Roman Empire as a positive event. Older eschatology had established the notion that the Roman Empire was the unnamed agent who was described as holding back the tide of Antichrist in II Thessalonians 2:7.[58] For Hildegard and the German reformers of her period, the Roman Empire was anything but a positive force. Once the empire has been dispersed, it will never be able to be rebuilt. After the division of the empire, the papacy will also fall,[59] having deteriorated from its pristine dignity to such an extent that only Rome and a few neighboring regions will remain under its jurisdiction.

The visionary prophecy of Hildegard of Bingen

With the disappearance of these two great medieval institutions, which Hildegard obviously thought hopelessly corrupt, spiritual strength will reach unprecedented heights: the abundance of the earth, harmony of the elements and prophetic revelations once again mark this kind of change (col. 1027C). Princes and ecclesiastics will reprove each other and cooperate in maintaining good government and morality (col. 1027B). Most interesting is the comment that men will return to the "antique" disciplines: Hildegard here harks back to the pristine dignity of early Christianity (col. 1027B).

At the same time, however, many heresies and much iniquity will develop as Antichrist approaches, this being, appropriately enough, the time of the pig in the *Scivias* vision (*Liber divinorum operum*, col. 1027D). As if to justify these extreme changes in her apocalyptic program, Hildegard explains here that "the world at no time remains in one state." From here until the end of the *Liber divinorum operum* she returns to a nearly standard eschatology of Antichrist's life, reign and defeat. This is the time of the wolf for Hildegard, because the sheep of Christ will be devoured in the persecutions of Antichrist and the great number of martyrs of this era will bring to fulfillment the number of the saints since the primitive Church (col. 1034A–B). After the defeat of Antichrist Hildegard ends the prophecy, and the *Liber divinorum operum* itself, with the mass conversion and renewal of the Church, giving her version of Salvation History a truly comedic form. The song of praise she uses comes from Apocalypse 12: "Now is come salvation and strength and the kingdom of our God and the power of his Christ; because the accuser of our brethren is cast forth . . ." (Apocalypse 12:10). This renewal is an optimistic extrapolation of the exegetical "refreshment of the saints" tradition, which marks Hildegard as an optimist, if not a full chiliast.[60]

Summarizing Hildegard's complete program into the form of a schedule we get a detailed system of good and bad times to come – and *much* to come – before Antichrist:

Symbol		Description of time period
fiery hound	1	Time of spiritual weakness of "feminine debility" ("tempus muliebre") –clergy are "perversi mercenarii," simoniacs and heretics are forerunners of Antichrist –both secular and spiritual leaders are corrupt (emperor and pope) –Church has fallen away from pristine apostolic discipline
lion	2	Time of chastisement and disendowment of Church and purgation through tribulation for all –"tempus utile" or "tempus virile" –renewal of spiritual strength revealed through prophecy, abundance and peace – utopian vision –conversion of pagans
pale horse	3	Time of sorrows –Church polluted –persecution of Christians by heathens

>   –Christians saved by miracle and conversion of heathens
>   –Papacy and Empire dispersed
>   –Church returns to pristine discipline
>   –renewal of spiritual strength again revealed through prophecy,
>   abundance and peace

black pig   4   Reign of heretics and forerunners of Antichrist
                    –many Christians desert orthodoxy
                    –moral decay and spiritual decline
                    –signs of the End

grey wolf   5   Antichrist's "ministry"
                    –persecution of faithful and traditional eschatological events

                  Death of Antichrist
                  Renewal of Church and spirituality
                  Last Judgment

The pendulum effect of such an apocalyptic program is immediately evident: the swings between periods of good and evil show that the optimism of millenarian dreams soon gives way to pessimism, and vice versa. What Rauh (*Antichrist*, p. 510) has referred to as the cycle of Build-up, Decay and Restitution (paralleled by the biblical cycle of Creation, the Fall and Salvation) is at work here all the time. It is informed by the apocalyptic writer's sense of the weakness of human nature and human institutions, and the strongly ingrained medieval notion that no perfection is possible on earth where man is only a pilgrim. All this is set over against an indomitable sense of hope.

However, perhaps the most important thing to note about such a program is the important place which it gives to Church renewal. Hildegard's scheme differs from the "old" eschatology and the Augustinian scheme of the seven ages in that she sees spiritual renewal occurring before the End of the World, both before and after Antichrist. Although, like Marjorie Reeves, I do not see in Hildegard's scheme the full-blown historical optimism of Joachim of Fiore (Reeves, "Originality," p. 286), it must be conceded that Hildegard's vision of the future is a radical departure from the old view of the close of history. Her post-Antichrist chiliasm (to use Lerner's terminology, "Black Death," pp. 541ff.) differs from Joachim's, as Reeves says, in that "this last period is seen not so much as a new epoch in history as the rounding off of the work of the Son" ("Originality," p. 286). Later medieval readers coupled her apocalyptic program together with Joachim's and saw no discrepancy between the two. As Langland's contemporary, Henry of Hassia, wrote: "Est verum quod Hildegardis et Abbas Joachim sonant quasi finem mundi et adventum antichristi precessure sint una vel plures reformaciones ecclesie seu reduciones in statum primitive sanctitatis."[61] The point for medieval readers seems to have been that these reformist apocalyptic writers saw hope for the Church in the future and placed this hope in chastisement and reform of the clergy in particular; whether this would happen before or after Antichrist was perhaps of less importance to them than it has been to modern scholars. To a medieval reader, prophecy of the

Church's apocalyptic renewal was sufficiently startling in itself, it seems, and this is a point which should interest Langland scholars.

Let us now try to patch together from some of Langland's prophecies the scheme with which he was working – however unconsciously. The first passage which reveals something of this fragmentary schedule is in the prophecy at the end of Passus III (lines 436–81). Conscience has been trying to show how dangerous a desire for "mede" can be and he uses the exemplum of Saul's disobedience to God in not killing Agag, king of the Amalekites, after Samuel had told him to do so. The prophecy into which Conscience breaks at this point indicates that at some future time an unrighteous king will once again be overcome and a true Christian king will reign over a unified world (III. 436–41, quoted below). The prophecy ends, as a number of apocalyptic prophecies of this type do, with a "dark," foreboding reference to future times which seems to be based on an obscure sense of an apocalyptic program: "Ac ar this fortune falle fynde me shal the worste . . ." (lines 477–81, quoted below). I have made an attempt to reconstruct this fragmentary schedule below in a form in which it can be compared with reconstructed fragments from other passages:

> I, Consience, knowe this, for Kynde Wit me tauhte
> That resoun shal regne and reumes gouerne
> And riht as Agag hadde happe shal somme;
> Samuel shal sle hym and Sauel shal be yblamed
> And Dauid shal be ydyademed and adaunte alle oure enemyes
> And o cristene kyng kepe vs echone . . .
> [Here follows a lengthy utopian vision.]
> Ac ar this fortune falle fynde me shal the worste
> Be sixe sonnes and a ship and half a shef of arwes;
> And the myddell of þe mone shal make þe Iewes turne
> And Saresines for þat syhte shal syng *Credo in spiritum sanctum*,
> For Machameth and Mede shullen mishap þat tyme,
> *Quia melius est bonum nomen quam diuicie multe.*   (III. 436–41, 477–81b)

Reconstructed schedule
1 Time of evil ("the worste")
2 Conversion of Jews and Saracens
3 Death of Saul and reign of David.

Langland repeats this same formula ("Ac ar") at the end of his prophecy of Church reform by a coming king (B. x. 322–35, and C. v. 168–79, quoted below). Once again the prophecy ends with an obscure reference to an assumed time schedule: "Ac er þat kyng come Caym shal awake,/ [Ac] dowel shal dyngen hym adoun and destruye his myȝte" (B. x. 334–35). In the C-text version of this prophecy, these lines have been altered. The reference to Cain has been removed and now there is a direct mention of Church renewal, "clerkes and holy churche shal be clothed newe" (line 179), in place of the more general reference to Dowell. The reconstructed schedules of both versions must assume a lapse of spiritual or moral fortitude to account for *both* times of renewal which these fragments indicate:

B. X. 322–35

Ac þer shal come a kyng and confesse yow Religiouses,
And bete yow, as þe bible telleþ, for brekynge of youre rule,
And amende Monyals, Monkes and Chanons,
And puten [hem] to hir penaunce, *Ad pristinum statum ire*;
And Barons wiþ Erles beten hem þoru3 *Beatus vir*res techyng;
[Bynymen] that hir barnes claymen, and blame yow foule:
Hij in curribus & hij in equis ipsi obligati sunt &c.
And þanne Freres in hir fraytour shul fynden a keye
Of Costantyns cofres [þer þe catel is Inne]
That Gregories godchildren [vngodly] despended.
And þanne shal þe Abbot of Abyngdoun and al his issue for euere
Have a knok of a kyng, and incurable þe wounde.
That þis worþ sooþ, seke ye þat ofte ouerse þe bible:
*Quomodo cessauit exactor, quieuit tributum? contriuit dominus baculum impiorum, et virgam
dominancium cedencium plaga insanabili.*
Ac er þat kyng come Caym shal awake,
[Ac] dowel shal dyngen hym adoun and destruye his my3te.

Reconstructed schedule
1 Time of evil (Cain awakes)
2 Time of good (Cain conquered by Dowell)
3 [Lapse?]
4 King comes to reform clergy.

C. V. 168–79
– first section much the same as B, but C finishes:

Ac ar þat kyng come, as cronicles me tolde,
Clerkes and holy churche shal be clothed newe.   (lines 178–79)

Reconstructed schedule
1 Renewal of Church
2 [Lapse of Church?]
3 King comes to reform Church.

It is easy to overlook these allusions to a fragmentary time schedule and regard them as simply fillers or tags. Certainly, it is obvious that Langland had not thought these comments through very carefully, but I believe that it must be conceded that these are allusions to an apocalyptic schedule of sorts. Here we have fragments of the usual cycles of decay and renewal that one comes to expect in such prophecies.

Finally, there is further proof of Langland's understanding of the fluctuations of religious reform prophecies and this occurs in the last two passus of the poem, where he uses a good deal of eschatological allusion to portray "a coming of Antichrist." I wish to stress·"*a* coming of Antichrist" as opposed to "*the* coming": like most other later apocalyptic writers, Langland probably believed in waves of evil or waves of "Antichrist" (although not all writers chose to use the term) that would rise, be combated and rise again at significant points in history. What Langland portrays in the last passus of *Piers Plowman* is not the End of the World, but it is very likely one of the great battles for Church reform further up the schedule.

Since this is not the place to treat all the complexities of the last two passus of the poem and since our main concern is to try to sift out an overall pattern, what follows is only a summary of the main events of this section:

Summary of Passus XXI–XXII

XXI.	1ff.	Piers appears as risen Christ at Mass
	199	The Pentecost
	207	Scene of mass devotion of people
	215	Grace gives out weapons to fight against Antichrist and warns of false prophets (alluding to friars) and of an antipope
	262	Piers and Grace establish "Unity" and "sow" Christianity
	336	Attack of Pride's army on Unity
	356	Strengthening of Church against attack and brief vision of renewal: "Clannesse of þe comune and clerkes clene lyuynge / Made Vnite holi churche in holinesse stande" (379–80).
	396	Beginning of breakdown (brewer, vicar, king)
XXII.	51	Coming of Antichrist, welcomed by all except a few "fools"
	74	Conscience collects "fools" into Unity
	80	Pestilences come and sins are temporarily subdued
	109	Sin on the rise again
	215	Sins now described as corrupt clerics attacking Unity
	228	Friars answer Conscience's call for help
	242	Conscience attempts to reform friars
	273	Attempt fails because friars are sent "to scole"
	297	Conscience bars gates of Unity and tries to hold out with traditional methods of confession and penance (without friars)
	332	Friars gain entry (Langland uses traditional anti-mendicant eschatology) and the last stronghold (that is, sincere penance) is down
	380	Conscience is forced to leave in search of Piers Plowman and a solution to the friars' corruption.

A number of the elements in this summary of events are reminiscent of an apocalyptic program. Passus XXI opens with the dreamer's vision during Mass of Piers as the risen Christ coming before the people. Mass was probably the most popular setting for prophetic visions during the Middle Ages and Langland must have been aware of this tradition.[62] Then comes a Pentecostal scene, which doubles allegorically as both a portrayal of the historical Pentecost and a vision of Church renewal for Langland's own time. After a typically apocalyptic scene of mass devotion, Grace gives out weapons to strengthen the Church against Antichrist. He also warns that "Pryde [shall] be pope and prince of holy chirche" (XXI. 223), a clear reference to the apocalyptic antipope tradition of which we have seen something in Hildegard and which we will see more clearly in Joachite writers.

After Grace's warning about Antichrist's infiltration of the Church and the establishment of Unity,[63] there is the first attack on the Church by Pride's army at lines 336ff. The Church withstands the attack and there is a brief vision of the

Church Militant: strong, secure and holy (lines 379–80). However, cracks begin to show soon enough and the beginning of Passus XXII brings the coming of Antichrist himself. From this point until the end of the poem, the Church becomes weaker and weaker and its defenses fall back further and further. This antichrist is clearly a religious antichrist – an "anticleric," the personification of all corrupt ecclesiastics. Friars and other religious join him as soon as he appears and Langland tells us that only a few fools are left to be taken into Unity as the crowd welcomes Antichrist. These are, of course, the "fools for Christ" that St. Paul talks about and such fools have a long history in the religious prophecy tradition.[64] At line 215, the sins who have been attacking Unity are described as corrupt clerics. Conscience has no alternative but to retreat into Unity and bar the gates, where he tries to hold the fort, as it were, with the traditional methods of penance and contrition. At this point Langland's anti-fraternalism comes into play and he portrays the disastrous entrance of the friars into Unity and their insidious attack on penance, which leaves the future of Unity in doubt. With Conscience's last weapon destroyed, he has no choice but to become a wanderer in search of Piers Plowman, "who will destroy Pride" and find a solution to the fraternal problem. Piers here is some kind of reforming Church leader – possibly a pope, possibly even a *papa angelicus*; whoever he is, Langland definitely sees him as the last hope for the healing and restoration of the Church.[65]

Critics have always been baffled by Langland's use of eschatological elements in this section. Most commentators on the poem use only the traditional eschatology,[66] where there is one Antichrist and he directly precedes the End of the World. Yet Langland is clearly not thinking of the End of the World here, because when the poem ends Conscience is looking to Piers to reform the Church. In order to solve this apparent discrepancy, Frank has suggested that 'antichrist' is merely a term of abuse and pointed to Wycliffite writings in which the term is clearly used in this way (See his "Conclusion"). It seems to me that neither explanation is entirely satisfactory. However inexplicit and vague Langland's apocalyptic system may be, it looks very much as if he is referring to the kind of schedule which the "new" apocalyptic theory of the later Middle Ages popularized. There are enough bits and pieces of this tradition scattered throughout the last two passus to indicate that Langland's Antichrist has a real, apocalyptic significance but that he is not *the* Antichrist of the old tradition. Either, like the "new" apocalyptic writers, Langland believed in a renewal after this Antichrist that would last until the Second Coming, or (like Hildegard) he saw a series of forerunners of Antichrist or, like the Joachite writers, he foresaw multiple antichrists and this particular "Antichrist" could be any one of them.[67] Whatever he believed, it is clear that Langland, like Hildegard, saw his own time as apocalyptically significant. Although not the End of the World itself, obviously for him it merited a place on the schedule.

Before we leave the question of Langland's schedule, an attempt should be made to try to correlate the fragments we have. The patterns hinted at the ends of the prophecies in C. III, B. X and C. V all have in common an imminent time of evil ("the worste" or a time of the awakening of Cain) followed eventually by a just king

(David or a reforming king who will give the friars a "fyndynge"). The last passus of the poem ends with the search for Piers, who is expected similarly to solve the problem of the friars. Whether Piers is to be the reforming king, or whether Langland had by the end of the poem shifted this image to a papal figure or other religious leader, or whether he just did not notice the discrepancy, it is hard to say, but there is something of a consistent pattern among these fragments in the motif of the expected reforming leader. Some of the short fragments also suggest that there will be more than one renewal – something we have seen in Hildegard's apocalyptic schedule, certainly; but it is hard to know whether Langland's multiple renewals arise from a considered sense of the apocalyptic future or from a failure to work out a consistent program of events. Whatever the meaning of these fragments, it seems clear that what Langland is describing in the last two passus is a process which he believes to be already under way and which will reach its climax in the immediate future. This lavishing of detail on the implications of present troubles for the immediate future is what we have already come to expect from Hildegard's prophecies. Whatever the imperfections of Langland's apocalyptic architecture, the implications for the near future are clear enough.

We have only to look at Langland's and Hildegard's schemes for the future in comparison with the Augustinian scheme of Salvation History and the traditional eschatology[68] to see how radical their visions of the Last Times were:

1 Sons of Ishmael, or Gog and Magog, invade Christendom
2 Christendom saved by a great king and conqueror, "Last World Emperor"
3 Period of prosperity under Roman Emperor
4 Arrival of Antichrist: Last Emperor lays down crown on Mount Olivet and is taken up into Heaven
5 The reign of Antichrist, deception of many Christians and persecution of faithful remnant
6 Enoch and Elijah preach against Antichrist; conversion of the Jews
7 Death and resurrection of Enoch and Elijah
8 Death of Antichrist (killed by Michael/God/Christ)
9 Fifteen signs before Doomsday
10 Resurrection of the Dead and the Last Judgment.

We can also see how much more detailed they are, how high a profile the Church and the ecclesiastical orders have in the program of events and how much more time is given over *before the final End* to cycles of decay and restitution. Unlike some apocalyptic writers, Hildegard does not confuse the reader by referring to evil figures or groups of figures as Antichrist until she gets to *the* Antichrist; rather she refers to the forerunners of Antichrist (the heretics and simoniacs or pseudo-prophets). Langland's "Antichrist" may well be such a forerunner too, or he may be a Joachite antichrist but, in that he *precedes* renewal, he can be best read as part of the reformist apocalyptic tradition. By the end of the poem the clerical reform of Langland's schedule is still wanting. The great reforming leaders, Langland's Piers or his king of the prophecy of Passus v, are still being sought. The traditional events of the conversion of the Jews or Saracens, or the less traditional coming of an age of renewed spirituality, are also still to come. In both Langland's and

Hildegard's apocalyptic program, the end is a long way off – but the implications of mankind's sins and the wrath they provoke *sub specie aeternitatis* are not. Herein, for these writers, lies the *sententia* for their own age.

WHY VISION? STYLE IN MEDIEVAL APOCALYPTIC VISION LITERATURE

Late medieval apocalyptic visionary writing like Hildegard's not only has a distinctive ideology, but distinctive literary characteristics as well. In Chapter 3, a broader selection of these characteristics will be discussed as features inherited from the early apocalypses; however, two main features will interest us here: a particularly shifting, fluid use of allegory and typology common in such writers, and in the next section, the ambivalent handling of the visionary narrator within the vision which the more sophisticated writers exhibit. The question which will concern us in this section is: why vision? Why would a writer choose the visionary mode? What were the motivations of such a choice and how did these writers hope that their audiences would view their works?

It is first of all important to realize that the visionary experience was by no means the most highly regarded of religious experiences. For example, the twelfth-century mystic, Richard of St. Victor, distinguished four types of vision: ordinary physical vision, physical vision of a supranatural significance (such as Moses' seeing of the burning bush), symbolic vision and, finally, anagogic or contemplative vision which is non-imagistic.[69] As Dronke has pointed out, Hildegard's vision is clearly of the third or symbolic type (*Women Writers*, pp. 146ff.). Retaining all her normal faculties of perception, she describes her vision, in a well-known letter to Guibert of Gembloux, as a seeing "in the soul":

> The brightness that I see is not spatial, yet it is far, far more lucent than a cloud that envelops the sun . . . and I call it "the shadow of the living brightness." And as sun, moon and stars appear [mirrored] in water, so Scriptures, discourses, virtues, and some works of men take form for me and are reflected radiant in this brightness.
>
> (trans. Dronke, *Women Writers*, p. 168 [Latin text, p. 252])

Her mode of vision might be described as meditative rather than contemplative, symbolic rather than mystical.[70] In a brief passage in the *Pentachronon* (from *Scivias*) God explains to her that He speaks to her as He does because mortal men are weighed down by the weight of their mortality, and for as long as this is so He must manifest Himself "in a darkening" ("obumbratione"), just as a painter manifests the invisible through his images (III, 11, 28: 595ff.).

But to medieval theorists of religious experience visions were not as exalted a gift as the contemplative, non-imagistic variety of mystical experience.[71] The visionary is too closely tied to this world by concern for its problems to be helpfully identified with the contemplative. Lina Eckenstein, in her classic study *Woman Under Monasticism*, wrote that later inspired nuns "have neither the hold on outside events nor the wide outlook which give such a deep interest to the writings of Hildegard of Bingen and Elizabeth of Schönau" (pp. 284–85). Similarly, in his study of William Blake, the English writer most like Hildegard, Northrop Frye has suggested that what characterizes visionary writing is the visionary's special view of the objects of this world: "A visionary creates, or dwells in, a higher spiritual world in which the objects of perception in this one have become transfigured and charged with a new intensity of symbolism . . . It is a perceptive rather than a contemplative attitude of mind."[72] This notion is echoed by the Jewish theologian of prophecy, Abraham Heschel (*Prophets*, vol. II, p. 147): "What makes the difference between the prophet and the ordinary person is the possession of a heightened and unified awareness of certain aspects of life." A writer like Hildegard would herself have defined prophetic vision as a special insight, visually perceived, into the meaning and course of things and events, a capacity which is present to a greater or lesser extent, she stresses, in all human beings.[73] Visionaries, then, may be seen as comprising the "lower" rank of those who have transcendental experiences. Theirs might be described as the "active" life of the supranaturally inclined. This position makes for certain kinds of literary characteristics in visionary writing, influencing form, content, style and the visionary narrator's own stance, all of which are evident in both Hildegard's and Langland's works.

The main problem in comparing two writers like Langland and Hildegard is that it is difficult to establish criteria for distinguishing the relating or even imitating of "real" vision from the exploitation of literary conventions. On the one hand, a self-acknowledged prophet like Hildegard can be seen to have made use of all the appropriate literary conventions and to have exercised a great deal of control over the presentation of her vision in many of her prophetic passages. On the other hand, a more obviously literary writer like Langland, as critics have observed, can be seen in certain passages to manifest some of the features of an altered state of consciousness, of the kind we might associate with accounts of "real" visionary or dream experience (for example, in his use of abrupt and disjointed movement, sudden appearances and disappearances and the like). Langland's use of such techniques even seems to go beyond the requirements of "dream realism,"[74] which sophisticated medieval writers so successfully mimicked. However, since we are never likely to know what experiences really formed the basis of such writing perhaps it is better to approach the problem by asking what, if anything, a close look at avowedly visionary literature, like Hildegard's, can teach us about dream-vision allegory.

Both Langland and Hildegard used allegory extensively in creating the visual effects of their visions. Peter Dronke in his study of the rise of the religious lyric comments that "poetically, the finest allegory is closest to pure vision" (*Medieval Lyric*, p. 79). Speaking of one of Hildegard's own lyrics he comments on the "cascade of images" (*ibid.*, p. 77) she uses to enrich the central theme of the poem in several directions at once, giving the work the kind of multivalency which we see so often in Langland's use of images. This fusion (and profusion) of imagery in Hildegard's lyrics, "taken to an unparalleled visionary extreme" (*ibid.*, p. 75), Dronke has elsewhere noted as the main feature of Langland's most explicitly visionary vision, Will's dream of the Tree of Charity: "We can see, then, that what is new in Langland's vision lies not so much in the components as in the movement and structure . . . The scope of Langland's transgressions of known, systematic allegory, fusing traditional elements unpredictably, is startling . . . Whether we view the transgressions as so many sins against an allegorical norm, or as imaginatively valid ways of stepping beyond that norm, is something each reader, in each context, must decide" ("*Arbor*," p. 220). Following Walter Benjamin, Dronke refers to this type of allegorical writing as "disordered scenery," stressing "an element of fluidity and unpredictability." He sees a process of "'scattering' and 'gathering' at work. Things are gathered according to their signification; the lack of concern for their reality scatters them again" (Dronke, citing Benjamin, in "*Arbor*," p. 208). In order to illustrate the existence of this "disordered scenery" in medieval dream-vision allegory, Dronke calls to witness a number of apocalyptic and visionary writers who make use of a similar fluidity of allegory in their visions,[75] among whom are Hildegard, Joachim of Fiore and *The Shepherd of Hermas* author. Hildegard's vision, which draws on literary conventions but also in places bears the marks of "vision realism" or of an altered state of consciousness, reflects this fluidity to a greater extent than Dronke's treatment of a single passage could suggest, and this will be further explored here.

Although it is difficult to say exactly what the relationship *is* between allegory and vision, a study of writers like Hildegard does suggest some common characteristics: visionary writing is (or is expected to be) vividly visual; thus we have an abundance of images, which may or may not be worked into coherent allegory. We also have a fusion of these images in surprising ways and a tendency toward abrupt, disjointed movement between these fusions. Dream-vision allegory also indulges in sudden appearances of unexplained or unintroduced characters or objects.[76] Add to this some of the characteristics of apocalyptic writing, such as a strong dependence on typology for explanations of past, present and future events (a dependence which allows for a blurring of distinctions between times, historical ages and places),[77] and one has indeed a recipe for "disordered scenery." Finally, we have the contribution of biblical prophetic literature[78] to visionary style, which gives it its terse, aphoristic, unreasoning quality. The message of the vision is presented with the conviction of assertion, not suggestion. All these aspects seem to suggest a literature which emanates from the intuitive rather than the logical perceptions of the writer.[79]

Many of these characteristics apply equally to "literary" (or more consciously artificed) visions and to apocalyptic visions, but with the difference that the latter type of vision makes fewer concessions to the reader – or, to put it more bluntly – the author is less considerate of the difficulties which the reader might have in following the sense of the vision. (Some readers respond better than others to this type of treatment – *Piers Plowman* has certainly had its fair share of indignant reader-reaction.) In fact, medieval visionary literature could be ranked in terms of difficulty from the least difficult type, the didactic vision, through the carefully crafted literary type, to the more unpredictable variety, which seems to be recording or imitating actual religious experience; the apocalyptic variety discussed here falls into this last category. The didactic vision,[80] which was so popular in chronicles, sermons, and religious writings, usually had a purely edificatory intent, while the

The visionary prophecy of Hildegard of Bingen

apocalyptic vision is highly polemical. In the latter, writers are free to be (and usually are) opinionated, partisan and "political" in what they say and this, too, will affect the literary character of the vision. Impassioned and often obscure, this type of vision once again shows up as less comprehensible and coherent as further reasons for the disordering of the scenery are brought to bear upon it.

The first passage we will consider is taken from Hildegard's fiery letter to Pope Anastasius. Having rebuked him for the state of the clergy and the Church which he directs, she then breaks into an apocalyptic sequence:

Omnis terra turbatur per magnam vicissitudinem errorum, quia quod Deus destruxit, homo amat. Et tu, o Roma, velut in extremis jacens, conturbaberis ita, quod fortitudo pedum tuorum super quos hactenus stetisti, languescet, quoniam filiam Regis, videlicet justitiam, non ardenti amore, sed quasi in torpore dormitionis amas, ita ut eam a te expellas: unde et ipsa a te fugere vult, si non revocaveris eam. Sed tamen magni montes maxillam adjutorii tibi adhuc praebebunt, te sursum erigentes, et magnis lignis magnarum arborum te fulcientes, ita quod non tota in honore tuo, videlicet in decore desponsationis Christi omnino dissipaberis, quin aliquas alas ornamenti tui habens, usque dum veniat nix morum diversarum irrisionum, multam insaniam emittentium. Cave ergo ne ad ritum paganorum te commisceri velis, ne cadas. Nunc audi illum qui vivit et non exterminabitur. Mundus modo est in lascivia, postea erit in tristitia, deinde in terrore, ita ut non curent homines se occidi. In omnibus his sunt interdum tempora petulantiae, et interdum tempora contritionis, et interdum tempora fulgurum et tonitruum diversarum iniquitatum. (Ep. ii, col. 152B–D)

In this brief passage we see some of the fluidity of allegory of which Dronke spoke: Rome, the seat of the Church, is pictured as lying at the point of death ("in extremis"), because it neglects *Justitia*, the King's daughter, though there can be little reason for making this connection. A few lines later the Church is the Bride of Christ, but this image soon gives way to a vaguely angelic or bird-like image with the promise that it will retain "aliquas alas ornamenti tui." In an abrupt and unexplained shift within the same sentence, Hildegard refers ominously to the coming snow which will fling out mockeries against these wings, ending the whole section with a warning against mixing with pagan rites, for which the reader is equally unprepared. All the elements of Hildegard's vision of the coming chastisement of the Church are here but they are couched in very obscure terms: the diseased state of the contemporary Church, the storm of the coming chastisement, the promise that a remnant will be saved – here symbolized as a remnant of the wings of its former distinction. Finally, the "pagan rites" must refer, as they do in her other prophecies, to the practice of simony. This is easy enough to see after reading and studying several of Hildegard's prophecies, but one wonders what Pope Anastasius made of it. If we remember that correspondents received these letters singly and would not likely have had access to her other works, the problem of understanding Hildegard to which Gebeno referred takes on another dimension. This is a good example of the kind of visionary apocalyptic writing which is not particularly concerned to take the reader with it.

In the very apocalyptic and striking image of the mountains and trees offering support to the faltering Church, *if Rome will only try*, Hildegard holds out hope in the midst of recrimination and despair. This rapid fluctuation between the poles of despair and hope is typical of prophetic literature; authors of this kind of prophecy always seem to have some reserve of optimism to draw upon. Also typical is the envisioning of the sympathy or participation of the great forces of nature, a motif common to much biblical writing but especially to prophetic and apocalyptic literature, in which it serves to create a sense of the universal and contributes to the heightened, dramatic intensity which the writer so fervently wishes to convey.

Hildegard achieves this heightened, dramatic effect partly through her choice of diction, as well as through imagery. The lexis of the first section could only be described as apocalyptic: "turbatur," "vicissitudinem," "destruxit," "in extremis," "conturbaberis," and so on. The prophecy ends with two storm images (the coming of the snow flinging mockeries and insanities and, at the end of the passage, the time of lightning and thunder), reinforcing the sense of impending turbulence.

The second section of the prophecy, which Hildegard separates from the first with one of her usual formulas "Now hear Him who lives . . ."[81] is again a shift in focus to futuristic prophecy ("Mundus modo est in lascivia, postea erit in tristitia, deinde in terrore . . ."), but it goes on to blur the distinctions between these times in an ominous fashion ("In omnibus his sunt interdum tempora petulantiae, et interdum tempora contritionis . . ."), a favorite trick of prophetic writing. The portrait of the future is appropriately vague and foreboding, spoken with the terse, aphoristic quality that Old Testament prophecy often has. This kind of obscure and summary assessment of present and future time often concludes a larger prophetic section in medieval apocalyptic writings and it is one of the patterns which Langland makes use of in his own prophetic passages, as, for example, he does at the end of the prophecy which itself forms the end of Passus III, "Ac ar this fortune falle fynde me shal the worste . . ." (lines 477ff.).[82] Although Langland himself did not write a great many prophecies, he certainly was familiar with the conventions of the genre, even some of the more subtle ones.

One might compare the style of the foreboding prophecy at the end of Passus VIII, where similarly abrupt shifts from the unexplained to the unexplained also occur. In the B version especially, even the syntax is obscure (B. VI. 328–29), never mind the problematic symbolism. The prophecy has the genre's terse, aphoristic qualities, with the same mix of pessimistic warning and tentative hopefulness:

And thenne shal deth withdrawe and derthe be iustice
And Dawe þe deluare dey for defaute
But yf god of his goodnesse graunte vs a trewe.   (VIII. 352–54)

The same fluidity of allegorical technique is present, as Dronke has shown (in his "*Arbor*"), in passages like the Tree of Charity episode, where, within a few lines, the fruits of the Tree shift from representing the three grades of perfection, to fruits which Will desires to taste (echoing the sin of Adam), to lives which Elde can cut down, to pre-Christian souls who, because of Adam's sin, can be claimed as the Devil's booty (XVIII. 101–17). The richness of the passage is, by this point, so multifaceted that it is difficult to say precisely what sets off the Annunciation which follows: the "fortunate fall" of Adam, which has in a sense just been allusively reenacted by Will, or the stealing of the fruit which moves an indignant wrath "in magestate dei" or, on the individual level of the allegory, Will's own burgeoning sense of salvation, triggered by his discovery of the *Ymago-dei* within himself (line 7), a sign of growing self-awareness in medieval thought.[83] Whatever the case, Langland's handling of it is brilliant, and by the time he shifts from allegorical to biblical history ("And thenne spak *Spiritus Sanctus* in Gabrieles mouthe . . .", line 124), the reader's mind is resonating with powerful associations, not the least of which is the central image of the fruit itself, about to become the fruit of the womb of Mary. Never satisfied for long without a new resonance, Langland leaps immediately to wordplay upon "chamber," by association with "womb," and the cascade of images continues.[84]

We should note here another aspect of this fluidity of allegory common in visionary writing: a very loose use of typology. Both in the Tree of Charity passage, and again in the final Antichrist episode of the poem, for example, Langland deliberately conflates biblical episodes or characters proper to one time period with another, so that he can suggest the significance of current events in striking, even shocking ways. So effective is this strategy that, in discussions of the final section of the poem, many critics have assumed that Langland was intending to portray the End of the World[85] rather than simply exploiting the biblical imagery of the pseudo-prophets and followers of Antichrist to comment upon the current clerical crisis. Similarly, in a letter to the clergy of Mainz on the growing number of heretics, Hildegard cryptically alludes to the idolatry of Baal and to the hypocrisy of the Pharisees, implying that since 1139 all *three* of these groups of forerunners of Antichrist have been loosed on the world through the perverse works of men.[86] In so doing she uses the typological figures in such a way that time distinctions are blurred and all the historical figures of evil are seen to be present at once in the age she elsewhere described as "the worst" – her own. Similarly, Langland superimposed the signs of Doomsday upon his own times in order to demonstrate the seriousness of the current crisis. As Hildegard suggests at one point, the forerunning signs of the End will have been seen more than once on earth by the time history closes.[87]

Peculiar to apocalyptic style, then, is the way typological figures in this kind of prophecy are spilled forth with little or no attempt to explain their significance and with no concessions to history, circumstance or place. The main lines of a prophecy like Hildegard's Mainz prophecy would have been clear enough to a clerical audience with some knowledge of current reform literature or of Hildegard's other writings.[88] The fine points would have seemed obscure and enigmatic, no doubt, but as Gebeno says in his commentary on the *Pentachronon*, this style is the reader's assurance that the prophecy is the product of the true finger of God! One wonders to what extent Langland hoped to create this impression.

We will finish this brief discussion of apocalyptic visionary style with a look at a delightful prophecy from Hildegard's *Prooemium vitae s. Disibodi*, which is similar in its flight of idealism to Langland's millenarian prophecy at the end of Passus III. It illustrates many of the most characteristic features of the genre: its participatory appeal, its fluid use of loosely associative biblical imagery, its tendency to play elusively upon a central idea or image, its concern with warning as it struggles between hope and foreboding. We have noted before that the new apocalyptic schemes which concentrated on highlighting the pattern of events and their spiritual significance before the End arose out of a sense that contemporary man needed to know how he could participate in his destiny. The very knowledge of what lies ahead, narrated in graphic detail and coupled with denunciation of the sins of the present, could provide a kind of crisis of experience or encounter with conscience for the credulous and stimulate a change of heart. In the following passage from the *Prooemium* Hildegard says as much herself: she is aware that her prophecies, in delimiting the times of evil and good, not only provide reassurance, but also provide a kind of *speculum* in which the spiritually aware will see the coming wrath and prepare to flee it:

Tempus pressurae et destructionis, videlicet ponderis illius, quo uva in torculari premitur, nondum venit. Sed tamen nunc vilissimum tempus est; quapropter ad priora tempora aspicite, et in quali honore fuissent, considerate, et ab inimicis vestris vos defendite, et Deus vos adjuvare non recusat.

Tempus enim bonae intentionis et conversationis quandoque veniet, et ad primam auroram aspicient, et saeculum pro amore tunc relinquent; ad Deum anhelabunt, et sic in bono perseverabunt.

Et tunc de ipsis clara voce populi in Spiritu Sancto dicetur: *Vox turturis audita est in terra nostra*. Quod est: Vox heremitarum et hujus mundi peregrinorum, tam fortiter in coelum aspicientium, quod arctam viam, quae ad coelum tendit, ire volunt. Et hi omnia transacta et praeterita, quae vel prospera vel adversa fuerunt, inspiciunt, quatenus praecaveant quomodo acerrimo accipitri se surripiant, quemadmodum columba ab isto fugit, cum ipsum in speculo aquae viderit.   (pp. 356–57)

There is little here in the way of denunciation of abuse (writing for the monks of her beloved monastic home at Disibodenberg, Hildegard clearly thought it was not necessary), but there is gentle advice and warning mixed with the assurance that she offers. The prophecy maintains a perfect balance between authoritative pronouncement and a sense of intuitive fluidity. Allegorical images emerge and recede with the fluency of a natural language, images like the terrible reminder of the winepress, or the striking image of the first dawn. Some are only suggestive of allegory, like "ad Deum anhelabunt," an allusion to Psalm 41: "As the hart panteth after the fountains of water: so my soul panteth after thee, O God" (verse 2). Symbols of hope abound in this passage: Hildegard speaks not only of the first dawn, but of love and of springtime in her "*Vox turturis* . . .," an allusion to Canticles 2: "My beloved is like a roe or a young hart . . . Arise, make haste, my love, my dove, my beautiful one, and come: For winter is now past, the rain is over and gone. The flowers have appeared in our land: the time of pruning is come: the voice of the turtle is heard in our land" (verses 9–12). The context of this quotation, which Hildegard would have expected the monks to recognize immediately, probably prompted some of the other symbols in the prophecy, like that of the dove, while the hart of Psalm 41 may have in turn prompted the Canticles verse itself. The invitational impetus, implicit in the allusion, adds to the galvanizing effect of the prophecy, which assumes that the reader is, like the writer, yearning for the period of spiritual serenity she portrays. Like Langland, Hildegard "speaks Bible,"[89] and the Scriptures supply a rich fund of material for the movement by association from image to image which is an identifiable characteristic of the "vision realism" of this type of writer. Hildegard's technique of joining loosely connected symbols together around a central theme was thought by Liebeschütz (*Weltbild*) to stem from her reading of contemporary theology, but there is no doubt that it serves to add a visionary quality to her work. The central theme in this passage is surely the often repeated motif of watching or looking for something: the imperative "aspicite" comes near the beginning of the passage and the same verb is repeated twice more, along with forms of *considerare, inspicere* and *videre*. To Hildegard, for whom everything spiritual was visually perceived ("as sun, moon and stars appear [mirrored] in water, so Scriptures, discourses, virtues, and some works of men take form for me and are reflected radiant in this brightness"),[90] her prophecies also provided a *speculum* for others who were willing to *look*, like the dove hovering over the water. The emphasis on looking for or watching for something creates and articulates the sense of expectation which characterizes prophecy itself, but in this passage it has a still richer meaning. The pilgrims and hermits of this world are not just watching in the negative sense of "watching out," they are also "looking for" in the positive sense of yearning or seeking: "ad primam auroram aspicient, et ... ad Deum anhelabunt ... tam fortiter in coelum aspicientium, quod arctam viam, quae ad coelum tendit, ire volunt." Hildegard captures in the duality of this central image the duality of the visionary experience which encompasses both a horrifying awareness of future doom as well as an equally strong awareness of the possibility of spiritual renewal.

Like her contemporary Joachim of Fiore,[91] Hildegard anticipates a period of the pouring forth of the Holy Spirit, a new generation peopled by the most fervent of the cenobites, that is, hermits and pilgrims, any who realize that this world is not their true home. These predictions are basically the same as all the other Hildegardian visions we have looked at, but the tone and style and emphasis differ remarkably. Hildegard obviously tailored her writings to her audience, but she also shows an amazing flexibility of imagination. No matter how many times she laid out her apocalyptic scheme, there were new images and new emphases to renew each telling and I submit that there is the same impetus at work in the various apocalyptic passages of *Piers Plowman*. No doubt some of the discrepancies of detail we find in the prophecies of visionaries like Langland and Hildegard result from the agility with which they shifted from image to image, and from the fluctuations of their fears and desires for the future.

The question we asked before looking at these few passages of Hildegard's from a literary point of view was what, if anything, the writings of a "professional" or "real" visionary like Hildegard teach us about dream-vision allegory, as it is manifested in a poem like *Piers Plowman*? That these are two distinct types of writing is immediately evident and no one would wish to push any comparison too far, but I think it is obvious that they have many characteristics in common –

stylistic and literary characteristics as well as attitudinal and ideological ones. Perhaps the main literary characteristic could be described as a certain looseness or freedom with imagery, a freedom which seems to spring as much from "honest indignation" (as Blake would say) as visionary agility, sometimes even from an exhilarating or impatient bursting of the bonds of reason. Peter Dronke characterized this freedom or looseness with imagery as a fluidity of allegory, which it definitely is, although the word "fluidity" may disguise the fact that the images shift abruptly and disjointedly as often as they move "fluidly" or gracefully. The point is that they often do move quickly and there are a great many of them and that we do not often get this type of vividly visual, imagistically indulgent allegorical writing in many other authors.

We do not and cannot know whether Langland had "visionary" (that is to say spiritual) experiences, as Hildegard claimed to have. What we can assume is that he could have learned to write the way he did in certain passages from reading apocalyptic vision literature. This type of literature would not, of course, be the only source for his visionary style – scholars have firmly established the place of the thirteenth-century French dream-vision literature, for example, among sources for the tradition in which Langland writes – but I suggest that apocalyptic-vision literature accounts for some of the darker, looser, more "fluid" aspects of his writing, aspects which we do not see in the artistically controlled visionary style of the *Pearl* poet or the delightful dream mimicry of Chaucer. There is a sense of movement by intuitive perception in Langland's visionary writings for which we must turn elsewhere to find a model.

VISIONARY SELF-IMAGE

It is some decades ago now that Leo Spitzer published his important "Note on the Poetic and the Empirical 'I' in Medieval Authors," in which he demonstrated that even though the medieval view of the purpose of autobiography was fundamentally different from our own (medieval writers were even capable of plagiarizing autobiography!) it was also more complex than scholars had assumed: "I submit the theory that, in the Middle Ages, the 'poetic I' had more freedom and more breadth than it has today" (Spitzer, "Note," p. 415). Postulating the presence of both the "poetic" (participatory) and the "empirical" (actual, historical) "I" in Dante, Spitzer argued that

Dante does not allow us to forget that his empirical . . . personality is also included in this "I" . . . For the story that Dante had to tell, both aspects of his composite "I" were necessary: on the one hand, he must transcend the limitations of individuality in order to gain an experience of universal experience; on the other, an individual eye is necessary to perceive and fix the matter of experience. (p. 416)

In spite of Spitzer, the trend in criticism until recently has been to deny the empirical "I" to the extent that, as John Burrow has recently shown, "it now seems necessary to argue that not all autobiographical passages are simply conventional" (Burrow, "Autobiographical Poetry," p. 390). Preferring to consider the problem from the standpoint of the authorial *purpose* of the work in question, Burrow suggests that medieval autobiography can best be read as "written versions, albeit elaborated and formalized, of an everyday self-referring speech-act" (*ibid.*, p. 410), which frequently take the form of a genre like the *consolatio* or, following Augustine, the *confessio*.

Like Dante's, Langland's self-referring passages use a mixture of both poetic and empirical "I"'s. R. W. Chambers once challenged those who believed the most famous of these passages, in *Piers Plowman* C. v., to be fictional "to produce a precedent,"[92] and E. T. Donaldson pointed out that no one had ever explained what purpose it was meant to serve if it was fictional.[93] Furthermore, the main self-referring passages in the poem can be readily analyzed, following Burrow, as *confessio* and *consolatio* outbursts, and in any case give the impression of recording real issues with which Langland could well have struggled: the illegitimacy of writing poetry, of attacking the sins of others and of his own manner of earning a livelihood. In what follows we will try to understand Langland's self-references in the light of the mix of conventional and autobiographical self-reference of the religious visionary, particularly as represented in Hildegard.

The self-image portrayed in Langland's works shows neither the confidence nor the self-professed prophetic stance portrayed in Hildegard's writings.[94] Hildegard uses (and exploits) the modesty topos persistently, both in her insistence that she is unlearned and incapable of eloquence, and in the assertion that she writes under divine compulsion:[95]

Nam mystica verba a me non profero, sed secundum ea in viventi lumine video, ita quod saeþe quae mens mea non desiderat, et quae etiam voluntas mea non quaerit, mihi ostenduntur, sed illa multoties coacta video. (Ep. cxcvii, col. 157c–d)

However, she never leaves any doubt of her prophetic vocation. The visionary ground that Langland staked out for himself, on the other hand, is poetic ground, and, although it must be admitted that he eventually grows impatient with some of the literary conventions of his choice,[96] he obviously feels more comfortable with the poetic medium as a vehicle for his message than he does with the setting down of direct divine revelation.[97] Hildegard's works are related to her by the "Living Light" or "the voice of I Who Am" but one senses that Langland would never have allowed himself overtly to adopt such a position. *Piers Plowman* is a much more earthbound work: the supranatural beings who speak to Will are facets or faculties of the mind of man or personifications of spiritual but earthly authorities or virtues. Even Peter and Christ himself are presented to Will in the more earthly, figural form of Piers. Through Piers, Christ and the apostle become accessible to the dreamer without the necessity of the dramatic divine apparitions or locutions of the mystic-visionary tradition.

For this reason Will's encounters with the different authority figures of his vision are very different from the type of encounters typically recorded by monastic writers and lay mystics in which angels, saints, apostles and even Christ himself appear to the visionary in order to teach or admonish.[98] Even when it is compared to other more literary religious visions, *Piers Plowman* appears more humble and earthbound: Will is neither granted a vision of Heaven, as the *Pearl* narrator is, nor does he mingle with the dignitaries of Heaven and Hell the way Dante does. Langland chose the dream-vision form, but his dreamer does not commune with the highest. Will muses over the value of visions (IX. 298ff.); he does not confidently proclaim them as divine revelation. Langland hopes for the reader's assent, whereas Hildegard commands it.

For all that, however, both writers expect to be taken seriously in their critique of abuse and this is where their prophetic stances converge. Furthermore, it is surprising to find, in spite of what has just been said, that Hildegard makes much of her insecurities – more than the conventions of the modesty topos would seem to demand – and Langland fills his poem with authoritatively prophetic passages. What seems to emerge from a study of the stances of these two writers is that both used a visionary-prophetic persona to deal with, among other things, their insecurities about speaking out from the social and personal positions they found themselves in and, furthermore, that both seem to have used autobiographical elements along with that persona: in short, we find that mixture of the poetic and the empirical "I" which Spitzer postulated in Dante. In investigating these stances we will look at the theme of knowledge, which is an obsessive problem with both writers, and we will also look (here, and in Chapter 3) at a few of the possible sources or traditions behind the enigmatic visionary personas which both visionaries set up for themselves, personas which reflect both prophetic self-assurance and self-deprecation. However, whether Langland ever came in direct contact with Hildegard's works or not, it is evident that he took for granted some aspects of the visionary-reformist tradition, both literary and ideological, which her works crystallized, and thus Hildegard's visionary stance can provide us with a good starting point in reconstructing the visionary tradition behind his poem.

One of the persistent themes of both vision tradition and *Piers Plowman* is the question of the right place of learning and knowledge on the road to salvation. The question takes many forms. Langland attacks what he sees as the destructive learning of the friars (see, for example, XI. 54ff. or XXII. 273ff.) and he also condemns as presumptuous the fashion of mealtime theological disputations:

> Nowe is þe manere at þe mete, when munstrals ben stille,
> The lewed aȝen þe lered þe holy lore to dispute,
> And tellen of þe trinite how two slowe þe thridde
> And brynge forth ballede resones, taken Bernard to witnesse,
> And putten forth presumpcioun to preue þe sothe.
> Thus they dreuele at the deyes, the deite to knowe,
> And gnawen god with gorge when here gottes fullen. (XI. 35–41)

At the center of much of Langland's treatment of this theme is Will, whose curiosity – from his desire to "hear wonders" (Prol. 4) to his over-zealous desire to learn everything – is consistently frowned upon. On the other hand, however, Will's humbly proffered requests for knowledge of salvation (for example, I. 80 and XI. 88ff.) are welcomed and encouraged. As Hildegard does in *Scivias* (the title itself means "Know the Ways"), Langland seems to make distinctions between the kind of thirst for knowledge which may be approved as worthy and the kind which cannot.[99]

One aspect of this question of right knowledge is Langland's view of the role of academic learning in salvation. In the Recklessness interlude, Will plays the devil's advocate and takes a profoundly anti-intellectual position, a position which, although it is eventually overturned by Imaginatif's voice of sanity, rings true in some places, in spite of the exaggeration and bravado with which it is pronounced.[100] He argues at one point that "Austyn þe oelde"

> Saide thus in his sarmon for ensaunple of grete clerkes:
> *Ecce ipsi idiote rapiunt celum ubi nos sapientes in inferno mergimur.*
> And is to mene no more to men þat beth lewed,
> "Aren noen rather yraueschid fro þe rihte bileue
> Comuneliche then clerkes most knowyng in konnyng,
> Ne none sonnere ysaued ne none saddere in bileue
> Then ploughmen an pastours and pore comune peple." (xi. 290–95)

Even though Imaginatif is able to bring a sense of moderation to the discussion (xiv. 43–53), Recklessness's assertions are not entirely forgotten and form part of the rich, dialectical complexity of the poem, which always struggles toward truth by examining every facet of a problem.

For all that Recklessness's arguments are presented *as reckless*, they reflect a certain pragmatic skepticism which pervades the poem concerning some aspects of contemporary theological studies. Conscience's advice to the friars to "leue logyk" illustrates this anti-academic (here anti-scholastic) attitude:

> Y wol be ȝoure borwh; ȝe shal haue breed and clothes
> And oþere necessaries ynowe; ȝow shal no thyng lakke
> With þat ȝe leue logyk and lerneth for to louye.
> For loue lefte they lordschipe, bothe lond and scole,
> Frere Fraunceys and Domynyk, for loue to be holy. (xxii. 248–52)

Dame Study, after listing her many fields of intellectual endeavor, says of Theology:

> Ac Teologie hath tened me ten score tymes;
> Þe more y muse þeron the mystiloker hit semeth
> And þe deppore y deuine the derkore me thynketh hit.
> Hit is no science sothly bote a sothfaste bileue,
> Ac for hit lereth men to louie y beleue þeron þe bettere,
> For loue is a lykyng thyng and loth for to greue.
> Lerne for to louie yf þe lik Dowel,
> For of Dobet and Dobest here doctour is dere loue. (xi. 129–36)

And even Langland's Christ shows a somewhat anti-academic attitude in the Harrowing of Hell scene when he says:

> For y þat am lord of lyf, loue is my drynke,
> And for þat drynke today y deyede, as hit semede.
> Ac y wol drynke of no dische ne of deep clergyse,
> But of comune coppes . . . (xx. 403–06)

The advice is similar to Piers' advice as it is related by Clergie at the Feast of Patience:[101]

> For Peres loue þe palmare ȝent, þat inpugnede ones
> Alle kyne connynges and alle kyne craftes,
> Saue loue and leute and lowenesse of hert. (xv. 131–33)

Langland's point in these passages seems to be not so much perhaps a problem with "clergie" itself as with the assumption that one can come to faith through academic knowledge. This type of external knowledge in itself will not suffice unless it can be internalized and personally experienced or lived. This lesson is, as we shall see in Chapter 3, a key feature of the early apocalypses, and it is also the main reason for the presentation of autobiographical elements in religious literature, as Spitzer suggested.

Langland was obviously a man who was both fascinated by knowledge and wary of its abuse. Therefore, to stress the anti-academic tendency in the poem is obviously to tell only part of the story, but there is a definite sense in which, as the *Vita* progresses, Langland places increasing emphasis on inner, spiritual knowledge and on self-knowledge. As Scripture says to Will, echoing the popular Pseudo-Bernard treatise, *"Multi multa sciunt et seipsos nesciunt"* (xi. 166).[102] Will gradually learns to leave off his clerkish disputations and listen with patience in order to learn. The emphasis shifts from the acquisition of knowledge to the development of *understanding*. This intensely spiritual approach to knowledge displaces the perceived source of knowledge itself in the poem from the schools and the educated to the Holy Spirit: by the end of the poem the purveyor of all skills and knowledge is no longer Dame Study (xi. 119ff.), but Grace (xxi. 213ff.). This orientation toward inner illumination, complemented by skepticism of the "clergie" of the schools, is precisely what one would expect of a prophetic writer and does, in fact, stand out as one of the most persistent characteristics of the apocalyptic reform writers from Hildegard and her contemporaries onwards.[103] It is also reflected in the evangelical impetus that characterized so many religious movements both inside and outside the Church.[104] Anti-academic thought had, by Langland's time, become firmly entrenched as a trademark of prophetic reform ideology, which in turn emphasized prophecy and revelation over scholarly knowledge (Töpfer, *Reich*, p. 39). At least some of Langland's struggles with the problem of the proper place of knowledge in attaining salvation must be seen in this context.

Hildegard must have possessed no small amount of bookish learning, yet she never, or rarely ever, mentions a source or cites an authority outside of the Bible.[105] In everything she wrote upon the subject, she was at pains to credit her vision with all the knowledge she had acquired, always minimizing anything learned from earthly teachers.[106] She constantly refers to herself as a "poor little feminine form" ("paupercula feminea forma"), often adding the adjective "indocta" and insistently giving over all credit (and thus all responsibility) for her writings to divine revelation.[107] The reasons for such a strategy are fairly obvious, and it is absolutely consistent with the conventions of the modesty topos, but one suspects that insecurities about the inflammatory nature of some of her material would also be considerations. Langland may have chosen the dream-vision form for similar reasons, among other more literary ones.

The choice of the visionary form often goes hand in hand with a certain amount of anti-academic feeling. Time and again Hildegard denounces the *doctores* for their failure to teach the people, as this exhortation she receives in *Scivias* suggests:

O frail human form from the dust of the earth, ashes from ashes: cry out and proclaim the beginning of undefiled salvation! Let those who see the inner meaning of Scripture, yet do not wish to proclaim or preach it, take instruction, for they are lukewarm and sluggish in observing the justice of God. Unlock for them the treasury of mysteries, which they, the timid ones, bury in a hidden field without fruit. Therefore pour out a fountain of abundance, overflow with mysterious learning, so that those who want you to be despicable on account of Eve's transgression may be overwhelmed by the flood of your profusion.

(trans. Newman, *Sister of Wisdom*, p. 4, from *Scivias*, I, I, 8)

Not only does Hildegard castigate the learned clergy for their lack of productivity in the vineyards of the Lord, but she almost seems to imply in places that they have deliberately concealed these things, and to suggest that God is now forced to speak through one (that is, Hildegard herself) who is neither eloquent nor learned, in order to reveal "many mystical things" which have remained hidden in books until now (*Scivias*, III, I I, 18: 385 ff.).[108] We have seen elsewhere that Hildegard felt that the clergy misused their special powers over others, and more of the same distrust is implicit here. Now (in Hildegard's own age), the spokesperson of God will not be a member of the elitist circle of academics. As Töpfer (*Reich*, p. 38) has suggested, Hildegard sees her own prophetic preaching as an example of the new, more penetrating form of instruction in the faith, for which no learning is necessary. In the seventh age, she says, the meaning of the Scriptures will be opened up, offered "in gentle words just as the words of this book" (*Scivias*, III, I I 23: 453–55), that is, they will become accessible to the less learned.

The same sense of dissatisfaction with and rebelliousness against those who hold the power of teaching and spiritual guidance in the Church is evident in Langland's writings, but there is not the same overt claim of a prophetic vocation. Like prophetic literature, however, *Piers Plowman* expresses autobiographical concerns. In a passage in the B-text, Imaginatif rebukes Will:

And þow medlest þee wiþ makynges and myȝtest go seye þi sauter,
And bidde for hem þat ȝyuep þee breed, for þer are bokes y[n]owe
To telle men what dowel is, dobet and dobest boþe,
And prechours to preuen what it is of many a peire freres.
I seiȝ wel he seide me sooþ, and somwhat me to excuse
Seide, "Caton conforted his sone þat, clerk þouȝ he were,
To solacen hym som tyme; [so] I do whan I make:
Interpone tuis interdum gaudia curis.
And of holy men I her[e]," quod I, "how þei ouþerwhile
[In manye places pleyden þe parfiter to ben].
Ac if þer were any wight þat wolde me telle
What were dowel and dobet and dobest at þe laste,
Wolde I neuere do werk, but wende to holi chirche
And þere bidde my bedes but whan ich ete or slepe."

(B. XII. 16–28)

The *consolatio* function of this passage is, in fact, typical of medieval autobiographical traditions, as I mentioned earlier, and, furthermore, it is difficult to see what function this passage would have as purely fictional: it certainly fills no didactic function (as the more obviously *poetic* uses of the "I" in the poem so frequently do). What it does do is set out, very clearly, both authorial intention and authorial qualms – as such, its frankness makes a refreshing change from Hildegard's more conventional assertions that she writes under divine compulsion. Langland's compulsion to write as here described seems to have come from a personal yearning for understanding of Dowell or of the different ways of salvation. This yearning was clearly not being fulfilled, despite what Imaginatif says, by the books already written or the preaching of the friars. For Langland, the available contemporary spiritual aids to understanding, human or literary, were obviously bankrupt. And so he took up his pen, for himself – and for others (his many direct second-person addresses to various social groups, most notably the rich and the clergy, betray a sense of audience which goes far beyond the self-help therapy which his reply to Imaginatif suggests).

Interestingly, in the reworked passage in the C-text (that is in the autobiographical section of Passus v),[109] the question of the validity of Langland's writing does not come up again. Whether this means that he acquired a stronger sense of purpose and self-confidence, even of mission, it is hard to tell. We do have one instance of audience reaction at the beginning of this passage in the C-text, however, which may supply a clue:

> Thus y awakede, woet god, whan y wonede in Cornehull,
> Kytte and y in a cote, yclothed as a lollare,
> And lytel ylet by, leueth me for sothe,
> Amonges lollares of Londone and lewede ermytes,
> For y made of tho men as resoun me tauhte. (v. 1–5)

If this can be relied upon to be literally true, then Langland had attained something of the reputation of a moralist or reformer already on the basis of the A- and B-texts, albeit a grudging one.[110] It may not be simply empty speculation to suggest that he no longer needed the passage of apology for writing in B. xii. The apology that he no longer needed the passage of apology for writing in B xii. The apology he seems to need at this point is now *pro vita sua*. As we shall see in Chapter 3, the C-text shows a new concern with the credibility of his own manner of living, reflecting another aspect of vision convention, that of the examination of the appropriateness of the visionary's mode of life to his vocation.

In another passage Langland actually portrays this sense of hesitancy with respect to another aspect of his writing, his open criticism of certain moral failings in others, most notably the friars:

> "Y wolde it were no synne," y saide, "to seien þat were treuthe;
> The sauter sayth hit is no synne for suche men þat ben trewe
> To segge as they seen and saue only prestis:
> *Existimasti inique quod ero tibi similis; arguam te et statuam contra faciem tuam.*
> Thei wolle allegge also and by þe gospel preuen hit,

70

The visionary prophecy of Hildegard of Bingen

Nolite iudicare quemquam."
"And wherof serueth lawe," quod Leaute, "and no lyf vndertoke
Falsnesse ne faytrye? for sumwhat þe apostel saide:
Non oderis fratrem tuum secrete in corde.
Thyng þat al þe world woet wherfore sholdest thow spare
To rehercen hit al by retoryk to arate dedly synne?
Ac be neuere more þe furste the defaute to blame;
Thouh thowe se, say nat sum tyme, þat is treuthe.
Thyng þat wolde be pryue publische thow hit neuere,
Nother for loue labbe it out ne lacke hit nat for enuye."   (XII. 27–38)

What he is establishing here through Leaute is both the legitimacy of the moral reformer's stance as "sothsegger" and the ground-rules for such activity. Although Leaute's answer seems to settle the question quite nicely, there can be little doubt that the very existence of the passage suggests that Langland struggled with doubts or fears about what he was doing.

In analyzing Hildegard's prophetic stance, Liebeschütz (*Weltbild*, pp. 163–66) has made the very helpful comparisons of certain of Hildegard's attitudes with those characteristic of what he calls the "monkish autobiography" ("mönchisch[e] Autobiographie"). The relevance of this literary genre is perhaps even more apparent in relation to Langland. The greatest model for this type of writing was, of course, Augustine's *Confessions* and certainly the confessional approach remains the most pervasive influence in this genre. This type of spiritual autobiography, which narrates, often amid prayers, tears and thanksgiving, the story of how the writer learned first this truth, then the next, how he was proven a fool in this situation and was inspired to change for the better in that one, has two main features which we can see in both Langland and Hildegard. The first Liebeschütz describes as a negation or deprecation of self; the second is an intense interest in the role of studies and intellectual development in the life of the autobiographer.

The first notion involves a tendency toward self-deprecation at every point in favour of stressing the role which the writer believes God has ordained for him or her. Only the gradually unfolding divine teachings are realistic for the writer, who thus writes a life story told from a peculiarly interior and spiritualized point of view. The second notion involves the process by which the autobiographer comes to grips with the proper place of knowledge and study in life and the effect of these studies upon him or her. Liebeschütz notes that one of two scenarios occurs in monastic autobiographies (p. 165): either the individual is miraculously stricken at one blow with an understanding of profound spiritual knowledge or he is drawn back gradually to more "useful" spiritual thinking from a dangerous indulgence in idle questioning, speculation and superfluous knowledge. To some extent, the latter theme is reflected in Will's struggles with learning in *Piers Plowman*; the former experience is definitively recorded by Hildegard.[111]

These attitudes are well illustrated in the famous monastic autobiography of Guibert of Nogent.[112] Guibert deals at great length with the problems that his desire for learning involved him in: spiritual pride, persecution by fellow monks and, perhaps most interestingly, his abbot's annoyance with Guibert's agreement

71

to write a treatise on sermon preparation at the request of another prior, an episode which illustrates the kind of anti-academic and anti-literary attitude which a monk could encounter in his superiors (Book 1, ch. 17). The passage in which Will is attacked by Imaginatif ("and þou medlest þee wiþ makynges . . ." B. xii. 16) bears some of the marks of this monkish attitude toward writing. What is perhaps most interesting, however, about Guibert's account is that he uses the excuse of the task of writing a treatise on sermon preparation to write on a much larger subject in order to settle his mind about matters which (as we learn from passages just previous to this one) were of special concern to him at the time, notably questions about the psychology of man, particularly the relation between appetite, will, reason and intellect, and problems of morality. All this he works into a treatise on the Six Days of Creation. While this plays havoc with our modern sense of unity of theme and appropriateness of genre, it does provide a contemporary example of the type of "writing as process" which we see in *Piers Plowman*. Other passages in Guibert's autobiography, as well as his description of the writing of his little treatise, show the "monkish" mind struggling with and through and against knowledge toward some kind of inner awareness.

The influence of the "monkish autobiography" on both Langland and Hildegard is apparent in an examination of their prophetic stances. The weakness, ignorance, even the feeble-mindedness of the visionary's persona is stressed in order that the teaching can be seen to pass directly from its "divine" or authoritative source to its audience, with no interference from or by the messenger, the implication being that the messenger is just too limited to meddle with anything so far above his or her capacity. The presentations of this stance in the two writers are, obviously, different – Langland dramatizes Will's ineptness through the narrative of the poem while Hildegard simply avows her ineptness before or after her report of the prophetic teaching – but the impetus is the same. The whole thing is, of course, a literary convention – not to say a hoax – but it does serve some useful functions. First of all, and most obviously, it shelters the visionary from responsibility. Secondly, and less obviously, it subtly connects the visionary with a long line of "simple fools" traditionally hailed as prophetic figures. The association of the fool with the prophet or wiseman or holy man probably finds its origin in Christian thought in the words of Paul: "Where is the wise? Where is the scribe? Where is the disputer of this world? For seeing that in the wisdom of God, the world, by wisdom, knew not God, it pleased God, by the foolishness of our preaching, to save them that believe" (1 Corinthians 1:20–21). Here, the "foolishness" of the Christian is metaphorical but the later tradition branches out in many directions to include the simple rustic and even the literally mad or imbecilic.[113] Langland makes a good deal of use of the fool figure, much of it ironic, of course, in his portrayals of Will, but perhaps his most extreme use of this motif occurs in his passage about the "lunatik lollars," who wander as witless beggars:

> Careth they for no colde ne counteth of non hete
> And aren meuynge aftur þe mone; moneyeles þey walke,
> With a good will, witteles, mony wyde contreyes,

The visionary prophecy of Hildegard of Bingen

Riht as Peter dede and Poul, saue þat þey preche nat
Ne none muracles maken – ac many tymes hem happeth
To profecye of þe peple, pleyinge, as hit were.   (IX. 109–14)

What Langland admires most about these men is their capacity to live a life of perfect apostolic poverty (that is, of total dependence on God), but it is interesting that he should also focus on their ability to prophesy. What they say sounds like nonsense ("pleyinge, as hit were"), but Langland seems to imply that because of the perfection of their lives (he later calls them God's "privy disciples" and apostles, IX. 118), they reflect, and have the capacity to utter, divine truths. The literal incoherence of the imbecile is analogous to, or becomes a metaphor for, the "darkness" or difficulty of all prophetic utterance, which always sounds like nonsense, literally or logically, to the casual observer.

Langland's use of Will's apparent simplicity is far more sophisticated than anything Hildegard does with her prophetic persona. For example, Will's literal-mindedness can be used to point up ironies in what has just been asserted or to dramatize the difficulty that certain divine truths present to the common man, but Hildegard's persona, too, is an elaborate construct with an evident mix of autobiographical elements.

Hildegard constantly downplays her own intellectual capacities. Describing the period of her life before she began to write down her visions she says (speaking of herself in the third person as she often does), "ab infantia sua usque in XL aetatis suae annum imbecillis."[114] In one of her visions God tells her that literary competence in the use of language is not among her capacities (Ep. II, cols. 152D–153A). The self-portrait she paints in prefaces and epilogues to her works is that of a child-like, frail, idiosyncratic and unstable person. Again speaking of herself in the third person, she writes movingly in the final passage of the *Liber divinorum operum* (cols. 1037C–1038B) that this work has been published by God through a "pauperculam femineam formam", who has never been edified by scriptural learning, and who has been weighted down by infirmities since birth. This last assertion, a persistent theme in her writings, stands out from the modesty topos clutter as distinctively autobiographical: again, if it is fictional what purpose does it serve? She distinguishes her own behavior from that of other people, portraying herself as an infant who looks at those around her in semi-bewilderment. But God, "qui omnem fatigationem passionis ejusdem hominis veraciter cognovit," has always sustained her, and, in a very Hildegardian touch she adds, "quasi rore cujusdam refrigerii a morte suscitat." The entire passage is a gentle reminder, perhaps as much to God as to man, of what her visions have cost her.

Yet in many ways the opposite of this frail, encumbered image must have been evident. In Hildegard's prophetic denunciations, business affairs, travels, defenses of her abbey, correspondence and scientific writings, she seems to have been energetic, self-preserving and forthright.[115] In fact, the old spirit revives even in these somewhat self-pitying portraits when she reaches the point of pronouncing a curse on any who would alter her writings, a curse which subtly associates her writings with the Apocalypse of St. John:

73

hanc scripturam per nullam doctrinam humanae scientiae, sed per simplicem et indoctam femineam formam ut sibi placuit mirabiliter edidit. Unde nullus hominum tam audax sit, ut verbis hujus scripturae aliquid augendo apponat, vel minuendo auferat, ne de libro vitae, et de omni beatitudine quae sub sole est deleatur[!]   (*Liber divinorum operum*, col. 1038B–C)

The main complaint, if indeed it is a complaint, in this self-portrait is of insecurity. She gives a "scientific" explanation of her physical instability and frailty, based on her theory of complexions and humors,[116] but the instability goes beyond the purely physical and the self-denigration beyond the purely conventional. She compares her behavior and perception to those of a child and describes herself as living without any security or knowledge. Like Langland, Hildegard shows a mixture of pugnacious outspokenness and timorous insecurity; like Langland her writings betray more than one voice.

Liebeschütz (*Weltbild*, pp. 159ff.) has suggested that this belittling or negation of any strength or independence of the self is necessary to the prophetic stance which Hildegard takes up. After describing, in one of the autobiographical excerpts in her *Vita*, the mockery she suffered when God told her to move her nuns from their fatherhouse of Disibodenberg to an independent monastery at Rupertsberg, she says, "Nonetheless, God did not want me to remain steadily in complete security: this he had shown me since infancy in all my concerns, sending me no carefree joy as regards this life, through which my mind could become overbearing" (in Dronke, *Women Writers*, p. 151 [Latin text, p. 234]). Hildegard had obviously come to believe that insecurity was the way of life most suited to a servant of God; only insecurity provided the conditions for the total dependence on God necessary to the prophetic stance.

The influence of the monastic spiritual autobiography in both writers can be seen, then, in the persistent self-denigration and the reduction of the autobiography to a history of spiritual encounters. The distinction between natural knowledge and revelation is sharpened and only the unfolding of spiritual teachings is ultimately significant to the writer. We see something of this perspective in *Piers Plowman*, in the autobiographical passages, for example, or in descriptions of Will between dreams or encounters, particularly as his search becomes more obsessive.[117] The influence of the prophetic visionary tradition carries this autobiographical concern one step further, exacerbates it with a sense of insecurity in the face of such a vocation.[118]

Critics have often argued that it is the narrator who holds *Piers Plowman* together. Mary-Jo Arn has recently made this point with regard to the dreamer in *Piers Plowman*:

Episodes do not relate to each other; they relate, each in turn, to Will. This allows Langland a more radical departure from discursive exposition than is evidenced by any other Middle English poet. It also raises the narrator to an altogether new plane of importance. It is overstating the case only a little to say that without Will the action of the poem *as a whole* has little meaning.[119]

One genre of medieval literature in which the narrator had already been raised to this "altogether new plane of importance" is the religious visionary literature.

The visionary prophecy of Hildegard of Bingen

Here the visionary is "the medium through which the authoritative story [that is, the revelation] had become available to the reader," at the same time as he or she provides "a role with which the reader could identify in his reading" (Ellis, "*Flores*," p. 169). As Spitzer suggested, both the empirical and the poetic "I"s are necessary to the effectiveness of this type of religious literature (see pp. 64–65, above).

Langland never overtly assigned the grandiose, uncompromising role of God's prophet to the "I" voice (or voices) of his poem, but prophecies *are* given voice throughout and his prophetic proclamations are no less earnest for the evasion. His frank confessions of inadequacies and frustrations are reminiscent of nothing so much as the self-confessed insecurities, hesitations and excuses of the visionary tradition in which autobiography plays such a key role. The ironic undercutting of the dreamer throughout the poem does much to mitigate the effects of all this, and is probably calculated to ward off charges of presumption, but the ambiguity cuts both ways, to force us to allow for the possibility of prophetic wisdom from the mouth of a wayward fool.

3

Piers Plowman and the medieval visionary tradition

INTRODUCTION: THE APOCALYPTIC VISIONARY TRADITION

In this chapter we will examine some of the literary features of the Hildegardian tradition of visionary writing, beginning with the pre-medieval apocalypse genre. Hildegard, who is probably the single most influential figure in the development of a Northern European apocalyptic visionary tradition, was consciously imitated by later visionary writers. The tracing of the Northern tradition is made all the more difficult because, unlike Southern visionary writing, it has never really been studied as a coherent tradition, largely because no study of Hildegard's influence exists.[1] However, when entering upon such uncharted territory, it is reassuring to note that medieval writers and readers were aware of the development of this kind of visionary literature, even if modern scholarship has largely neglected it.

In 1513 the philosopher and theologian Jacques Lefèvre d'Etaples published the *Liber trium virorum & trium spiritualium virginum* as part of his campaign to make medieval spiritual works available to a larger public.[2] Among the works he printed were visions by Hildegard, Elizabeth of Schönau, the anonymous *Shepherd of Hermas* and the visions of the Dominican Robert of Uzès. All six works were visions or revelations[3] and it is clear that Lefèvre had a strong sense that they formed a literary and spiritual tradition (Dronke, "*Arbor*," p. 221). It is also clear that he felt that the publication of visions required some justification, or even defense, especially the publication of visions by women. Anticipating their detractors he asks, "Will they deny such revelations, because they themselves have never experienced them? Will the owl dispute with the eagle about the radiance of the sun and moles deny the beauty of the day?"[4] Lefèvre's defensiveness reflects medieval sensitivity about this controversial and idiosyncratic genre, an issue which, as we will see in the last section of this chapter, itself illuminates *Piers Plowman*.

The idea of a Northern visionary school makes sense because Hildegard's influence is unmistakeable in a chain of later writers. Hildegard's own writings show the inspiration of the second-century apocalypse, *The Shepherd of Hermas*, which was itself most popular in Northern Europe.[5] After Hildegard, there is a link to the Dominican visionary, Robert of Uzès (d. 1296), who seems to have known both. The same "chain" of apocalyptic visionaries continues in the early fourteenth century with the Joachite John of Rupescissa, who had studied

Hildegard and Robert with enthusiasm[6] and ends (for our purposes) with Langland's contemporary, St. Bridget of Sweden, who seems to have read John and most certainly knew Hildegard. All of this literature was well known in Northern Europe (including England). It will be some time yet before we are able to be more explicit about what I have called the Northern European visionary tradition, but it seems to be at least the right area to be exploring as background to Langland.

The first section of the chapter involves a study of some literary and visionary features of pre-medieval apocalypses, once again those which were well known in medieval England: *The Apocalypse of Esdras* (or *Ezra*) and *The Shepherd of Hermas*. Although it is difficult to say for certain that Langland was influenced by the apocalypse form itself, some of the formal and stylistic parallels between the apocalypses and *Piers Plowman* are striking, especially in the areas of the role of the visionary and the use of allegory within the vision. The second section deals with two important medieval visionaries in the Northern apocalyptic tradition, Robert of Uzès and Bridget of Sweden, and notes some parallels with Langland. The third section deals with some of the theories, literary conventions and attitudes prevalent in the Middle Ages with regard to visions, with a view to what evidence we have in *Piers Plowman* that Langland was aware of these. While scholars have concentrated on the parallels between *Piers Plowman* and other medieval literary, usually secular, dream visions, there has been less concern to relate the poem to the medieval religious vision tradition. This study makes a start in this direction. religious vision tradition. This study makes a start in this direction. considered or even represented in this chapter. For example, the most obvious type not included here is the literary dream vision of Middle English writers like Chaucer and the *Pearl* poet, or the earlier French dream allegories. Critics have given us many studies in this area and there seems little need to tackle the problem afresh here.

Another group of writers who could well have been included in a study of the medieval vision are the visionary mystics of the period. These are not at first easy to distinguish from visionary prophets, but there are profound differences in point of view between the two groups. The operative distinction is between vision and contemplation: visionary experience may sometimes be *meditative* but it is never *contemplative*. The visionary experience explodes with visual imagery; the mystical experience seeks wherever possible to surpass images and do without them.[7] However, there were a few mystics who tended toward the visionary side of religious experience, for example, Mechthild of Magdeburg (1210–94), Ramon Lull (*c.* 1231–*c.* 1316), Jacopone da Todi (1228–1306) and Ubertino da Casale (1259–1330). Certain stylistic features of their works make it tempting to associate such writers with Langland,[8] but it is difficult to say, given the paucity of their works in English manuscripts, how Langland could have come in contact with most of them. The mystical tradition native to England positively discouraged visionary experience[9] and so it is not surprising that there is no real English visionary tradition to speak of here.

Among medieval prophetic writers there was a tendency to refer to any kind of cryptic prediction as a revelation or a "vision."[10] Many of these writings are patently not visions in any meaningful sense of the word and so this is another group of "visions" which will be excluded from discussion here. The "Cedar of Lebanon Vision," a very popular religious prophecy which survives in countless manuscripts, provides a good instance of a pseudo-vision. Supposedly revealed to a Cistercian monk during Mass, the vision is nothing more than a prophecy written in the usual prophetic idiom (that is, future events are predicted but not *visualized*).[11] Visionary status could be claimed for almost any type of prophecy if the circumstances of revelation were appropriate. As Lerner writes, "medieval prophecies often begin with a prologue explaining that the course of the future was made clear in a vision granted to the prophet while he or she was lying in bed (sometimes a sickbed), participating in mass, or reading psalms. If the setting seemed right and the prophet worthy, the vision might be widely accepted . . ." ("Medieval Prophecy," p. 9). As we will see, the appropriateness of the setting *and* of the prophet was of utmost importance in claiming visionary status. In assessing visionary credibility, the medieval mind seemed as much concerned with these external aspects as with internal criteria of the message itself.

Finally, a distinction should be made between the prophetic and the non-prophetic religious vision. Visions which treat topics such as the welfare of a certain soul in purgatory or conversion experiences of individuals were extremely common in the Middle Ages, especially among regular clergy and devout laymen (see Holdsworth, "Visions"). The final section of this chapter deals with some characteristics of religious visions in general, but for the most part our concern here is with apocalyptic vision, that is, visions which are directed to a wider audience than the individuals who receive them and which, generally, have some kind of polemical purpose or motivation beyond simple didacticism.

My working definition of a visionary writer involves two criteria. First, such a writer records the ideas presented to him (or her) by the religious experience in a vividly visual fashion. The images may arise from the process of creative problem-solving, in meditation or in actual (or feigned) religious experience, but the revelation must be conveyed imagistically. Such visions are often susceptible to quick shifts and changes or even to total obliteration because of the way the mind works.[12] But however the images are arrived at – and this is the second criterion – they must be intrinsic to the writer's mode of thinking, not simply a form of ornamentation. Since a visionary writer dramatizes in imagistic terms what he or she is trying to say, allegory is, *par excellence*, the visionary mode, and has been since biblical times. Most of the writers we will look at in this chapter do not share Langland's poetic skills with allegory, but to a great extent they all share his allegorical way of thinking and his spiritually charged perspective on the world. It is hoped that their presence here will serve as a reminder that vision literature is not simply the preserve of poets and that the religious visionary tradition is also part of the literary legacy which produced *Piers Plowman*.

ALLEGORY OR APOCALYPSE? APOCALYPTIC FORM IN *PIERS PLOWMAN*
AND SOME OF THE PRE-MEDIEVAL APOCALYPSES

The apocalypse can be most simply defined as "a genre of revelatory literature within a narrative framework" (Hayes, *Introduction*, p. 366), because all apocalypses are or include visions of one sort or another. For many scholars the essential requirement of the genre seems to be that of a human encounter with the supra-human world; however, this does little to explain the peculiar ideological thrust of most apocalypses. E. P. Sanders' recent observation that (Palestinian Jewish) apocalypses combine "revelation with the promise of restoration and reversal" illuminates this aspect of the problem,[13] and suggests where the roots of what I have called medieval reformist apocalypticism lie. It does not, however, illuminate the literary and structural problems of the apocalypse genre: to deal with these scholars have developed a variety of dishearteningly long lists of characteristics, and categories of types and sub-types.[14] We will very shortly examine the most relevant of these features to medieval apocalypticism, but for the moment it is perhaps easiest to summarize by saying that all apocalypses involve the disclosure of a hidden divine purpose.

Certain commentators on *Piers Plowman*, from Robert Crowley to Morton Bloomfield, have viewed the poem as "an apocalypse,"[15] and it should be stressed that this is a different proposition from saying that the poem has apocalyptic passages.[16] Many medieval writers wrote apocalyptic prophecies or saw visions on apocalyptic themes, but few attempted to write *an apocalypse* – a full-fledged revelatory literary work within a narrative framework. In order to find out whether this is what Langland himself was trying to achieve, the literary form and style of some of the apocalypses available to him have to be analyzed and this is what we will attempt to do now.

Unfortunately, it is just about as easy to define the apocalypse as a literary genre as it is to define the novel or the epic. However, by selecting some characteristics of genuine apocalypses, we will be able to throw light on certain literary freatures of *Piers Plowman*. We will begin by looking at two apocalypses which were certainly known to or *knowable* to Langland: *The Apocalypse of Esdras* (also known as *Ezra*), and *The Shepherd of Hermas*,[17] the following characteristics of which, I think, are of especial interest to readers of *Piers Plowman*:

1 a haphazard mixture within the same work of visionary (usually allegorical) passages with non-visionary (usually didactic and dialectical) sections, resulting in a total absence of visualization in some parts;
2 a mixture, again within the same work, of characteristics which may be associated with both "real," "experienced" visions or with literary, conventionalized visions;
3 a striking degree of variation in the extent to which the dreamer or visionary participates in particular passages or sections of the work;
4 a somewhat troubled or argumentative or unpredictable relationship between the visionary and certain supernatural figures of authority;
5 a tolerance of a certain amount of confusion or structural looseness on the surface level of the narrative or allegory, and in the treatment of topics or ideas throughout.

Biblical scholars have commented on some of these features, but remain silent on others.[18] R. H. Charles has commented that something which "the reader of the Apocalyptic Literature must be prepared for is the frequent inconsistency of thought to be found there, together with variableness of teaching often involving contradiction."[19] Charles explains this phenomenon with reference to the observation that the apocalypses involved an undigested mix of both traditional and newer conceptions. In fact, Michael Stone suggests that the apocalypse was originally created as a vehicle for presenting speculative questions.[20] Certainly Langland scholars can attest to these features in *Piers Plowman*.

With regard to the visionary aspects of apocalypses, Morton S. Enslin notes that "vision" and "seeing" are conventionalized terms for the apocalypticist:

What he wishes to express he reports as having "seen." Thus the author of Rev. can see a scroll that is rolled up and sealed with seven seals, yet can see that it is "written within and on the back" (5:1). He can turn around to see the voice which is talking to him (1:12) and see the Son of man holding seven stars in his right hand yet placing that same right hand on the author's head (1:16–17) . . . Failure to understand this convention of apocalyptic imagery has led to most unwarranted conclusions.[21]

On the other hand, certain features in the apocalypses, such as many of the apocalypticists' descriptions of their physical state during or after their visions, sound convincing enough to "suggest that the reported dream or vision may well have had genuine inspirational experience behind it" (Russell, *Method*, p. 165). The vivid descriptions of Esdras' emotional state, for example, coupled with his long bouts of prayer and fasting, might have given rise to psychic experiences in anyone:

And so I fasted seven days, mourning and weeping, like as Uriel the angel commanded me. And after seven days . . . my soul recovered the spirit of understanding [*spiritum intellectus*] and I began to talk with the most High again. (II *Esdras* 5:20–22; Klijn's edition, p. 35)[22]

As Holdsworth says, speaking of the medieval experiences in the cave known as the Purgatory of St. Patrick:

It is significant too that no one could enter the cave called the Purgatory of St. Patrick until they had spent fifteen days fasting and praying in the nearby church, and that they finally entered fortified by communion and elaborate ritual. Prepared in such a way it would take an unimaginative person not to believe that he saw visions once he had crossed the threshold of the cave. ("Visions," p. 144)

There are also literary indications of actual psychological experience in the genre, or convincing *imitations* of such experience, as for example the chaotic use of imagery and disrupted narrative line.

Biblical scholars speak (though not always appreciatively) of the profusion of symbolism, allegory and imagery in apocalypses, but there is less comment on the chaotic use of such things within the framework of what are usually very untidy narratives. However, Austin Farrer writes, in his study of St. John's Apocalypse, which is surely one of the most chaotic visions ever written,

Piers Plowman and the medieval visionary tradition

The Apocalypse has a great deal of framework; no one can miss that. It bears the promise of formal consistency, of a continuous grand architecture spanning the whole book, into which all the visionary detail is to be fitted. Yet, as we advance . . . the work seems in danger of disintegrating into a mere pile of visions and oracles. Must we conclude that St. John attempted form and broke down in the execution of it? Or must we accept the supposition of a demon-editor who has broken up St. John's noble building by his senseless omissions, rearrangements and additions?   (*Rebirth*, p. 36)

Piers Plowman critics have been haunted by similar problems for years.

Two aspects of the apocalypse which will interest us here are the treatment of the narrator and allegorical style, the same two features which I discussed in Hildegard's writings in chapter 2. The apocalypse is a completely literary form, a message disseminated through a book: "What thou seest, write in a book" (Apocalypse 1:11) is the watchword. The effect is to shift responsibility for the content of the work onto supranatural authorities and this may well account for the apparent stupidity or short-sightedness or even "amazement" with which the visionary characterizes himself within the work: it is safer and more effective for the visionary to be taught certain things than it would be for him to espouse them personally. The scribal character of apocalypses, then, contributes to a strong self-consciousness of literary activity, perhaps the antecedent of this feature in writers like Hildegard and Langland. The two predominant sub-forms within apocalypses, the allegory or similitude on the one hand and the disputation or dialogue on the other, are both used as vehicles for resolving the conflicts within the visionary's mind (Hayes, *Introduction*, p. 366). This is nowhere more evident than in the first apocalypse we shall look at, the apocryphal *Apocalypse of Esdras*. Called by Charles "one of the most remarkable of Apocalypses," the core of the work (chapters 3–14) consists of seven visions,[23] of which three are visions in the strict sense, that is, they are allegorical dramas which must be interpreted to Esdras afterwards. Three further visions are "extended philosophical colloquies" between Esdras and a divine authority.[24] The final vision consists of Esdras' commission to rewrite the sacred books which were destroyed in the burning of the temple, including seventy apocalyptic books. Even from this brief summary the mixed nature of the apocalypse genre can be seen: it divides itself almost evenly between allegorical and dialectical vision.

Esdras was not considered canonical by the Church, but it became attached to the Vulgate as the apocryphal IV Ezra and Latin manuscripts are numerous.[25] In the Middle Ages the Latin text in circulation would have been equivalent to chapters 3–14 of the King James translation. It was not until 1875 that R. L. Bensly published a missing section of chapter 7 (verses 36–196), which was probably excised early on for doctrinal reasons. In what follows I have used the King James translation, which was made from the version the Middle Ages knew, followed by page references to the Latin text in Klijn's edition.

Let us look first at Esdras' role as visionary within the work. In chapter 3 (the beginning of the original apocalypse proper) Esdras,[26] who narrates the work in the first person, writes "In the thirtieth year after the ruin of the city [Sion] I was in

81

Babylon, and lay troubled upon my bed, and my thoughts came up over my heart" (II *Esdras* 3:1, Klijn's edition, p. 25). Lamenting the desolation of Sion and the prosperity of Babylon, he challenges God to justify what he views as His unreasonable treatment of Israel (3:30–36; Klijn's edition, pp. 27–28). At this point the angel Uriel appears and the bold, indignant Esdras takes on the role with which we have become so familiar in medieval dream visions: "And the angel that was sent unto me, whose name was Uriel, gave me an answer, And said, Thy heart hath gone too far in this world [Excedens excessit cor tuum in saeculo hoc], and thinkest thou to comprehend the way of the most High? Then said I, Yea, my lord" (4:1–3; Klijn's edition, p. 28). However, Esdras' confidence evaporates as Uriel tells him that he will grant his desire if Esdras can "weigh me the weight of the fire, or measure me the blast of the wind, or call me again the day that is past" (4:5; Klijn's edition, p. 28). Esdras, of course, cannot, and although he has clearly lost the first round of the fight, he perseveres in his questioning of God's purpose in allowing the present state of affairs. Esdras reminds us here of Will "aresoning" Reason or pestering *Liberum Arbitrium* for endless answers. For example, when Will jokes about the number of names he has, *Liberum Arbitrium* responds with a sudden anger which surprises most modern readers:

> "Now y se thy wille:
> Thow woldest knowe and conne þe cause of all here names
> And of myn yf thow myhteste, me thynketh by thy speche."
> "3e, sire!" y sayde, "by so no man were ygreued,
> Alle þe sciences vnder sonne and alle þe sotil craftes
> Y wolde y knewe and couthe kyndeliche in myn herte."
> "Thenne artow inparfit," quod he, "and oen of Pruydes knyhtes;
> For such a lust and lykynge Lucifer ful fram heuene." (XVI. 205–12)

In an age which applauds intellectual curiosity it is hard to understand this reaction, although the hyperbolic way in which Will describes his thirst for knowledge in his reply to it is a good clue. Like Esdras, Will "would comprehend the way of the most High" in his pursuit of knowledge but in his present state of mind even all this knowledge would not likely bring him understanding, a distinction which he is unable to see. This type of encounter between visionary and guide is a common motif in apocalypses, as we shall see with *The Shepherd of Hermas* especially. Critics of Middle English dream-vision literature have not usually realized that the convention of the blundering, inquisitive dreamer goes back so far in literary history.[27]

Esdras then tries to change the tenor of the discussion by asking, "O Lord, let me have understanding: For it was not in my mind to be curious of the high things, but of such as pass by us daily, namely, wherefore Israel is given up as a reproach to the heathen . . ." (4:22–23; Klijn's edition, p. 30). A discussion of sin ensues in which Uriel promises worse to come for Israel. Esdras asks, "How and when shall these things come to pass? wherefore are our years few and evil?" and he is rebuked again, "Do not thou hasten above the most Highest [Non festinas tu super Altissimum]: for thy haste is in vain to be above him, for thou hast much exceeded"

(4:33–34; Klijn's edition, p. 31). As the apocalypse continues the reader is consistently struck by the portrait of Esdras as sincerely and desperately seeking understanding, on the one hand, and being consistently made to play the fool, on the other hand, with his indignant and essentially unreflective reactions to his own thoughts and emotions. As always in religious writings, similitudes serve as surrogate answers to the unanswerable questions of faith, and the effect is often one of disjointedness as this oblique way of proceeding masquerades as logical discussion. But logical progression is quite simply not to be had. Esdras, like Will, does not see that faith is not settled by disputation:

And he said unto me, I will liken my judgment unto a ring: like as there is no slackness of the last [Sicut non novissimorum tarditas], even so there is no swiftness of the first [sic nec priorum velocitas]. So I answered and said, Couldest thou not make those that have been made, and be now, and that are for to come, at once; that thou mightest shew thy judgment the sooner? Then answered he me, and said, The creature may not haste above the maker . . .   (5:42–44; Klijn's edition, p. 37)

Like Will, when he "aresonede Resoun" (XIII. 243), in this passage Esdras even tries to make suggestions to God about how he should organize the world, but for all his boldness, his desperation to understand is touching:

. . . then said he unto me, Thou art sore troubled in mind for Israel's sake: lovest thou that people better than he that made them? And I said, No, Lord: but of very grief have I spoken: for my reins pain me every hour [torquent enim me renes mei per omnem horam], while I labour to comprehend the way of the most High, and to seek out part of his judgment. And he said unto me, Thou canst not.   (5:33–35; Klijn's edition, p. 36)

It is difficult not to sympathize with Esdras; from a human point of view his questions are just, but Uriel is only one in a long line of supranatural authorities in the visionary tradition who view the searchings of a human visionary with disapproval. The relationship between visionary and guide in apocalyptic tradition is unpredictable and uneasy. While at one point the visionary's questions will be welcomed and the answers delivered with grace, shortly afterwards he or she will meet with a rebuke and the relationship seems about to dissolve in bad temper. The technique – if it is intentional – may be an attempt to instill fear and meekness in the reader, who will usually identify with the human protagonist. There can be little doubt that it adds to the sense of instability which these visions create in so many different ways.

Another of the *Esdras* visions illustrates the characteristically fluid use of allegory in apocalypses. Esdras receives this vision, as he has the others, after seven days of fasting and praying out in a field. While praying he sees a woman who mourns and weeps aloud in rent clothing and ashes. Esdras asks her why she mourns and she responds, after some coaxing, with a tale that is absolutely coherent on the literal level: after thirty years of praying for a child, she and her husband were graced with a son who grew up and took a wife, but this son died at the wedding feast. The woman has fled to the field to mourn and fast until death releases her from her pain. Esdras reacts to this story by rebuking her for mourning one son when "Sion our mother" is desolate (using a metaphor of which he does not see the significance himself). After a lengthy attempt to bring her around to his point of view, she suddenly begins to change:

And it came to pass, while I was talking with her, behold, her face upon a sudden shined exceedingly, and her countenance glistered, so that I was afraid of her, and mused what it might be. And, behold, suddenly she made a great cry very fearful: so that the earth shook at the noise of the woman. And I looked, and, behold, the woman appeared unto me no more, but there was a city builded, and a large place shewed itself from the foundations . . .

(10:25–27; Klijn's edition, p. 70)

This is the kind of allegorical shift one finds in the Tree of Charity passage in *Piers Plowman*. It is as if the woman brings forth the city in labor, but Esdras is incapable of understanding the significance of what is now, obviously, a vision and not a chance encounter. Panicking and desperately calling for Uriel, he faints. Upon Uriel's reappearance he pleads with him for an interpretation of the vision, still frantic that he will be abandoned: "Speak on, my lord, in me; only forsake me not, lest I die frustrate of my hope. For I have seen that I knew not, and hear that I do not know. Or is my sense deceived, or my soul in a dream? Now therefore I beseech thee that thou wilt shew thy servant of this vision" (10:34–37; Klijn's edition, p. 71). Esdras here emphasizes the interior nature of this experience. Langland may also have used these devices of swooning and desperate searching for the figure of authority who can explain all that disturbs and obsesses the visionary. This obsessive, even physical reaction to intense desire for spiritual understanding is characteristic of apocalyptic visions.[28] As Uriel explains, the woman whom Esdras rebuked was indeed Sion herself. The city was barren until Solomon built it up and began to present offerings; the death of the son was the destruction of Jerusalem which Esdras himself so laments: "For now the most High seeth that thou art grieved unfeignedly, and sufferest from thy whole heart for her, so hath he shewed thee the brightness of her glory, and the comeliness of her beauty" (10:50; Klijn's edition, p. 72).

We can see within this allegorical vision episode a number of features of the apocalypse: the dream-like mid-vision shift of symbol (the woman becomes the city), the troubled state of the visionary in being unable to comprehend anything beyond the literal level of what he perceives. And, comparing this to other allegorical visions in the apocalypse in which Esdras is just an observer, we note the degree to which he participates in this one. Although the elements of the allegory are simple and very conventional there is also the suggestion – deliberate or otherwise – of actual visionary experience, especially in the confusion of Esdras (Russell, *Method*, p. 165).

There is much in *Esdras* which is typical of apocalyptic prophecy such as we find in later medieval productions. The book abounds with doom and gloom predictions, unnatural signs and portents, obscure similitudes and common motifs such as the persecution of the faithful, the stubbornness of the unrepentant even after repeated divine chastisement, a pessimistic sense of history winding down to a close, a periodization of world history (proving that the world is in its eleventh hour) and the usual exhortations to repentance. But perhaps most interesting from our point of view is the handling of the visionary narrator and the striking use of visionary allegory which signal that we should beware of too narrow a definition of what might constitute apocalyptic influence in a poem like *Piers Plowman*.

These same features are apparent in the early Christian *Shepherd of Hermas*, an endearing allegorical work which seems to have had a profound influence on Hildegard, Robert of Uzès and a number of later medieval visionaries. The apocalypse was perhaps written by Hermas, brother of Pius, who was Bishop of Rome in the mid-second century, or it may have been written by an otherwise unknown writer as early as AD 90–100.[29] The name "Hermas" may or may not be an assumed name. As Taylor suggested (*Shepherd*, vol. 1, p. 9), a number of early Christian writers, like Origen, identified the name with the Hermas to whom St. Paul sends greetings in Romans 16:14, and this may be what the anonymous writer intended: most apocalypses are pseudonymous but more recent opinion has suggested otherwise in the case of Hermas (McGinn, "Early Apocalypticism," p. 24). Many biblical scholars have tended to view the work as allegorical fiction (Taylor compared it with *The Pilgrim's Progress*, *Shepherd*, vol. 1, p. 10), although it may well be founded at least in part on fact. The problem presented by the autobiographical elements in the work which relate to the visionary narrator, Hermas, is similar to the problem of assessing the historical reality of Langland's Will. For example, Hermas is rebuked in his visions for the misconduct of his children and his wife (Vision I), and is told that when he was a rich man he was unprofitable to God (Vision III), whereas now in poverty and old age, he is a more worthy servant. As Taylor suggested, "a didactic purpose being here so evident, Hermas may be illustrating ideas rather than recording mere facts" (*Shepherd*, vol. I, pp. 11–12), but many of the facts connected with Hermas' life seem too specific to be fictional.

Whether *The Shepherd of Hermas* should be regarded as an allegory or as an apocalypse is a problem that was debated in older scholarship. If the question itself seems outdated now, the method used to arrive at a solution is still pertinent, as will be suggested below with regard to *Piers Plowman*. Scholars sought to solve it by looking at evidence concerning the reception of the text during the early years of its existence. The witness of the second-century *Muratori Fragment* shows that *Hermas* was then grouped with other apocalypses, and although it was canonically disallowed at this point, it is clear that it was associated, at least in literary if not in canonical terms, with other works of the genre[30] and that it continued to be read down through the Middle Ages as such. Medieval manuscripts are numerous and emanate especially from Northern Europe: Switzerland, South Germany, Northern France and England,[31] a fact which is especially interesting to the student of medieval apocalyptic writings. It is becoming increasingly evident that while Joachite works were extremely popular in Southern Europe, a Northern European apocalyptic tradition, which, as I mentioned in chapter 1, above, was much more visionary in orientation, was flourishing with the impetus of a very different set of works. It would seem that England was more a part of this Northern European tradition because, almost without fail, the pattern of dissemination in England resembles that of Northern Europe more closely than its Southern counterpart (although there is obviously no hard and fast rule). This is precisely what the pattern of extant *Hermas* manuscripts shows and it therefore provides external evidence for the conclusion one often reaches on the basis of internal evidence: that Northern prophets like Hildegard and Robert of Uzès knew and were influenced by Hermas' archaic apocalypse. Possibly Langland knew it too.

We have spoken of the varying degree of participation of the visionary (or visionary persona) within different parts of an apocalypse, as well as of the somewhat volatile relationship he carries on with his guide from above. No apocalypse illustrates these characteristics so well as *The Shepherd of Hermas*, whose author, apparently, knew *Esdras* well (Joly's edition, p. 12). Critics have occasionally mentioned this work in connection with *Piers Plowman*,[32] but only Peter Dronke has given it any prolonged attention. This critical neglect is odd because the work is without doubt an important antecedent to the spiritual-quest visions of the later Middle Ages. The very central role which Hermas himself plays in the vision exemplifies beautifully the autobiographical soul-searching of the visionary tradition which we have come to know through Middle English poems like *Piers Plowman* and *Pearl*.

Hermas is a remarkably insightful work with regard to the psychological aspects of spiritual growth and it is this dimension of the work, as it relates to the role of the visionary, on which we will concentrate. Piehler's notion (*Visionary Landscape*, p. 9) of the dream vision, as offering the reader a chance to participate in a process of psychic redemption, is extremely apt with regard to *Hermas*. The opening of the work sets out, within the compass of a few lines, both the autobiographical elements of Hermas' life and the background to a visionary incident which precipitated his revelatory experiences and spiritual growth. At the opening of the dream vision the visionary finds himself, like Will, in the midst of "a wildernesse, wiste I neuere where" (*Piers Plowman*, B. Prol. 12). In Christian religious literature from the Bible to Dante the wilderness is a symbol both of spiritual lostness and spiritual potential for those who find themselves there, and Hermas is no exception. What is most effective about this opening, however, is its succinct telling of an event which gives Hermas cause to worry about the insidious and unconscious nature of personal sin and guilt. Hermas relates an incident in which he saw Rhoda, the mistress he served (apparently, as a slave), bathing and thought to himself "Happy were I had I such a one for beauty and disposition to wife. That only I thought to myself, and nothing more" (Taylor, vol. 1, pp. 57–58; Vision 1, ch. i; *PG* 2, cols. 891–92). Later, while traveling to Cumae, he falls asleep, and Rhoda appears to him and charges him with having had lewd desires, asserting that even the merest thought of such things is a sin. As the vision evaporates the troubled Hermas is left to wonder: "And I said within myself, If even this sin is laid to my charge, how is it possible I should be saved? How shall I make atonement to God for my sins that are full grown?" (*PG* reads: "Aut quomodo exorabo Dominum pro peccatis meis abundantissimus?") (Taylor, vol. 1, pp. 58–60; Vision 1, ch. ii; *PG* 2, cols. 893–94). This is an insightful opening to a work on the theme of repentance, and this motif of self-confrontation does indeed recur throughout the work at crucial points in a way which makes the apocalypse the record of one individual's spiritual growth. It is a role in which the reader finds himself participating and one wonders whether *Hermas* provided a model not only for the representation of psychological and spiritual growth in later visionary narrators, but also for the tradition of monastic autobiography which, as we have seen, is closely related to medieval vision literature.[33]

The reader may feel that Rhoda's accusation is rather unfair and may even wonder if the incident is as much a divine revelation as the result of over-wrought soul-searching. Taken to its logical conclusion the "revelation" certainly gives more cause for despair than hope and this is indeed the state which Hermas is in when a second revelation comes to him. The second revelation shows him a woman in bright garments, who asks him why he is sorrowful. The old woman, who is later identified as *Ecclesia*, seems almost to make light of the Rhoda vision. Instead, she points him toward the real reason why God is angry with him: he has not corrected his children or turned them toward Christianity, but she promises, "God will heal all the former ills of thine house" (Taylor, vol. I, pp. 60–61; Vision I, ch. ii; *PG* 2, cols. 894–95). There is a definite sense of gradation of the visions in the work, as each previous vision becomes a psychological and spiritual stepping-stone to the next. Langland, of course, makes use of a similar pattern of development.

From this point on *The Shepherd of Hermas* concerns itself with somewhat less subtle (if more difficult) problems in Hermas' spiritual growth, but this initial episode has set the tone for a work which demands that a high standard of self-knowledge be required of the Christian for salvation. While Hermas receives much encouragement he also receives many rebukes and one senses the process of spiritual renewal is a painful one and, as in *Piers Plowman*, one which staggers toward its goal partially subconsciously.

Hermas has two further visions of the woman during which her appearance changes and she gradually becomes younger. In the second vision Hermas, like Langland's Will, does not recognize *Ecclesia* and has to be told who she is (Taylor, vol. I, p. 70; Vision II, ch. iv; *PG* 2, cols. 897–99). This is, of course, a religious-vision convention. For example, in *The Vision of Tundale*, the narrator is told, upon the appearance of his angel-guide, that the angel has been Tundale's companion since birth. Tundale's inability to recognize the angel is then explicitly attributed to his sinful past (ed. Mearns, lines 299–304). In this context one immediately recalls Holy Church's response to Will's question in which she identifies herself and adds "þou oughtest me to knowe; / Y undirfenge þe formeste . . ." (*Piers Plowman*, I. 72–73). This lack-of-recognition motif, like a number of other small details in Langland's visions, has a clear visionary lineage. Both Will and Hermas begin to receive their revelations at crucial points during their lives when they are stirred by a sense of spiritual need but have little notion of how to go about finding the right path. The similarities are striking: both are earnest and inquisitive, eager to learn but slow to think for themselves, both are visionaries hampered by literal vision. In his second vision of *Ecclesia*, Hermas' personal life again becomes the point of departure. After revealing the misdeeds of his family and urging them to repent, *Ecclesia*'s message is broadened to all the Christian community: the Lord has limited to the very day the time left for repentance and that day is at hand. At this point the message becomes truly apocalyptic with the motif of preparation for coming tribulation: "Happy are all ye that endure the great affliction which is to come, and that shall not deny their life" (Taylor, vol. 1, p. 68; Vision 11, ch. ii; *PG* 2, cols. 897–98). The seeming inconsistency in the duality of the message which is both a personal and a general revelation goes to the heart of apocalyptic literature as a genre: the apocalypse is very much a scribal text in that the visionary is only a mouthpiece of higher forces, but the visions themselves are traumatically personal experiences and record not just a divine message but a process of personal growth as well.[34] Even the unobtrusive St. John, who for the most part hides himself behind the Apocalypse he relates, cannot wholly keep himself back emotionally from the action of the revelation itself, as, for example, when he weeps because no one is worthy to open the sealed book (Apocalypse 5:1–5). Similarly, at the end of the vision John can no longer contain his awe; falling down at the feet of his angel-guide, he is rebuked: "See thou do it not; for I am thy fellow-servant, and of thy brethren the prophets and of them that keep the words of the prophecy of this book. Adore God" (Apocalypse 22:8–9). Even in John's visions there is the sense that his reactions are being monitored. Upon seeing the woman drunk with the blood of the saints, John is awed and the angel asks, "Why dost thou wonder? I will tell thee the mystery of the woman . . ." (Apocalypse 17:6–7).

If even John, the least demonstrative of all apocalyptic narrators, can be seen to be undergoing a personally traumatic experience, with which the reader will naturally identify, it is in this sense that apocalypses are both autobiographical and universal documents. However, they so often appear chaotic because these two interests are not well delineated. The reader can often justifiably ask whether the writer wished to write a spiritual autobiography or to document a universal prophetic message when, at times, he seems to be doing both incoherently or haphazardly. The only answer (and this is not so much an answer as an observation) is that the apocalypses that have come down to us do try to do both and do not seem either concerned to or able to control both forms. Difficulty seems almost to be a requirement of the genre.[35] Apocalypses always read as works of passion, urgency and compulsion. At the same time they are works of process: as the visionary tries to grapple with the message he feels compelled to convey, he records his experience and the growth of his understanding. But works of process are not always "reader-friendly," and perhaps this is something which readers of apocalypses must simply accept.

In the third vision *Ecclesia* shows Hermas a tower being built of square stones. Stones which are of the proper shape fit together so that no trace of a joint can be seen, but many types of stones are rejected by the builders. Having shown these things to Hermas, she prepares to leave, but Hermas asks her,

Lady, what doth it profit me to have seen these things and not know what they mean? She answered me saying, Thou art a knavish fellow, desiring to know all about the tower. Yea, quoth I, lady, so that I may tell my brethren . . . Then quoth she . . . Hear then the parables of the tower, for I will reveal all things unto thee; and then trouble me no more about revelation . . . Yet thou wilt not cease to ask for revelations, for thou art shameless.

(Taylor, vol. 1, pp. 78–79; Vision III, ch. iii; *PG* 2, cols. 901–02)

This last comment cannot fail to remind Langland scholars of Will, with his persistent appetite for "wonders" and knowledge. This scene and others in the book are, again, very much like the beginning of Will's vision of the Tree of Charity or his discussion with Holy Church in that Hermas' questions are sometimes encouraged and answered with patience and sometimes met with impatient disapproval because of their inquisitive nature. In the B-text version of the Tree of Charity vision, the dreamer tells Piers that he has "þou3tes a þreve" concerning the three props which support the Tree, but soon realizes that Piers is becoming intolerant of his boundless questioning. Piers tells him,

> "And I haue told þee what hi3te þe tree; þe Trinite it meneþ."
> And egreliche he loked on me and þerfore I spared
> To asken hym any moore þerof . . .   (B. XVI. 63–65)

From the standpoint of the visionary, the unpredictability of response to his questions serves to heighten the awesome superiority of the other-worldly guide. From the standpoint of the guide, the questions do, at times, reveal the dreamer's inability to think for himself. It is possible to sympathize with both views, but as the reader often identifies unconsciously with the dreamer or visionary figure in any given vision and as our own age views intellectual curiosity in a more positive way, it is perhaps easier to understand the dreamer's sense of intimidation than his guide's exasperation. But modern readers are not alone in their tendency to identify with the visionary figure: medieval authors apparently counted on this humanizing effect to engage their audience for didactic purposes.[36]

There are many parallels in *Piers Plowman* to Hermas' relationship with his various guides. At one point when Hermas complains that he is foolish and cannot understand, his guide (the Shepherd this time) tries to suggest *why* he finds himself so hampered. Upon the Shepherd's advising him to "put away sorrow," for it is "sister" to fickleness and impatience, Hermas complains:

Sir, quoth I, I am foolish and understand not these parables . . . Hear, quoth he; they who never searched about the truth nor enquired diligently concerning the things of God, but believed only, and were mixed up with . . . affairs of this world; such, I say, as are intent upon these things understand not the parables of divinity, for they are darkened by these employments, and they decay and grow barren.

(Taylor, vol. 1, pp. 144–45; Mandate x, ch. i; *PG* 2, cols. 939–40)[37]

The message is clear: parables are not understood by those who put no effort into searching out the truth or living a Christian life. Readers of Langland cannot help but recall Will's refrain, "I haue no kynde knowyng," which always crops up when he seems unwilling to exert his mind to grasp some new teaching. His exchange with Holy Church furnishes a typical example:

> "I haue no kynde knowyng," quod y, "3ut mot 3e kenne me bettere
> By what wey it wexeth and wheder out of my menynges."
> "Thow dotede daffe," quod she, "dulle aren thy wittes.

To lyte lernedest þow, y leue, Latyn in thy ʒowthe:
Heu michi, quod sterilem duxi vitam iuuenilem!
Hit is a kynde knowynge that kenet in thyn herte . . ." (I. 136–40)

Like Hermas' Shepherd, Holy Church seems to understand what she perceives as willful ignorance by putting it down to lack of application – a lack of application which betrays a lifelong habit. Instances of this rebuke in *Hermas* are legion.[38]

Hermas is eventually made to recognize the power of his own mind over what he sees and learns. Upon fasting and praying in order to gain understanding of the series of visions of *Ecclesia* Hermas sees a young man who, after the usual admonition of his incessant curiosity, explains the three visions in such a way that they now appear as mirrors of the state of Hermas' soul at the time of seeing (Taylor, vol. 1, pp. 94–95; Vision IV, ch. xi; *PG* 2, cols. 907–10). *Ecclesia* first appeared elderly and feeble because of Hermas' spiritual weakness – in what is a nice comment on spiritual perception, vitality is in the eye of the beholder. The increasingly youthful appearance of the woman in the second and third visions is likewise interpreted as reflecting Hermas' increasing ability to comprehend spiritual truth and utilize his own spiritual strength: they are a mirror of his own rejuvenation.

At this point the visions of the apocalypse themselves are almost wholly a reflection of the visionary's spiritual state and the broader apocalyptic message seems in danger of being swallowed by a purely subjective vision. There is something of this mirror effect in the early sections of the *Vita* of *Piers Plowman*. At this stage many of Will's guides are reflections of certain facets of his own mind and his ability to provide answers for himself is thus consistently restricted to his own mental capacities for vision. *Piers Plowman* illustrates this rather more subtly and at greater length than *Hermas* does, but the point is the same: Will encounters a number of personifications in this section, many of whom, like Thought (X. 68ff.), Wit (X. 114ff.), Recklessness (XI. 196ff.) and Imaginatif (XIII. 217ff.), are more or less projected fragments of his own limited world view. He is only freed to move onwards by being cast out of the visionary world in a confrontation with his own impudence: both literally and metaphorically Reason gets the better of him (XIII. 193ff.).

The self-confrontation which so unlocks his mind is thus brought on by shame and humiliation. When Imaginatif, as yet unidentified, rebukes him for his impatience and "entermetynge," Will admits,

"ʒe seggeth soth, be my soule," quod y, "I haue sey hit ofte:
Ther smyt no thyng so smerte, ne smelleth so foule
As Shame; ther he sheweth hym, vch man shoneth his companye.
Why ʒe worden to me thus was for y aresonede Resoun." (XIII. 240–43)

The dreamer has come far enough by this point in the poem to be able to offer his own definition of Dowell: "To se moche and soffre al, certes, is Dowel" (XIII. 219). The definition is hopelessly inadequate, but it is nevertheless a benchmark in Will's spiritual growth, which has been much hindered up to this point by his inability to listen patiently and think *independently* toward an understanding of what he is told. A similar turning point comes for Hermas when he feels the sting of shame:

> Again he said unto me, Love truth, and let all be truth which proceedeth out of thy mouth . . . Now when I heard these things I wept bitterly. And seeing me weep he said, Why weepest thou? Because, sir, quoth I, I know not whether I can be saved. Wherefore? quoth he. Because, sir, quoth I, never yet in my life spake I a true word, but I lived always knavishly with all men, and displayed my falsehood as truth to all; nor did any one ever gainsay me, but my word was believed. How then, sir, quoth I, can I live when I have done these things? Thou thinkest well and truly, quoth he; for it were fit that thou as a servant of God shouldest walk in truth, and that an evil conscience should not dwell with the spirit of truth, nor bring grief upon the reverend and true Spirit. Never before, sir, quoth I, did I hear such words aright. Now therefore that thou hearest, quoth he, keep them.
>
> (Taylor, vol. i, pp. 115, 116–17; Mandate iii, ch. i; *PG* 2, cols. 917–18)

Hermas is very harsh on himself here, but what he has achieved is more than simple penitence, it is a whole new awareness of self: "Never before . . . did I hear such words aright." Shortly after this episode Hermas' Shepherd underlines the point for Hermas that repentance *is* understanding:

> I asked him again saying, Since the Lord counted me worthy that thou shouldest always dwell with me, bear with yet a few words from me, for I understand nothing, and my heart is grown dull from my former doings. Give me understanding, for I am very foolish and apprehend nothing at all. He answered and said to me, I am set over repentance, and to all who repent I give understanding. Seemeth it not to thee that this very repenting is understanding? To repent, quoth he, is great understanding.
>
> (Taylor, vol. i, pp. 121–22; Mandate iv, ch. ii; *PG* 2, cols. 919–20)

Perhaps Will's foolishness in his visionary role should be understood as Hermas' is: as a marker of the moral and spiritual weakness which clouds his vision.

There is more than one such turning point for Will in *Piers Plowman*. There are, for example, beside the encounter with Imaginatif, the brief episode in which Will is made to weep upon hearing Repentance's call to repentance, and the autobiographical passage, new to the C-text, in which Will tries to justify his life, but goes away ashamed (v. 102–08). This kind of episode, in both *Piers Plowman* and in *Hermas*, is a good example of the effort to humanize the narrator which seems to have become conventional for didactic purposes in visionary works, because it offers the reader the chance to participate vicariously in the experience of turning over a new leaf. It is interesting to note that Langland seems more rather than less concerned in his additions to the C-text to heighten some of the religious-visionary aspects like this one.

The Shepherd of Hermas makes much use of the kind of vision which we see in Will's interchange with Holy Church or at the beginning of the Tree of Charity episode, and which I call deictic vision. In this type of vision the guide points out a visionary scene to the dreamer and explains its significance, as for example in Holy Church's first appearance: ". . . 'Wille, slepestow? seestow þis peple,/ Hou bisy þei ben aboute þe mase?'" (i. 5–6). When Will asks Holy Church to "Kenne me by sum craft to knowe þe false" (ii. 4)[39] she responds by showing him the Lady Mede vision: "Loke vppon thy left half and loo where he standeth . . ." (in medieval vision convention, the left generally represents evil, the right good). After this early stage in the poem, Langland more or less abandons this directly didactic type of vision, preferring to have his dreamer observe without the benefit of an interpreter (as, for example, in Will's vision of the pardon episode) or to have Will participating directly in the action of the vision (as in the Feast of Patience).

Certainly the abandonment of this purely didactic format for alternative approaches is the mark of a more sophisticated writer. The deictic type of vision in which the visionary stands outside the action of the vision and listens to his guide's interpretation of what he sees is perhaps one of the least helpful modes of visionary writing for Langland and he seems to have realized this early on in the development of the poem. Many non-apocalyptic visions of the Middle Ages, especially those which German scholars call *Jenseitsvisionen*, other-world visions, rely almost entirely on this type of convention.[40] Indeed, the masterpiece of *Jenseitsvisionen*, Dante's *Divine Comedy*, makes much use of this visionary convention in its basic structure. However, Langland was obviously dissatisfied with this mode of proceeding and does not sustain it. He reverts to it again at the start of the Tree of Charity vision and this perhaps contributes to our sense of this episode as distinctively visionary: it makes use once again of the deictic visionary-guide convention at its opening, but swiftly moves to an abrupt and highly associative chain of allegorical events which better suit Langland's purposes in conveying the dream-likeness of the episode. Still, the formal, static beginning, with its diagrammatic allegory, sets this vision apart from previous "participatory" visions and Langland may have intended this. The "Tree of Life" vision is an important and often climactic convention of formal apocalypses and Langland's reversion to the deictic convention here may indicate that he is consciously drawing on this tradition.[41]

Although apocalypses like *The Shepherd of Hermas* make more use of this particular convention than *Piers Plowman* does, they too exhibit a wide variety of approaches to the visionary's participation in his vision. Dialogues concerning doctrinal problems, especially those which the visionary narrator finds hard to fathom, take up as much space in these apocalypses as the allegorical or "visualized" visions and the result is long stretches of text in which any would-be illustrator would not find a scrap of visual material to fasten on. Rosemary Woolf, in her seminal article on some of the "non-medieval" qualities of *Piers Plowman*, relates this absence of visualization in parts of the poem to its "abrupt shifting of time and place, which is so familiar from actual dreams, and so extremely unlike any other Medieval use of the dream convention" (Woolf, "Qualities," pp. 116–17). It is hard to find models or analogues in vernacular literature for both this periodic lack of visualization (alternating, of course, with the vividly visual sections) and for the instability of narrative framework in *Piers Plowman*, and we are left to wonder, as Rosemary Woolf does, what literary paradigms Langland was influenced by: "Langland's avoidance of the common need to lay a foundation in reasonable plot for the appearance or conduct of any character is clearly related to his indifference to the literal level of his allegory, and his suggestion of the disorganized nature of real dreams gives at least a technical plausibility to the inconsistencies of the literal level of the poem" ("Qualities," p. 118).

Every individual has experienced dreams and it is therefore not necessary perhaps to seek for an explanation in literary history for Langland's use of real dream-likeness. The extent of it, however, is unusual and one genre of literature to which he could have turned as a model for his dream realism is the apocalypse. We have already noted the mixture of visualized and non-visualized (usually dialectical or hortatory) passages in the two early apocalypses *Esdras* and *Hermas*, as well as the uncertainties involved in the visionary's relationship with his guide. Let us look now at some of the features in *Hermas* which produce this dream-likeness, notably the work's structural looseness, shifting symbolism and the changing states of some of the characters.

The Shepherd of Hermas is divided into three discernible sections of five Visions, twelve Mandates (or commandments) and ten Similitudes (or parallels). Certain allegorical symbols serve to provide the work with some cohesion, such as the allegory of the Church as a tower under construction. Hermas sees the tower for the first time fairly early on in the work (in the third vision) and the allegory recurs in several places, is explained *ad nauseam* in its various forms and finally comes to rest with the end of the work itself, at which point the reader is exhorted: "Do good works therefore, ye who have received from the Lord, lest while ye delay to do them the building of the tower be finished; for your sakes the work of the building of it hath been delayed. Except then ye make haste to do ought, the tower shall be finished and ye shall be shut out" (Taylor, vol. II, p. 131; Similitude x, ch. iv; *PG* 2, cols. 1011–12). The tower, then, provides a measure of cohesion within the work, but even this is limited. The main themes of *Hermas*, exhortation to repentance and concern with the requirements of the spiritual life, are introduced and represented and discussed in a myriad of ways and any number of images and similitudes are pressed into service in the process. As in *The Apocalypse of Esdras*, similitude after similitude is produced and images are heaped one on top of another in order to solve the unsolvable or express the inexpressible. There is little or no attempt to reconcile symbolic incongruities or relate similitudes to one another.

Critics have frequently complained about this "problem" in *Piers Plowman*; many regard it as a lack of authorial control or even of literary ability. David Mills, for example, complains of the "inadequacy of imagery" in both Holy Church's explanation of love and in the Tree of Charity vision: "When Holy Church attempts to explain love to the Dreamer, she is compelled to use images, but shifts reference so frequently that the image breaks down . . . On a larger scale, the same inadequacy of imagery can be seen in the description of the Tree of Charity, which, even in its poetically superior form in the C-text, utilizes an inadequate image."[42] Mills takes the trouble to show in each passage how the chosen allegorical image with which the passage begins "breaks down" ("Role," p. 204) and he implies that these passages are therefore poetic failures. Interestingly, he despairs of the Tree of Charity vision just at the point when it becomes truly fascinating, when the falling fruits become the Old Testament patriarchs. As Peter Dronke has suggested ("*Arbor*," p. 220), this may well be a matter of personal taste ("Whether we view the transgressions as so many sins against an allegorical norm, or as imaginatively valid ways of stepping beyond that norm, is something each reader, in each context, must decide"), but critics like Mills would do well to remember that there is plenty of absolutely consistent and well-sustained allegory which is no longer read. Allegoric consistency and artistic genius are not necessarily found together. This technique of heaping images is, however, a common feature of apocalypses and it may be this eccentric form of literature which gave Langland a paradigm for his allegorical transgressions.

This looseness of structure is marked in other ways in *Hermas*. The key guide figures do not maintain their presence throughout the work, but appear and disappear almost arbitrarily, often in changing forms. The woman who represents the Church, as we have seen, consistently appears to Hermas during the first visions in different forms and Hermas is later told that this shifting of forms reflects his changing capacity for vision. The Shepherd himself, who is most comparable to Piers, and for whom the work is named, does not enter the drama until the fifth vision (much as Piers does not enter the poem until it is well under way). Hermas is told that the Shepherd, who is also the Angel of Repentance, has been given to him as a guide "for the rest of the days of his life" and yet he appears in different forms and Hermas does not at first recognize him, even suggesting at one point that it is a deceiving spirit:

He said unto me, Knowest thou me not? Nay, quoth I. I, quoth he, am the Shepherd to whom thou wast delivered. While he yet spake his visage was changed, and I took knowledge of him that it was he to whom I had been delivered; and immediately I was confounded, and fear took hold upon me, and I was quite overcome with grief at having so answered him wickedly and foolishly. Then he answered and said to me, Be not confounded, but strengthen thyself in my commandments which I am about to command thee.   (Taylor, vol. 1, pp. 107–08; *Prooemium* to Mandates; *PG* 2, cols. 913–14)

The shifting appearance of the Shepherd's face and Hermas' concern that he is being deluded are both markers of vision convention. It is perhaps overly generous to say, as Peter Dronke has, that the two protagonists, *Ecclesia* and the Shepherd, "are in their ways as richly elusive as Piers Plowman in Langland's poem" ("*Arbor*," p. 221); however, it is certainly true that they exemplify the dream-like shifting of shape with which we are familiar from Langland's poetry.

Placing these apocalypses, then, in the background to *Piers Plowman* provides us with a different perspective on some of what Rosemary Woolf calls the "unique" aspects of Langland's poetry, especially those which we associate with "dream-likeness," with "lack of artistic control" and with the "non-medieval" way in which Langland treats his visionary narrator ("Qualities," pp. 116–17). In the final section of this chapter we will look further at this problem of the "non-medieval" qualities, but enough has been said for the moment to help us make an assessment of what is involved in the suggestion that *Piers Plowman* might, in literary terms, be called an apocalypse.

At the beginning of this section "apocalypse" was defined most basically as "a genre of revelatory literature within a narrative framework" (Hayes, *Introduction*, p. 366) and we set ourselves the problem of trying to determine whether this literary model was in the back of Langland's mind as he wrote. As I mentioned above, earlier biblical scholars disputed about whether *Hermas* should be regarded as an allegory or an apocalypse and the same question has been asked of *Piers Plowman*. From a literary viewpoint it seems that the question can partly be resolved for *Piers Plowman* as it was for *Hermas*: on the basis of audience reaction, that is, how was the work *read* by a contemporary audience, simply as an allegory or as an apocalypse? In the case of *Hermas*, it is clear from the *Muratori Fragment* that, whatever the canonists decided, *Hermas* was thought of and mentioned in the context of other apocalypses. In other words, similarities in form and message placed it in the same category as other apocalypses in the minds of contemporaries. For the literary historian this is important testimony, and it would be nice to have such conclusive evidence for *Piers Plowman*. What fragmentary evidence we do have suggests that it was read as an apocalypse by its sixteenth-century editor, Crowley; that it frequently appears in manuscripts with other works concerned with the course of Salvation History; and that the prophecies are frequently picked out for marginal commentary by medieval readers.[43] Furthermore, the apocalypse was well enough known as a genre to have been parodied in the *Apocalypsis Goliae*, a work to which Langland may well be alluding in the Feast of Patience scene (xv. 99). And there are a number of parallels in style and convention between formal apocalypses and the poem, as we have seen. Perhaps whether or not we call *Piers Plowman* an apocalypse, however, is not as important as whether we recognize the elements of the apocalypse genre within the poem, and especially the visionary conventions which fall under this heading, as part of a distinct tradition in literary history.

Before leaving the question of whether *Piers Plowman* is an apocalypse, we should look at what Morton Bloomfield had to say about the problem which, after all, gave him the title of his book on *Piers Plowman*: "A simple answer to the question of the genre of *Piers Plowman* would be to say that it is an apocalypse. The classic Judeo-Christian apocalypse is cast in dream form, or consists of several dreams, is a revelation from some superior authority, is eschatologically oriented, and constitutes a criticism of, and warning for, contemporary society" (Bloomfield, *Apocalypse*, p. 9). However, he dwells more upon the differences than the similarities between *Piers Plowman* and the apocalypse genre as he sees it:

The emphasis on the quest is foreign to the apocalypse as we know it. There is no single guide in *Piers*, but rather a search for guides, although Holy Church and Conscience have a certain authority. The use of personifications is not a characteristic of the apocalypse, and there is a strong vein of irony in the figure of Will that is not consonant with the apocalypse. Although *Piers* does criticize contemporary society, is in dream form, and is eschatologically oriented, these characteristics of the apocalypse can be accounted for otherwise.

(Bloomfield, *Apocalypse*, pp. 9–10)

I hope it is now clear that this assessment is inadequate: whether we wish, in the last analysis, to consider *Piers Plowman* an apocalypse or not, the only way to assess the problem is to look closely at what an apocalypse, in literary terms, really *is*. What has been done here in this regard is at best a beginning, but it has been enough to make Bloomfield's objections seem questionable. As we have seen, the quest, as a spiritual quest, is *not* foreign to the apocalypse. Neither of the apocalypses we have looked at has a single guide. There is much use of personification: Sion in *Esdras*, *Ecclesia* in *Hermas* or even Babylon in St. John's Apocalypse, to mention only a few

95

examples. Even the "vein of irony in the figure of Will" has important antecedents in the figures of visionary narrators like Esdras and Hermas.

Bloomfield ends his short discussion of the problem with the suggestion that the notion of the apocalypse as genre is unhelpful:

> The chief objection to taking the form of *Piers* to be an apocalypse is that it is doubtful whether such a literary form existed. I agree with Father H. Musurillo when he writes, "The form known as 'apocalypse' creates a problem, and perhaps no useful purpose is served in making the term a technical one applicable both to the Revelation of St. John and the so-called *Shepherd of Hermas*." He says that the *Shepherd* is rather "allegorical fiction disguised as a primitive Christian prophecy."[44]

It is doubtful that the author of *Hermas* was trying to disguise allegory as prophecy and this seems a rather perverse way of posing the problem: the author of *Hermas* would no doubt have thought the scholarly opposition of allegory to apocalypse somewhat ludicrous. He was writing within a literary genre (the apocalypse) which was by definition visionary and the way that visionary experience had always been related in the Judeo-Christian tradition was by the use of allegory – as works like the apocalypses of Daniel, "Esdras" and St. John all show. Allegory is, *par excellence*, the visionary mode of writing and this literary tradition has been preserved even in post-medieval visionary works like those by Bunyan and Blake.

The form known as "apocalypse," as Father Musurillo says, does create a problem, but so does every other literary form worth mentioning. Have genres like the lyric, the novel or the epic not "created problems" for literary critics? One may well "doubt" whether it is helpful to try precisely to define the novel or the epic, but as long as works are created which remind readers of other works in a literary tradition, we will have to grapple with these problems of categorization as best we can.

The apocalypse, as *the* mode of fully developed visionary narrative within the religious tradition, is perhaps the best term we have for describing these qualities and tendencies in *Piers Plowman*. Until more scholarly work is done on the literary characteristics of the religious visionary tradition, it is unlikely that our primitive system of literary labeling will offer a better term than "apocalypse" for Langland's revelatory allegory.

"VISIONARY DENUNCIATION OF ECCLESIASTICAL ABUSES": ROBERT OF UZÈS AND BRIDGET OF SWEDEN

In this section two visionary apocalyptic writers who seem to be direct descendants of Hildegard's visionary prophetic line will be examined. Similarities in ideology are the most obvious points of comparison between this "school" of writers and Langland's own prophetic brand of vision, but from a literary point of view there is also a similarity in the use that each of these writers makes of, to use Northrop Frye's vivid phrase, an apocalyptic grammar of images (*Anatomy*, p. 141). While the choice of images often differs from visionary to visionary, the archetypes of apocalyptic thought are remarkably stable.

An examination of the apocalyptic visions of Robert of Uzès and Bridget of Sweden reveals the same sense of crisis of leadership within the Church, reflected in the figures of ideal popes and chastising reformers which people their visions. These, in turn, are opposed by various Antichrist figures, or forerunners of the same, all of whom have a place in a perceived pattern of current and future history. The state of the friars, which Bridget explains allegorically as the infiltration of the devil ("Brother Adversarius"), is of paramount concern to both. Moreover, she and Robert persistently reflect the anti-materialism and anti-intellectualism common to all such prophets.

The similarities between this Northern European visionary prophetic "school" and *Piers Plowman* make it obvious that Langland must have known *something* of this type of literature, but it is not the purpose of this book to argue for the influence of any particular work or author on *Piers Plowman*. Time may well reveal other visionary writers in this "school" deserving of comparison with Langland, but for the present this brief look at Robert of Uzès and Bridget of Sweden will provide some sense of an alternative tradition of visionary writing, one which urges reform in an apocalyptic manner just as Langland does.

Robert of Uzès (d. 1296)

Robert is usually described as "little-known" (when he is described at all) by modern scholars,[45] but it would seem that he was not as obscure a figure in his own time. In fact, his visions seem to have enjoyed a certain vogue from the fourteenth to the sixteenth century.[46] Jeanne Bignami-Odier, who edited Robert's meagre works in 1955, first drew attention to him as one of two visionaries (Hildegard of Bingen being the other) who had greatly influenced John of Rupescissa.[47] As she has shown, Robert must have been considered a man of some importance during his own lifetime. Having become a priest as a young man, Robert did not join a religious order until 1292, after he had received many of the visions which he records in the *Liber visionum*.[48] But even by the time of his profession he seems to have attained a degree of recognition within his order.[49] No less an authority than Bernard Gui devoutly recorded Robert's death in 1296; "Vir fuit in etate florida plenus Spiritu Dei, cui multa Dominus revelavit et predixit futura; et evenerunt; diem et horam mortis sue in infirmitate qua obiit socio suo predixit, sicut ab eodem fratre audivi" (quoted in Bignami-Odier, "Robert," p. 263). This note by Bernard Gui certainly sets a seal of orthodoxy upon Robert's reformist denunciations: like all the prophets discussed in this study, Robert was an orthodox radical.

In the second half of the fourteenth century the English chronicler Henry of Herford recounted a miracle which occurred at Robert's funeral, noting first that Robert had predicted the general pestilence thirty years before its occurrence as a chastisement against the avarice and simony of the papacy.[50] Any prophet who could be seen genuinely to have predicted the great plague of 1348 was destined, in the latter half of the fourteenth century, for some degree of popularity even outside apocalyptic circles, and this is certainly true of Robert. His prophecies seem to have influenced some fourteenth- and fifteenth-century reformers,[51] especially John of Rupescissa, who was particularly impressed with Robert's angelic-pope figure, as well as his many attacks on ecclesiastical corruption; John even tried to imitate Robert's style.

The question of the dissemination and influence of Robert's works is a difficult one. During the fifteenth and sixteenth centuries, when the popularity of apocalyptic collections and compilations reached its zenith, Robert persistently appears with his better-known fellows of the prophetic company: Hildegard, Joachim, John of Rupescissa, St. Vincent and others.[52] However, the circulation of Robert's works in the fourteenth century is less obvious, and tracing it is made more difficult by the fact that sometimes they were copied anonymously (Bignami-Odier, "Robert," p. 271). The Augustinian friar John Erghome (d. 1385), author of the "John of Bridlington" commentary and avid collector of prophetic material at York, owned a manuscript which contained "prophetia Roberti de Usecio," and there is other evidence of his being known in England.[53] However, since his writings are short and the visions easily excerpted, they are more likely to be embedded in a collection than to stand on their own.[54] It will be some time yet before we will be able to say with more certainty how well Robert was known in fourteenth-century England (or anywhere else, for that matter).

Robert's visions show all the classic hallmarks of reform apocalyptic. His concern is primarily about the decay of the Church and about its coming humiliation, which he predicts over and over again. Central to this concern is the figure of a pope whom he portrays as a *papa angelicus*, a humble, poorly dressed spiritual man, a stranger to the glitter, pomp and intrigue of the papal *Curia*. Moreover, this pope is closely associated with the figure of the apostle Peter, whom Robert portrays as the simple working man of the Gospels. Robert was clearly much affected by the events of 1294–96, which saw the eventual abdication of the holy hermit-pope Celestine V and the enthronement of "one of the least spiritual men to hold the papal office," Boniface VIII (McGinn, *Visions*, p. 188). The episode gave rise to quite a prophetic legacy because Celestine and Boniface provided apocalyptic reformers with the most dramatically opposed images of pope and antipope that history could possibly have produced. Many of Robert's visions are peopled with these two powerful figures; characteristic of this type of apocalyptic thought is this persistent focusing on the crisis of leadership, and the related tendency of marking out a special group or order as forerunners or embodiments of Antichrist, in Robert's case, as in Hildegard's, a heretical group.

Let us begin by looking at one of Robert's visions of the "angelic-pope" figure. The reader will be struck immediately by how much the vision reads like an account of a real dream and yet, at the same time, by the evidence it shows of attention to allegorical structure:

In the same place I saw in a dream that I was with my oldest brother and sister. While we were walking we came to a door and heard the words: "The pope is inside, if you wish to see him." We entered and kissed his feet as he stood on the ground. I was amazed that he would sit upon the ground and looked upon his short narrow bed with its very poor covering. I said: "Why is it, Father, that you have such a poor bed? The poorest of the poor bishops of the world would not have a meaner one." The pope said to me, "We must be humbled."

Suddenly we were on our way down a mountain and I saw him in the habit of the Friars Minor. I fell upon my face and kissed his naked foot; then I held him up on the right side. As we began to ascend the mountain, I held the pope up on the left side and a secular priest supported him on the right. While we ascended, the pope began to limp badly so that he would not have been able to go up had we not carried him. While we carried him, we entered a hospice at the top of the mountain; there were kettles and pots there, but the fire was out. We glanced all around and saw no one, but when we entered we looked in a small place as through a window and saw some women looking at the pope. He lifted up his hand and blessed them.[55]

There are many elements of actual dream-likeness here, as, for example, the mention of being with a brother and sister[56] or the lack of narrative cohesion: these are striking enough that one suspects that the vision, as it is written, does have its roots in a real dream. The sudden and unexplained shift of location and pervading sense of arbitrariness contribute to the dream-world effect. And yet Robert's imagery in places suggests deliberate allegory: "As we began to ascend the mountain, I held the pope up on the left side and a secular priest supported him on the right." This vision must have been written after Robert had joined the Dominican order, because he distinguishes himself from the secular priest and they are both, obviously, symbols of the two groups of clergy, secular and regular, who should be helping the crippled Church (or the Head of the Church) in the uphill struggle towards reform. The meanness of the pope's personal appearance and living conditions suggests Robert's idealization of him as a poor hermit, a practitioner of the apostolic poverty so idealized by such reformists, including Langland. Other visions portray even more graphically the humiliation of the Church and the stripping away of the papal materialism.[57] In accordance with Robert's view of the current spiritual crisis, the pope is symbolically crippled and one of the last images is of a fire that has died out, although all the utensils are ready and waiting. The whole vision conveys a sense of poverty, emptiness and struggle which is more than the sum of its confused parts.

Another of Robert's visions is as interesting for its use of visionary tradition as for its emphasis on ecclesiastical crisis. Imitating Hildegard's use of dryness and disease as an image of spiritual aridity, Robert also draws on the visionary convention of placing the divine interpreter of the vision on his right, as Langland does when Holy Church speaks to Will. The vision of a rough, irate St. Peter, which occurs in one of the most powerful of visionary settings, at Mass, is no doubt intended to affirm Robert's orthodoxy. He sees:

sanctum Petrum apostolum papalibus indumentis rubeis vestitum tyaramque in capite eius. Et ecce yrsutus incomptus et iratus aparuit, tenens claves magnas ferreas in manu sinistra. Cumque inspicerem ad dexteram eius, vidi brachium eius dextrum nigrum siccum et quasi aridum miratusque dixi: "Que sunt hec, Domine Deus?" Dixitque mihi Spiritus, qui michi hoc ostendebat, a dextris stans: "Pars dextra, ecclesia, nigra facta siccaque et quasi arida, non tamen amisit ecclesia clavium potestatem."   (Bignami-Odier, "Robert," p. 277)

St. Peter appears, in spite of the papal robes, as the simple working man of the Gospels; he is angered and debilitated, but he still retains the power of the keys. As Bignami-Odier indicates ("Robert," pp. 277–78, n. 21), Robert, like so many apocalyptic reformers of the period, vehemently criticizes the ecclesiastical hierarchy but always remains a true son of the Church. She opposes this type of reformer to those revolutionaries who challenged the rule of the powerful and the entire fabric of the social and religious order. This is the same opposition as we have, in religious terms, between Langland and Wyclif, and in secular terms, between Langland and John Ball. Langland, too, cannot be as successfully associated with religious heretics or social revolutionaries as he can with the radical but orthodox apocalyptic reform writers.

Robert is similarly concerned with decadence within certain orders of the clergy, even the Dominican order. In Vision 36, headed "concerning the Order of the Preachers," he writes:

Accidit una dierum per signum, comedente panem cum fratribus meis irruit in me spiritus Domini et vidi in spiritu virum unum in habitu virorum evangelizantium, habentem maculas magnas tam in capite quam in membris. Dixitque spiritus Domini: "Ordo hic maculatus est, tu autem serve meus dic ei ut mundetur."

(Bignami-Odier, "Robert," p. 287)

The image of the blemished head and limbs is once again very Hildegardian, and Robert is given a suitably Hildegardian mandate as prophet or spokesman of God to his order.[58] We note that this is the first vision in which he is specifically told to preach a message to others.[59] Vision 23 (Bignami-Odier, "Robert," p. 283) is similarly prophetic but this time more pessimistic with regard to the fate of another group of clergy. The rubric reads "on the destruction of the prelates" and the entire vision is contained within one stark sentence: "Vigilans vidi quasi cumulum in terra mitrarum et baculorum pastoralium sine episcopis et prelatis, in multitudine fere innumerabili."

One of Robert's most significant visions comes at a dramatic moment in his own life. In Vision 17 (Bignami-Odier, "Robert," p. 281) he is shown some enigmatic symbols which, he is told, represent the End of the World. He then records two events which, for him, are foreboding signs. The whole set of events occurs shortly after he has relinquished all the possessions which were his by inheritance to pursue his religious vocation. Robert pointedly mentions this at the beginning of the vision, something which exemplifies the close relationship between the personal and spiritual lives of religious visionaries:

Factum est autem, cum cepissem verbum Domini ardentius predicare, semper inserens de preparatione ad tribulationes futuras, circuiens castra et villas, perveni ad Avinionensem civitatem, eadem praedicans ibi. Et facta est indiscreta commotio virorum ac mulierum ac periculosa valde, vocataque est congregatio eorum a vulgo Saccatorum secta. Et factum est temporo illo: mortuus est dominus Nicolaus papa quartus.

(Bignami-Odier, "Robert," p. 281)

Robert seems to have picked out the Saccantes[60] as the most dangerous group threatening the Church at the time. The apocalyptic mentality seems to work this way: some group is always identified and charged with "anti-Christian" activity. For many writers the orthodox friars themselves fill this position; for other writers heretical groups or corrupt forces within the Church supply the targets.[61]

Piers Plowman and the medieval visionary tradition

Antichrist himself is the subject of many of Robert's visions, some of which read not so much as prophetic visions as personal nightmares. One such vision is in fact Robert's first, and gives the strong impression of having originated in a real dream. In it, Antichrist appears in the same dishevelled appearance that Robert so often attributes to his holy pope (Bignami-Odier, "Robert," p. 273), suggesting that ambiguity between true and false apostles which Langland too exploits.

Also reminiscent of Langland is Robert's contempt for vain philosophical speculation. The last vision in the *Liber visionum* concerns "the investigators of inane philosophies." Robert reports that one day while he was "seeing in the Spirit," he saw a man in fraternal habit gnawing a stone, all the while ignoring delectable bread and wine. Two serpents' heads emerge from the stone,

Et instruebat me spiritus Domini dicens: "Lapis hic questiones sunt inutiles et curiose quibus famescentes elaborant, animarum substantialia relinquentes." Et dixi: "Quid ergo capita illa dicunt"? Dixit Spiritus Domini michi: "Nomen uni: vana gloria, alteri vero: dissipacio religionis dicitur." (Bignami-Odier, "Robert," pp. 287–88)

Robert once again constructs his vision around an emblematic allegory. However awkward the device may seem to us today, the message is clear enough: his condemnation of intellectual curiosity and warning of the coming destruction of the religious are, for him, closely related.

The last vision at which we will look is heavily steeped in the visionary allegorical tradition of the apocalyptic writers. While saying Compline, Robert records that he was

videns in spiritu Dei et ecce facta est ecclesia ante me ex albis constructa lapidibus, super quam erecte stabant columpne alte valde ad modum capitellorum, in quibus erant quasi poma coloris crocei. Fundata autem erat in monte lapideo ostium habens ab occidente altum et latum, caliginosum et nigrum, similiter et fenestras. Egressaque est caligo illa ab ecclesia per portam sicut fluvius usque ad aquilonem commixteque sunt aque non multum clare caligini et redundaverunt simul super ecclesiam, adeo ut eam fere penitus operirent, sed non potuerunt intantum ascendere, quin columpnaris pars licet modica appareret. (Bignami-Odier, "Robert," p. 287)

This image of the Church, constructed of white stones, on a mountain of stone and having a high, wide gate comes originally from *The Shepherd of Hermas*,[62] and is used extensively in Hildegard's *Scivias*. It was not by coincidence that Lefèvre d'Etaples published these works with Robert's in his 1513 edition of the writings of three men and three women visionaries; he had certainly identified the tradition to which they belong. The whole vision is highly reminiscent of Hildegard, as is much of Robert's visionary writing, right down to his use of directions (north, south and so on) to reconstruct the placement of objects in the mental picture. Langland, too, uses this method, especially in the Prologue where he places the tower in the east and the "depe dale" in the west (lines 14–18), although, as we have seen, he largely abandons this traditional deictic form of vision as the poem progresses. Although Robert portrays the Church as still bearing good fruit (that is, good clerics), it is, however, engulfed in darkness which threatens but cannot entirely swallow it.[63] Like Langland's Unity, the Church is seen as besieged and threatened on all sides, but not wholly defeated.[64]

In the last section of this chapter we will return to Robert in our consideration of medieval visionary conventions and the problem of distinguishing fictional or literary visions from the "real" variety. But it should be stressed here that Robert's visions show the hallmarks of both kinds of vision. His attention to allegorical detail (some of it politically as well as religiously motivated, if Mme Bignami-Odier is correct) betrays the polemical purpose behind these seemingly guileless, homespun visions and nightmares. Robert usually provides the reader with an interpretation, given by the "Spirit of God," but much is left unexplained. Perhaps, as in Langland, there are times when he dares not interpret. Writers like Robert seem to have had a keen sense of how to maintain the balance between reforming zeal and fanaticism – prophets like John of Rupescissa wrote from prison because they lacked this.

There are few similarities between the actual images and details in Robert's writings and in Langland's, but after one has read several such prophetic writers, the archetypes and ideological similarities begin to emerge from the visionary clutter. This is above all a literature of archetypes and patterns, from which each writer creates individual visions: the humbly attired, God-fearing and frustrated spiritual-leader figure, the group or order who are seen as precursors of Antichrist, the expected chastisement of the corrupt clergy, the belief that the *renovatio* must and will come, the use of "dark" symbols or emblems to convey the sense of outrage, fear or fervor. Only a full-scale study of Robert's visions would do justice to his own apocalyptic grammar: what is offered here is simply an attempt to highlight certain characteristics and patterns in order to exemplify the kind of prophetic visionary thought which Langland must have known in some form.

Bridget of Sweden (1303–1373)

The revelations of St. Bridget (or Birgitta) of Sweden are easily comparable in size, scope and popularity to the works of Hildegard. These two women visionaries dominated the non-Joachite prophetic tradition of Northern Europe and Great Britain for the better part of the later Middle Ages, but, surprisingly, they have less in common than one would expect. Bridget has little of Hildegard's literary ability and she is altogether less likeable than the serene, compassionate twelfth-century abbess. While Hildegard's experience of the divine is often dignified by her detachment of herself from the action of the vision, Bridget engages in direct dialogue with a vindictive Christ who denounces the unhappy works of men, presaging ghoulish torment in the depths of Hell. The literary abilities required for the successful rendering of a divine figure, which even Milton could not effectively master, are nowhere evident in Bridget's visions. Her visions of individual torments are similarly sensational, crude and ruthless. However, if Bridget was neither a Dante nor a Milton, she was nevertheless highly popular in England in the decades after her death and she left a mark on papal history which few women of any period could match.

Piers Plowman and the medieval visionary tradition

One of the main goals of Bridget's life was to persuade the Avignon popes back to the "true seat" in Rome. She regarded this as the "prerequisite for the reformation of Christendom" (Colledge, "*Epistola*," p. 21) which she so earnestly desired. Born into a family of the highest nobility of Sweden, Bridget was a member of the royal court and the mother of eight children. The death of her husband in 1344 marked the beginning of her visionary role as "spouse" and prophetess of Christ (Cumming's edition, p. xxiv). Her initial contact with the papacy came in 1347–48 when she sent a delegation to Clement VI in Avignon to make known certain of her revelations to him. The revelations were unsparing in their attack on the papacy. Instead of promoting the cure of souls, the pope is described as a hindrance. Instead of being a shepherd and a servant, he is a scatterer and destroyer of the sheep, worse than Lucifer, less just than Pilate. Judas sold only Christ, but the pope sells the souls of the elect for filthy lucre (I, 41, p. 362).[65] The delegation also carried with it the projected *Rule* for the order which Bridget hoped to establish to leaven the bread of decadent monasticism. It is perhaps no wonder, however, given the tone of these early revelations to Clement VI, that the delegation returned without approval for the order (Colledge, "*Epistola*," p. 22).

In 1349 Bridget herself went to Rome, accompanied by a secular priest, Master Peter Olafsson, and by another Peter, prior of a Cistercian house in Alvastra. These men were to be her translators and secretaries for most of her life. They were later joined by Alphonse of Jaen, who is responsible for much of the editing and propagation of her later works, as well as for the active promotion of her canonization proceedings and for the *Epistola solitarii*, a spirited defense of her visions which will interest us in the next section.[66]

Once in Rome Bridget poured forth her *Revelations* to her secretaries and sent numerous threats to successive popes, urging them to return to Rome, to reform the Church and to approve her rule for the Brigittine order.[67] It is difficult to assess what influence, if any, the seemingly simplistic warnings of a relatively unlearned and uncompromising woman had upon decision-making processes in the powerful political world of the *Curia*.[68] There is certainly evidence that they were received with skepticism in many quarters (Colledge, "*Epistola*," p. 38), but as Colledge suggests, "In all the documents in the case of St. Bridget we have the clearest proof that popes and kings could not always deny audience to those who came to speak to them of death and judgment, hell and heaven, that 'even as constrained to hear they heard them'" (*ibid.*, p. 49).

If the powerful had, in many cases, to be "constrained to hear," the reading public in the Middle Ages, it seems, did not. The popularity of Bridget's *Revelations* after her death is easily attested to by the dozens of manuscripts which survive. In England she was especially popular in the fifteenth century, but evidence for the dissemination of her work there before her death is a little harder to come by. F. R. Johnston has shown that Bridget made a lasting impression on at least two Englishmen who encountered her in Europe.[69] Cumming, who edited a fifteenth-century Middle English translation of a selection of Bridget's *Revelations* for the Early English Text Society in 1929, notes in his Introduction that before her death in 1373 Latin texts of the *Revelations* had found their way to England and were being studied with great interest in Oxford and London. Johnston notes that theologians were studying full texts of the *Revelations* in England before the end of the fourteenth century.[70] John Bale writes that the *Revelations* were being explicated "in scholis Oxoniensibus & in cathedris publicis" by the great masters of the time, notably, the Dominican Thomas Stubbes (d. 1373), the Carmelite Richard Lavenham (d. 1381) and "many others of that type besides" around the year 1370 (Cumming's edition, p. xxix). Ellis makes it apparent in his illuminating study of the textual tradition of Bridget's works in fifteenth-century England that the first seven books of the *Revelations* were virtually all that were available to most English readers even during the fifteenth century ("Flores," p. 166). This suggests that texts of Bridget's *Revelations* came to England before Book VIII was added, perhaps long before, and remained in circulation in this form for decades to come.[71]

It is virtually impossible to say exactly how early Bridget's works began to circulate in Britain. The first collection of *Revelations* was brought from Sweden to Rome in 1347, although it is likely that this consisted only of what is now the first book of the full work (Jorgenson, *St. Bridget*, vol. I, p. 301). Sometime between this date and Bridget's death in 1373 at least some of her works began to be read in England, but Bridget herself was definitely known there by 1347 because of a revelation which she had regarding the Hundred Years War, which was particularly friendly to England (Book IV, chapters 103–05). These chapters from the *Revelations* did themselves become well known to the English. Hoccleve wrote a verse paraphrase of Bridget's account of Christ's judgment in his *De regimine principium*, and many other fifteenth-century English writers used it for various political purposes.[72]

The witness of Bridget's *Revelations* is important in a study of the religious vision tradition of *Piers Plowman* not so much as a possible source, but because many of the themes and concerns are similar; in some cases they even use the same imagery and some of the same phrases to express their desires and fears about the state of the Church and the urgent need for reform. Bridget was more concerned with Rome and the papacy than any English writer ever could have been, but her orientation to Church reform is otherwise very similar to Langland's and she is very much a part of the visionary apocalyptic tradition which Hildegard, Robert of Uzès and John of Rupescissa represent. While it is almost impossible to know how many books of the *Revelations* were available in England before Bridget's death in 1373, we do know that the upper limit is definitely the first seven books and excerpts in what follows will be restricted to these.

In this brief study reference will also be made to the *Onus mundi*, a compilation done by the Leipzig theologian John Tortsch in 1433 of prophetic passages from the voluminous *Revelations*. Although the *Onus mundi* itself is too late to be of precise relevance to the study of *Piers Plowman*, it is important in its own right as a near-contemporary commentary on prophecies of Church reform and as a specimen of that "much neglected medieval genre, the prophetic compilation."[73] Tortsch had read Hildegard, Joachim and a number of other medieval prophets and he was well able to set Bridget's prophecies within the context of the tradition to which they belong. In fact he was so proficient at his task that he is positively dangerous – unlike Gebeno of Eberbach, Tortsch wove a great deal of his own commentary into Bridget's prophecies and one must always go back to a full edition of Bridget's *Revelations* in order to verify precisely what is hers and what is Tortsch's elaboration.[74] As Ellis says of the *Onus mundi*: "In his prologue (f. 2), the author shows a great concern that the book should come in its present form of a single *libellus* to as wide a public as possible. His desire that his own text would be handed on unchanged contrasts strikingly with his treatment of the *Revelations* material he is using . . ." ("*Flores*," p. 169).

Tortsch was certainly fanatically enthusiastic about the prophetic reform material in the *Revelations*, but as Ellis has shown, he was not alone in regarding these passages as the most significant of Bridget's literary offerings. In fifteenth-century England compilers went to the *Revelations* for three main purposes: (1) for their prophetic and eschatological material, (2) for material on the requirements of the spiritual life and (3) for information about the life of Christ and the Virgin (Ellis, "*Flores*," p. 166ff.). Prophetic and eschatological elements were a factor for some compilers in the selection of revelations translated into Middle English (*ibid.*, p. 171), while others used this material to emphasize the evils of the corrupt clergy and the Lollards (*ibid.*, p. 172). The prophetic passages, then, were certainly among the more popular excerpts from the *Revelations* and in this Bridget's works are similar to Hildegard's, which survived mainly because of their prophetic content.

Let us now look at some passages from the *Revelations* themselves which highlight Bridget's apocalyptic view of the need for Church reform. Like most apocalyptic writers, Bridget focuses time and again on the crises of leadership within the Church and, like most apocalyptic writers, this concern originated for her with a sense of indignation about clerical corruption. We have already noted Bridget's vehement denunciation of the papacy in the early revelations sent to Avignon in 1347. These are contained in Book 1, chapter 41 of the *Revelations*, which deserves to be looked at more closely as one of the starting points of Bridget's apocalypticism. In this chapter Christ appears, as he so often does in Bridget's revelations, as a judge who brings down a harsh verdict on various groups in society. While our concern here is primarily with Bridget's view of the clergy, it should be noted that Christ also speaks out against the laity, the Jews and the heathen, and before beginning his condemnations he expressly exempts those Jews and pagans who live justly (1, 41, p. 361). The righteous heathen seems to have been a concern of Bridget's, as well as Langland's; this is so often the case in reformist prophets, because of the special role that non-Christian peoples are given in apocalyptic thought. In this revelation Christ's judgment is viciously pronounced in macabre threats against the pope; he promises hellfire and eternal torment and threatens the clerics with removal of their ecclesiastical dignities and possessions by an explication of verses 9 and 11 of Psalm 108: "May his children be fatherless: and his wife a widow . . . May the usurer search all his substance: and let strangers plunder his labours." In exchange for their dignities, he threatens, they will inherit eternal confusion. Tortsch refers to this passage in his discussion of Bridget's prophecies against the corruption of the various clerical orders (in

105

Montag, *Werk*, p. 300) and it is no doubt partly on the basis of this revelation that he later associates Bridget's predictions of clerical chastisement with the confiscation prophecies of Hildegard (*ibid.*, pp. 324–26) and (Pseudo-)Joachim (*ibid.*, p. 328).[75]

Like Langland, Bridget looked for a reforming king who would take the clergy back to their pristine state of unworldliness. In fact, she uses various images to describe this expected reforming leader. In at least one revelation he is a king (VI, 26), in other revelations the pope is to fulfill this function himself, in still others the great leader is more vaguely cast in symbolic terms as a plowman (*arator*), a hunter (*venator*) or as simply a conqueror.

In *Revelations* VI, 26, Christ explains to Bridget exactly how this king should go about reforming the Church. The revelation opens with Christ's lament that the vessels and instruments of his Church have been carried off to Babylon, these things representing allegorically the (former) holy life of the clergy. In a passage which echoes both the language of Hildegard and the imagery of *The Shepherd of Hermas*, the king's instructions for rebuilding the Church (VI, 26, p. 436) are laid out. He continues with an *ad pristinum statum* prophecy:

Inquirat etiam quomodo vasa domus meae restituantur in pristinum statum, scilicet, vt clerici, & religiosi relicta superbia resumant humilitatem, innocentes diligant castitatem, cupidi & mundiales abstineant a nimio mundi appetitu . . . Vere ecclesia mea nimis longe recessit a me, in tantum quod nisi praeces matris meae interuenirent non esset spes misericordiae.   (VI, 26, p. 436)

The final comment is typical of the tension one often finds in reformist apocalypticism between the promise of certain chastisement and the hope that repentance will forestall it, or in biblical terms, the tension between the prophetic and the apocalyptic. The tension is similar in Langland. The phrase "restituantur in pristinum statum" is also very close to Langland's *"ad pristinum statum ire,"* which he uses in his own prophecy of the reforming king (*Piers Plowman*, v. 171). This passage from Bridget is not as clearly a disendowment prophecy as Langland's is, but the basic pattern is the same. This phrase emerges again in a revelation in which Christ threatens to give up trying to save Christians altogether and make the heathen his chosen people (*Revelations* VI, 44, pp. 464–65; in Montag, *Werk*, p. 270), lamenting that Christians are now degenerating from their former state ("a priori statu degenerantes"). This sense of the decline of spirituality in recent history is, of course, endemic in apocalyptic thought, and the concept of going back to a first, more pristine, state is often the cornerstone of reform ideology.

Tortsch himself uses the phrase ("ad pristinum statum bonum reducere") to summarize the contents of another revelation (IV, 49) in which Bridget sees and hears a discussion in Heaven on the state of the Church in Rome. The vision takes place after Urban V has returned to Rome in 1367, a triumph for Bridget which is obviously marred by her view that the ecclesiastical hierarchy is still in as bad a state as ever. In this revelation she uses the decaying church of St. John Lateran, which had been burnt out in 1361, as an emblem of the corrupt hierarchy. The question Bridget hears asked in Heaven is, "But how can the pope come into the church?" The doors are hanging crookedly, the hinges rusted and deformed, the floor is full of holes so deep that they have no bottom, the roof is smeared with pitch and burns with a sulphurous flame, and so on. This image of the Lateran church is interpreted in profuse allegorical detail in the revelation, beginning with the doorposts, which represent the pope himself. Urban is to begin by reforming his own life, stripping away the wealth and retinue that accompany him, and leaving himself with necessities only. Then he must turn his attention to the hinges, *id est*, the cardinals, by force of a play on the Latin word *cardines* in which Langland too indulges (Prol., 132). The pope must take up hammer and forceps and bend the hinges to his will, not allowing them to have many worldly things (clothing, servants, and so on) but, once again, only the necessities they require. He should seek to bend them with kind words and divine counsel, but if they do not wish to obey, he must use the hammer and by showing them his severity and doing whatsoever he is able ("as long as it is not against justice," Bridget qualifies) bring them to bend to his will. The floor of the Church is represented by the bishops and secular clergy, whose cupidity, like the holes in the Lateran floor, has no bottom. The revelation ends with a reiteration of the basic principle that each group should be permitted to have *necessities only* and no superfluities, and that anyone who does not wish to amend his life will be utterly deprived of his ecclesiastical office (IV, 49, p. 251).

This notion that the *modus vivendi* of the clergy should be reduced to a provision for necessities only is most often associated with such radical groups as the Franciscan Spirituals; however, as we have seen in Hildegard's and now Bridget's works, the notion is very much a part of visionary prophecy outside of the Franciscan Joachite circle.[76] Langland too is concerned with the limitation of the clergy to necessities[77] and, although he may have been influenced by Franciscan Joachite ideology, the use of this notion by writers like Hildegard and Bridget shows that he could have acquired the idea of a coming clerical chastisement and reform from any number of prophetic sources.

After Urban's death in 1370, the undaunted Bridget began working to persuade Gregory XI to return the papal seat to Rome and reform the decaying Church. In Book IV, chapter 142 of the *Revelations* another *ad pristinum statum* prophecy occurs, this time addressed to Gregory. It begins with a strongly worded condemnation of the pope's pride and cupidity and of the state of the *Curia* ("indeed it is as if all who come to your *Curia*, you send into the fires of Hell" [p. 359]), which again oscillates between bitter denunciation and a desire to encourage reform. The pope is both threatened and entreated to come to Rome in language which sometimes echoes Hildegard's: "consurge viriliter, & induere fortitudinem confidenter, incipe renouare Ecclesiam meam, quam ego acquisiui meo proprio sanguine & renouetur & spiritualiter reducatur ad pristinum statum suum sanctum, quia iam nunc magis veneratur lupanar quam sancta mater Ecclesia" (*Revelations* IV, 142, p. 359). If he does not obey, Gregory will be condemned in the *Curia* of Heaven (p. 360). Brandishing threats of eternal torment, Bridget nevertheless ends with the assertion that Gregory is God's chosen pope and there is still time for reconciliation.

The most interesting of Bridget's reforming figures for students of *Piers*

Plowman, however, is the plowman (*arator*), whom she uses as agent of the coming chastisement and reform. Both the plowman and his plow recur in a number of her visions and are perhaps among her favorite images. Bridget's plowman, who is somewhat more aggressive than Langland's, is a reformer and a chastiser, a man who will set the world right. One of the clearest statements about this figure comes in Book IV, chapter 22, in which Christ breaks off a typical Brigittine complaint about the sad state of humanity to make the following prophecy:

Ideo veniet arator a potentissimo, exacuatus a sapientissimo, qui non quaerit terras, & pulchritudinem corporum, non veretur fortitudinem fortium, nec timet minas principum, sed nec accipit personas hominum, . . . Ideo amici mei ad quos te mittam laborent viriliter, & celeriter, quia non erit istud quod dico in nouissimis diebus, vt dixi prius, sed in diebus istis. Et multorum iam viuentium etiam hoc videbunt oculi, vt impleatur quod scriptum est. Fiant vxores eorum viduae, & filii sine patribus.   (IV, 22, pp. 232–33)

This plowman will have divine wisdom as well as power, and will not be swayed by worldly attributes of any kind, be they beauty, riches or power. The fact that he will not be a respecter of persons not only establishes his credentials as a true Christian (James 2), but makes him an antitype to the pseudo-prophets as well.[78] Perhaps most interesting, however, is Christ's comment that this will occur not in the Last Days, but imminently. Although Bridget's apocalyptic program is far less developed than Hildegard's or Joachim's, she too shifts the weight of apocalyptic foreboding away from the Last Days and towards the present.

A note to this passage in the Durante edition of 1611 directs the reader to chapter 28 of the Book of Isaias and to Jerome's commentary on it. This is no doubt the source of Bridget's plowman figure, and it will remind Langland scholars of the imagery in John Ball's well-known letter alluding to *Piers Plowman*. The biblical passage concerns God's chastisement of the Israelites:

Shall the ploughman plough all the day to sow, shall he open and harrow his ground? Will he not, when he hath made plain the surface thereof, sow gith, and scatter cummin, and put wheat in order, and barley and millet and vetches in their bounds? For he will instruct him in judgment: his God will teach him. For gith shall not be threshed with saws, neither shall the cart-wheel turn about upon cummin: but gith shall be beaten out with a rod, and cummin with a staff. But bread-corn shall be broken small; but the thresher shall not thresh it for ever: neither shall the cart-wheel hurt it, nor break it with its teeth.   (Isaiah 28:24–28)

The plowman is the man who will put everything right, "sharpened by the most wise" ("exacuatus a sapientissimo"), instructed by God Himself. The threshing and grinding images are clearly images of chastisement and purification but, the prophet asserts, this will not be done with instruments which are too heavy or too sharp (the cart-wheel or the saw), but with the appropriate tools, the rod and the staff. Even though the corn will be ground small, it will not be ground forever, "neither shall the cart-wheel hurt it, nor break it with its teeth." To paraphrase, the business of purification, of separating kernel from chaff, is not intended as a process which will destroy the kernel, nor will it go on forever. Coming as it does at the end of a prophecy of retribution (Isaias 28:1ff.), the allegory of the plowman's work is intended as a reassurance: the Lord does not seek to destroy, only to purify.

The passage also speaks of the proper treatment of different types of grains, something in which the plowman is instructed by God himself. St. Jerome's commentary on this passage (*PL* 24, cols. 337–38) picks up this notion by stressing that gith and cummin are weaker seeds than the others; the wheat may be ground but the gith and cummin must only be beaten (col. 337C). Jerome suggests that these weaker seeds represent the Gentiles who have not received the Law, while the grains represent the Jews, who will suffer greater torment (col. 338A). Others interpret the passage as referring to the common people and the clergy, Jerome continues. On the Day of Judgment, the common people will be corrected with the rod and staff, like the gith and cummin. The clergy, however, will suffer greater torture for their sins because they were in full possession of the knowledge they needed to avoid sin. This interpretation would certainly have appealed to clerical reformers like Bridget or Langland. Jerome's whole interpretation has eschatological overtones,[79] but also stresses the notion of consolation and refreshment after sorrow and chastisement ("post tormenta, refrigeria," col. 338C),[80] which is also a key apocalyptic theme of reform-oriented prophets.

The apocalyptic overtones of the passage also parallel John Ball's use of the image of grinding "smal" in the obscure prophetic letter which is attributed to him by Walsingham: "Iohan the Mullere hath ygrounde smal, smal, smal; / The kynges sone of heuene schal paye for al."[81] The harsh treatment of the bread-corn as a symbol of divine chastisement in the Isaias passage may well have been suggested to the rebel priest by his use of the figure of Piers the Plowman just prior to this couplet ("and biddeth Peres Ploughman to to his werk, and chastise wel Hobbe the Robbere").[82]

Although Piers himself is not obviously a chastising figure in *Piers Plowman*, he does direct a chastising figure, Hunger, who is in turn associated with an apocalyptic prophecy (VIII. 343–55). He does try to set the world straight in the *Visio*, on the basis of his knowledge of Truth's teachings. It is Piers who attempts to get everyone in society working productively; it is Piers who tries to curb the Wasters and put the idle back to work. When they are chastised it is through his strategy of calling in Hunger (VIII. 167ff.), but Piers also calls *off* Hunger when he feels they have been punished enough. Like the biblical plowman, Piers controls the "threshing." In the *Vita*, after Christ's death and Resurrection, it is again Piers who is called to set the new Church in motion. In a return to the agricultural imagery of the *Visio*, Piers once again ploughs and harrows and sows, not seeds this time, but truth (XXI. 260ff.).

At the end of *Piers Plowman* the purification of the clergy is yet to come and it is Piers whom Conscience seeks to carry this out. As Rosemary Woolf has suggested, the power of the figure of Piers in the poem lies in the fact that his allegorical significance is not as explicitly defined as is usual in medieval literature (Woolf, "Qualities," p. 113) and this looseness of definition is certainly true of the many apocalyptic associations with agricultural imagery in the poem. Agricultural imagery is very common in bibilical apocalyptic writing and the figure of Piers is powerfully but evasively suggestive of all the richness of this tradition.[83]

Unlike Hildegard and Joachim, Bridget shows little interest in the kind of exegesis which produces historical and futuristic patterns, although in one chapter of the *Revelations* she explicates her own periodization of the past and future. This revelation shows the influence of apocalyptic sources; in fact, at one point Bridget mentions a source. The revelation begins with Christ's statement that the world is like a ship having three parts, the prow, the middle and the stern. So too it has three ages, the first closing at the time of the Incarnation:

Prima erat ab Adam vsque ad incarnationem meam, hac signatur prora, quae alta erat, & mirabilis & fortis. Alta in Patriarcharum pietate, mirabilis in Prophetarum scientia, fortis in legis obseruatione; sed hec pars tunc paulatim descendere cepit, quando populus Iudaicus contemptis mandatis meis, miscuit se sceleribus, & impietatibus, propterea abiectus est ab honore, possessione.   (VI, 67, pp. 499–500)

The middle part of the ship, the lowest, began with the Incarnation and was a time of humility (*ibid.*, p. 500), now however, because of the present pride and impiety, "ideo tertia pars incipit ascendere, quae durabit vsque ad iudicium, & in hac aetate per te misi verba oris mei mundo" (*ibid.*).

This is a very conventional apocalyptic program which shows surprisingly little of the optimism one would expect in such a tireless reformer as Bridget. However, it does demonstrate that as with so many apocalyptic thinkers, the perception of present evil is the foundation upon which Bridget sees herself called as a prophet at this special moment in time. At this point in the revelation Christ explains to Bridget that Antichrist will be born at the end of the present age and concludes with an interesting comment, "but the time of this Antichrist will not be just as that friar, whose books you have seen, has described it, but in a time known to me" (*ibid.*). Although "that friar" could be almost any of the Joachite-influenced Franciscans, it seems likely that the friar in question is John of Rupescissa. John was a near-contemporary of Bridget's and wrote many books which were extremely popular. He also attempted the business of prophesying exact dates for the coming of Antichrist, something not all prophets did, and it would seem to be this that Christ is objecting to in his statement to Bridget ("not . . . as that friar . . . described it, *but in a time known to me*"). Whether or not this refers to John's writings, it is interesting evidence of current attitudes on this controversial kind of speculation.[84]

Like many apocalyptic writers, Bridget was especially concerned with the state of the mendicant orders. Book VII, chapter 22 contains a revelation on the Franciscan order in which Christ says that there are two types of Franciscans, those who followed Francis' *Rule* and those who followed the rule of "Brother Adversarius" (the devil). The chapter describes the penetration of the devil, under the guise of humility, into the order, and in Roger Ellis' edition of the Middle English translation of the *Revelations* in British Library MS Claudius B 1 a passage condemning the anti-intellectualism of the friars sounds even more reminiscent of *Piers Plowman* (XXII. 273ff.). Among other hypocrisies Friar Adversarius says, "Also I will go to þe scole and lere, þat I mai hafe wirshipe in þe worlde and in mine ordir . . ."[85] Like Langland, Bridget saw the downfall of the friars as being in large part due to their zeal for university studies. Anti-intellectualism is as much a part of Bridget's prophetic point of view as it is of the other visionaries we have looked at.

In a revelation concerning a foreign ecclesiastic Bridget is asked, "Will he stake his esteem as a scholar, and exchange his seat among the other supporters of culture for the humble place of a poor Franciscan among the simple-minded and the foolish? For only then can he stand fearlessly . . . and speak the truth . . ." (*Revelations* III, 8; trans. Jorgenson, *St. Bridget*, vol. II, p. 10). Like Langland, Bridget calls upon the ideal of the holy fool or simpleton in order to counter what she sees as the excesses of intellectualism. Furthermore, in spite of the decadence, which she severely castigated, in the Franciscan order, Bridget maintained a certain idealization of these friars which we rarely see in Middle English literature. One can only assume that the struggle of the Franciscan Spirituals on the Continent left its mark on the imaginations of many religious thinkers there. What is particularly interesting about Langland is that he, too, shows all the signs of this idealization of poverty and simplicity at the same time as he heaps scorn upon the faults of the fraternal orders and it is the apocalyptic aspect of this problem which will be taken up in chapter 4. For the time being we should consider these characteristics as part of the visionary apocalyptic tradition to which they also belong – and to which they belonged even before the formation of the fraternal orders in the thirteenth century.

In *Revelations* IV, 22, Bridget's Christ idealizes intellectual simplicity in the same manner as we witnessed earlier in Hildegard and Langland:

Venite idiotae, & simplices, & dabo vobis os, & sapientiam, quibus linguosi non poterunt repugnare. Sic feci iam diebus istis impleui simplices sapientia mea, & resistunt doctis. Evulsi magniloquos, & potentes, & subito decesserunt. (IV, ch. 22, p. 233)

The original notion is, of course, Pauline, but the implied challenge to the academic and clerical establishment is typical of medieval apocalyptic visionary thought: visions, after all, were an alternative form of expression for those barred from the circles of intellectual and ecclesiastical power. One of the most famous images from Bridget's *Revelations*, immortalized in an excellent woodcut in Gothan's 1492 Lübeck edition, is of a monk on a ladder. The whole fifth book of the *Revelations* records the questions of an arrogant university professor who, from a heightened position on a ladder, challenges God on the imperfections of the world and of Christian doctrine.[86] Will's "aresoning" of Reason (*Piers Plowman*, XIII. 243) would seem to be part of a long and lively prophetic tradition which scorns the intellectual pride and presumption of mankind.

Like Hildegard, Robert and Bridget suggest a number of parallels with Langland in that, when they are considered together, it becomes apparent that all of these writers were working with a similar apocalyptic grammar. Bridget's prophetic visions show the same preoccupation with reforming and chastising leaders, with *ad pristinum statum* prophecies, with the state of the friars, with the course of history and with anti-intellectualism which, increasingly, becomes a trademark of late medieval prophecy. Both Robert and Bridget are also illuminating witnesses to medieval attitudes toward the visionary experience, a topic to which we will turn next.

PIERS PLOWMAN AND SOME PSYCHOLOGICAL, LITERARY AND SPIRITUAL ASPECTS OF MEDIEVAL VISIONARY TRADITION

In this section we will look briefly at the theories, conventions and attitudes toward visions and visionaries in the Middle Ages with a view to how these might illuminate *Piers Plowman*. This takes in many different subject areas, including medieval psychology, theology and literary and social history; obviously, it will be necessary to generalize about some very complex issues.

Although there was a variety of theories in the later Middle Ages about the sources, workings and characteristics of visions, all writers seem to have agreed that the imagination was the workshop for such productions, no matter what spiritual or psychic forces caused the visions themselves. Medieval psychological theory distinguished between the *imaginatio* and the *vis imaginativa*. The former was simply a storehouse of sense data which had no power to form judgments about what it received but did have the capability for long-term retention (Harvey, *Inward Wits*, p. 44). The *vis imaginativa*, on the other hand, had the power to combine and divide images at will. Theorists postulated that it was because of this power that man could imagine things which he had never seen, like an emerald mountain or a flying man (*ibid.*, p. 45; Minnis, "Ymaginatif," pp. 72ff.; Bloomfield, *Apocalypse*, pp. 170ff.). The *vis imaginativa* works by looking into both the *imaginatio* and the *memorialis* for forms and images, and in sleep when the external senses are cut off and the control of reason is lifted it "meddles" with these stored images to produce visions (Harvey, *Inward Wits*, p. 49).

As Bloomfield pointed out in his excellent short study of "The Problem of Imaginatif," "it is clear from the adjectival form of the word that Langland is using 'Imaginatif' as a translation of (*vis*) *imaginativa*"[87] and this means that it is the creative one of the two imaginative faculties which is being referred to. As Bloomfield and others have suggested, however, even the *vis imaginativa* was considered something of an inferior faculty by medieval theoreticians and yet it is given a key role in *Piers Plowman*. At the end of the lengthy and confusing Recklessness section of the poem, Imaginatif is able to shake Will from a number of unhelpful attitudes as he summarizes and answers the vexing questions of previous passus. Bloomfield suggests that the "manner whereby the imagination could be elevated [to a more prestigious role] is through the medieval theory of prophecy" (*Apocalypse*, p. 172) and that this was Langland's purpose in portraying Imaginatif as he does in the poem. As we shall see shortly, Langland's use of Imaginatif here is closely related to his use in the same passage of various conventions of the visionary tradition, all of which shows that Langland was very conscious of current thought on the subject of visionary experience.

Alastair Minnis has taken up the problem in a study of medieval theories of the imagination which brings to light a number of reasons why this particular faculty would be so important for Langland's purposes. The Imaginatif episode marks the end of the disputative phase of Will's journey (Minnis, "Ymaginatif," p. 71), and though the imagination is normally the servant of reason, Imaginatif dominates the poem at this point because Will must learn that not all questions can be settled by reason (*ibid.*, p. 75). Minnis shows that the imagination was thought to enable one to form hypotheses about the consequences of wrongdoing, by working from knowledge of past sins, a suggestion which fits Langland's Imaginatif very well (*ibid.*, p. 77). Minnis further suggests, citing a passage from Froissart, that "imaginatif implies a prudence based on far-sighted grasp of a situation" (*ibid.*, p. 78). All three qualities, it should be noted, are relevant to the role that the imagination was thought to play in prophecy, where it becomes a vehicle for sophisticated insight into spiritual and moral problems of the mind. As the workshop of dreams, the imagination is, as Minnis points out, the medium through which everything in the poem passes (*ibid.*, p. 94), a fact which alone would serve to underline the importance of Imaginatif in the poem and Langland's concern with vision theory.

The importance of the imagination in medieval prophetic theory becomes evident when one looks at the different types of prophetic revelations to which mankind was thought to be susceptible. Various medieval writers suggested various categorizations of such revelations, but virtually all agreed that vision, for one reason or another, was a necessary part of prophecy. Almost all attempts at categorization tried to distinguish visual from non-visual types of revelation: Augustine suggested a threefold distinction between corporeal, spiritual and intellectual revelation (Minnis, *ibid.*, pp. 92–93); Richard of St. Victor distinguished between two types of bodily and of spiritual vision (Dronke, *Women Writers*, p. 146); Thomas Aquinas distinguished between infused representations, supernatural light and the kind of revelation which includes both (Synave and Benoit, *Commentary*, p. 33), or between sensible, imaginative and intellectual revelation (*ibid.*, p. 177). Medieval religious visionaries were very aware of these categorizations. Robert of Uzès opens the *Liber visionum* with the following descriptions of his visions: "Placuit Domino Jhesu Christo michi omnium peccatorum vilissimo sua beneplacita revelare, nunc in sompnis per ymaginativas visiones, nunc in vigilia per easdem visiones, nunc in verbo exteriori aut interiore per metaphoras multas cum declaracionibus earundem" (Bignami-Odier, "Robert," p. 272). Langland's use of Imaginatif would suggest that he, like Robert, would describe his revelations as occurring 'in sompnis per ymaginativas visiones." Similarly, Tortsch says that Bridget of Sweden's prophecies were received "in revelatione et visione imaginaria et intellectuali" (in Montag, *Werk*, p. 320).

As I have suggested earlier, while there is often a prejudice, stated or implied, which places the intellectual vision above the imagistically conveyed vision, there is also a recognition on the part of theorists that the imagistically conveyed vision is most accessible to the human mind. Aquinas felt that the notion of prophecy is more properly realized in imaginative vision (Synave and Benoit, *Commentary*, p. 177). Hugh of St. Cher recognized that prophecy usually occurred "per impressionem, ymaginis in spiritu" (Torrell, *Théorie*, p. 209). Furthermore, he distinguished two different types of prophecy by images: in the first, the prophet does not have need of the images for understanding God's message himself, but God wishes him to announce it with the help of the images in order that it can be made accessible to the common man (*ibid.*, p. 211). In the second case, the prophet does not himself completely understand what he is told and the images are purposely given to veil the divine mystery (*ibid.*, p. 212). Prophecy through images and similitudes, then, was the most common kind recognized in medieval thought, making prophecy virtually synonymous with imagistic vision.

Hugh of St. Cher's second distinction brings us to another problem in medieval prophetic theory: to what extent can a prophet be said to be prophesying if he does not understand the full import of what he says? It seems that medieval theory allowed for a whole spectrum of levels of understanding on the part of the prophet, ranging from a case like Pharaoh, who perceived only images without understanding them, to Daniel or Isaiah, who perceived images, understood them and interpreted them.[88]

The narrators of later apocalyptic texts, as we have seen, do not claim to be prophets in the fullest biblical sense: they are portrayed, rather, as groping or fumbling desperately and at times blindly for an understanding of their revelations. Both Esdras and Hermas, for example, are portrayed as participating in the learning process of their revelations, not as confidently telling forth a revealed message. The relevance of this prophetic model to *Piers Plowman* is obvious: Will is not a prophet in the traditional Old Testament sense of a man with a direct message. Like the seers in these early apocalypses he gropes toward understanding, "musyng on this meteles" (IX. 298), acknowledging that "mony tyme this meteles hath maked me to studie" (IX. 299). Aquinas felt that the prophet who did not fully grasp the meaning of his prophecy was an instrument of the Holy Spirit, but not a proper prophet (Synave and Benoit, *Commentary*, p. 82). He has another category, however, for the prophet with partial knowledge and that is the man with "a certain instinct" ("quidam instinctus") for God's message, "a certain impulse, a certain prophetic instinct, a certain divine influence."[89] Such a prophet will lack the certitude of divine command, but may nevertheless have an important message. The point for readers of *Piers Plowman* is surely that there was plenty of room, even in theological conceptions of prophecy, for a prophet to be in some way or another speaking on behalf of God without claiming too much for himself, that is, without claiming the same status as a fully fledged biblical prophet.

To summarize briefly, then, the relevance of all this theory for a consideration of the visionary aspects of *Piers Plowman*: (1) prophecy in the Middle Ages was conceived of as being usually and most properly *visionary*, that is, making use of "similitudes," images and the like; (2) Langland gives a special authoritative role to the imagination and this is probably because he saw himself as writing visionary prophecy of some sort; (3) the imagery of prophetic vision was seen as a useful tool for teaching the common people; (4) a prophet could prophesy in many ways without claiming full prophetic status (that is, status equivalent to the biblical prophet's). Minnis has put this last point from a different angle in his considerations of medieval literary theory:

Certain exegetes were so impressed with the literary qualities which many prophetic writings seemed to have that they came to regard the *modus prophetialis* as a possible genre or style of writing. In such an intellectual climate, a writer could imitate biblical "modes of treatment" without in any way offending against the great authority of the Bible, or appearing to claim divine inspiration of the kind possessed by the authors of holy Scripture.

Piers Plowman and the medieval visionary tradition

Therefore, there seems to be no *a priori* reason against regarding *Piers Plowman* in the light of the *triplex genus visionum*. The poem can be described as a "spiritual vision or imaginatif" in so far as the Dreamer sees images and figures of various things; it can be said to have an element of *visio intellectualis* in so far as Langland's personifications explain their significance.
("Ymaginatif," p. 94)[90]

These, then, are some of the limitations within which *Piers Plowman* may be considered as a prophetic work. Further evidence that it is not inappropriate to speak of *Piers Plowman* as a prophetic poem lies in the fairly broad definition which many medieval writers gave prophecy. Aquinas, for example, defines prophecy as "all those things, the knowledge of which can be useful for salvation . . . whether they are past, future, or external, or necessary, or contingent."[91] Synave and Benoit have summarized Thomas' view of prophecy further, stressing the social and pedagogical vocation of the prophet: "By 'prophecy' St. Thomas understands essentially knowledge, supernaturally given to man, of truths exceeding the present reach of his mind, which God teaches him for the benefit of the community" (*Commentary*, p. 61). This second definition stresses the difficult nature of prophecy which deals in "truths exceeding the present reach of the prophet's mind" – a statement which suggests that a certain amount of confusion on the part of the prophet was thought inevitable. The definition also suggests that visionary texts could really only be regarded as prophecy if they somehow reached beyond the didactic to the genuinely revelatory. *Piers Plowman* does, at times, do this as well, both in revelation of the future and in what is in many ways a more profound form of vision, revelation of divine truths through only partially understood figures like Piers (Woolf, "Qualities," p. 113).

The poem can also be spoken of as prophetic in more specific ways, however, and it is to these aspects that we should turn now. Langland not only includes overtly prophetic passages in his poetry, but he also uses many of the literary conventions which in his time signaled the recording of serious visionary experience. This is an aspect of the literary history of the poem which has been left virtually unexplored by critics of *Piers Plowman*: the relationship between the medieval religious visionary tradition and the visionary character of the poem.

For many years now critics have treated the visions of Langland in much the same way as the dream visions of Chaucer, that is, as literary inventions which provide the writer with a vehicle for satirical comment and with freedom from the tyranny of narrative realism. Comparisons with Chaucerian dream visions and other visions of the Middle English literary tradition can certainly be enlightening, but they do not and cannot provide a full context for the consideration of certain visionary aspects of Langland's poem. Some of these visionary aspects are so different from anything we find in other Middle English works that many critics have come to accept Rosemary Woolf's description of them as the "non-medieval" qualities of *Piers Plowman*. But, as I have suggested earlier with regard to the apocalypse genre, these visionary aspects are not so much non-medieval as non-Middle English: if we go outside of Middle English literature to the Latin religious prophecy of the Middle Ages we will find much that explains these so-called "non-medieval" qualities in the poem.

We have already noted some of these "non-medieval qualities" which can be

115

explained with reference to the apocalyptic tradition, for example, Langland's enigmatic and evocative handling of allegorical figures, the looseness of his allegorical structure and his chaotic mixture of vision of external events with internalized, psychological vision. Another of Woolf's "non-medieval" qualities is Langland's peculiar treatment of his visionary narrator in what seems to be his mixing of autobiographical elements with a highly conventionalized literary persona. It is the autobiographical phases of Langland's Will which surprise Woolf, who suggests that even a partially personalized "I" does not develop in English literature before the Renaissance (Woolf, "Qualities," pp. 119–20). However, George Kane, recognizing that while the name and historical details of a dream-vision author often accord well with his portrayal of the poem's dreamer, also cautions against identifying dreamer and author because of "the fact of the literary occasion, the artificial circumstance of the narrative being in verse, the degree to which the reported dream must surpass any actual dream in organization, coherence, and circumstantial character, the known use of the dream setting for fictional representation" (Kane, "Autobiographical Fallacy," p. 13).[92]

A study of the religious visionary conventions behind *Piers Plowman* does indeed support this mix of the historical and the fictional in the narrator, but it seems to me that Rosemary Woolf was still correct in her assessment that Langland's "autobiographicalization" of his narrator was unparalleled in Middle English literature. Especially in parts of the C-text, Langland's treatment of Will is much more specific than anything Chaucer does with Geoffrey. The autobiographical passage in C. v in which the dreamer asserts that he has learned "witterly what holy writ menede / And what is . . . sykerost for þe soule" (lines 37–39) stands in sharp contrast to the "dotede daffe" who has no grasp of the fundamentals of Christianity which Holy Church teaches. And the itinerant cleric who reproves the lollars of Cornhill in his verses similarly jars with the hermit "vnholy of werkes" (Prol. 3) who wanders the Malvern Hills. The autobiographical and the fictional are related to each other by a series of ironically cast similarities in appearance – but they are not quite the same figure. The Middle English literary tradition does not furnish us with much precedent for such specific autobiographical portrayal;[93] however, the Latin religious visionary tradition does. Against this background, in which the narrator figure is usually based on truly autobiographical detail that has been shaped by its own structure of visionary conventions, Langland's narrator looks surprisingly at home.

Like Chaucer, Langland exploits the visionary mode for literary purposes, and both authors portray their dreamers as musing on the question of the validity of dreams, but for Langland there was an added dimension to this musing: satirist though he was, he also broke into earnest prophecy, urgent admonition and authoritative doctrinal teaching at various points in the poem. As there can be little doubt that he intended his poetry to provoke serious religious thought, we must ask ourselves to what extent Langland sought to establish visionary credibility for himself and his poem. I would like to approach this problem in two ways: first, by looking at what guidelines we have for distinguishing between "real" or actual vision, as it was recorded by those who believed themselves to have had religious experiences, on the one hand, and purely literary or fictionalized visions on the other; secondly, by looking at the extent to which the life and demeanor of the visionary was judged in the Middle Ages to reflect the credibility and validity of his visions. The question in both cases is one of authorial intention – what type of poem was Langland trying to write, and how did he hope that it would be received by his audience?[94]

Before going further, I would stress that "real" or "experienced" visions *and* their fictionalized counterparts exhibit a powerful tendency toward conventionalization in the Middle Ages. Religious visionaries seem to have labored under as many constraints with regard to the recording of their visions as any "literary" writer working in the most conventionalized of traditions. To see this point one has only to consider one of the most famous passages from the annals of medieval religious writing, St. Augustine's description of the religious experience which finalized his conversion. While lamenting his inability to let go of the world, he suddenly hears a voice chanting, "Take it and read."[95] The account reads in many ways like a real experience: Augustine first wonders, upon hearing the voice, whether he is overhearing a child at play – details such as this give the passage an air of autobiographical realism. However, certain stylistic features and a number of phrases are lifted directly from biblical sources. Furthermore the whole scene has been typologically arranged: for example, throughout the *Confessions* Augustine refers back with shame to a boyhood incident when he had stolen pears from a pear tree. The conversion takes place under another tree, a fig tree – one of the most typologically resonant of biblical plant symbols. Augustine arranges his autobiography in such a way that it echoes man's first Fall, at the Tree of Knowledge, and his redemption, at the tree of the Cross.

To point out Augustine's use of biblical phrases and typological parallels is not to deny that he really underwent some kind of religious experience – or even that he really stole pears as a boy; it is to show that such writers were less concerned with the experience of the individual and more concerned that anything which was recorded – even autobiographical experience – be made a vehicle of religious truth through the imposition of typological patterns.[96] If we were honest we would acknowledge that even modern autobiographies betray the same myth-making tendencies (although the motivation behind this creative activity may no longer be religious edification), so it is perhaps wrong for us to pity or condemn the medieval tendency to adapt historical truths or sacrifice personal experience to the purposes of edification. Nonetheless we should be aware that when we speak of recorded religious experience we are dealing with a species of conventionalized work.[97] The question for us is not so much whether a religious poet like Langland could be recording "real" religious experience, as whether there is any evidence in his poem that he opted for the conventions which in his time signaled the recording of "real" (or experienced) *religious* vision as opposed to literary (or fictional) vision.

The only scholar who has tried in any systematic way to set out some guidelines for distinguishing between literary and "experienced" visions is the German historian Peter Dinzelbacher. Although we should be grateful to Dinzelbacher for tackling a problem which other scholars have been content to skirt around, his guidelines present us with some problems when we attempt to apply them to apocalyptic visions. This in itself, however, is instructive and gives yet another justification for looking at apocalyptic vision as a type of literature unto itself. In order to illustrate some of the differences between experienced and fictionalized visions and the difficulties of categorizing apocalyptic visions as either, we will look first at Robert of Uzès' visions in light of Dinzelbacher's guidelines and then at *Piers Plowman* itself. The following chart is abstracted from Dinzelbacher's discussion of the literary vision and its "real" religious counterpart:[98]

"Real" religious vision	*Fictional vision*
−occurs within an autobiography or contains autobiographical elements, autobiographical narration	−non-biographical, "Everyman" narrator
−prose	−poetry
−waking vision or state of ecstasy, visionary disturbed by the experience	−dream vision, visionary shows no signs of disturbance
−realistic, biographical setting for visions (e.g. church, home, etc.)	−idyllic natural setting
−rarely uses allegory, symbolism, etc.	−usually uses allegory
−religious content	−secular content, often uses pagan myth
−asserts validity of visions	−narrator muses on validity of visions, expresses doubt
−experience results in change in the visionary's life or conversion of some kind	−vision does not result in change in the visionary's life

Let us look first at how a writer like the apocalyptic reformist, Robert of Uzès, who at first glance appears to be a writer of "real" rather than fictionalized visions, measures up to these categorizations. Robert serves as a good example because he is always careful to record the circumstances of his vision. The settings of Robert's visions are often biographically oriented, occurring, for example, while he is "eating bread with [his] brothers," visiting the home of a nobleman, sleeping between the two bells for Prime, or saying Mass.[99] Furthermore, many of the dream visions contain references to his paternal home and family (for example, "I saw in a dream that I was with my oldest brother and sister"), suggesting a great likelihood of their having been experienced.[100] In this Dinzelbacher's analysis is apt. They are indeed written in prose, but show a concerted use of enigmatic allegory and symbolism (some of which is obviously derived from visionary literature like *The Shepherd of Hermas*), something which, Dinzelbacher says, is rare in medieval religious visions. Robert does talk about "seeing in the spirit" and is often troubled by what he sees, but he never describes a traumatic or difficult transition into a different state. He does not give us any information about how his visions affected him while awake, but many of his visions come to him while he is doing very "normal" activities: eating (as in Vision 36, in Bignami-Odier, "Robert," p. 287), speaking with someone (as in Vision 10, *ibid.*, p. 287), resting in bed but awake (as in Vision 3, *ibid.*, p. 274). This, I suspect, reflects the influence of Hildegard, whom he had obviously read with care.[101] In fact many of Robert's visions seem to come to him the way a modern person would describe an idea "coming to him." As Jean Leclercq said about Hildegard, she envisions what others would express in another way (Leclercq *et al.*, *Spiritualité*, p. 224). Although many of Robert's visions show marks of real visionary experience, especially some which he describes as dreams, they also show the effect of conscious imitation of a literary tradition, conscious development of religious and political allegory and conscious reforming or didactic intent. Robert's visions, then, transgress the boundaries between "real" and literary visions in several areas.

Dinzelbacher's guidelines for "experienced" and literary visions work very well when applied to most medieval vision literature, from *The Vision of Tundale* to St. Jerome's famous dream to Chaucer's literary masterpieces. He does not consider much apocalyptic vision literature, however, and admits difficulty with writers like Robert.[102] Medieval apocalyptic vision literature seems to be best described as a mixture of "experienced" and literary constructions, perhaps because writers of such visions found themselves trying to relate what they hoped would be a convincing autobiographical experience to an audience they hoped to persuade, on the one hand, and working within the confines of a strong literary tradition on the other – as biblical scholars so often stress, there is nothing more "literary" than an apocalypse.[103] Perhaps the single most important feature which distinguishes apocalyptic visions from their fictional and "real" counterparts is the polemical motivation of the apocalypse. This is what separates Robert's, Hildegard's and Langland's visions from Tundale's on the one hand and Chaucer's on the other. The polemical element does not explain all the differences, but does provide us with an important focus.

Checking *Piers Plowman* against the list of some of Dinzelbacher's guidelines we find, similarly, that the poem is a mixture of both. As in the fictional visions of the Middle Ages, the narrator of *Piers Plowman* dreams his visions and never goes into a state of ecstasy, although some of the waking episodes are distinctly visionary in quality, which may suggest that Langland was reaching beyond secular literary conventions to religious ones.[104] Like many literary visions *Piers Plowman* is written in verse rather than prose, although this is perhaps the least reliable of the criteria, as Dinzelbacher says. As in other literary visions some of Will's dreams are set in idyllic natural surroundings, although it is evident that Langland was not much interested in this stylized literary convention and with the C-text revision of the poem he excised more of the natural description of flowers, trees and bird songs, finally leaving his dreamer to fall asleep in some of the barest natural settings in dream-vision literature. Another relevant aspect of Langland's use of setting is that for later visions in the poem he totally abandons the idyllic natural world and begins to set Will's dreams in contexts which are usually only associated with the recording of real religious visions, notably his vision weeping before the Cross in Passus v, and the vision from which he awakes at home among his family on Easter morning (Passus xx). A third vision (xxi. 4ff.) is received during Mass, a visionary setting usually reserved for prophetic visions in the Middle Ages.

It would seem then that we do have certain indications that Langland was playing with the idea that some of his visions were to be read as the real, religious variety. This is hardly surprising given the strong sense of spiritual urgency the poem leaves with the reader. *Piers Plowman* differs from almost all the literary dream visions of the Middle English period (except, perhaps, for *Pearl*) in that it is much more religious in character than it is secular (although this is more true of the C-text than it is of A and B); we should note that Langland never uses pagan mythology in his visions, as Chaucer does: it is only the Christian world view which interests him. This is especially true of the C-text, which condenses and clarifies and spiritualizes many of the confusions and mental wanderings of the B-text. While Langland no doubt began writing the poem with the more secular dream-vision model in mind, his work soon became a quest for moral and spiritual reform.

As Dinzelbacher suggests (*Vision*, p. 69), the literary *religious* vision is a rare phenomenon; he cites the *Divine Comedy* as the type of work which is both uncommon in medieval literature and difficult to produce, being a literary work of sustained religious vision. When he mentions *Piers Plowman* it is always in the context of the secular, literary vision tradition, but this may be partly because of the unequivocal way modern criticism has received *Piers Plowman* as a purely literary vision and also partly because Dinzelbacher uses the B-text rather than the C-text. Certainly, a key feature of *Piers Plowman* which suggests that Langland had the "real" religious vision model in mind is the emphasis throughout the poem on Will's spiritual growth, and this is more dominant in C than it is in B. Literary visions such as the ones Dinzelbacher discusses (those in Latin and also those in various vernaculars) do not result in any change in the visionary's life or any conversion experience, whereas the religious vision on the contrary seems often to be motivated by this factor (*Vision*, p. 75). This emphasis on the spiritual growth of the visionary brings us to two key features of the religious vision at which we will now look in more depth with regard to *Piers Plowman*: the autobiographical elements of such visions and the state of the visionary (awake or asleep) when the vision occurs.

Robert of Uzès' visions provide interesting information about this question of the mode of receiving visions. As I have mentioned above, some of his visions come to him almost casually; others are the result of intense prayer (he usually describes himself as prostrate when receiving a vision during prayer, as in Vision 17, in Bignami-Odier, "Robert," p. 281, or Vision 22, *ibid.*, p. 283). Many of his waking visions occur during Mass or during a service such as Matins (Vision 2, *ibid.*, p. 273) or Compline (Vision 35, *ibid.*, p. 287). This scenario was a favorite with visionaries, especially in prophetic circles. Some prophets mention the exact point during the Mass when the vision occurred; we notice that Robert mentions a vision occurring at the elevation of the body of Christ in Visions 17 and 22; other times he simply states that it happened during Mass. Langland may have this convention in mind when he has Will begin to dream "In myddes of þe masse, tho men 3ede to offrynge" (xxi. 4) or in v. 108, when he falls asleep while praying. It is interesting how Langland uses these moments to create ambivalence with regard to dreams: from the secular standpoint his falling asleep in church is morally, if somewhat comically, reprehensible; from the standpoint of religious vision convention it heralds a vision of some spiritual significance.

Piers Plowman and the medieval visionary tradition

Unlike a number of other medieval visionaries, Robert has both waking and dream visions. A rough count shows that the waking ones predominate, which may indicate that Robert was aware that these were more prophetically prestigious than the ones which occur during sleep. Medieval psychological theory held that:

Sleep is an affection of the body: damp humours rise to the brain and cut off the external senses, but they do not silence all the internal powers. This is an opportunity for *virtus imaginativa* to meddle with the images stored up in the *imaginatio*. Normally, in waking, the rational powers command both of these wits; but when the control of reason is lifted, *imaginativa* can make new shapes and forms by combining and separating the images . . . Some men who have a particularly strong *imaginativa* can see waking what others see only when sleeping. This kind of prophetic experience is to be distinguished . . . from a higher prophecy . . . which is a direct insight by the strong and pure soul . . . Prophetic dreams belong to the lower kind of imaginative prophecy. (Harvey, *Inward Wits*, pp. 49–50)

The fact that Robert has both waking and dream visions shows that the dream vision could be a respectable form for certain religious visionaries and that it was not just limited to literary usages.

In the early Middle Ages there was a great distrust of the dream and this negative attitude was to some extent perpetuated to the later period through the writings of Augustine, Gregory and Jerome (Le Goff, "Dreams," p. 203). However, as Le Goff writes, "the twelfth century may be considered the age of the reconquest of the dream" (*ibid.*, p. 203). With twelfth-century writers like Hildegard of Bingen, the dream came to be seen as a more healthy phenomenon (*ibid.*, p. 204) and was no longer regarded with as much suspicion. There is no clear distinction between a dream and a vision throughout the Middle Ages, but an essential distinction between receiving of visions when asleep or awake.[105] For example, the anonymous author of the *Vita* of Christina of Markyate is often at pains to assert that the religious experiences he recounts are of the most respected sort, carefully using the terminology of Macrobius' commentary on the *Somnium Scipionis* to stress that Christina's visions were not "fantasma" (Holdsworth, "Christina," p. 200). As Holdsworth points out, it is clear that her biographer did not have "a well-judged standard by which he judged the quality of the experiences he recounted" (*ibid.*) and this is the whole visionary problem in a nutshell. By Langland's time there was a sophisticated literature about visions and a well-established visionary tradition, but religious visionaries were still haunted by the ambiguities inherent in their mode of revelation.

There are waking episodes in *Piers Plowman*, which might well be described as waking visions, in the sense that Will encounters personified abstractions (like Reason and Conscience in v, and Nede in xxii), thus continuing the visionary allegorical mode of the poem. Will's encounter with Imaginatif is similar to these waking episodes in that, even though here the dreamer only "wakens" from a deeper dream (xiii. 213), the symbolism of awakening is highly suggestive. In fact, the half-waking state was sometimes used in medieval religious literature to underline the movement to greater spiritual awareness.[106] In this passage it looks as if Langland plays on this convention and on the medieval conviction of the superiority of waking over dreamed visions. And given the fact that the Imaginatif encounter constitutes one of the major turning points in Will's spiritual growth, it seems pertinent to look for features of the religious vision tradition at this point. The passage does indeed record what is at least a minor "conversion" experience for Will.

The passage begins as Will has been literally cast out of the visionary world because he has rebuked Reason for what Will sees as his unreasonable treatment of mankind:

> Tho cauhte y colour anoen and comesede to ben aschamed,
> And awakede þerwith; wo was me thenne
> That y ne hadde met more, so murye as y slepte,
> And saide anoen to mysulue, "Slepynge hadde y grace
> To wyte what Dowel is, ac wakynge neuere!"   (C. XIII. 212–16)

Wakened and sobered by shame and remorse for his presumptuous behavior, the dreamer cries, "Slepynge hadde y grace / To wyte what Dowel is, ac wakynge neuere!" Ironically, it is in his "awakened" state in the episode of Imaginatif that follows which gives Will the spiritual grace he needs to transcend his own narrow perceptions of the spiritual life and move on to greater understanding. This is, both literally and metaphorically, the passage in which Will *wakes up*. By shifting this important revelation from a sleeping to a "waking" vision, if we may use the term, Langland is playing off two different vision conventions against each other, and not without some irony. The one convention, popular in the secular literary tradition, is the receiving of revelations during sleep. This is set over against the theologically orthodox view of the religious visionary school that dreams received during sleep are the least reliable form of revelation – the waking vision being the more respected of the two. Add to this the widespread use in religious literature of sleep as a symbol of spiritual torpor from which a man must be awakened to save his soul, and we have a powerful set of ironical implications clustered around Will's cry. Langland would certainly have expected his audience to be aware of the spiritual implications of the sleeping and waking (and perhaps even half-waking) states and would also have expected them to pick up the important shift he makes at this point in the poem through this juxtaposition of secular and religious vision conventions. Indeed, Langland's awakening on Easter morning, with its jubilant recognition of the significance of Christ's Passion, is reminiscent of the medieval vision convention of the narrator's waking to conversion, normally after three days.[107] This motif of awakening as a new man, so common in the one-vision, one-waking pieces of vision literature, is less suitable, however, to a spiritual realist like Langland, who clearly does not see a one-time conversion experience as a state which can be sustained. Will, more realistically perhaps, is forced to return to vision again and again.

A further clue that Langland is concerned here with the question of visionary convention is that he gives such an exalted role in the poem to the personification Imaginatif. As we have seen, the only place in medieval theory in which the imagination was thought to be involved in spiritual affairs was in discussions of its role in visionary prophecy. As the workshop of dreams and prophetic visions, the *vis imaginativa* had a widely divergent reputation, which ranged from the observation that it made a nuisance of itself by producing unreliable and nonsensical images during sleep and contemplation to the belief that it was the faculty which enabled the holiest souls to receive prophetic visions. This is the background against which literary writers like Chaucer and Langland portray their dreamers as musing about the validity of visions. The implications for visionary credibility created by these ambiguities are obvious – they are the ironist's delight but the bane of the religious visionary's existence – and the ground Langland occupies is somewhere *between* these two positions. His delight in irony and his skill in creating irony are every bit as evident as Chaucer's, but Langland's poetry is far too didactic to exist for art's sake alone. Langland clearly highlights the visionary conventions in this encounter between Will and Imaginatif to some purpose. He may have been drawing attention to the whole visionary question in this passage, to the issue of the status of his poetry as revelation and of his own credibility as a visionary. The veins of irony which riddle the passage do not alter this suggestion in the slightest; they only complicate it.

A study of some of the episodes in which the dreamer is indisputably awake further supports the notion that Langland is concerned with visionary conventions and self-credibility. The waking episodes are often somehow self-revelations: in the C-text the most important of these are the dreamer's confrontation with Conscience and Reason in the autobiographical passage in Passus v and his encounter with Nede at the beginning of Passus xxii. In both cases Will is reproved for his manner of living and accused of being a false beggar:

> And hit neyhed neyh þe noen and with Nede y mette
> That afrounted me foul and faytour me calde:
> "Couthest thow nat excuse the, as dede the kyng and oþere,
> That thow toke to lyue by, to clothes and to sustinaunce,
> Was bi techyng and by tellyng of *Spiritus temperancie*
> And þat thow nome no more then nede the tauhte?"   (xxii. 4–9)

There have been many critical attempts to interpret Nede's dubious advice to the dreamer, but not much notice of the fact that Nede begins by accusing Will of being a "faytour," a point which hardly seems to further Nede's argument. Conscience and Reason make the same accusation in Passus v, but argue that the dreamer should remedy the situation by performing some socially useful labor. Clearly the dreamer's manner of living and role in society are recurring concerns for Langland throughout the poem. He seems to have a vague sense of uneasiness about his association with the various "faytours" of medieval society and, whatever the rewards of this association in terms of the riches of irony and literary ambiguity, he seems to need consistently to try to clarify his own position. The waking (or semi-waking) episodes, like the autobiographical passage in v, the Imaginatif passage in xiii–xiv and the Nede passage in xxii, are all somehow self-confrontational and one wonders if there is not a reason for this.

There is much in Langland's treatment of his dreamer-narrator which shows that he was concerned with his self-image as a writer of visions. Langland must have known from his acquaintance with serious religious visionary literature that, because of the ambivalence with which visions were viewed, judgments as to the credibility of any revelation usually fall back upon an attempt to discern whether the manner of living of the visionary himself (or herself) was credible. This process was part of what medieval theologians referred to as *probatio*, a series of tests whereby one could tell a true visionary from a fraudulent one. In testing the validity of any vision, much weight was placed on the moral and spiritual character of the visionary.

Edmund Colledge's study of the medieval issue of *probatio* with regard to Bridget of Sweden is useful in illuminating this concern in the autobiographical passages of *Piers Plowman*. Not much is known about Bridget's actual mode of receiving visions, but the controversy which surrounded Bridget both during her lifetime and after her death provided a great deal of material reflecting a variety of medieval attitudes towards the visionary experience. Some of the most eminent theologians of the fourteenth and fifteenth centuries became involved in commentary on Bridget's claims in particular and the problem of visionary validity in general.[108] The proliferation of prophecy of all types at this time no doubt made religious thinkers from a variety of backgrounds aware of both the dangers and possibilities inherent in this question.

Bridget's visions were received when she was awake, not asleep, "rapt and caught away from the senses of the body in ecstasy and spiritual contemplation."[109] In *Revelations* IV, 77 she writes, "O dearest God, strange it is what thou dost to me. For when it pleases thee, thou dost awaken my spirit to see and hear and feel with the powers of the Spirit . . ." (trans. Jorgenson, *St. Bridget*, vol. II, p. 231). Alphonse of Jaen, an amanuensis who was responsible for much of the publication of her work and promotion of her canonization process, wrote a defense of Bridget's visionary status, the *Epistola solitarii*, in which he says that whenever he is asked for an account of Bridget's manner of receiving her visions, he cites this passage. He adds that, after a vision, she often feared to have been "deluded by the devil" (Colledge, *"Epistola,"* p. 42).

All medieval visionaries lived with this ever-present fear of being duped by diabolical frauds. In *Revelations* IV, 38 Christ warns Bridget against too easy a trust in dreams and reminds her that the devil is the father of lies. As Colledge notes, Bridget was on various occasions required to undergo *probatio*, that is, to be "tested" as to the validity of her revelations (*"Epistola,"* pp. 39–40). By Bridget's time a considerable literature had grown up concerning this problem of telling a true visionary from a fraudulent one and it is this literature which Alphonse summarized and called to witness in his defense of Bridget. There are two aspects of the *probatio* problem which we will look at, the first spiritual and the second polemical: how does one go about distinguishing a true visionary from a fraudulent one, and, secondly, why does God choose to reveal himself in this way to the simple and not to the learned?

Drawing on Augustine, Jerome, Gregory, Thomas Aquinas, Nicholas of Lyra, Hugh of St. Victor and St. Anthony, Alphonse deals in the *Epistola solitarii* with the first problem under the heading of "discretio" (Colledge, *"Epistola,"*

Piers Plowman and the medieval visionary tradition

pp. 41–42). In discerning the validity of any vision, much weight was placed on the moral and spiritual character of the visionary or visionaries in question:

Are they spiritually-minded or of the world? . . . Do their lives bear fruits of obedience, humility, charity, prayer, or are they marked by pride, vanity, ambition? . . . Have they continued for long in spiritual life and in visions, or are they only beginners? Are they of sound intelligence and judgment, or are they giddy, easily moved, fantastic? (summarized by Colledge, "*Epistola*," p. 41, from Durante's edition, ch. 2, pp. 576–77)

The visions themselves should then be examined:

Were they received in waking, in sleeping or in dreaming? Are they corporeal, imaginary and spiritual, intellectual and supernatural? Were they received in ecstasy? Have mysteries and doctrines of the faith been revealed in them? Has divine truth been illuminated or illustrated? Do the visions accord with Scripture? Do they promote virtue and the health of souls, or do they lead to error, teaching that which is monstrous and irrational? Are they always true, or do they sometimes deceive? Do they foretell worldly honours and riches, or humility? Do they encourage pride or meekness, disobedience or obedience? (*ibid.*)

Even these indications, however, are full of ambiguous implications for the Church, and medieval theologians who distrusted visionaries and prophets were quick to point these out. Revelations had, on the one hand, to accord with Scripture and the Church's received tradition of faith; on the other hand, they could hardly be considered as revelations if they added nothing to current knowledge or awareness.[110] The illuminating or illustrating of divine truth was a tricky business: what accorded with present faith and knowledge could hardly be regarded as "revelation" (except to a previously untaught individual) and what did not could easily be seen as heresy. As Gerson said in his attack on Bridget's revelations, too many supposed visionaries had turned out to be heretics in the last analysis (in Colledge, "*Epistola*," p. 46). Furthermore, as Alphonse himself said, one had to be learned and experienced in the spiritual life in order to be able to judge visionaries in the first place. Gerson took the problem even further: not all men are capable of such proofs; rather, it is a gift of the Holy Spirit in itself to be able to make such judgments (*ibid.*, p. 45). At this point we may rightly ask how one can assess the validity of the *judge* and/or his judgments. The solution seems only to spawn fresh problems.

The whole question was magnified in Bridget's time by the presence of a plethora of prophets and visionaries often giving contradictory advice. In *Revelations* IV, 141 Bridget makes excuses for Pope Gregory, whom she had exhorted through her prophecies to return to Rome, by explaining what hinders him: "I have heard that many oppose him, saying that they have the Spirit of God, and that they have received divine revelations and visions; and that they use these as a pretext to dissuade him from coming" (trans. Colledge, "*Epistola*," p. 38). For Bridget this was obviously an embarrassing situation and one can see why visionaries in her position were often tortured with insecurity. As Colledge suggests, however, even detractors of such visionaries often espoused prophecy when it suited their purposes,[111] a fact which suggests that, even with the skeptical, prophecy still carried some weight, whether for its spiritual or polemical potential.

It is clear from what has been said in this brief summary of the problem that prophets found themselves under constant scrutiny both regarding their own way of life and demeanor and regarding the orthodoxy and credibility of what they prophesied. One wonders to what extent Langland, as a serious religious writer, felt that his own way of life and writings required the kind of justification which Alphonse sought for Bridget? I think that we may have the reason here for some of Langland's autobiographical additions to the C-text.

A stereotypical image of the true visionary or prophet had been evolving in medieval minds since the evangelical movements of the twelfth century had sprung into being.[112] These groups put much emphasis on apostolic poverty, rigorous asceticism and evangelical teachings. They roamed the countries of medieval Europe preaching the Gospel, urging poverty and repentance and (often) prophesying doom, especially against the wealthy and corrupt clergy of the established orders.[113] There is much evidence within *Piers Plowman* that Langland was strongly attracted to both the ideology and the manner of life of such evangelical figures: for example, there is the amount of space he gives to the discourse of Patience, who is a holy wanderer, and Piers' own dramatic conversion to the evangelical life in B. xii. 121ff., which (although the passage disappears in the C-text) he nevertheless fulfills in the C *Vita* (see xv. 33ff.), as in B. There is also much to support the argument that Langland wanted his dreamer-narrator to be somehow associated with this apostolic image. For example, Langland goes out of his way to stress that many of his dreamer's visions are received when he is hungry – wandering "meteles and moneyles on Maluerne hulles," as he puts it in one place (ix, 297). Fasting was considered highly efficacious for the receiving of visions: medieval vision theory held, for example, that the only true dreams were those which occurred in the morning, when the body was free from the physiological effects of food.[114] Early theorists on visions believed "that the soul could reach its greatest power when it was independent of the digestive activity of the body and, therefore, most free from bodily influence."[115]

These notions give the enigmatic section in which Nede appears to the dreamer and tempts him to steal food to satisfy his hunger a new kind of complexity. Nede's argument is convincing, but we must note that the dreamer does not give in. Although Langland portrays Will's "meteles"-ness as the accident of his wandering lifestyle, sometimes even implying that it is Will's own fault because of his idleness (as in v. 5–10), Will's hunger does have more positive associations within the poem, as the hunger of the lunatic lollars does (ix. 105–27). One may not always plan to be a prophet, but certain conditions of life and point of view can *predispose* one to the role! Langland's emphasis on Will's hunger and the fact that all of his visions (so far as we can tell) are daytime or early morning visions (these were regarded as the most propitious times) are perhaps part of a subtly drawn visionary self-portrait.

Langland drops other hints in this direction. Through the course of the *Vita*, Will's search for Truth drives him to a state of alienation from society; he stops noticing physical discomforts and this obsession with the search becomes almost a form of madness:

Ac after my wakynge it was wonder longe
Er I koude kyndely knowe what was dowel,
And so my wit weex and wanyed til I a fool weere.
And some lakkede my lif – allowed it fewe –
And lete me for a lorel and looþ to reuᵉrencen
Lordes or ladies or any lif ellis,
As persons in pelure wiþ pendaunt3 of siluer;
To sergeaunt3 ne to swiche seide no3t ones,
"God loke yow, lordes," ne loutede faire,
That folk helden me a fool; and in þat folie I raued
Til reson hadde ruþe on me and rokked me aslepe.   (C. xv. 1–11)

This and other self-portraits correspond closely to the portrait of the lunatic
lollars, even in small details. Here, Will becomes a type of the "holy fool," and
stresses that people took him for a lunatic, a village idiot, but society is not his real
concern any more. Similarly, Richard Rolle of Hampole asserts in his *Incendium
amoris* that the man who is led by the Holy Spirit will become a social outcast,
paying no special respect to anyone (ed. Deansley, p. 238). It was said of the holy
hermit, Robert of Arbrissel, concerning his ragged appearance that only a club was
missing from the outfit of a lunatic (Leyser, *Hermits*, p. 68). Clearly there are strong
associations, both literary and social, between the lunatic and the holy man upon
which Langland is drawing.

But is Langland's dreamer a true prophet or a visionless, wayward wanderer? In
the B-text in particular, Langland toys with both ideas. In the C-text, however, he
seems to have taken steps to eliminate some of the ambiguities and the result is that
he comes down even more heavily on the serious religious visionary side. Two
new passages appear in the C-text which may have been written expressly for this
purpose. The first is the autobiographical passage in C. v. Here Langland the poet
once again merges with his fictionalized narrator figure to expose certain details of
his manner of living – the poem's Everyman becomes a specific man, the poet
himself. The passage is expanded and reworked from a shorter *apologia pro vita sua*
which occurs in the dreamer's confrontation with Imaginatif in the B-text. In the
original passage, Imaginatif accuses the dreamer-poet of "medd[ling] with
makyngs" (B. xii. 16) when he should be praying for those who give him bread.
Many critics have taken this to mean that Langland was a beggar – and they have
read all kinds of ironies and inconsistencies into these lines because this would
place the poet among those in society against whom he spends most of the poem
inveighing, the idlers and wasters and fraudulent clerics who preyed upon
medieval society. Some of that irony is certainly there, but a close examination of
these passages shows that this is partly a misconception. This misconception about
Langland's manner of living which has misled modern critics may have misled
some of Langland's contemporary audience and it may be because of this that he
rewrote and clarified the passage in the C-text. In the new passage he makes it quite
clear that, although he is bothered by Conscience for having wasted time in his life,
he is not in fact a beggar. He makes his living, as did many other unbeneficed lower
clergy, by making the rounds of various homes of benefactors who provide him

with sustenance to say prayers for their souls and the souls of dead relatives (Donaldson, *Piers Plowman*, pp. 219ff.). When Conscience and Reason ask him why he cannot make himself useful by doing manual labor, he replies with a defense of his life and means of livelihood, which implies that the learning he gained as a youth has set him apart from common laborers and given him the vocation he labors in now:

> And so y leue yn London and opelond bothe;
> The lomes þat y labore with and lyflode deserue
> Is *pater-noster* and my prymer, *placebo* and *dirige*,
> And my sauter som tyme and my seuene psalmes.
> This y segge for here soules of suche as me helpeth,
> And tho þat fynden me my fode fouchen-saf, y trowe,
> To be welcome when y come, oþer-while in a monthe,
> Now with hym, now with here; on this wyse y begge
> Withoute bagge or botel but my wombe one.   (C. v. 44–52)

To understand this passage fully it must be placed alongside Langland's description of the lunatic lollars, who in his view are God's own disciples because they live in a state of total dependence on God for their livelihood.[116] Like Christ's apostles, they do not beg with bags either, but take from their benefactors only what suffices for today, leaving the problem of sustenance for tomorrow up to God. Distinguishing them from idle beggars Langland writes:

> And ʒut ar ther oþere beggares, in hele, as hit semeth,
> Ac hem wanteth wyt, men and women bothe,
> The whiche aren lunatyk lollares and lepares aboute,
> And madden as þe mone sit, more other lasse.
> Careth they for no colde ne counteth of non hete
> And aren meuynge aftur þe mone; moneyeles þey walke,
> With a good will, witteles, mony wyde contreyes,
> Riht as Peter dede and Poul, saue þat þey preche nat
> Ne none muracles maken – ac many tymes hem happeth
> To profecye of þe peple, pleyinge, as hit were.
> And to oure syhte, as hit semeth, seth god hath þe myhte
> To ʒeue vch a wyht wyt, welthe, and his hele,
> And suffreth suche go so, it semeth, to myn inwyt,
> Hit aren as his postles, suche peple, or as his priue disciples.
> For a sent him forth seluerles in a somur garnement
> Withoute bagge and bred, as þe book telleth:
> *Quando misi vos sine pane et pera.*
> Barfoot and bredles, beggeth they of no man.
> And thauh a mete with the mayre ameddes þe strete,
> A reuerenseth hym ryht nauht, no rather then another.
> *Neminem salutaueritis per viam.*
> Suche manere men, Matheu vs techeth,
> We shoulde haue hem to house and helpe hem when they come.
> *Et egenos vagosque induc in domum tuam.*
> For hit aren merye-mouthed men, munstrals of heuene,
> And godes boys, bourdyors, as the book telleth.
> *Si quis videtur sapiens, fiet stultus vt sit sapiens.*   (C. ix. 105–27)

Like the dreamer-poet, they wander "meteles and moneyles." Like him they are perceived as lunatics. Like him they beg without a bag and trust Providence for tomorrow. Like him they do not salute the great ones of society when they meet them on the street – they are social outcasts, whose wits wax and wane, as the poet's do, with the moon. Like the poet they sometimes prophesy: "ac many tymes hem happeth / To profecye of þe peple." They are God's minstrels, poets of heaven, as (I suspect) Langland himself wanted to be. But the holy fools are also "merye-mouthed men," "bourdyors" – jesters – and when they prophesy it is as if they are playing, Langland tells us. Perhaps like Langland they too delight in the profound ironies which a spiritual point of view on life is forever revealing to the thoughtful man. Finally, he ends the passage with St. Paul's admonition, "If anyone among you is seen to be wise, let him become a fool that he may be wise." Perhaps Langland would have glossed this text by saying, "Let him become a dreamer and a visionary."

I have referred at many points to Rosemary Woolf's analysis of the character-istics of *Piers Plowman* which she calls "non-medieval" and which I have contended are not so much non-medieval as simply non-Middle English. With reference to Latin religious literature of Langland's day many of these supposed anachronisms can be seen to have parallels in other medieval works. To summarize some of these "non-medieval" qualities which we have touched on: Langland's "inconsistent" handling of allegorical figures and themes (Woolf, "Qualities," pp. 111ff.), the absence of visualization in parts of Langland's otherwise visionary writing (*ibid.*, pp. 116ff.), his dreamlike shifting of time and place (pp. 117ff.), the autobiograph-ical features of the dreamer (pp. 119ff.), the extent to which the dreamer's participation in the visions varies (pp. 118ff.) and Langland's entangled com-pression of allegorical ideas (p. 124).

Woolf particularly fastens on Langland's handling of the figure of Piers, the many forms he takes throughout the poem and his sudden appearances and disappearances: "The combination in Piers of uncertain significance with deep emotional power is exactly the reverse of what is normally found in Medieval allegory" (*ibid.*, p. 114). We have seen that this type of elusive handling of supranatural authority figures is a characteristic of apocalypses like *The Shepherd of Hermas*, but it is also similar to the treatment of Christ figures in certain medieval religious visions. For example, Mechthild of Magdeburg (1210–79), whose writings, as Dronke has suggested ("*Arbor*"), are similar to Langland's in their "loose" treatment of allegory, represents Christ as appearing to her in different guises, notably as a "working man" or as a pilgrim. Her vision of Christ as a working man deserves to be quoted in full, not only because it exemplifies the recurrent vision motif of the seer's inability to recognize divine figures in some appearances, but also because the exchange between Christ and the visionary illustrates this structural looseness:

Our Lord showed me in a parable what He has fulfilled and still fulfils in me. I saw a poor man raise himself from the ground. He was dressed as a working man in poor linen clothes. He had a crowbar in his hand on which there lay a burden as big as the earth. I said, "Good man! What art thou lifting?" He said, "I am lifting thy sufferings. Turn thy will towards

129

suffering! Lift it up and carry it!" Then I said, "Lord, I am so poor that I have nothing." Then He said, "Thus did I teach My disciples when I said *Blessed are the poor in spirit*, for when a person would fain do something and has not the power, that is spiritual poverty." THE SOUL. – "Lord! Is it Thou? turn Thy face to me that I may know Thee!" Then He said: "Learn to know Me inwardly!" THE SOUL. – "Lord! if I saw Thee among a thousand, yet would I know Thee!" Then my heart tempted me inwardly to a small dissimulation, but I did not trust myself to say to Him, "Thou art the Lord!" I said: "Lord! this burden is too heavy for me!" And He said, "I will clasp it so close to Myself that thou canst easily bear it. Follow Me and see how I hung before My heavenly Father on the Cross and endured!" Then I said, "Lord, give me Thy blessing." He answered, "I bless thee without ceasing. Thy sufferings shall give thee good counsel." And I replied, "May this help all those who gladly bear suffering for Thee!"[117]

One wonders whether Rosemary Woolf would say of this passage that it "lacks the typical Medieval virtue of clarity" ("Qualities," p. 124). It would appear that some religious writers were simply trying to express the partially inexpressible when they recorded certain mental and spiritual experiences, and Langland may well have been as familiar with this type of writing as he was with lucidly consistent allegories.

A modern theologian uses much the same language to describe the character-istics of Hildegard's mystical writings as Rosemary Woolf uses to describe Langland's allegory. David Baumgardt talks about the "density and compactness" of Hildegard's recording of her experience (Woolf speaks of associated ideas being "interwoven and compressed together," "Qualities," p. 124), and he explains that Hildegard records "a diversity of insights in one instant . . . what modern psychology would describe as the peculiar contraction and stratification of intuitive and highly emotional thinking, and what Jakob Boehme once called being caught in an intellectual downpour."[118] Memories, observations and conscious interpretation of the observed and remembered, Baumgardt writes, "are squeezed together in one moment." There are many instances in *Piers Plowman* in which one feels that one has been caught in an intellectual downpour (the Tree of Charity vision comes instantly to mind). Perhaps one of the best known of these is Christ's speech in the Harrowing of Hell passage (Woolf, "Qualities," p. 124):

> For y þat am lord of lyf, loue is my drynke,
> And for þat drynke today y deyede, as hit semede.
> Ac y wol drynke of no dische ne of deep clergyse,
> Bote of comune coppes, alle cristene soules;
> Ac thy drynke worth deth and depe helle thy bolle.
> Y fauht so, me fursteth 3ut, for mannes soule sake.
> *Sicio.*
> May no pyement ne pomade ne precious drynkes
> Moiste me to þe fulle ne my furst slokke
> Til þe ventage valle in þe vale of Iosophat,
> And I drynke riht rype must, *resureccio mortuorum*.
> And thenne shal y come as kynge, with croune and with angeles,
> And haue out of helle alle mennes soules. (xx. 403–14)

As Salter and Pearsall have suggested, what we have in this passage is the complete range of the four levels of biblical exegesis,[119] yet it is so unforced, so totally lacking in the mechanical abstractionism one normally associates with such exegetical exercises. The comfortable mixing of abstract and concrete (for example, "Ac y wol drynke of no dische ne of deep clergyse / Bote of comune coppes . . .") suggests a mind which uses both allegory and literary realism as readily as a bilingual man who has forgotten which language was his mother tongue. This, I submit, is the result of the visionary habit of mind.

Mechthild also sees Christ as a poor pilgrim, and except for the direct nature of the exchanges between the soul and Christ, these incidents are reminiscent of the multiple appearances of Piers. The English recluse Christina of Markyate similarly sees a Christ-like wanderer. Holdsworth describes the account in her *Vita* of three appearances of a "certain pilgrim" to Christina as follows:

The first time he comes he is received hospitably but goes on his way. "After a while" he returns again, talks with her, and sits down whilst she and her sister prepare refreshment for him. This he scarcely tastes, but after blessing them he goes on his way. The two sisters are left longing to see more of him; finally he turns up the day after Christmas day, attends services with the nuns and then disappears, although the church door had been locked so that no one could get in or out. At this point the author adds "Who else could we say he was, except the Lord Jesus or one of his angels?" ("Christina," p. 192)

Holdsworth refers to the vision as Christina's "Emmaus experience" and one wonders whether the evocative biblical tale of Christ appearing to his disciples as an unrecognized traveler is not at the root of many of these enigmatic appearances in medieval literature. As Holdsworth remarks, the stranger who joins the disciples in the Vulgate account is a *peregrinus* (*ibid.*, p. 191), a linguistic point which supports this notion. The mysterious and elusive appearances of Piers as a pilgrim, as, for example, in the Feast of Patience episode, may stem from a long-standing visionary tradition, examples of which we have seen in *Hermas* and *Esdras* earlier. In *The Vision of Tundale* there is similarly an appearance of a palmer "of parfyt lyf" (ed. Mearns, line 470) who passes mysteriously through the dangers of Hell unscathed. Langland's handling of the figure of Piers, then, does not appear to be entirely as "non-medieval" as one might initially think.

Clearly, where one should go to find parallels to some of the vision-like qualities in *Piers Plowman* is to those writers who believed themselves to have had real visions, who were steeped in the literature of the earlier visionaries and who formulated their religious ideas in terms of visual experience. As David Baumgardt says, "The mystical vision, like the aesthetic one, seeks something quite different from the observation of the bare given facts of existence . . . [it] seeks, rather, to grasp the inner import, the living impact and meaning of these facts."[120] If there was ever an intersection of spiritual and aesthetic vision, it is in *Piers Plowman* – literary critics always pride themselves on their sensitivity to the latter, but we ignore the former at our peril. The tradition of visionary writing behind *Piers Plowman* is much broader than the one literary scholarship has illuminated for us in studies of the secular literary dream vision of the Middle Ages. The emphasis in this study on the religious visionary tradition is by no means an attempt to displace that, only to broaden our view to further possibilities for influence among those writers who, believing themselves to have experienced visions of significance, not only wrote but *thought* in images, who spoke a visual language. None of the writers discussed here spoke that language as eloquently as Langland, but all of them, in one way or another, strove, as C. S. Lewis said, to render "imaginable what before was only intelligible" to visionless humanity.[121]

4

Leaven of malice: false apostles in the anti-mendicant apocalypticism of later medieval England

INTRODUCTION: "ORDO" PROPHECY IN MEDIEVAL APOCALYPTIC THOUGHT

For there shall arise false Christs and false prophets and shall shew great signs and wonders, insomuch as to deceive (if possible) even the elect.   (Matthew 24:24)

Apocalyptic thought is concerned mainly to distinguish the false from the true. At one point Hermas asks the Shepherd to teach him to distinguish between true and false prophets;[1] Langland's Will pleads with Holy Church, "Mercy, madame, for Mary loue of heuene . . ./ Kenne me by sum craft to knowe þe false" (II. 2–4). The apocalyptic mentality, urged on by multiple New Testament warnings like the one quoted from Matthew above, is ever on the alert for signs of both spiritual fraud and messianic leadership. Medieval apocalypticism, therefore, can be read as a history of groups which were considered to be either the new apostles or the much-feared pseudo-apostles of any given author's time. In the later Middle Ages many new groups or clerical orders were heralded as true apostles and seen as a long-awaited leaven of hope for the future. Equally, apocalyptic thinkers warned of other orders or groups whom they believed to be the pseudo-apostles, forerunners of Antichrist and false brethren. Often, one man's hope for the future was another man's despair. This mentality was fed by the rise of new religious orders and by the controversies and rivalries which they sparked as groups both old and new tried to justify their particular choice of path to Christian perfection.[2] In the twelfth century, apocalyptic thinkers who were members of newly founded religious orders often incorporated their own order into a future plan for renewal, resulting in some of the first traces of apocalyptic optimism in medieval thought.[3] This phenomenon is referred to here as *ordo* prophecy, my own term for the expectation that either crisis or renewal will come to the Church through the agency of a new order. The new tendency to read current events into an apocalyptic scheme of history allowed for much labeling of various groups as either the new apostles or pseudo-apostles of the day. However no *ordo* ever received as much apocalyptic attention, both positive and negative, as the fraternal orders did. They appear at the center of much apocalyptic prophecy and controversy, either as the order upon which the future renewal of the Church depends or as the malignant disease which will be its scourge or downfall.[4] From the perspective of medieval apocalyptic thought, then, it is not at all unusual that Langland should have given the friars the key role he did in *Piers Plowman*.

Joachim of Fiore had prophesied the coming of two new orders who would guide the Church through imminent crisis (see chapter 5, below). Although many orders claimed for themselves the role of these "viri spirituales," none were so strongly associated with this role in the medieval mind as the fraternal (especially the Franciscan) orders. By the mid-thirteenth century, Joachim's prophecies of the coming of two new orders of "viri spirituales" had been claimed by the Dominicans and Franciscans. In 1255 Humbert de Romanis and John of Parma, Generals of the Dominican and Franciscan orders respectively, issued a joint encyclical in which they stated that their orders had a mission to save the world in these Last Days (Reeves, *Influence*, p. 146). The friars were hailed by other religious groups as the leaven of Church renewal and it was precisely these apocalyptic claims which were so skillfully overturned by anti-mendicant propagandists to redefine the friars as the pseudo-apostles of the End Time. Langland presents an interesting case in the context of thirteenth- and fourteenth-century pro- and anti-fraternal apocalyptic thought because he fits none of the ideological categories which one routinely sees in this literature. His anti-mendicantism is mixed with what seems to be a genuine hope for the reform of the friars and a surprisingly "fraternal" view of clerical poverty and the evils of Church endowment.

To complicate the situation even further, one must beware of limiting consideration of the background to this problem in *Piers Plowman* solely to the well-known Joachite and anti-mendicant prophetic traditions. Hildegard of Bingen, as we will see, also contributed (unwittingly) to the mendicant controversies and there is also to be considered the virtually untapped literature of the shorter religious and political prophecies which carried pro- or anti-mendicant material as well.[5]

Langland's particular apocalyptic view of the mendicant orders could have come from a variety of prophetic sources. The one school of apocalyptic (or pseudo-apocalyptic) thought with which we know him to have been in contact is the anti-mendicant one, and the first section of this chapter will deal largely with the apocalypticism and ideology of this type of literature. It is important, however, to realize that anti-mendicant literature initially arose out of an apocalyptic controversy sparked by the Joachite expectation of new "spiritual men" and was fired for decades by medieval clerical concerns with the relative merits of the paths to perfection chosen by rival orders. In this sense anti-mendicant eschatology can be viewed as a type of *ordo* prophecy, a negative response to the positive claims of the Joachite groups (to be discussed in chapter 5, below). Langland's concerns with the issues of *ordo* prophecy, therefore, can be seen as inextricably tied up with the apocalyptic expectations which this type of prophecy produced.

Not all of Langland's fraternal prophecy is anti-fraternal – this is at first startling, because we think of him so much in the context of other anti-fraternal writers. The disendowment prophecy, for example, in Passus V is not anti-fraternal at all; in fact, it suggests a constructive solution to what Langland sees as the friars' predicament. Langland did not go as far as some prophetic thinkers in foreseeing the reformed friars as the hope of a new age, but he was desperately concerned with their reform and this is perhaps why it makes more sense to consider *Piers Plowman* from the standpoint of the wider tradition of *ordo* prophecy. As we shall see, there are many things which distinguish Langland's anti-fraternalism from that of the propaganda he drew upon and not the least of these is his sense that the friars had a rightful place within the Church after their reform.

THE IDEOLOGY OF WILLIAM OF ST. AMOUR AND *PIERS PLOWMAN*

Beware ye of the leaven of the Pharisees, which is hypocrisy.   (Luke 12:1)

If there is one type of apocalyptic literature which we can be reasonably certain Langland knew in some form, it is the anti-mendicant prophecy written during the thirteenth-century clerical conflicts at the University of Paris.[6] The prophetic motifs used with such effectiveness by William of St. Amour and his circle as a weapon against the friars were to be the mainstays of anti-mendicant literature and propaganda for decades to come. Although these motifs were taken up by many poets, satirists and propagandists who had no apocalyptic expectations themselves, the conventional charges laid against the friars continued – from Rutebeuf to Dunbar – to be those derived from biblical descriptions of the pseudo-prophets or false brethren who would plague the Church during the Last Days.[7] Until quite recently, scholars have not been sufficiently aware of the exegetical foundations of anti-mendicantism and have persisted in reading what is essentially a biblical typology as social history.[8] In the case of a writer like Langland this has led to a good deal of misunderstanding of both his apocalypticism and his attitude toward the fraternal orders. Recent scholarship has done a great deal to untangle some of these threads, but it is not yet altogether clear why a writer like Langland holds the peculiar mix of attitudes he does. The great clerical issues of the fourteenth century – mendicancy, poverty and the apostolic life – generated a huge literature, the marks of which are everywhere evident throughout *Piers Plowman*. But anyone familiar with the battlelines of the monastic, fraternal and secular camps can only be amazed at the way they have been scrambled in *Piers Plowman*. Langland's views on poverty and mendicantism could be the subject of any number of volumes – here we can only stress the association of these themes with medieval apocalypticism and the complexities of his ideas on these subjects.

We will look first at the beginnings of anti-mendicantism in the eschatology and ecclesiology[9] of William of St. Amour and his circle in order to establish the similarities and, more surprisingly, the differences between his point of view and Langland's. Then we will turn briefly to the transmission of these ideas in fourteenth-century England, and finish with a reading of Langland's own anti-mendicantism in the last passus of the poem.

The eschatological basis of anti-mendicant propaganda was a response to both ecclesiastical and apocalyptic tensions which were rife during the 1250s at the University of Paris. The apocalyptic expectations of Joachim of Fiore had infiltrated especially the young Franciscan order by this time. Many Franciscans, and by no means the extremists only, believed that Francis was the angel of the sixth seal (Apocalypse 7:2) who had brought about the renewal of Christ's teachings which Joachim expected (Leff, *Paris*, p. 258). With both the Franciscans and Dominicans claiming the role of Joachim's predicted new orders and the ominous prospect of the year 1260 (thought by Joachites to herald the traumatic transition period before the new age) coming upon them, apocalyptic tensions were high.[10]

To these were added the ecclesiological tensions created by the arrival of the friars into the pastoral domain. The secular clergy were not used to having to share pastoral duties, or the income they generated, with anyone else and both the growing numbers and popularity of the new orders began to pose a threat to those who had previously controlled the cure of souls. At the University of Paris, traditionally dominated by secular masters, the friars were making significant inroads. When in 1250 they tried, with the help of the pope, to increase the number of magisterial chairs held by friars, a dispute arose which exacerbated the already all-too-evident problem of the friars' capacity for attracting large numbers of students (and thus tutorial fees) away from the secular masters (Szittya, "Antifraternal Tradition," p. 295). Commanding papal and royal favor, as well as a general and ever-growing popularity, the friars became the cause of a good deal of jealousy and paranoia on the part of the seculars. The uneasiness of the secular clergy was further exacerbated by the knowledge that the friars were not subject to any diocesan authority in the pastoral field (Leff, *Paris*, p. 259). From the standpoint of those in the traditional hierarchy of the episcopal system, the friars appeared to be dangerously footloose. One of the main characteristics of anti-mendicant thought is precisely this sense of threat and paranoia which stems partly from confronting a force outside of the traditional system. So pervasive was this mentality that it was to survive long after the reasons for many of the charges had disappeared, as the work of Penn Szittya and other scholars has shown.

In the midst of this unstable situation an overly zealous Franciscan, Gerard of Borgo San Donnino, launched his *Liber introductorius* to the works of Joachim of Fiore[11] in which he claimed, among other things, that there would soon be no further need for the secular clergy in the coming new age (Szittya, "Antifraternal Tradition," p. 291). Guided by the new "viri spirituales" (the friars themselves, Gerard claimed), the Church was about to enter the Age of the Holy Ghost, in which the New Testament would be superseded by the *Evangelium aeternum*, in the same way as the Old Testament was once superseded by the New. This *Eternal Gospel* was none other than the works of Joachim prefaced by Gerard's *Introduction*. The situation at the university, which had seethed for so long, now boiled over. The secular masters had acquired a stick with which to beat the friars and, with William of St. Amour as spokesman, they lost no time in developing their own apocalyptic propaganda with which to fight this new apocalyptic threat. In the scandal that ensued the seculars tried as much as possible to associate the friars with this heretical brand of Joachimism and, for reasons which are still unclear, the Joachite Minister General of the Franciscan order, John of Parma, was forced to resign, while Gerard himself ended his days in prison. Shortly after these events

Leaven of malice: false apostles

William of St. Amour published his *Tractatus de periculis novissimorum temporum*, in which he showed that Gerard's *Eternal Gospel* heralded the coming of Antichrist and that the friars were none other than his precursors, the pseudo-apostles of the Last Days of the world. The biblical typology upon which William drew to paint his portrait of the friars as the hypocrite false prophets of the End comprises the set of conventions by which the fraternal orders were to be caricatured by satirical and polemical writers throughout the next two hundred years.

The *De periculis* was, at the friars' request, condemned by the pope and William was exiled in 1256, but by then the damage was done. William had scored a propaganda victory which was to last for decades. According to Matthew Paris, public opinion was swayed by the *De periculis* and people began to ridicule the mendicant orders: "alms which had heretofore been generously given were now refused; they were called hypocrites, successors of Antichrist, false preachers, flatterers and advisers of kings and princes, scorners and usurpers of priests, skilful intruders of royal apartments, prevaricators abusing the confessional . . ." (McDonnell, p. 458, from *Cronica maiora, MGH SS*, xxviii, p. 363). These charges and this tone, even this style of epithet-mongering, stuck. The animosity of the secular clergy knew no bounds. There is no other chapter in the history of apocalyptic literature which deals in such shrill and vitriolic material, even though apocalypticism has always attracted urgent and fanatical polemicists of all kinds. As Penn Szittya has remarked, anti-mendicantism is not a very noble chapter in the history of mankind ("Antifraternal Tradition," p. 313).

There are several themes in the *De periculis* which should be highlighted in view of Langland's overt use of this material: William's biblical typology, his periodization of history and eschatology, his views on the ecclesiological issues which first put the seculars and mendicants at loggerheads and finally his marked paranoia. Only the first of these, the biblical typology, has been discussed in much detail with regard to *Piers Plowman*, and it will therefore receive the briefest notice here. The other three themes are of interest in highlighting Langland's view of Salvation History and his clerical ideology. Penn Szittya has done very illuminating work on the eschatological typology of anti-mendicant prophecy, first in his unpublished doctoral thesis, "'Caimes Kynde': The Friars and the Exegetical Origins of Medieval Antifraternalism,"[12] then in subsequent articles and in his recent book, *The Antifraternal Tradition in Medieval Literature*. On many details, I refer the reader to his studies; for the brief summary which follows I am much indebted to his work and to the work of other scholars whose names appear in the notes.

Of William's typology Szittya writes,

The exegetical method of William of St. Amour is a direct corollary of his attitude toward history, which is, it should be stressed, symbolic, not empirical. His frame of reference for understanding the friars is not recent history but Salvation History, and it is therefore natural that he should turn to Scripture to explain events around him which were unsettling, even terrifying, because symbolic of the End.   ("Antifraternal Tradition," p. 291)

William used three main biblical texts as the basis for his portrait of the pseudo-apostles, which he was able to superimpose over the public's image of the contemporary friars without once mentioning the friars by name or directly referring to current events.[13] Drawing upon Christ's denunciation of the Pharisees in Matthew 23, William charged that the pseudo-apostles feign piety and only do good works "to be seen of men" (verse 5). Furthermore, they "love the first places at feasts and first chairs in the synagogues, salutations in the marketplace, and to be called by men, Rabbi" (verses 6–7).[14] This last charge proved a goldmine to William. "Rabbi" being rendered "magister" in the Vulgate, William could relate the command "ne vocemini magistri" directly to the friars' zeal to take up magisterial chairs at the university – and as it was the only biblical verse which could be made relevant to current university politics he had to make the most of it.

William attacked the friars' doctrine of mendicancy and the novelty of their evangelical way of life by drawing on a passage from St. Paul:

Now we command you, brethren, in the name of our Lord Jesus Christ, that ye withdraw yourselves from every brother that walketh disorderly, and not after the tradition which he received of us . . . Neither did we eat any man's bread for nought; but wrought with labour and travail night and day, that we might not be chargeable to any of you . . . For also, when we were with you, this we declared to you: that, if any man will not work, neither let him eat. For we have heard there are some among you who walk disorderly; working not at all, but curiously meddling. (II Thessalonians 3:6, 8, 10–11)[15]

From the reactionary viewpoint of the secular masters, the very fact that the friars stood outside of the ecclesiastical tradition was a condemnation in itself – a condemnation which verse 3:6 of the Pauline Epistle seemed to support. It is a short step from being outside the received tradition to being perceived as "disorderly" and "curiously meddling," and this was a step which William was only too willing to take: the theme of idle curiosity recurs throughout the *De periculis* at every opportune moment. The question of the relative merits of begging and manual labor was an issue which had always divided the seculars and mendicants. The Thessalonians passage gave William all the ammunition he needed to condemn the fraternal orders for meddling and idleness.

Finally, drawing upon II Timothy 3, William tagged the friars with all the characteristics of the pseudo-apostles whom Paul had warned would come to plague the Church at the End Time:

Know also this, that in the last days shall come dangerous times. Men shall be lovers of themselves, covetous, haughty, proud, blasphemers, disobedient to parents, ungrateful, wicked, without affection, without peace, slanderers, incontinent, unmerciful, without kindness, traitors, stubborn, puffed up, and lovers of pleasure more than of God, having an appearance indeed of godliness, but denying the power thereof. Now these avoid. For of these sort are they who creep into houses and lead captive silly women laden with sins, who are led away with divers desires. (II Timothy 3:1–6)[16]

The central point here, as in the other passages, is the characteristic hypocrisy or feigned piety of the pseudo-apostles. In part the friars had laid themselves open to such charges by the indiscreet manner in which some had claimed the status of the Joachite "viri spirituales," and in which fraternal apologists had stressed the mendicant ideal as both the highest mode of perfection and a return to the true apostolic life. Such claims for the apostolic perfection of one's order were commonplace throughout the Middle Ages – in fact it is hard to overestimate medieval concern for this subject – but obviously the conspicuous zeal – and success – of the fraternal orders on this score had irritated the seculars deeply. The type of the false magician, upon which Langland may be drawing in *Piers Plowman* XXII. 377–79, also derives from William's use of II Timothy 3, as does his use of the *penetrans domos* motif and his condemnation of fraternal learning. Paul writes that the pseudo-apostles will be: "Ever learning and never attaining to the knowledge of the truth. Now, as Jannes and Mambres resisted Moses, so these also resist the truth, men corrupted in mind, reprobate concerning the faith. But they shall proceed no farther; for their folly shall be manifest to all men, as theirs also was" (II Timothy 3:7–9).[17] Note that Paul promises that these pseudo-apostles will be found out and "proceed no farther." This was obviously one of the attractions of the identification for William, who dearly hoped for the demise of the friars and hoped that his "exposure" of their "true" colors in his treatise would do the trick (*De periculis*, p. 30).

William finished the *De periculis* with his famous forty signs that the friars are indeed false apostles. These have received much attention from literary scholars and we need not pause long over them here. The signs include various themes culled mainly from biblical texts, as, for example, the assertion that true apostles do not penetrate houses (no. 1), or seduce the innocent (no. 2), or commend themselves (no. 4), or devour the goods of others (no. 13), or breed strife if they are not received (no. 15), are content with the food and drink offered them (no. 24), do not apply or depend on logic or philosophy (no. 37) and so on. Many of the signs are repetitive and many are obvious jibes at the friars' popularity (for example, no. 20 states that true apostles are badly received at first!) or their rivalry with the seculars for clientele (for example, no. 21: true apostles do not preach to those who already have apostles, or no. 34: true apostles do not preach to converts but to those as yet unconverted). Finally, in keeping with William's recurrent pretense that the seculars' attack is simply an objective attempt at *probatio*, there are signs like number 33, which asserts that true apostles do not persecute those who try their validity.

In spite of the fact that the *De periculis* was condemned and William exiled from France, his eschatological charges persisted and, as any student of fourteenth-century English literature knows, these caricatures were alive and well, virtually unaltered, over one hundred years after the Parisian disputes. The fact that so many of these charges made against the friars have their sources in biblical typology is highly suspicious and has led recent scholars to question seriously their value as social or ecclesiastical history. The work of Arnold Williams has shown that non-polemical and non-literary historical sources, such as bishops' registers, give a very different picture of the activities of the fraternal orders and even, in some cases, of clerical attitudes toward them.[18] Why intelligent, perceptive and *thinking* men like Chaucer, Gower or Langland chose to perpetuate what was in large part a mythopoeic structure, and not a very nice one at that, is a fascinating question, the answers to which could range from personal animosities to the irresistibility of the satirical conventions. Here we can only speculate on Langland's motivations, which I suspect were threefold: I believe that he had reformist, apocalyptic and possibly even personal reasons for his anti-mendicantism and it is the basis for these views which will occupy much of the rest of this discussion.

It is so rarely that Langland scholars are able to treat any medieval work as a likely source for *Piers Plowman* that it seems especially fortunate to have something so obvious as anti-mendicantism to add to our otherwise highly tentative knowledge of Langland's apocalyptic reading. However, in spite of what critics have assumed, Langland does not exhibit perfect agreement with the most popular anti-mendicant work, the *De periculis*, in spite of many obvious parallels in symbolism. I think that Langland, oddly enough, would have disagreed even more with the English anti-mendicant writers of his own century.[19] Most of the studies of *Piers Plowman* and the *De periculis* so far have concentrated upon similarities in symbolism,[20] which is certainly useful, but I would like to turn now to more ideological questions.

As McDonnell has pointed out (*Beguines*, p. 459), William of St. Amour saw a twofold menace in the rise of the new fraternal orders: evangelical poverty and a share in pastoral activity. All those who attacked the mendicant orders from William to Richard FitzRalph knew themselves to be treading on dangerous ground because the new orders had been firmly established and their privileges granted by a series of papal decrees: to attack the friars was, in one sense, to attack the papacy. William therefore couched his criticisms in an attack on the ideology of voluntary poverty, as well as developing a radically restricted reading of the structures of Church government. These ecclesiological positions, overlaid by an eschatological garment, were meant as proof against counterattack by papal authorities. The two themes (poverty and ecclesiastical jurisdiction) are closely related and it is worth following William's arguments in some detail because he raises a number of points which readers of *Piers Plowman* will find familiar.

William begins by asserting that the friars cannot earn their livelihood from pastoral work; in his words, they cannot "live from the Gospel" ("de Evangelio vivere") because they are not true apostles (*De periculis*, p. 31), that is to say, secular priests. If they are evangelizers, ministers at the altar, dispensers of the sacraments, then they are true apostles, William admits, but "Si haec officia non habent, nec vivendi de Evangelio potestatem habent." James Doyne Dawson explains William's position as follows:

> The main issue raised by the tract was the right of the friars to administer the *cura animarum*, a right which no one had seriously questioned before, since the friars were priests and operated under papal license. William's essential argument was a simple one. He asserted that all power to preach and administer the sacraments had been invested by Christ in the apostles and disciples and in their successors, who are the bishops and the parish priests respectively. These are the only two *ordines* in the Church which possess the *cura animarum*, and no other such *ordo* can ever be instituted. (Dawson, "William," p. 233)

William argued that in order to take on the responsibility of the cure of souls, one had to be "sent," but the friars had not been sent and therefore were usurpers. As Gordon Leff explains:

Leaven of malice: false apostles

[William] put forward a doctrine of extreme diocesan autonomy that effectively gave the clergy the power of deciding who could engage in pastoral activities in their dioceses – by invitation. William also divided the ecclesiastical hierarchy into two classes: the upper, consisting of seculars – bishops, priests, and deacons; and the lower, composed of faithful laymen and catechumens (including the regulars). As ordained by God, none of the lower class could act among the upper class. (*Paris*, pp. 260–1)

Categorizing the friars as regulars, William could argue that they were overreaching their station, as it were, in their bid to do pastoral work and *live from the Gospel* – that is, claim livelihood from the alms or oblations of the laity. This strict ecclesiological hair-splitting has some illuminating implications for two important issues in *Piers Plowman*: first of all, for Langland's recurrent anxiety over the question of a "fyndynge" for the friars and secondly, for his anxiety – if the C-text autobiographical passage is indeed autobiographical – over his own "fyndynge." As a member of the lowest rank of the secular hierarchy, by William's definition Langland himself would not have had any right to "live from the Gospel" – that is, from the oblations of the laity. As we will see shortly, William's categories could give pause to a cleric in minor orders living by alms.[21]

William goes on to argue that involvement in "foreign" (or "worldly") business ("de curando negotia aliena") is not an acceptable way for "viri religiosi" who do not have cure of souls to earn their keep. "Work with your hands, just as we taught you," he quotes from the passage in II Thessalonians and emphasizes that those who do not work will not eat. Throughout this section William is relying heavily on Augustine's *De opere monachorum* and here he is especially careful to quote Augustine's gloss on this passage and the saint's assertion that to do bodily labor is not against the commandment, "Nolite soliciti esse, dicentes, quid manducemus?" (Matthew 6:25), as some have thought; rather, in many places in the Epistles Christians are urged to do bodily labor "lest they be compelled by need to ask for necessities" ("ne compellantur egestate necessaria petere") (*De periculis*, p. 32). William is obviously trying to answer all the standard biblical texts used by the mendicants in their justifications of begging in this section of the *De periculis*. He continues to defend the notion that there is danger in begging for necessities by saying that those who wish to live from begging become flatterers, liars and worse (*ibid.*).[22]

William now moves to demolish one of the most important set-texts of mendicant apologist literature: "Sed dices: Nonne opus perfectionis est omnia relinquere pro Christo, et postea pro Christo mendicare?" (alluding to Luke 18:22). He responds by shifting the emphasis from poverty to good works and asserting that "Omnia pro Christo relinquere, et ipsum sequi, imitando in bonis operibus, opus perfectionis est" (*De periculis*, p. 32). Not only is begging nowhere implied in the command to "sell all you have and give to the poor and follow me," William says, but begging has been prohibited by the apostle Paul. How therefore does the perfect man live after he has relinquished everything? William offers only two options: he may live by manual labor or by entering a monastery where he may have the necessities of life (*ibid.*, p. 32). He has succeeded in leaving no room at all for begging as a clerical option. It is precisely this problem which seems to concern

Langland in Passus v. Here, Conscience's and Reason's confrontation with Will in the "autobiographical passage" centers on the question of Will's method of earning a livelihood which is, they charge, by begging – once Will has rejected their suggestion of manual labor, they turn to the question of where he fits into the ecclesiastical hierarchy in order to ascertain whether in fact he does have the right to "live from the Gospel." We will return to this complex passage and the questions it raises in this context a little later.

William now has the task of disproving that Christ ever begged – this particular question being among the most hotly debated in all the exchanges of polemical literature.[23] When Christ sent the disciples out with "neither purse, nor scrip, nor shoes" (Luke 10:4), William insists that they were not living as mendicants because they deserved to have their necessities provided by the people to whom they ministered. He also insists that they did not ask for anything but were content with offerings, providing the remaining necessities by manual labor (*De periculis*, p. 32). "Who feeds the sheep and does not partake of the milk?" he asks, and stresses that he can find nowhere an account of the Lord having begged. Some of his arguments smack of the speciousness for which both sides of this controversy are known: Christ did not beg water of the woman at the well because the water was for communal use, William insists. When Christ told Zacchaeus, "this day I must bide in your house" (Luke 19:5) this was not begging, William insists, but pleasantry ("urbanitas")!

A closely related issue, which also crops up in Passus v of *Piers Plowman*, and which gave rise to much strained argumentation, was the constant warring about the two Gospel references to Judas' purse or bag ("loculus"). Here the anti-mendicant propagandists were not on entirely sure ground: both times Judas' purse is mentioned (John 12:6 and 13:29) it is in close connection with his betrayal of Christ (Szittya, *Antifraternal Tradition*, pp. 49ff.). St. Francis had therefore come to associate the purse with false apostles like Judas. True apostles, he argued, following Christ's directions in Luke 10, carried nothing. Traditionally Judas' purse had been seen as a testimony that Christ and the disciples held goods in common and had been used to support notions of corporate ownership. But the coming of the mendicants did much to upset traditional notions of the necessity and appropriateness of clerical wealth and one of the consequences of such controversies was the growing discussion of clerical disendowment. William himself must have felt defensive about the long-accepted tenet of clerical ownership, because he asserts that even though the mendicants say they are more perfect than monks (having neither goods of their own, nor in common), having goods in common does not impede or diminish the perfection of the regular orders (*De periculis*, p. 33).

William concludes that the friars, since they cannot live from the Gospel, should follow Paul's instruction to do manual labor and suggests that "we should not give to them, but rather correct them" (*ibid.*). As Dawson has pointed out, William and later secular propagandists had no small difficulty in sustaining what was by this time a rather strained and outdated argument for manual labor:

Leaven of malice: false apostles

In support of the view that religious are required to maintain themselves by their own labor, they cited Paul's epistles, the Benedictine Rule, Augustine's *De opere monachorum*, and appropriate passages from the *Decretum* and the standard *Gloss* to the Scriptures . . . But the seculars had no strong case here, because it had also been accepted for about a century that this principle applied only to *lay* religious . . . Since the mendicant frairs were clerics (even the Franciscans had become overwhelmingly clerical long before 1255), no one had questioned their right to receive alms, and William's opponents had little difficulty with this argument.
(Dawson, "William," pp. 229–30)

In his *Questio de evangelica paupertate*, for example, St. Bonaventure had argued that if, as William suggested, the endowments of the Church were simply alms for the maintenance of those charged with the cure of souls and the destitute of society, then the monks as well as the friars should live by manual labor.[24] However, since the contemplative life had always been regarded as valuable for its own sake, neither the monks nor the friars (who combined the active and contemplative life) should have to labor. Bonaventure goes on to argue that the seculars should be grateful that so many clerics preferred mendicancy to competition for the limited number of benefices and that even though St. Paul had labored for a living those who were less spiritually gifted had to study in order to acquire the skills to fulfill their duties and so had no time to earn their living as the apostle had (Douie, "Conflict," pp. 10–11).

In his treatise *Contra impugnantes cultum dei*, Aquinas similarly attacked William's argument that the friars should live by manual labor by demolishing his carefully constructed distinctions between a religious and a priest.[25] He argued that manual labor was neither a precept nor a counsel; and, in any case, it would have applied universally had it been either (Leff, *Paris*, p. 267). Aquinas put his finger on the aspect of this issue which particularly concerned Langland when he pointed to the number of secular clerics who had neither cure of souls nor lived by manual labor (*ibid.*, p. 268).

We have seen that William went to great lengths to prove that Christ never begged, that begging was a highly suspect way of life for an able-bodied man to lead and that it would likely land him in sin. Langland sympathized with this view, but he was also drawn to the ideal of mendicant poverty. Bourquin has shown that Langland's Patience can be seen as a powerful embodiment of the Franciscan ideal of patient poverty and mendicancy (Bourquin, *Etudes*, p. 698). At the very least it is obvious that Patience's view is in agreement with the Franciscan ideal, although such ideology was not peculiar to the Franciscans alone. Furthermore, it seems that Langland knew the ideas set out in Bonaventure's *Apologia pauperum*, at least as they were embodied in the papal bull *Exiit qui seminat*,[26] and there are many echoes of Franciscan ideology in *Piers Plowman* that could likely be traced to Langland's intimate knowledge of the defenses of Bonaventure and other prominent mendicant apologists. For example, since all the goods of the Franciscan order were owned by the papacy, Bonaventure "sought to establish that the goods the order consumed were only those of 'simple use,' the bare essentials necessary to preserve mortal life in this world" (Leff, *Paris*, p. 266). This notion of the spiritual

143

efficacy of voluntary poor living as a remedy against pride and avarice is at the heart of Langland's portrayal of Patience.[27]

Langland's anxiety about the question of a "fyndynge" for the friars is, I believe, closely related to his preoccupation with his own mode of livelihood (or, at least, with that of "Will"). We saw that William of St. Amour sought to restrict the clerical hierarchy to two classes: the prelates and priests of the secular clergy, and in a lower class, the regular clergy and the laity. Anyone in the lower class could not "live from the Gospel" and was therefore restricted to living by manual labor or entering a monastery, according to William.

This gives us some perspective on Conscience's and Reason's confrontation with Will in the autobiographical passage of the C-text of *Piers Plowman*. The view of the ecclesiastical hierarchy and rights of livelihood within it expressed by the allegorical figures in this passage are not dissimilar to William of St. Amour's. It would seem that Will is too far down the ecclesiastical ladder to perform even minor clerical duties[28] and yet considers himself too far up to do manual labor (v. 13ff.), although his reply to these queries is rather apologetic and oblique (v. 35ff.). It is clear from Reason's questioning of him that it is difficult to tell whether Will is a layman or a cleric and, if he is a cleric, what means of livelihood he is entitled to. If only those with cure of souls can live from the Gospel and Will neither performs manual labor nor is a member of a monastic order, his claim to beg his "bylyue" (v. 29) is tenuous indeed by strict ecclesiastical standards.[29] As Donaldson (*Piers Plowman*, pp. 208ff.) has shown, clerics in Will's position had to forge a livelihood for themselves on the fringes of the ecclesiastical hierarchy, which is what Will has done and is trying to do – and to justify. But as a would-be reformer and critic of clerical corruption, his need for self-justification becomes paramount and although the passage is riddled with self-doubt and ambiguity, Will does eventually manage a kind of *apologia pro vita sua*. The tools he labors with, he asserts, are in his prayerbook:

> This y segge for here soules of suche as me helpeth,
> And tho þat fynden me my fode fouchen-saf, y trowe,
> To be welcome when y come, oþer-while in a monthe,
> Now with hym, now with here; on this wyse y begge
> Withoute bagge or botel but my wombe one. (v. 48–52)

Using the metaphor of manual labor, Langland skillfully walks a tightrope between the various doctrines and charges of the mendicant controversies. He manages to cut a path for himself, carefully avoiding excesses and carefully upholding ideals.

The compromise is in fact surprisingly Franciscan in point of view, while remaining acceptable (or nearly so) to the ground-rules of secular ecclesiology. Will describes a means of livelihood which, following the tenets of Franciscan evangelical poverty, takes no care for the morrow. In fact he performs a type of spiritual labor in exchange for goods received. This scrupulous definition of what is essentially a lower-order secular-mendicant manner of living is, I suspect, original to Langland.[30] It comes of his close knowledge and perpetual preoccupation with the literature of the mendicant controversies and is, incidentally, one of a number of passages in the poem which reveal as much sympathy for the mendicant point of view as others show for the anti-mendicant one. It strives to be acceptable to both sides – and perhaps more importantly, to conscience.

Langland's extraordinary emphasis on begging without a bag comes, I think, as much from the Franciscan notion that only false apostles – like Judas – carry bags, as from anti-mendicant attacks on lax friars who do. Both stem, of course, from Christ's prohibition against bags when he sent the apostles out to minister, but Langland seems to come down here much more clearly on the fraternal side with its distrust of all worldly baggage (as symbolized by Judas' purse) than on the side of William of St. Amour and his followers in their elaborate defenses of Judas' bag and clerical endowments. It seems to have taken Langland some years – and two previous versions of *Piers Plowman* – to find himself ready to delineate his own stand. Whether it is simply a symbolic one – a symbol of voluntary clerical poverty which abhors worldly baggage and is not afraid to face tomorrow without it – or whether this is a mode of life which Langland actually practised or believed was practicable, is difficult to say. If Conscience and Reason are commenting on realities external to the poem, then it sounds as if this is a manner of life which Will (or Langland) had trouble living up to. Like the friars, Will's will to adhere to this supremely challenging regime at times slips. As Penn Szittya has pointed out, Langland tries in many ways to associate Will with the friars throughout the poem: both have a dubious "appearance of godliness" (to quote William of St. Amour), both wander,[31] both are always learning but never understanding, as William of St. Amour says.[32] But if Langland is harsh on both the friars and the dreamer at times, he also shows a deep awareness of the ideals to which both are trying to live up and from which both constantly fall.

If one views Will's personal situation from the standpoint of William of St. Amour's attacks on the validity of clerical mendicancy (or *any* mendicancy of ablebodied men, for that matter), it becomes easy to see why Langland is so worried about the question of begging. If Langland himself lived or tried to live the life he describes in Passus v (a possibility which, as we saw in chapter 2, p. 65, many critics have advanced), then it is clear why he was so sensitive to the issues of apostolic poverty and mendicancy – this would have put him in precisely the same position as the mendicants in having to request sustenance from the laity in return for pastoral services which fell outside traditional secular ministerial duties. His odd combination of views on the fraternal orders, poverty, manual labor and clerical endowments is just about what one would expect of someone caught in this socio-ecclesiastical position. His first loyalty would seem to be to the secular ideology, but his precarious existence on the bottom rung of the secular ladder may have driven him to his idealization of mendicant or eremitical poverty. Part of the motivation for his interest in all this may have been an attempt to understand and come to terms with his own position, or the position of unbeneficed secular clergy, as well as his all-consuming reformist zeal.

We could take our speculation one step further to suggest that his own predicament accounts for Langland's anger with the friars' abuses of mendicancy, as well as with the abuses of the various false hermits and minstrels. It would be most aggravating to see others abuse the goodwill and charity by which one must live and by which one has *tried* to live honorably. Whatever the case may be, it should be stressed that Langland's ideology of poverty is most likely, given his wide knowledge of the mendicant controversy literature, derived largely from fraternal counter-arguments, which, it should be stressed, often occur in the same manuscript collections or anthologies as the anti-mendicant material. The writings of the mendicant apologists and especially the Franciscan Spirituals are very charismatic – it is hard to imagine anyone with the spirituality Langland exhibits not being moved by them. Langland knew that mendicancy was a morally dangerous way for most men to try to live and he seems to look forward to a world without it – for both laity and clergy – but he seems also to have valued its symbolic and didactic power as a vivid way of expressing man's ultimate dependence on God and the tendency of worldly goods to disrupt that relationship. And with his great sensitivity to the possible gradations of perfection, he may well have believed that some few might still achieve the "dobest" of Patience.

However, in the main, Langland seems to have believed that neediness was morally dangerous and that moderation was the best guarantee of moral soundness. His sympathies with the anti-mendicant position seem to be rooted in this concern. As the strategic anti-mendicant text from Proverbs has it:

Remove far from me vanity and lying words. Give me neither beggary nor riches. Give me only the necessaries of life. Lest perhaps being filled I should be tempted to deny, and say: Who is the Lord? Or being compelled by poverty, I should steal, and forswear the name of my God. (30:8–9)

Langland must have created the figure of Nede partly as a specter of the result of mendicant poverty: as the verse from Proverbs says, those who are needy may be compelled to desert integrity in order to fulfill their need. There has been much discussion among *Piers Plowman* critics about the "specious" nature of Nede's arguments[33] and certainly some suspicion is justified because Langland clearly associates Nede with the "Kyng and oþere" who have just demonstrated some of the perversions of the cardinal virtues possible to straining self-justifiers (xxii. 4–9). However, there is much more to the Nede episode than this – as if demonstrating the potentialities for subtle moral perversions and deceptions (even self-deceptions) were not enough for any passage to bear. Pamela Gradon has suggested that Nede is a friar[34] and shown briefly that his speech "is largely concerned with those controversial concepts 'necessity' and 'temperance' enshrined in the Bull *Exiit qui seminat*" – the bull issued by Pope Nicholas III which officially embodied St. Bonaventure's philosophy of Franciscan poverty as set out in his *Apologia pauperum*.[35] As such, everything Nede says is entirely orthodox and, although it is controversial, as Gradon says, Langland could not have despised or disagreed with it – nor, I think, does he. What I believe he is questioning here is not the validity of those primarily Franciscan teachings, so much as their inevitable potential for perversion in the hands of fallen man. In this sense I would adapt

Leaven of malice: false apostles

Gradon's view that Nede is a friar to say that he is the embodiment of the *fraternal predicament*. The distinction is subtle but useful.

Langland's view of the friars is basically that they are trying to live up to an ideal which is humanly impossible to sustain – the exigencies of their way of life lead them, however subtly or self-deceivingly, to desert the path of integrity in order to fulfill their need. The fraternal predicament is also, as we have seen, Will's predicament. Wandering and without a formal method of earning a living, he too must confront Nede. There are two ways of viewing such poverty and both were accepted teachings in medieval theology. One was the view stressed by the anti-mendicant writers that need is dangerous because it may compel a man to sin – this is the main reason why, in Langland's view, the friars need a "fyndynge." The second view, put forward by mendicant writers, was that complete, voluntary poverty conquered cupidity, helped a man set his sights on spiritual rather than material goals and promoted humility. As Nede says,

> And Nede ys nexst hym [i.e. Temperance], for anoen he meketh
> And as louh as a lamb for lakkyng þat hym nedeth,
> For Nede maketh neede fele nedes louh-herted.
> Philosopheres forsoke welthe for they wolde be nedy
> And woneden wel elyngly and wolden nat be riche.
> And god al his grete ioye goestliche he lefte
> And cam and toek mankynde and bicam nedy. (XXII. 35–41)

Langland sympathized with this view too; countless passages throughout the poem could be cited to bear witness to his reverence for the virtue of patient poverty. The Nede passage is so difficult partly because it records the confront-ation of these two opposing views – in partisan terms, the anti-mendicant and mendicant views of poverty – and the dreamer is paralyzed by the confrontation because he can neither wholly accept nor wholly reject either. We noted earlier that this episode is one of the handful of vision-like waking episodes which seem to bear personal as well as more general significance for the dreamer. On the personal level of the allegory (that is, the significance for the dreamer's own life) the passage recalls the conflicts with regard to begging which come up in the autobiographical passage. The dreamer has been trying to live out his recently learned belief[36] that God provides for the faithful, and has run up against the reality that in many cases God does not – at least not in the direct and miraculous way which the charming tales of the Desert Fathers might imply.[37] Just as the passage reveals a conflict between ideology and reality on the level of the question of fraternal mendicancy, it reveals a similar conflict between ideology and reality in the dreamer's mode of living. The conflict is between the relative merit (or even validity) of two kinds of spiritual *ascesis*: encountering need leaves the dreamer to wonder whether it is better to live in faith that God will provide and thus endure hunger as an *ascesis* or whether it is better to endure the shame of begging as an *ascesis*, the latter being, as Nede suggests, the humbling experience so valued by St. Francis.

When the scene opens, Will is disturbed and anxious about his predicament and it seems to be partly this anxiety which arouses Nede's anger:

> And as y wente by the way when y was thus awaked,
> Heuy-chered y ȝede and elyng in herte,
> For y ne wiste where to ete ne at what place.
> And hit neyhed neyh þe noen and with Nede y mette
> That afrounted me foule and faytour me calde.   (xxii. 1–5)

Clearly a calm and willing acceptance of neediness is the preferred attitude,[38] and in Nede's final words to the dreamer,

> Forthy be nat abasched to byde and to be nedy
> Sethe he þat wrouhte al þe worlde was willefolliche nedy,
> Ne neuere noen so nedy ne porore deyede . . .   (xxii. 48–50)

he suggests that an attitude of patient poverty and Christ-like humility would better suit the dreamer's neediness. Clearly the dreamer has been "abasched to byde and to be nedy" and, as the rhetorical question in line 6 suggests ("couthest thou nat excuse the . . ."), the dreamer has also been reluctant to take what he needs or even ask for it – the relative validity of these inhibitions is as difficult for us to judge as they are for the dreamer himself. Is it more meritorious to put aside all pride and to beg, as St. Francis would have it, or is it more meritorious to suffer hunger indefinitely and wait upon God's mercy? Is Nede's exhortation to abject humility a more worthy path than the path of resisting the temptation he enjoins? And why does Nede call the dreamer a "faytour"? Is Will a false beggar because he does not suffer need in the right spirit and is therefore not a holy beggar? Or is he a false beggar because he begs when he has no need? Nede's ensuing comments suggest the former reason, but both meanings may be implied in the charge. Presumably Nede would be the best possible judge of "faytours" – that is, of how needy beggars really are and how patiently they suffer that need. Nede is, after all, an allegorical representation of the state of want (and as such is neither moral nor immoral). He is, rather, an expert on the condition of neediness.

This passage presents us with many questions but few answers and I believe this is what Langland intended. The warning signals with regard to the potential of Nede's argument for perversion, both for the dreamer's own life and for the broader question of the fraternal ideology, are all there and flashing – but the warning signals do not tell all. The complexity of this passage should never be underestimated and we may never be able to plumb its depths sufficiently.

Robert Adams has argued on the basis of medieval exegesis of Job 41:13 that Nede should be seen as a harbinger of Antichrist (Adams, "Need," pp. 298ff.) and it seems likely that this is yet another face of Nede to be added to the list. Yet just because Nede "goes before the face of Antichrist," there seems little reason to believe – as Adams finally argues – that he is the "Noonday Demon" of the commentary tradition on Psalm 90:5–6. In the exegetical tradition of Job 41:13, need is simply a neutral misfortune that will herald the coming of Leviathan (Antichrist) and it is therefore important to distinguish between Nede, whom Will meets as "hit neyhed *neyh* þe noen" (italics mine) and the noonday demon himself. On one level of the allegory Langland has subtly arranged for this perfectly orthodox but heavily Franciscan spokesman for patient poverty to arrive just before Antichrist and just before his poetic reworking of William of St. Amour's anti-fraternal motif of the pseudo-apostles. However, Langland does not confuse the friars with Antichrist and, unlike William of St. Amour, he does not cast friars alone in the role of harbingers of Antichrist: a good number of secular clergy share this honor in Passus XXII.

Nede's second appearance is as counselor, this time to Conscience, whose main problem at this point is not the friars but "inparfit prestes and prelates of holy churche" (XXII. 229) – that is, the secular clergy. Finding the friars willing to help but incompetent (line 231), Conscience receives some advice from Nede. It is for covetousness that the friars wish to have cure of souls, Nede says, and because of their poverty they will end up flattering:

> Late hem chewe as thei chose and charge hem with no cure!
> For lomere he lyeth þat lyflode moet begge
> Then he þat laboreth for lyflode and leneth hit beggares.
> And senne freres forsoke the felicite of erthe
> Lat hem be as beggares or lyue by angeles fode!   (XXII. 237–41)

Just as in his confrontation with Will, Nede is here once again a good judge of "faytours," but something we must realize about Nede is that, as with other personifications, his point of view is strictly limited to the point of view of what he personifies. Nede is someone who *approves of need* and who therefore wishes to *promote need*. A poetic personification functions by self-promotion (hence the popularity of this form in medieval satire) and if we lose sight of this *modus operandi* of personification allegory in judging Nede, he becomes simply an inexplicable turncoat, seeming to propound fraternal ideology in his first appearance and anti-fraternal ideology in his second.[39] In fact, in both cases he is simply being true to himself. In his advice to the dreamer he gives counsel on neediness and mendicancy, drawing upon orthodox doctrines of poverty; in his advice to Conscience he opposes the notion of the friars having cure of souls because this would remove their need – and Nede would have lost a lot of clientele. Ironically, although the point of view he expresses here is an anti-mendicant propagandist one, St. Francis himself would have sympathized with it. Francis envisioned the Minorites as an order which would hold to abject poverty as an assurance of humility and a foil against cupidity and the distractions of worldly goods. Francis himself might have said, "Lat hem be as beggares or lyue by angeles fode!" He believed that if the brothers were true to their ideals, God would provide. Still more ironic is the fact that for all the critical accolades Nede's advice to Conscience has received, in fact it runs counter to Langland's hope for the friars. Only a steady income will solve the fraternal problem in Langland's view, and although he is not clear about whether this should come through the friars having cure of souls (like secular clergy) or simply through Constantine's coffer (like regular clergy), or both, the basic message is obvious enough. The ideology of abject poverty – need – will have to go. There are too few men who can master this *ascesis* without perversion of its ideals.

Reformist apocalypticism and *Piers Plowman*

When, in the 1270s, the controversy reached what Gordon Leff calls its second phase (*Paris*, pp. 263ff.), the attacks of the anti-mendicant propagandists were becoming more and more shrill. In 1269 Gerard of Abbeville preached a sermon in a Franciscan church in which he claimed that the pastoral office was the highest degree of perfection and he laid much stress on the importance of temporal goods:

[He] accused the mendicants, in having renounced possessions, of attacking the position of the church; its endowments had been sanctioned both in scripture and by the Donation of Constantine. To demand their abdication was to undermine the church's authority and so fall into heresy. The church's care of souls depended on its being able to minister to those in need. It was upheld in this by the example of Christ's purse; why should he have had it if not because it was his intention also to bear it? ʼ (Leff, *Paris*, p. 264)

The secular polemicists, then, reached a position in which they had strenuously to defend ecclesiastical endowments and temporalities at the same time as they were drawing a number of invidious (and unpopular) distinctions between themselves and fellow clerics. Langland would have had trouble with a number of these arguments, notably their position on clerical temporalities and the view that unordained clerics should earn their living by manual labor, a point he counters in no uncertain terms in v. 61ff.

Therefore, even though Langland was no defender of the mendicant cause, we are left with the fact that the anti-mendicant propagandists held some key positions with which Langland would not have been totally comfortable. It is fair to say that his concerns were largely their concerns, and in many things they were his tutors, but he often arrived at rather different conclusions than they espoused. It is perhaps worth stressing once more that the mendicant literature often traveled in manuscript anthologies which carried *both* pro- and anti-mendicant treatises, so that anyone who was an avid reader of the one type of literature would also have known the other.[40] The issues of clerical *modus vivendi* and reform which the two sides hotly debated have so often in this literature an apocalyptic edge that by the fourteenth century poverty and prophecy were common polemical bedfellows.[41]

Although there is much in the seculars' polemics with which Langland would have disagreed, their pro-endowment stance perhaps stands out as the clearest issue which would have kept Langland out of their camp. Langland seems to have believed that the secular clergy should live by tithes and first-fruits and that their endowments were a corrupting force (XVII. 218ff.), while he felt that the excess in monastic endowments should go toward providing for the friars (v. 173ff.).

The concept of voluntary poor living as a remedy against pride and avarice obviously gripped the imaginations of thinkers like Langland, even though it was impossible for him finally to concur with the realities of mendicancy as a means of livelihood. Langland was completely different from William of St. Amour and his party on this score. If his means were often the same, his ends were totally different from theirs. While the anti-mendicants sought the dissolution of the mendicant orders (as we shall see, William's eschatology allows for the Church authorities to use their powers to stem the "Antichristian" flow), Langland seems to have thought them worth reforming. This difference in attitude becomes clearer when Langland's views are set against those of the leading anti-mendicant polemicist of his time, Richard FitzRalph.[42]

FitzRalph began his career with strong reformist ideals, not unlike Langland's. Although a detailed study of the thought and writings of the prelate cannot be undertaken here, a few brief observations on how FitzRalph's anti-fraternalism developed can be made, and these are illuminating for Langland scholars. To begin with, FitzRalph's abrasive, not to say pugnacious, personality and his purist or even literalist tendencies were probably the predisposing factors in his anti-mendicantism (Walsh, "Archbishop FitzRalph," p. 245). His rather sudden conversion to anti-fraternalism in 1350 (when only months before he had been on the friendliest terms with the friars) is explained by his latest biographer as having its roots in reformist interests: "on acquiring a large diocese to administer he was faced in an acute form with the problem of enforcing episcopal authority. The problem of the exempt religious who exercised a pastoral ministry was made more difficult by the tensions of a racially divided community" (Walsh, *Fitzralph*, p. 363). Scholars have tried to demonstrate that a growing anti-fraternalism is evident in his sermon-diary entries before this period,[43] but as Walsh points out, this is not easy to uphold: "The general criticism of ecclesiastical failings, of licentious and ignorant clergy, negligent prelates, greedy benefice-hunters, and pluralists which he repeatedly expressed in the Avignon sermons of 1338–44 might be deemed to apply more appropriately to the secular clergy" (Walsh, *FitzRalph*, p. 363). Like Langland, then, FitzRalph's attacks on ecclesiastical abuses had been non-partisan, a position which Langland, unlike FitzRalph, was able to maintain alongside anti-mendicantism. However, at about the same time as FitzRalph's change of heart occurred, he was appointed by Pope Clement VI to a commission "to investigate certain topics of dissension among the mendicant orders concerning property, dominion, possession, and the right of use, furthermore to examine that apostolic or evangelical poverty professed by the Franciscans" (Walsh, *FitzRalph*, p. 366). If Walsh is correct in her argument that FitzRalph's appointment to the commission predated his first dramatic anti-fraternal sermon, then it seems likely that it was his close study of the ideological basis of fraternalism and the literature of the extremist Franciscan Spiritual positions which turned his head. As John Fleming has suggested ("Antifraternalism"), scholars have too often ignored the "anti-fraternal" literature of the Franciscan Spirituals themselves as a source for anti-fraternalism in England. The purist severity and seemingly suprahuman expectations of the Franciscan Spirituals in their requirements for observance of St. Francis' *Rule* no doubt struck a sympathetic chord in FitzRaph as he studied their literature. It seems likely that Langland might have undergone a similar experience through his own reading of this literature, which looks to have been thorough. Where it brought out only wrath in a literalist like FitzRalph, in Langland it seems to have induced an equally intense but mixed reaction. Alongside his anger there is a strong attraction to the ideals which the friars had tried, and failed, to uphold. These stringent ideals are imaginatively gripping, but, probably, realistically impossible to most men. Still, to the perception of an urgent reformer and idealist, such literature could have fostered the impression that the whole fraternal community had flagrantly deserted the precepts of Francis. As Walsh says of FitzRalph, "His attitude to what had become a raison d'être of the mendicant orders seemed to be based on a rigid and literal interpretation of the rule of St. Francis which would have done credit to the extreme fundamentalists among the Fraticelli a generation earlier" (Walsh, "Archbishop FitzRalph," p. 231).

Certainly, FitzRalph begins the *Defensio curatorum* under the pretext of a simple desire for reform: "it is nou3t myn entent to counsaile, noþer axe destruccioun & vndoyng of þe ordres of beggers . . . but [to] consaile þat þese ordres schulde be brou3t to þe clennesse of her first ordenaunce" (Perry edition, p. 39, lines 5–10). However, FitzRalph's extremist tendencies soon emerge as it becomes apparent that, for him, there is no room in the Church hierarchy for the services of the friar; he even goes so far as to suggest that a parishioner commits deadly sin in allowing a friar to hear confessions or bury the dead (*ibid.*, p. 40ff). To maintain his extreme anti-fraternal position, FitzRalph must defend endowments (*ibid.*, p. 85, lines 18ff.) and denounce poverty as an evil in itself: "But riches is good hauyng & worþi to be loved of God, for he is richest of alle, & pouert is contrarie & ys priuacioun of riches; þanne pouert is evel; þanne pouert is no3t worþi to be loued for hit-silf aloon" (*ibid.*, p. 80, lines 21–24). Although Langland wrote realistically of the privations of poverty among the involuntary poor, these notions would not accord with his views of voluntary poverty and perfection.

The fact that FitzRalph got little support for his campaign against the friars at Avignon from the English bishops is perhaps the most telling evidence of his extremism. Walsh suggests that "the reluctance of powerful interests to commit themselves to FitzRalph's extreme position of total condemnation of the mendicant orders gave the dispute a localised and personal appearance" ("Archbishop FitzRalph," p. 244). She indicates that the response of most concerned prelates was to avail themselves of canonical machinery already in place to control fraternal abuses. "Thus they could continue to profit from having in the pastoral field communities of religious whose level of education and commitment was so much higher than that of the average parish curate" (*ibid.*). We see some of this awareness of the potential usefulness of the friars in Conscience's welcome to them (*Piers Plowman*, XXII. 244ff.). There can be little doubt of Langland's hope for their reform. There is, furthermore, historical evidence about the friars and their work in the fourteenth century which also lends weight to the view that such extreme anti-fraternalism as FitzRalph's was unwarranted:[44] for example, his charge that the friars were not interested in performing the less lucrative pastoral duties such as baptism and the last rites, "an accusation which must have caused particular resentment among those who had seen their confreres succumb in large numbers to the recent plague precisely because they had devoted themselves to the latter task" (Walsh, *FitzRalph*, p. 371).

Finally, evidence for the dissemination and ownership of FitzRalph manuscripts reveals that his campaign was most popular with the *possessionati*, that is, with those likely to be most threatened by the rise of the fraternal orders.[45] The manuscripts were usually owned by members of the episcopacy, educated seculars or endowed religious (Walsh, "Archbishop FitzRalph," p. 227). The mendicant controversies, not to mention the very existence of the mendicant orders with their ideological position on clerical possessions, were giving rise to much speculation about the confiscation of clerical property on account of the sinfulness of the clergy. FitzRalph and later anti-mendicant writers were constantly supporting the *possessionati* side of the disendowment question.[46] This issue therefore seems to have been regarded as an extension of the anti-mendicant controversies, because the same antagonists and battlelines were involved, although not all calls for disendowment can be traced directly to fraternal sources.[47] The concomitant appeal to papal (as opposed to royal) power is another area in which Langland does not display the usual anti-mendicant positions. Outside of what both of them had inherited from William of St. Amour, Langland shows little in common *ideologically* with FitzRalph, or with the anti-mendicant polemicist Uhtred of Boldon, despite Marcett's assertions to the contrary.[48]

Unlike William of St. Amour, who would have (at the very least) totally removed the friars from the pastoral field and reduced them to the traditional equivalent of monastic lay brothers, supported by their own manual labor, or unlike FitzRalph, who would have legislated the friars out of any realistic right to the lucrative priestly duties such as confession and burial,[49] Langland seems to have envisioned a role for the friars once they had been suitably reformed by the provision of a "fyndynge." The B-text version of the disendowment prophecy, which promises the friars a share in what "Gregories godchildren vngodly despended" (B. x. 330), suggests that, for Langland at least, the friars were worthy to live from the offerings of the faithful in the same way as other members of the clergy. For all his criticism of fraternal avarice, Langland seems to feel that their problem – unlike that of the monastic and secular clergy – is rooted in their *need*, not their wealth, and it is this which he seeks to redress. It is worth noting that Langland brandishes the example of the Templars before the complacent secular clergy and not, as William of St. Amour and FitzRalph would have done, before the friars (xvii. 208ff.; lines 217 and 233 especially refer to secular clergy). Langland seems more concerned with the problem of fraternal perversion of confession, caused, in his view, by the necessity of begging, than with questioning the friars' ecclesiastical rights to do pastoral work.[50] It is worth noting that Conscience does not rule out the possibility that the friars could have "cure" (xxii. 253), although he laments their large numbers (xxii. 254–72) with reference to a common anti-fraternal motif (Szittya, *Antifraternal Tradition*, pp. 280–82).

The differences between Langland's point of view, in ideological terms, and those of prominent anti-mendicant writers being read in fourteenth-century England are, I believe, larger than has been previously suspected. It remains for us to look at the apocalyptic aspects of this problem.

ANTI-MENDICANT APOCALYPTICISM AND THE ENDING OF *PIERS PLOWMAN*

William of St. Amour's apocalypticism itself has received little attention. Some scholars have suggested that it is not to be taken seriously.[51] However, as Dawson remarks very perceptively in a footnote to his study of William's ecclesiology, "William's writings show a recurrent interest in schemes of historical periodization and a strong belief that the present age is the climactic age of world history." He goes on to say that his "apocalyptic expectations were derived from traditional sources and were of the traditional pessimistic sort" unlike those of his fraternal opponents (Dawson, "William," p. 235). William's apocalyptic expectations are really just eschatological; that is, he believes (or wants his audience to believe) that the End is near and all the signs are there, waiting to be read by a latter-day Daniel like himself. Langland may well have taken his anti-fraternalism from William and his school, but his apocalypticism is an entirely different brand.[52] There is not a scrap of reformist apocalypticism in William's thought: his reasons for attacking the friars, unlike Langland's, were annihilistic, not reformist. Langland's use of this heavily eschatological writer in the last passus of *Piers Plowman* has led many critics to mistake his own apocalyptic intentions, but a careful reading of the *De periculis* set over against the poem reveals a rather different point of view. On this score Langland has more in common with William's enemies, the Franciscan Joachites, than with William himself.

William's view of historical periodization is not highly developed and it is all backward-looking; that is, he does not project any scheme of periodization into the future. His only historical schema looks back into the past in order to explain the present. In his third chapter he suggests that the pseudo-apostles are the third great persecution of history, as represented by the pale horse of Apocalypse 6. Unlike the persecutions of the red and the black horses earlier, the current one is not an open attack, yet such an attack is the worst yet.[53] He reminds the reader of Gregory's comment that "Nemo plus nocet in ecclesia Dei, quam qui perverse agens, nomen habet sanctitatis & ordinis . . ." (*De periculis*, p. 23).

The paranoia in William's view of the friars runs throughout the *De periculis*. In Chapter 4 (pp. 23–24) William compares the pseudo-apostles with the false magicians of Pharaoh (a motif which Langland may have picked up in *Piers Plowman* XXII. 377 where Peace says "The frere with his fisyk this folk hath enchaunted"). Prophesying that the princes and people will be turned away from the counsels of the prelates of the Church by these seducers, William paints a grim picture of a coming persecution of the true apostles (the secular clergy) based on Christ's warnings to the disciples in Matthew 10 of how they will be maltreated for his sake. Treating the friars as a heretical sect, William speaks of how the people will be led into error and will "lose the name of sheep" because they permit themselves to be seduced (*De periculis*, p. 24). Obviously William felt a certain amount of bitterness toward the laity as well as toward the friars on the score of fraternal popularity. He spares no melodramatic detail in his bid to rouse the bishops and princes of the Church, whom he often exhorts by name, to act now to prevent this rising evil. He finishes his fourth chapter with the familiar apocalyptic refrain that this persecution will bring more tribulation than ever before in world history.

William's eschatology (and it is an *eschatology* because he is talking about only the Last Days) is, as Dawson says, a thoroughly traditional one, based entirely on standard biblical texts. In Chapter 8 of the *De periculis* he goes to great lengths to prove that the last age of the world is now come and he puts forward the standard Augustinian scheme of the seven ages of world history:

in ultima aetate seculi sumus: post enim istam sextam aetatem, quae est pugnantium: cum qua currit septima aetas, quae est quiescentium . . . Item Joachim super Jerem[*iam*].[54] Omne tempus a 1200 ultra aestimo periculosum. Item ad Hebr. 10. Adhuc aliquantulum modicum qui venturus est veniet, & non tardabit . . . Item Matth. 20. Circa undecimam vero horam exiit, &c. Gloss. Undecima hora ab adventu Christi usque in finem mundi: & certum est, quod hujus undecimae jam transacti sunt 1264 anni. (p. 27)

What is really surprising about this passage is that in the midst of so much standard eschatological pessimism, William throws in the name of Joachim of Fiore as an authority – in view of the Joachite scandal which gave rise to William's polemics in the first place the citation is almost unbelievable. Clearly the Joachites had made quite an impact and even William of St. Amour, avowed enemy and accuser of the fraternal Joachites, felt that the citation was likely to be convincing. Even this apparently earnest use of Joachite prophecy, however, betrays William's fundamental lack of understanding of Joachism. For Joachim the coming of Antichrist in the thirteenth century was to be a watershed of history to be followed by a glorious renewal of Christian spirituality, not so much an end as a new beginning. William seems to have understood nothing of this system of thought. Many scholars have remarked in passing on the irony of William's dispute with a group who shared his apocalyptic mentality, but beyond the fact that both William and the Joachites shared forebodings about their own time, there is little to compare between the two.

William then suggests eight signs that the dangers of the End "do now press upon us," rather cleverly making the *Eternal Gospel* itself a sign of the End (*De periculis*, p. 27). Having successfully made the connection between the *Eternal Gospel* and the perverted doctrine which was expected in traditional eschatology to be preached at the time of Antichrist, William underlines the fact that the scandal occurred in the most shocking of places – the university ("ubi viget sacrae scripturae studium"). The abomination of desolation is upon us, he suggests – or is it? Drawing upon a favorite eschatological text, II Thessalonians 2:7–8 ("For the mystery of iniquity already worketh, only that he who now holdeth do hold, until he be taken out of the way. And then that wicked one shall be revealed . . ."), William snatches back the suggestion that Antichrist is all but arrived and takes advantage of Paul's cryptic comment to establish the heads of the secular clergy (the pope and the bishops) as the forces which stand between Antichrist and the Church.[55] Exegetes from the earliest times had scratched their heads over Paul's enigmatic statement: given the polemical interests of many apocalyptic thinkers it is hardly surprising that the role of "he who now holdeth" was usually assigned to the powers to whom the exegete was well disposed. The view William espouses is a standard interpretation, although in these circumstances it becomes a pointed exhortation to Church authorities to act now and deter the forces of Antichrist. It should be noted that this is the type of apocalyptic ideology for which Langland would not have had much sympathy. The last passus of *Piers Plowman* portrays almost the exact opposite of the pope and the bishops (or secular clergy in general) holding out against Antichrist: if any Peter is the champion of the forces for good for Langland it is not the present Peter, but a new one – Piers. The marked difference between Langland and a number of other writers of *ordo* prophecies is that, unlike most of them, Langland is not writing in partisan support for any particular clerical group. In a sense this is what allows him his truly reformist stance.

The third sign has received substantial attention elsewhere and so needs little elaboration here.[56] Under this head William portrays himself as a latter-day Daniel who interprets the handwriting on the wall for the benefit of the Church. Each of the three mysterious words of the original text of Daniel 5:26–28 is interpreted by William as signifying some tenet of the scandalous *Eternal Gospel*. The other signs all elaborate William's theories of the workings of the pseudo-apostles: their self-glorification, twisting of doctrine, specious holiness, seduction of the laity and so on. Only the fifth sign holds out hope for the future in the midst of the gloom of unrelieved condemnation: it predicts that the pseudo-apostles will at some point be blamed for their false sanctity and, following Matthew 24:10, it says the Church will be scandalized. But William's prophecy of the fall of the friars is one of revenge, not reform. Defaming a group of opponents on the basis of a load of trumped-up exegetical charges of pseudo-apostleship has virtually nothing to do with the school of later medieval apocalyptic-reformist thought – however widely one has to cast one's net to "create" such a school for the purposes of historical study, it is hard to make the net big enough to take in William of St. Amour. Apocalyptic thought is no stranger to black and white, partisan world views, but truly apocalyptic thought is more than this. Where other prophetic thinkers have a vision – a plan – for the future, William has only a desperate hope of annihilation of his enemies. For all Langland's anti-mendicantism, he does not make the friars carry the whole blame for the corruption of the Church and he does not envision their demise. The difference in viewpoint is fundamental and helps us to understand Langland's essential independence of his anti-mendicant sources.

I would like now to look briefly at another anti-mendicant work which, following William's *De periculis*, makes use of apocalyptic propaganda, and which may well have been known to Langland. William's tenets, of course, became the standards of anti-mendicantism, but later polemicists often chose not to emphasize the apocalyptic side of the charges.[57] Because Langland *did* it is important to note that anti-mendicantism found its way into prophetic as well as polemical form. A short anti-mendicant prophecy called (by its incipit) "Insurgent gentes," for example, became very popular in medieval England, where it circulated under the name of Hildegard of Bingen.

Hildegard seems to have been best known in England as the prophetess who predicted the coming of the friars. Her name appears in this context in several works of English anti-mendicant literature like *Pierce the Ploughman's Crede*, which cites Hildegard as an authority and offers a Middle English paraphrase of the opening line of "Insurgent gentes": "Herkne opon Hyldegare hou homliche he telleþ / How her sustenaunce is synne..." (lines 703–04).[58] It is not easy to discover the exact process by which Hildegard, who died decades before the inception of the mendicant orders, came to be associated with anti-mendicant propaganda, but it looks as if the story begins with the independent circulation of extracts from her letter to the clergy of Cologne, which, as we have seen, prophesied the disendowment and chastisement of the clergy at the hands of a coming group of pseudo-apostles.[59]

The Parisian propagandists in William's circle certainly knew of Hildegard's prophecies and used them as ammunition against the friars, to the extent of provoking a response on the subject from the English Franciscan John of Pecham.[60] Some anti-mendicant zealot went so far as to forge a prophecy which ran along the same lines as Hildegard's predictions to the clergy of Cologne had, but which suited the anti-mendicant propagandists' purposes much more exactly. The result was the rather un-Hildegardian doggerel "Insurgent gentes," which, although it predicts the rise of a group of false apostles as the original prophecy to the clergy of Cologne had, could never be mistaken for Hildegardian prose. Nevertheless, the prophecy began to circulate under Hildegard's name and was snatched up eagerly by anti-mendicant anthologists everywhere.[61] One fourteenth-century English propagandist, Peter Pateshull, a prolific writer of anti-fraternal poems and treatises (according to Bale), even wrote a commentary on Hildegard's prophecies against the fraternal orders, the *Vita fratrum mendicantium*, now lost.[62]

"Insurgent gentes" is of interest to us not just because it catalogues all the standard anti-mendicant charges in the guise of a prophecy, but because Langland may have alluded to it in one of his most vivid anti-fraternal episodes, the Feast of Patience (*Piers Plowman*, Passus xv). In this passage, the disgruntled Will has been noticing that the friar requires "mete of more cost" (line 47) rather than eating what is set in front of him (line 45a), and he notes further that because these luxuries are purchased "Of þat men myswonne" (line 48), they will suffer "*post-mortem*" bitterness unless they "synge for tho soules [i.e. of the donors] and wepe salte teres." (Unlike other anti-mendicant writers, but like most reformist apocalyptic writers, Langland is always careful to add a qualifier like this one, which holds out hope of repentance.) He then quotes an unidentified Latin tag, which states almost the same thing, but in stronger terms: "*Vos qui peccata hominum comeditis, nisi pro eis lacrimas et orationes effuderitis, ea que in deliciis comeditis, in tormentis euometis*" (line 51a). The opening of "Insurgent gentes" in most manuscripts "prophesies" the rising up of a group who will similarly "eat [from or live off] the sins of the people" ("quae comedent peccata populi").[63] The similarity in phrasing may suggest that Langland is echoing the popular prophecy[64] and, in effect, subtly reshaping its message: Langland's line is cast in the second person and holds out the option of reform ("*nisi pro . . .*"), both of which are basic stylistic features of the prophetic voice. "Insurgent gentes" also stresses, as Langland does at xv. 48, that the friars accept donations which are "myswonne" and promises that they will suffer bitterly for their life of pleasure here below: "Heu eciam tollent res a miseris raptoribus, spoliatoribus, perdonibus, furibus, latronibus, sacrilegiis, usurariis [this list continues at great length] . . . propter suasionem diaboli et dulcedinem peccati (?) et vitam delicatam infra breve transituram in saciatatem et dampnacionem eternam."[65] The prophecy also dwells on other charges which particularly exercised Langland, including the problems of able-bodied begging, spiritual and physical wanderlust and the temptation to flatter in order to win the necessities of life. These are just the usual anti-mendicant charges masquerading as prophecy and there is no evidence anywhere in "Insurgent gentes" of the kind of hope for reform which one sees in Langland, or indeed, in Hildegard's genuine writings.

The eschatological elements in William of St. Amour's writings found a more elaborate and sophisticated home in the final passus of *Piers Plowman* than they ever did in the likes of "Insurgent gentes." Turning now to the poem's final scene, I would like to emphasize some of the distinctions between Langland's use of anti-mendicantism here and the vitriolic tradition of the propagandists upon which he was drawing. Although I do not wish to emphasize differences to the exclusion of similarities, it seems to me that Langland uses this tradition in a rather different way and for rather different purposes than he has been given credit for doing. Let us begin with his view of clerical corruption.

After the dreamer's encounter with Nede at the beginning of Passus XXII, he falls asleep and dreams that he sees Antichrist "in mannes fourme" come and overturn "the crop of treuthe" (XXII. 51ff.). Langland's Antichrist is the type which apocalyptic writers referred to as a mystic antichrist: his attack is moral and spiritual rather than social or political. This particular attack of Antichrist is primarily an attack on the Church and it comes largely from within the Church's ranks. Corrupt clergy form the vanguard of the siege, and, contrary to what other scholars have assumed, the friars are not the only – or even necessarily the most reviled – of the clerical *bêtes noires*. Although Langland wants to make the friars fill an important slot in apocalyptic typology – and the fact of a pre-existing tradition obviously suited his purposes here very well – a careful reading of the passus does not entirely warrant a statement like Frank's: "There are attacks on evil churchmen throughout the last vision, but the fiercest charge is against the friars. The narrative ultimately focuses on them. They cause the final catastrophe. They are villains" (Frank, *Scheme*, p. 112).

The friars do indeed weaken Conscience's last defense, but Langland attributes this more to the fact that "they couthe nat wel here crafte" (XXII. 231) than to overt maliciousness. Throughout the passus Langland is able to draw upon the long-standing association of the friars with the pseudo-apostles of the Last Days, but the satirical tone which he reserves for the fraternal orders is somewhat different from the tone he uses to describe the attacks of other clerics. Unlike William of St. Amour, Langland does not make the friars the sole followers of Antichrist among the clergy:

> Freres folewed þat fende, for he ȝaf hem copes,
> And religious reuerensed hym and rongen here belles
> And al þe couent cam to welcome a tyraunt
> And alle hise as wel as hym, saue onelich foles.   (XXII. 58–61)

Leaven of malice: false apostles

What is interesting about this passage is that the friars are the only ones who are provided with an excuse or rationale for following antichrist ("for he ȝaf hem copes") – again, fraternal need is their Achilles' heel. Although there is much severity in Langland's treatment of the friars at various stages in the poem, there is nothing to compare with the direct, sacrilegious onslaught on the Church which Langland creates for the *secular* clergy in the attack of the "proute prestes" in XXII. 218ff.:

> "By þe Marie," quod a mansed prest, was of þe march of Ireland,
> "Y counte no more Consience, bi so y cache suluer,
> Then y do to drynke a drauht of goed ale!"
> And so sayde syxty of þe same contreye,
> And shoten aȝeynes hym with shotte, many a shef of othes,
> And brode-hokede arwes – goddes herte, and his nayles –
> And hadden almost Vnite and holynesse adowne.   (XXII. 221–27)

Even as the poem progresses into the final scene, based as it is largely on anti-mendicant motifs, Langland shows more restraint than he has been given credit for. At this point Conscience cries for help against "imparfit prestes and prelates" (not friars) and the friars come forward to offer to help. Conscience complains of a series of typical anti-mendicant charges (flattery, lines 235ff.; over-indulgence in "logyk," lines 250ff.; uncontrolled numbers, lines 253ff.), but none which he does not seem to feel could be overcome if the friars lived according to their rule (line 247). Conscience thus welcomes the friars into Holy Church (despite Nede's warning), on certain conditions, such as the requirement that the friars "leue logyk." This is precisely the point on which Langland portrays the friars as falling. Langland's argument seems to be that logic gives the friars a method of twisting the truth to suit their own purposes:

> Enuye herde this, and heete freres go to scole
> And lerne logyk and lawe and eke contemplacioun,
> And preche men of Plato and preuen hit by Seneca
> That alle thynges vnder heuene ouhte to be in comune.   (XXII. 273–76)

But while the friars are learning philosophy, Hypocrisy is already attacking Unity and Frere Flaterare's eventual "attack" – if such a peaceable and legal entry may be called an attack – is only upon the already wounded. The fact that the friars' entry is "ecclesiastically legal" is, of course, part of William of St. Amour's point: the friars can do most damage, he says, because they are "familiar" enemies and their hypocrisy allows them this cover, but the friars have no monopoly even on hypocrisy in *Piers Plowman* and hypocrisy is the key charge of all anti-mendicant propagandists. It is interesting that Langland portrays the friar as going through all the right motions: he receives permission from the ecclesiastical authorities and enters through the front door.[66] Langland could well have charged the friars, as so many anti-mendicant writers did, with performing pastoral duties without episcopal license – but he does not. He shows none of the eagerness which the anti-mendicant writers did to lay blame everywhere it can be imagined.

Reformist apocalypticism and *Piers Plowman*

The poem ends with the best known of William of St. Amour's charges being played out within the walls of Unity. Sire *Penetrans-domos* enters and incapacitates Contrition by easy penance. In William's writings the *penetrans domos* charge works on two levels: the friars were thought to be illicitly entering not only the confessional but also the pastoral field. The *domus* that is being penetrated, then, for William, is on one level the individual conscience, on another level the pastoral work of the Church (Szittya, *Antifraternal Tradition*, p. 285). As Szittya says, the friars have forced themselves upon the collective conscience of Unity, and Piers, who is the head of all the confessors (see XXII. 320), is called upon to save the Church. To what extent Langland's treatment of Conscience is indebted to William of St. Amour it is hard to say. In *Piers Plowman* it is Contrition who "lyeth adreint" (XXII. 377) and Conscience is able to survive the attack and go on pilgrimage to seek Piers. If, as Szittya has suggested, Conscience is here as much a figure of the Church as of the individual Conscience, the last lines of the poem fall into a slightly different perspective. The Church does not, as in the *De periculis*, reject the friars and preside over their demise (*De periculis*, p. 30); rather it seeks the reform of the friars through providing them with a livelihood and, presumably, the reform of all clerics through Piers' destruction of pride.

In one sense the whole of *Piers Plowman* is, as Burdach says, written against false prophets,[67] and it was thus most convenient for Langland to make use of an already established eschatological tradition of pseudo-prophets coming before the End Time. Langland clearly drew upon the anti-fraternal tradition in order to make a reformist point, but we should not confuse his motives with those of the propagandists who preceded him. They sought revenge where Langland seems to seek only reform. Langland seems to have taken up anti-mendicantism, as I have said, for a number of reasons. Among those which I can discern (and there may well be others), are his desire to use it as a tool of reform and his irritation with the mendicants' abuse of mendicancy – a manner of living which he portrays his dreamer as leading and which he may himself have led and which, in any case, he seems to believe sanctifiable in the right hands. Finally, I believe that he took up anti-fraternalism as yet another apocalyptic tool. It suited his need to express the state of crisis he saw in the Church. Langland broadened his attack to include more than the mendicants in his portrayal of Church crisis in the last passus, but he was able to adapt William of St. Amour's schema to suit both his very different apocalyptic view of history and his more even-handed view of where the clerical corruption in the Church lay. Both his apocalypticism and his sense of clerical corruption are broader and less partisan than William's. As we have seen, Langland did not expect the Last Judgment immediately and he looked for a *renovatio* which is nowhere evident in William's use of traditional eschatology. William would have been scandalized by Langland's attacks on the secular clergy and FitzRalph would have classed Langland among the pseudo-apostles themselves for his attack on clerical endowments. Certainly, Langland has less faith in the Church hierarchy than they seem to have had.

Langland exhibits a stronger sense of justice and a greater soul than any of the propagandists he drew upon. And his sense of apocalyptic vision outruns the famous eschatology of William of St. Amour so fast as to make comparison difficult. We have come to expect from Langland a more subtle, thoughtful and evocative use of the intellectual traditions which came his way than most writers in those traditions ever mastered. His use of anti-mendicant material is no different. Langland is unhappy with fraternalism as it now stands and wishes fervently for change, but he rises above the cowering, acerbic hatred of the anti-mendicant partisans. The distinctions, however, are subtle, and though it is tempting to snatch up William of St. Amour as a key to all the anti-mendicant eschatology in *Piers Plowman*, the petty and vengeful eschatology which he bequeathed to the later Middle Ages cannot adequately illuminate for us Langland's larger, more constructive vision of the role of the friars in the divine plan.

5

Leaven of hope: new leadership and Joachite apocalypticism

INTRODUCTION: JOACHITE APOCALYPTICISM IN MEDIEVAL ENGLAND

. . . the problem of poverty and the nature of evangelical perfection introduced a new element into the outlook of the later thirteenth and fourteenth centuries. Largely under the influence of Joachism and the call for a return to first apostolic principles, the present church came increasingly to be contrasted to the life of Christ and the apostles. There was a growing sense that the church had betrayed its primitive ideal . . . A return could be made only by the disendowment of the church, taking it to the poverty, humility, and simplicity preached and practiced by Christ and his disciples. The disputes of the schools went far beyond their walls.   (Leff, *Paris*, pp. 269–70)

In this short paragraph Gordon Leff collects and focuses the issues and themes which will concern us in this section. By Langland's time so many apocalyptic strands were interwoven among these issues that it is impossible to study either separately. *Piers Plowman* reflects this faithfully. Among the issues that had coalesced around an apocalyptic sense of the need for reform were the problems of evangelical poverty and perfection, the sense that the Church had betrayed its primitive ideals and the related perception that this could be corrected only by clerical chastisement, disendowment and humiliation. The growing tendency among certain thinkers to compare the present Church, and especially the clergy, to the life of Christ and the apostles, and to question the discrepancies, came about, as Leff says, "largely under the influence of Joachism." Just *how* largely is a question that has excited much scholarly debate in recent years,[1] but even those scholars who have argued that the influence of Joachism has been overestimated would agree that its influence was considerable.

The dissemination of Joachite ideas in Southern Europe was widespread and has received much scholarly attention, but the influence of Joachism in Northern Europe, including England, is a much less well-charted territory.[2] England presents particular problems to the scholar of apocalyptic reform literature for a number of reasons. While the genuine works of Joachim were certainly available in thirteenth- and fourteenth-century England, they seem frequently to have been known or used in an edited form, perhaps, as Beryl Smalley has suggested, to avoid dangerous associations.[3] The result is that some of the most characteristically Joachite teachings, like the belief in a coming "age" of the Holy Spirit, are absent from a number of English treatments of Joachim's ideas.[4]

Furthermore, the radical, rigorist segment of the Franciscan Order, the so-called

Franciscan Spirituals, did not flourish in England the way they did in certain other countries.[5] The Franciscan Spirituals were among the biggest exporters or disseminators of Joachite doctrine and therefore, with a few exceptions, England missed out on – or partly missed out on – one of the main medieval sources of Joachism by its relative lack of contact with Franciscan Spiritualism. Heretical groups, whose affinities with reformist thought we have noted before, were also important disseminators of Joachite doctrine, albeit often in a rather distorted form, and England, once again, turns up virtually no evidence of heresy until the Wycliffite period.[6]

All this does not mean that there was no Joachism in England. It simply means that one cannot approach the study of Joachism in England in quite the same way in which Continental Joachism has often been studied by scholars. In England there are no easy answers or readily recognizable major sources of Joachism. Lacking either a strong fraternal or heretical tradition of Joachism, English Joachism expressed itself in other, and more fragmented ways. Several English chroniclers and writers mentioned or made use of Joachite material, as Continental chroniclers did. Prophecies, especially of the shorter semi-political Joachite variety, are legion in English manuscripts.[7] Certain Joachite writers did achieve a surprising degree of popularity in England (John of Rupescissa, for instance) and certain pseudo-Joachite works survive in numerous insular manuscripts (*Super Esaiam*, for example), easily outrunning the English survival rate of the genuine works of Joachim.[8] Finally, the apologetics and controversies of various clerical orders carried Joachism to England.[9] Though Joachism came up on the receiving end of anti-mendicant literature, which *was* popular in England, even this type of bad press played its part in the dissemination of Joachite ideas.

Morton Bloomfield turned to the English literature of monastic philosophy in his attempt to solve the problem of the comparative lack of insular sources for Joachite study and found evidence of the "quiet" apocalypticism characteristic of monastic circles and far removed from the active, sometimes revolutionary, roles which Joachism had played in the history of groups like the Fraticelli abroad.[10] Interestingly, this "quiet" apocalypticism of monastic ideology is probably truer to the spirit of Joachim of Fiore than the militant apocalypticism of many of the groups who marched under (or thought they were marching under) his banner. The strong interest in reading the meaning of history through the signs and patterns of biblical exegesis, the conviction that the coming Golden Age would represent not so much a material as a spiritual *renovatio* of mankind, the expectation of a new age of contemplation and intensified spiritual fervor in which all communities would become to some extent monastic communities, are all marks of true Joachite thought. There are certainly elements of what Bloomfield called "monastic philosophy" in *Piers Plowman* and the fact that this approach is not the one taken here should not be interpreted as casting doubt on its validity. Rather, I would like to pursue a different and, I believe, somewhat more direct route to understanding Langland's awareness of Joachism. In what follows we will be looking at some of the pseudo-Joachite prophecies which are known to have circulated in thirteenth- and fourteenth-century England and at the ideology, world view and prognosis for the future, especially for the future of the Church, which such prophecies reflect, in order to illuminate similar ideas in *Piers Plowman*. In so doing I will be using the term "Joachite" in its widest possible sense; moreover, works which are not really Joachite in ideology but which traveled under Joachim's name will also be discussed.

Even from the somewhat fragmented evidence of Joachism in fourteenth-century England, one can find ample testimony to English awareness of this type of prophecy and its ideological message. Among early pseudo-Joachite prophecies *Super Esaiam* and *De oneribus prophetarum* are well represented among surviving manuscripts, and seem to have been better known in England than even *Super Jeremiam*.[11] Also popular in insular manuscripts is the pseudo-Joachite *Vaticina de summis pontificibus*, as was the *De semine scripturarum*, which is not a Joachite work but rather a stray adopted pseudonymously into the Joachite family. John of Rupescissa, among the most popular of later Joachite writers, was frequently read in England; his *Vade mecum in tribulatione* survives in a large number of insular manuscripts and was even translated into English. Alongside the major works there are a number of short prophecies which traveled widely in English manuscripts and which carried the Joachite message to a wider audience in their concise, though often very obscure, form. For reasons of time and space we will be considering only some of the religious elements of these works and leaving aside the political concerns which so often obsessed their authors. Since Langland shows almost no interest in Continental politics, and a lively concern with the need for and possibility of Church reform, this approach seems justified.

As I suggested in chapter 4, anti-mendicantism exploited the apocalyptic tendency to divide the world into true and false apostles and to envision the future as a perpetual battle between the two – a battle which leaves the future renewal or destruction of the Church hanging in the balance. While this is by no means characteristic of Joachite prophecy only, it comes as close as any single notion to capturing the mentality of later Joachite thought as it developed in the hands of disciples and imitators less subtle than the abbot of Fiore himself. This perpetual battle between true and false apostles seems to be at the heart of Langland's apocalyptic message as well, as a study of the themes common to *Piers Plowman* and to Joachite thought shows. In what follows we will look at Joachite notions of crisis in the Church and expectations of renewal, themes of clerical chastisement, disendowment and hopes for radical new leadership from outside the established hierarchy of clerical power.

LABORING TOWARD SPIRITUAL UTOPIA: LANGLAND AND JOACHIM OF FIORE (1135–1202)

"Apocalypse," writes Frank Kermode, "depends on a concord of imaginatively recorded past and imaginatively predicted future, achieved on behalf of us who remain 'in the middest.'"[12] This perception of apocalyptic methodology is true of no writer so much as of Joachim of Fiore, abbot of Curazzo and later founder of the Florensian order. Joachim is perhaps now best known for his highly elaborate, rather academic systems of concords for the interpretation of the entire course of history, yet some of his writings also reveal the moralistic urgency of a practical prophet. Like Hildegard of Bingen, with whom his name was so often yoked in later writings, Joachim reflects some of the apparent contradictions of the prophetic personality. While yearning for the peace of study and contemplation, away from even the administrative duties of the monastery, Joachim was also an internationally known figure with an urgent message for the secular world and its leaders.[13] Both writers were primarily interested in the role of the reformed Church in future history and concerned to warn their fellow clerics especially of the tribulations soon to come upon them. Like Hildegard, Joachim was directly or indirectly responsible for much of the religious prophetic ferment of the later Middle Ages, especially for the growth of the notion that the Church must suffer a great purgation before reform could be effected. Despite a number of differences, both writers were essentially similar in believing that a great flowering of spirituality and clerical purity would come about before the book of history would close for good.

The student of *Piers Plowman* can see in Joachim a number of patterns of thought which will remind him of Langland: whether this is because Langland knew the works of Joachim directly or whether it is simply because he knew something of the apocalyptic reformist prophecy which Joachim helped foster, it is difficult to say. What we can say is that there are many elements in his apocalyptic thought which are difficult to explain without reference to the reformist prophetic tradition which Joachim so heavily influenced.[14] If Langland knew any of Joachim's ideas, I believe that it is more likely that they came to him through contact with some of the popular pseudo-Joachite works. However, as Bloomfield has suggested (*Apocalypse*, p. 160), there is at least a possibility that he knew something of the genuine works as well, although most of the parallels between Joachim and Langland seem too general to constitute definitive sources. Some of these will be noticed below, but a detailed study of the *genuine* works of Joachim in relation to Langland is not the purpose of the present book. The discussion of Joachim's ideas which follows is meant mainly as an introduction to the later Joachite thought known in England.

Joachim used several numerical patterns and typological concords between the Old and New Testaments to illuminate the course of history and to explain his sense of impending crisis.[15] His best-known pattern is based on a Trinitarian reading of history: the "age" of the Father or the first *status*, that of the Son or the second *status* and that of the Holy Spirit or the third *status* yet to come.[16] For Joachim, during the Old Testament period spiritual leaders had been laymen ("ordo conjugatorum") and had labored to reveal the Law; during the second *status* spiritual leaders had been clerics ("ordo clericorum") and labored to teach the message of Christ's Passion and Resurrection. During the third *status*, however, the spiritual leaders would be monks or hermits ("ordo monachorum" or "eremitarum")[17] and would oversee a new time in the liberty of the Spirit, because "Ubi spiritus domini, ibi libertas."[18]

This threefold shift from the labor of teaching the Law, to the Gospel, to the interiorized work of contemplation has certain general parallels in the development of *Piers Plowman*, especially in the progressive changes of Piers throughout the poem. A number of scholars have sought to pin down what Frank has called the "haunting through obscure harmonies" between Joachite doctrine and *Piers Plowman* by seeing parallels between Dowell, Dobet and Dobest and Joachim's Trinitarian scheme of history.[19] There are other possibilities, however, which do a little less violence to the poem and a little more justice to Joachim's sense of history. One of these is to focus on the role of Piers himself within the poem and the second is to view the end of *Piers Plowman* as occurring at roughly the same point of history as Joachim placed his own time, that is to say, at the *transitus* through crisis to a new age of renewal.[20] We will begin with the first of these possibilities.

For Joachim the three Trinitarian "ages" were an organic unity and a way of explaining what he saw as the grand movement of history toward spiritual freedom and from preoccupation with the "letter" to the "spirit." In *Piers Plowman*, Piers is first seen as a teacher of the Law and as one who is concerned with the literal and physical aspects of "doing well." His sudden "conversion" at the end of the *Visio* comes about as a displacement of physical concerns in favour of spiritual ones, a point which is evident in the B-text Tearing of the Pardon scene, with its implied denunciation of literalism, and in Piers' later teachings (and very comings and goings), which are both elusively eremitical and Christ-like. By the end of the poem Piers is sowing the Gospel rather than seeds and his agricultural tools have taken on a spiritual significance. Piers' movement from the labor of the *Visio* to an elusive mixture of itinerant eremiticism and Christian ministry in the *Vita* could be given a Joachite reading in the sense that Joachim perceived spiritual leadership as having left the duties of the "ordo conjugatorum" behind after the Old Testament period. In his view, another important shift would come in the transition to the third *status*, after which the emphasis in spiritual leadership would move from the "ordo clericorum" to the "ordo eremitarum." However, the seeds of the third *status* can be found, in his view, in earlier spiritual leaders such as Elijah and the Old Testament prophets, and later in St. Benedict and the monastic movement. The second *status* or "age" of the Son, then, for Joachim, had been a period of development for the spiritual life which would later come to full fruition in the *status* of the Holy Spirit and the entire course of history could be seen as the gradual blossoming of the eremitical life. After Piers apparently leaves behind his wife and family,[21] he takes on an increasingly clerical, even at times eremitical role in his appearances in the *Vita*, almost as if he were re-enacting the historical development of spiritual leadership as Joachim saw it.[22] Furthermore, Piers' anti-intellectualism (xv. 129ff.) and the very fact of Langland's choice of a reforming spiritual leader from outside of "establishment" circles could be markers of later Joachite thought and we will look at these themes more closely a little later. The point here is that Piers is partly a figure of the historical development of spiritual leadership through time, but we note that his full potential is only suggested and never realized in the poem itself.

There is a second possibility for a Joachite structural reading of the poem. In Joachim's terms, Langland breaks off the poem at the point of *transitus* into the third "age." For Joachim the *status* of the Spirit had not yet come, but it was imminent. To reach it the Church had to make a difficult *transitus* through the corruption and tribulation of the present times. Alongside his Trinitarian scheme he spoke of a pattern created by dividing the two Testamental ages into seven periods each. By drawing a series of concords between the patterns of persecutions in the Old Testament and the New Testament periods, Joachim could predict the future of the end of the New Testament period. He concluded that his own age was about to suffer the double tribulation of the sixth time in his exegesis in the *Liber figurarum* of the meaning of the seven-headed dragon of Apocalypse 12:3.[23]

Instead of trying to make *Piers Plowman* fit into a Trinitarian scheme of history in which the Dobest section of the poem has to be regarded as the "age" of the spirit *fully realized*, it might make more sense to see the *Visio* as a figural portrayal of the Old Testament period and the *Vita* of the New Testament period, with a vision of the Church in a state of crisis, making its difficult *transitus* into the seventh period of renewal,[24] a time which Langland talks about but does not portray. As Joachim says in the *Liber concordia* (Book II, pt. 1, ch. 2) the difference between the two ages "is that those of the Old Testament refer more to the flesh, these of the New more to the spirit, albeit it must be recalled that there were indications of the spirit in the former, reminders of the flesh in the latter" (in McGinn, *Apocalyptic Spirituality*, p. 122, translated from Daniel's edition). This qualification is important and Joachim is always stressing that the characteristic features of any later period have their roots in earlier ones. Likewise, a Joachite reading of *Piers Plowman* would, I believe, most helpfully identify the descent of the Holy Spirit and the passing out of the diverse gifts of Grace as the pentecostal roots of a coming dispensation of the Spirit *beyond* Passus XXII, not as the arrival of that dispensation in Dobest.

Indeed, Joachim's view of the *status* of the Holy Spirit is often similar to Langland's in that it tends toward chiliasm, or, to use a less suitable word, utopianism. Prefacing the diagrammatic explanation in the *Liber figurarum* of his "utopian" vision of the third *status*, Joachim quotes Ephesians 4, on the giving of spiritual gifts to the Christian community: "'He gave to some the gift to be Apostles, some to be Prophets, some to be Evangelists, others to be pastors and doctors, for the fulfillment of the saints in their ministry in the building up of the Body of Christ, *until we all come together into the unity of faith* and the recognition of the Son of God' (Eph. 4:11–13)" (emphasis mine; *Liber figurarum*, ed, Tondelli *et al.*, Table XII, trans. McGinn, *Apocalyptic Spirituality*, p. 142). In *Piers Plowman*, the building of Unity (which draws upon Ephesians 4 just as Joachim does) tries to achieve on the spiritual level what Piers' organization of the ploughing of the half-acre tried to do on the physical or "fleshly" level. It is, in fact, possible to read *Piers Plowman* as the progress of attempted utopianism through the literal and active stages to the spiritual and contemplative – although the word "contemplative' here, used in the context of Joachim's "ecclesia contemplativa," denotes not so much a *retiring from* society as a *reorganization of* society into various groups, each following a manner of life and devotional regimen appropriate to its level of "perfection." Joachim, like Langland, has the "utopian" tendency toward social and religious organization. In the *status* of the Holy Spirit Joachim foresaw what

McGinn refers to as a monastic utopia (*Apocalyptic Spirituality*, p. 111) in which all members of society can participate, according to their spiritual capabilities, in the "ordo eremitarum" (or "monachorum"). In the *Liber figurarum* diagram he divides society into seven groups,[25] each residing in a type of monastic oratory. Joachim sets out instructions, much like a monastic rule, for the behavior, dress and physical and spiritual labors of each group, and in so doing gives a sense of what is appropriate to the various degrees of active, mixed and contemplative lives. The oratory of the laity is reminiscent of Piers' attempt to organize the half-acre:

No idle person will be found among these Christians, someone who will not earn his bread that he may have that from which to help those in need (Eph. 4:28). Let each one work at his own craft, and the individual trades and workers shall have their own foremen. Anyone who has not worked up to capacity should be called to account by the Master and censured by all. Food and clothing will be simple as befits Christians. Worldly garb will not be found among them nor dyed clothing. Honest and approved women will spin wool for the need of Christ's poor, and they will serve like mothers of the other women, instructing the young women and girls in the fear of God. They will give tithes to the clerics of all they possess for the support of the poor and strangers, and also for the boys who are studying doctrine. They do this so that in case they have more than they need and the rest have less, at the command of the Spiritual Father the surplus will be taken from those who have more and given to those who have less so that there may be no one in need among them but all things held in common.

(*Liber figurarum*, ed. Tondelli *et al.*, Table xII, trans. McGinn, *Apocalyptic Spirituality*, p. 148)

Langland's utopian experiments both fail – or partially fail – but the poem ends with hope of a third attempt through the clerical reform which Piers will carry out. Langland realized that all attempts up to the present time to establish "Jerusalem" had been imperfect, but like Joachim he praises the courage and perseverance of those in earlier times who tried – whether they were founders of religious orders or the Desert Fathers or Old Testament figures like David or Moses. Only once does Langland make his typological view of history and its prophetic potential explicit in biblical terms, that is, in his prophecy of a new David to come, but Piers is the motivating force behind all three of Langland's reformist utopian experiments – the two portrayed in the poem and the one which Conscience seeks at the end. We will return to this problem later, but perhaps it should be said here that whether or not we choose to read these features in the poem as evidence of a genuine Joachism or as simply analogous to Joachim's kind of typological and historicist utopianism is perhaps a question for each reader to decide for himself. No Joachite reading of *Piers Plowman* that I know of is absolutely apt – but many of the parallels are, to use Frank's term again, haunting.

The notion of spiritual chiliasm is inextricably tied up with the important Joachite theme of Church reform and the question of reform brings us to the difficult issue of Joachim's relations with the Church. Joachim himself remained a loyal son of the Church and in his "Testamentary Letter" asserts that he wishes all his writings to be submitted to the papacy for correction.[26] However, his views on the Trinity were condemned at one point, and his career as a monastic leader and reformer was at times stormy.[27] Many passages in Joachim's works are quite radical in certain ways and often leave themselves open to revolutionary interpretations. As he proved in his own life, Joachim was not afraid of the idea of abandoning a traditional form in favor of something new if he thought that the quality of spiritual life would be enhanced. In this he differs from the kind of reformist thinker whose gaze only looks longingly back to a first pristine state either in the beginnings of an order or in the primitive Church itself.[28] In his *Tractatus super quatuor Evangelia* he discusses the transition in quality of religious life which will be created in the third *status* with a shift from the active, worldly preoccupations of the present (symbolized by Peter) to a more contemplative life (symbolized by John). To support this notion of "Peter" yielding to "John" he writes, "Can he who sees that he will be succeeded in such fruit grieve that partial perfection in him will cease when it is followed by universal perfection? No, no! Let such a thought be far from Peter's succession! Let not envy languish over the perfection of the spiritual order . . ." (trans. McGinn, *Visions*, pp. 135–36, from Buonaiuti's edition, pp. 87–88). In the hands of any disciple with a more literal mind than Joachim's (and there were many) this suggestion of the old order yielding to a newer one was heady stuff. As Bernard McGinn has said, "The Joachite tradition was a quasi-revolutionary element in the later Middle Ages, and though his would-be disciples went far beyond the Abbot of Fiore in many ways, he cannot be absolved of all responsibility for what was to come" (*Visions*, p. 129).

Not all those who took up Joachism did so in opposition to authority, but there can be little doubt that Joachim's writings appealed most to those who were dissatisfied with the institutionalized Church and the powers of its hierarchy. As McGinn has shown, certain of Joachim's ideas and symbols became instruments for criticism of the Church from the thirteenth century onwards: "Joachim's stress on the domination of the spiritual and charismatic over the institutional and rational in the future church was diametrically opposed to the forces that triumphed in the thirteenth century" (*Visions*, p. 129). Students of *Piers Plowman* are familiar with just such juxtapositions. Episodes like the Feast of Patience, for example, are virtually dramatizations of this conflict between "the spiritual and charismatic" on the one hand and the "institutional and rational" on the other. The latter is well represented by the cynical realism of the friar in response to Patience's idealism, "This is a *Dido* . . . a dysores tale!" (xv. 171). In spite of his realism, one usually feels, as in this scene, that Langland has given his heart to the idealists. Like Joachim, Langland's spirituality is intense and imaginative.

Important among Joachim's potentially revolutionary themes was the concept of the "Babylon" within the Church's walls. In an open letter to all the faithful, Joachim distinguished the hypocrites and backsliders as a separate group: "If you consider the crowd of those men who to the full measure of their damnation are counted as members of the Christian religion, you have what is called the first Babylon . . . The multitude of the wicked have prevailed because the just were tepid" (trans. McGinn, *Apocalyptic Spirituality*, pp. 115–16).[29] Babylon came to play an important role in the apocalyptic thought of later Joachite prophecies as a label for clerical corruption within the Church, against which a remnant of the faithful (a second important theme) would hold out until the coming age of spiritual renewal. In Langland's apocalyptic grammar this remnant is represented by the few "foles" who hold out against the "fendes lymes" for the love of Piers Plowman (XXII. 77). Joachim believed that Antichrist already stood upon the threshold of the age, but like Langland he did not see this as the End. In the *Liber concordia* he writes: "In this generation first of all the general tribulation will be completed and the wheat carefully purged of all tares, then a new leader will ascend from Babylon, namely a universal pontiff of the New Jerusalem, that is, of Holy Mother the Church" (trans. McGinn, *Visions*, p. 135; Book IV, pt. 1, ch. 45 in Daniel's edition).

A third apocalyptic theme, then, which Joachim left as a legacy to the later Middle Ages was the concept of a reforming (or "angelic") pope.[30] This notion is not fully developed in the original works of Joachim, but became an important concept in the thought of later disciples, giving rise to some of the most popular religious prophecies of the Middle Ages. It is certainly possible to analyze Langland's Piers from the standpoint of the Joachite vision of the reformed and spiritualized papacy. This is a point to which we will return after we have looked at some of the later developments of the angelic-pope themes, but for the present it can be said that Piers conforms to genuine Joachite thought in several ways. First of all, as we have noted, his dramatic conversion from social leader to spiritual leader, from plowman to "palmere," is reminiscent of the dramatic change in the papacy from "Peter" to "John" which would come about in the "age" of the Spirit. This change would bring about a more spiritualized, simplified role for the pope, who would now live a kind of eremitical life. But even though Langland really never shows us the post-reform Piers he so fervently hoped for, he does show us Piers' burgeoning development toward that powerful role of spiritual authority from his previous leadership of the half-acre society to his leadership in the building of Unity.

In Piers' changing incarnations, then, there could be something of the flavor of Joachite typology of the great spiritual leaders of history. Take for example Joachim's concord between Moses in the Old Testament period and St. Paul in the New Testament period (Reeves and Hirsch-Reich, *Figurae*, p. 7). A typological reading of Piers as the Moses who is both a lawgiver (VII. 213ff.) and a leader of a lost people through a wilderness,[31] or of Piers as a St. Paul whose mandate it is to build the post-pentecostal Church, would highlight both the development of Piers as a spiritual guide and the understated role of Old and New Testament history as one of the organizing principles of the poem as a whole. All of Joachim's typological figures, whether or not they were originally expressed in finite concords between the Old and New Testaments or in the open-ended series of concords which looked forward to the *status* of the Spirit, could (and did) create expectations of the rise of the type figure again in the future.[32] Piers too is ·perpetually expected: the Piers who will return to reform the Church has his roots, in Joachite terms, in the leadership of "Mosaic" and "Pauline" figures of the *Visio* and *Vita*.

Before there could be Church reform, however, Joachim, like most apocalyptic thinkers, believed that there had to be a chastisement and purgation. During the time of the opening of the fifth seal, "in qua nunc sumus," Joachim saw the persecution of the Church by the Roman Empire. He describes this in his "Commentary on an Unknown Prophecy" (edited in McGinn, "Joachim") in this way:

> There remains for us that other and worse Babylonian persecution, the fifth. "There has been an abundance of peace until the moon was taken away" (Ps. 71:7), that is, until the Roman Church, borne away in exile, lost the splendor of its brilliance. Since it is already in the cloud of darkness, there are persecutions left, the first of which will especially injure the clergy, while two following not long after will be against all in general . . .
> (trans. McGinn, *Visions*, p. 132, from "Joachim," p. 131)

This is the type of passage which later disciples were to fasten on, recycling and elaborating the imagery as well as the ideas, as we will see. It is evident from this passage that Joachim saw the fifth and sixth persecutions as coming in fairly quick succession, with the seventh added in upon the sixth to make the worst persecution in history.

Both the notion of an imminent persecution of the clergy (the fifth) and of a dual persecution (the sixth and seventh) which will be a *general* chastisement can be fit into Langland's apocalyptic scheme quite neatly. Especially at the end of the poem, the clergy are at the eye of the apocalyptic storm and Langland seems to feel that clerical rebuke is imminent, while apocalyptic events of a general or political sort are portrayed as somewhat more remote. As we have seen, the Antichrist of Passus XXII is largely a clerical demon, whereas "the worst" that is described in the "dark" prophecy at III. 477 is a general tribulation. Langland may even be alluding to the Joachite dread of the sixth persecution or, in a better-known periodization, of the sixth *age* in his symbolism of the "six sonnes" in III. 478.

It is possible to do a Joachite reading of Langland's prophecy involving many of these elements at the end of Passus III:

> Ac ar this fortune falle fynde me shal the worste
> Be sixe sonnes and a ship and half a shef of arwes;
> And the myddell of þe mone shal make þe Iewes turne
> And Saresines for þat syhte shal syng *Credo in spiritum sanctum*,
> For Machameth and Mede shullen mishap þat tyme,
> *Quia melius est bonum nomen quam diuicie multe.* (III. 477–81a)

As we have seen, "the worst" tribulation in Joachim's terms was the one expected in his own time. The six suns might be a reference to either the sixth persecution or the close of the sixth age – both dreadful times in Joachite theory. But tribulation always ultimately means renewal in this type of prophecy and Langland's hint that these obscure symbols will herald the conversion of the non-Christian peoples is typical of this mentality. The ship might, as J.A.W. Bennett suggested, represent the ship of Peter, which is also an important symbol in Joachite thought, a figure of the "ark" of the true Church being tossed on the seas of tribulation. The ship, especially in pseudo-Joachite prophecy, preserves the remnant who will save the world in the next age. The "half a shef of arwes" (that is, twelve arrows) may, as Schmidt suggests,[33] represent the twelve apostles who were to judge the tribes of

Israel at the Last Judgment (Matthew 19:28); however, since Langland is not talking about the End of the World here, it might make more sense to give this symbol a Joachite reading and see it as representing the twelve "spiritual men" ("viri spirituales") who, in concord with the twelve patriarchs of the Old Testament and the twelve apostles in the New Testament, would renew the faith in the "age" of the Holy Spirit.[34] The middle of the moon as a symbol of the Passover (Schmidt, *B-text*, p. 313), the one religious feast which Jews and Christians share, is typical of Langland's acute awareness of what Christians have in common with non-Christians.[35] It would certainly be appropriate that the Jews should be converted at the feast when both Jews and Christians give thanks for having been saved from the Angel of Death.

If this reading is correct (and we have no way of knowing whether it is or not), then all the symbols would be somehow associated with the saving of mankind from tribulation and death. The sixth period in any of the Joachite systems of periodization is always one of the expected dangerous *transitus* to freedom and salvation, and this is certainly what it heralds in Langland's prophecy.

THE CHURCH IN CRISIS: APOCALYPTIC THEMES IN *PIERS PLOWMAN* AND PSEUDO-JOACHITE PROPHECY

What follows is a survey of some of the most widely circulated pseudo-Joachite prophecies known to be generally available in fourteenth-century England. They have been selected with a view to providing some background to the key apocalyptic issues in *Piers Plowman*, notably, the concern with distinguishing false apostles, a sense of crisis of leadership, a preoccupation with clerical poverty and the need for repristination through (often) violence and disendowment and, finally, the attempt to periodize history, both past and future. We will consider, briefly, various prophecies or sections of prophecies which illuminate these themes, ending with a more detailed look at the most popular Joachite prophet read in medieval England, John of Rupescissa. Among the first crop of pseudo-Joachite works *Super Jeremiam*, *Super Esaiam* and *De oneribus prophetarum* were especially widely read. Such was the popularity of these works that by Langland's time they seem to have been more generally familiar and accessible than Joachim's own writings. This seems to have been particularly true of England, where copies of *Super Esaiam* and *De oneribus* especially were quite widely disseminated.[36] In these works one finds a heightening of Joachim's criticism of the "Babylonian" or "carnal" Church and a shift in emphasis toward political concerns.[37]

Most important from our point of view is the new attitude towards the papacy in particular and the wealthy Church hierarchy in general. From Joachim's more positive view of the papacy (Reeves, *Influence*, pp. 395–97), the early pseudo-Joachite texts have moved to a negative outlook. *Super Jeremiam*, a work which seems to have been known in England largely through secondary sources, opens with a prediction of disaster for the Church and sees this prefigured in the downfall of Eli and his sons – a theme and exemplum which we find in the Prologue to the C-text of *Piers Plowman* as well (lines 95ff.).[38] In the Prologue, the exemplum arises as

Leaven of hope: new leadership

Langland has been denouncing corrupt and irresponsible practices of the secular clergy. The story of "Offnies synne and Fines his brother" is told to suggest what mischief arises "thorwe two fals prestis" (lines 106–07). In *Super Jeremiam* the story is cited with a similar purpose: the two brothers represent the priests and bishops of the Church, and their unfortunate father, Eli, represents the pope. Just as in the biblical story, "Heli" will die, along with his two "sons," because he has been guilty of gross negligence and of conniving at clerical fraud. The anonymous Joachite writer therefore implies that the secular clergy, from pope down to parish priest, will be destroyed and that a new order, represented by Samuel, will take their place. All times after 1200, he warns in launching his exemplum, are suspect, just as Langland had earlier in the Prologue warned that "the moste meschief on molde mounteth vp faste" (line 65). The prophet goes on to urge preaching, voluntary poverty and purity of life against the impending ruin of the Church. Although Langland does not place his hopes in a new order, his message is very similar to (if somewhat less radical than) the Joachite prophet's. There is every chance that Langland encountered the prophecy in the final section of the *Speculum historiale*, which deals with eschatology and in which the *Super Jeremiam* prophecy occurs alongside one of Hildegard's.[39] Certainly the eschatological overtones of the section of the Prologue in which he cites it (lines 63ff.) make this possible.

Chastisement and disendowment are major themes in these pseudo-Joachite texts. As Marjorie Reeves says,

The attack on the wealth, worldliness, and pride of the Roman Church is developed and from this springs a more revolutionary attitude towards the transition from the second to the third *status*. A violent gesture, either by the papacy itself or by others towards it, begins to appear in the expected programme. Peter must cast off his coat and plunge naked into the waves, or the Church must "fall among thieves" on the road from Jerusalem to Jericho.

(*Influence*, p. 397)

There develops in these prophecies a specific imagery of the imminent stripping away of the Church's possessions,[40] and a growing sense of what one is tempted to call "garrison mentality," to borrow a phrase from Northrop Frye.[41] The notion of a remnant of the few faithful holding out against persecution from both within and without is common in these prophecies, and, although the metaphors differ, the idea is very reminiscent of Langland's few "foles" holed up in Unity (xxii. 74).

These prophecies were eagerly taken up by groups like the Franciscan Spirituals when they found themselves persecuted for clinging to their rigorist stances on clerical poverty; certainly, it is easy to see their attractiveness to any writer or group with such reformist notions.[42] Although these prophecies follow the Joachite pattern of belief in a renewal of the Church after it has made its hazardous crossing from the second to the third *status*, they seem primarily concerned to paint a portrait of the Church in crisis and to this purpose they return again and again to a cluster of related themes, namely clerical poverty and disendowment, condemnation of the Donation of Constantine and of clerical corruption in general, the renewal of religious orders after Antichrist and the pervasive tendency to separate the world into true and false apostles.

One is immediately struck by the harshness of the critique of the clergy in these prophecies. One motif, that became especially popular in later prophecies, has the cadavers of clergy stacked up like dung in the street,[43] although most passages are not quite this sensational. Very common, once again, is the charge that the clergy are mercenaries and hirelings[44] (for example, *Super Esaiam*, fol. 28ᵛ) and the hope that God will soon sort the hirelings from the true pastors (*De oneribus*, in Holder-Egger, "Italienische Prophetieen," p. 179). We have noted this motif before in Hildegard, Langland and Gower, where Gower actually attributes it to Joachim:

> For Joachim thilke Abbot tolde
> How suche daies scholden falle,
> That comunliche in places alle
> The Chapmen of such mercerie
> With fraude and with supplantarie
> So manye scholden beie and selle,
> That he ne may for schame telle.[45]

Super Esaiam speaks of the extermination of the "carnal Church," drawing upon the metaphors of the darkening of sun, moon and stars from Joel 2:10. In a reccurent motif in Joachite prophecy, the waxing of the moon is compared to the growth in prosperity of the prelates, who are soon to suffer eclipse in adversity (*Super Esaiam*, fol. 28ᵛ).

Most of these writers date the decline of the Church from the Donation of Constantine,[46] just as Langland does, even though for Joachim himself this was, historically, the high point of the Church's blessedness (Reeves, *Influence*, pp. 178, 395). As *De oneribus* so graphically puts it, in the time of Pope Silvester, Constantine subjected himself to the Church, "having deposited a leprosy" (Holder-Egger, "Italienischen Prophetieen," p. 158); the phrase recalls Langland's "*Dos ecclesie* this day hath ydronke venym" (xvii. 223). The Donation is often an important turning point in history for Joachite thinkers. The Franciscan Joachite Peter John Olivi,[47] for example, read papal history as three distinct periods: the first ran up to the time of Pope Silvester and Constantine, during which popes had maintained apostolic poverty; the second was a period of decline into worldly decadence and corruption, which would continue to the end of the fifth (that is, the current) age; and finally would come the third era, when after the persecution of the "mystic antichrist," the popes would return to a state of absolute poverty (McGinn, "Angel Pope," p. 167).

This type of periodization fits Langland's view of Church history almost precisely and there can be little doubt that it was this kind of thing which he had in mind in certain passages of *Piers Plowman*. Not only does he date the decline of the Church from the Donation, as we have seen, but like the Joachites he sees an imminent persecution of the clergy by a type of *antichristus mysticus* which will herald not the End of the World, but a new age of reform. This is not to say that Langland could only have derived these notions from Joachite sources, but at the very least he shows close affinities with a group of radical thinkers who, as Gordon Leff has shown, shared similar anti-papalist and historicist views about the primacy of the model of the early Church and who were themselves heavily influenced by Joachism. For example, Marsilius of Padua, leaning heavily on the arguments of Franciscan apologists, attacked ecclesiastical possessions and dated the Church's decline from the Donation of Constantine (Leff, "Apostolic Ideal," p. 69). His arguments for the limitation of papal and ecclesiastical power to strictly spiritual functions were based on that influential medieval reformist notion of the apostolic ideal of the early Church. They allowed a secular ruler full authority over the temporalities of the Church, even to the point of confiscation (*ibid.*, p. 71).[48]

After Marsilius, a number of other thinkers and groups expressed similar historicist views on the Donation and on temporalities, notably the Waldensians, the Franciscan Spirituals, Dante, John of Paris, Ockham and Wyclif (*ibid.*, pp. 75–79). Gordon Leff sees Joachism as one of the most powerful influences in shaping these historicist views of the apostolic ideal, the Donation and the need to curtail the temporalites and temporal powers of the papacy and the Church. Leff writes, "from the middle of the thirteenth century, if not before, it [Joachism] introduced a new element of historical criticism and prophecy into the outlook of time" (*ibid.*, p. 73). Some of the writers who took up these ideas were more radical than others; some were orthodox while others were heterodox; some had apocalyptic expectations and others had only political or reformist ones; but all show a debt to the Franciscan ideology of the thirteenth-century mendicant controversies and to the related phenomenon of fraternal Joachism.

The fact that Langland expresses his views on disendowment and the Donation in the form of prophecy (v. 168–79 and XVII. 208–32) suggests that he was in touch with the apocalyptic wing of this group of writers rather than just the polemical, non-apocalyptic ones. He may well have known Marsilius' and Ockham's writings or ideas on the subject, but neither of these writers would have provided him with a model for the prophetic form into which he cast his views. In the later Middle Ages the prophetic tradition fostered by Joachite thinkers is the most obvious source for a *prophetic* ideology comparable to Langland's on these points.[49]

Given the tensions between mendicants and possessioners in fourteenth-century England it is easy to see why such prophecies would have been of interest to Englishmen. The anti-papalism which Leff sees as characteristic of these historicist thinkers was rife in England and so it is not surprising that this fairly radical material found an audience here. Historical factors also contributed to the sympathy, especially among the nobility, for the taxation or even confiscation of clerical goods (Knowles, *Religious Orders*, vol. II, pp. 65ff.). Edward III's French wars were expensive and the coffers of the rich possessioner-clergy proved too tempting a source of revenue to be passed over. In the late 1330s Ockham, although now living abroad, addressed his polemical work "An princeps" to the English problem of whether Edward should be allowed to draw upon the purses of the clergy to support his "just" war.[50] Not only did Ockham support the notion of the secular power's rights to clerical revenue during time of war, but he also pushed the argument further to allow for the confiscation of goods from unjust clergy. In the "Octo quaestiones" he writes, "Therefore, all the more can the churches justly be deprived of the honors, rights, liberties, and privileges granted to them if they are not faithful to the laymen who have granted these things. Again, faith should not be kept with a faithless enemy . . ."⁵¹

Ockham's Franciscan viewpoint on clerical property and his disgust at the wealth and luxury of the papal court initially prompted such views, as David Knowles said (*Religious Orders*, vol. ΙΙ, p. 65), but they soon became influential in academic circles and even beyond. Knowles has tried to trace the development of this disendowment question in the years after 1360 and he consistently points to the friars as the instigators of the controversy:

Either in answer to further provocation of which nothing is known, or acting on the maxim that attack is the best method of defence, the friars began to take the offensive in academic circles with attacks upon the endowed religious bodies, known in the phrase of the day as "possessioners"; these were the older orders of monks and canons, among whom, in a dispute of this kind, the greatest and richest houses, such as Durham, Canterbury and Glastonbury, were obviously the most vulnerable . . . It would seem that the Minors at least had gone beyond a criticism of monastic property-holders to an attack, almost in the spirit of the *fraticelli*, on church possessions in general. , (*ibid.*, pp. 64–65)

It is interesting, in view of this situation, that Langland should have chosen to make the friars the benefactors of the monastic disendowment he prophesied. As we have said before, there is little evidence in England of rigorist Franciscan views, but this outburst in the 1360s shows that England was not immune to such ideas, even if they took a rather specific, one-issue form there. This is probably the context in which pseudo-Joachite prophecies on the theme of clerical decadence and the need for disendowment and Hildegardian disendowment prophecies began to be more widely disseminated in England.

In the 1370s the question moved from the academiç sphere to the wider realm of "practical politics," as Knowles says (*ibid.*, pp. 64ff.). While writers like Uhtred of Boldon and Bishop Brinton argued for the possessioners, a new opponent joined the fight on the side of the mendicant friars: Wyclif began to develop his doctrine of dominion during the 1370s, a doctrine of which C. H. McIlwain said, "There is scarcely one significant point in it which had not been elaborated again and again in writings resulting from the great controversy within or concerning the Franciscan order" (cited in Daly, "Wyclif's Political Theory," p. 181). As Pamela Gradon says, Wyclif's notions on disendowment and the Donation of Constantine were "neither new nor novel" when he advanced them ("Dissent," p. 186).⁵² The friars were still in the vanguard of the attack on the possessioners at this time and in 1371 two Austin friars laid a number of articles before Parliament in which, "in a curious example of the blending of practical politics and reforming zeal" (Gradon, "Dissent," p. 187), they proposed monastic disendowment in order to provide revenue for the French wars.⁵³ Gradon notes that the articles take the matter even further by citing Augustine on clerical poverty and concluding that "a powerful man who, for their unnatural behavior, would take from the monks their possessions and their liberty would be blessed by God."⁵⁴

This is the context in which Langland expresses the views he does on the Donation of Constantine and clerical disendowment; however, the immediate models for his reform prophecies are most likely to have been prophetic sources rather than simply polemical ones. One such work is *De oneribus prophetarum*, which seems to have been fairly well known in fourteenth-century England.[55] It prophesies the destruction of the corrupt clergy with reference to the same passage from Isaias to which Langland refers in his disendowment prophecy: "How is the oppressor come to nothing, the tribute hath ceased? The Lord hath broken the staff of the wicked, the rod of the rulers, that struck the people in wrath with an incurable wound, that brought nations under in fury, that persecuted in a cruel manner."[56] In another disendowment prophecy from the same work, this time involving the often-used Ship of Peter motif, the writer asserts graphically that the prelates should vomit up what they have drained from their temporalities: "aut quod exauserant de temporalibus presules evomant, aut ab erepti difficultate regiminis in subditorum iniuriam resipiscant" (ed. Holder-Egger, "Italienische Propetieen," p. 179).

The inevitability of disendowment, the constant charges of simony and "mercenary" interests among clergy, and ever more shrill descriptions of the extent of clerical wickedness fill the pages of these prophecies. Anti-papal prophecies, which predicted the victory of the secular powers over the Church, were especially popular in English chronicles, as were papal schism prophecies. For example, "Gallorum levitas," a short prophecy found in a legion of manuscripts in England[57] and on the Continent, ends with the following lines: "Papa cito moritur, cesar regnabit ubique, / Sub quo tunc vana cessabit gloria cleri" (ed. Holder-Egger, "Italienische Prophetieen," p. 126). As always in Joachite prophecy the state is the chastiser of the clergy. In England, where anti-papalism was especially rife, the prophecy was eagerly snatched up by chroniclers, as was another short Joachite piece found in numerous English manuscripts (incipit: "Corruent nobiles"). It focuses its future program on a papal schism, portrayed in terms of the classic apocalyptic opposition of the true and false apostle. In 1257, it predicts,

erunt duo pape, unus Lugduni et alter Rome. Lugdunensis erit iustus et equus. Alter vero iniustus et iniquus et mutuo sese excommunicabunt. Item LX anno erunt cotidie ecclesia et clerus in tanta vilitate et conculcacione in quanta non fuerunt a tempore Constantini qui dotavit ecclesiam residente Silvestro in Romana ecclesia. Item. LXV rediet [redibit] tota Grecia ad obbedienciam Romane ecclesie. Tunc audientur nova de predicatoribus antichristi. (In Reeves, *Influence*, p. 50)[58]

Although fastening on the typical Joachite themes of papal and clerical corruption, the decline of the Church since the Donation of Constantine and the healing of the Greek schism, this prophecy lacks the Joachite sense of optimism for the future. However, it does reflect the growing apocalyptic concern for the fate of the papacy, usually expressed, as here, in stark oppositions between good and evil papal figures. This kind of mentality is reflected to some extent in *Piers Plowman* as well, where Piers is the looked-for savior of the Church and, when Antichrist comes, "thenne shal pryde be pope and prince of holy chirche" (XXI. 223).

The possibility that Langland had been influenced by the angelic-pope tradition in his creation of Piers was first suggested by Burdach many years ago (*Dichter*, pp. 326–51). The first known record of this tradition occurs in the writings of the

Englishman Roger Bacon, who tried to encourage first Pope Clement IV and later Gregory X to take on this new role. He wrote to Clement,

Forty years ago it was prophesied, and there have been many visions to the same effect, that there will be a pope in these times who will purify Canon Law and the Church of God from the sophistries and deceits of the jurists so that justice will reign over all without the rumbling of lawsuits. Because of the goodness, truth, and justice of this pope the Greeks will return to the obedience of the Roman Church, the greater part of the Tartars will be converted to the faith, and the Saracens will be destroyed. There will be one flock and one shepherd, as the prophet heard (John 10:16) . . . [These things] could happen in your reign.[59]

In an even more apocalyptic mood he later wrote to Gregory X urging upon him the prophecies of the Sibyl, Merlin and others who

have thought that the days of the Antichrist would come in this period. Therefore it is necessary that evil be stamped out so that God's elect plainly appear. A very holy pope will first come who will remove all the corruptions in education and the Church and all the rest. Then the world will be renewed and the fullness of peoples will enter in; even the remnants of Israel will be converted to the faith.[60]

All such predictions rested on the central notion of the personal sanctity of the reforming pope. In a number of popular prophecies this idea was taken to quite an extreme. Just as in early Joachite writings, both genuine and spurious, the men of the new orders were conceived as leading a life of eremitical or apostolic poverty,[61] so too the new single-figure leaders, holy popes and even "Last Emperors" were now often visualized as eremitical figures. This tendency toward sanctification had always been present to some extent in Last World Emperor figures and now the two reformist leadership roles of pope and emperor came to resemble one another to the extent that they are sometimes conflated in later prophecies.[62]

Both these figures have parallels in *Piers Plowman*: both an unidentified king and Piers himself, who is an ideal, latter-day Peter, play a role in Langland's predictions of Church reform. Furthermore, there is evidence in the poem that Langland sometimes conflates the two roles – either deliberately or because it did not much matter to him whether a holy secular leader or a holy pope reformed the Church so long as it was reformed. We know that by the end of the poem Piers is to be read in many ways as a papal figure. In Passus xxi Langland noticeably switches from speaking of "Peter" (lines 163 and 169) to speaking of "Peres" (lines 183ff.) in the midst of his discussion of Christ's post-Resurrection appearance to the disciples and his founding of the Church upon the spiritual authority he gives to Peter.

> Thus hath Peres power, be his pardoun payed,
> To bynde and to vnbynde bothe here and elles
> And assoile men of alle synnes, saue of dette one . . . (xxi. 188–90)

while at xxii. 318–21 Piers is described as having power over all clergy. On the other hand in the "lewed" vicar's assessment of the current leadership crisis, Piers is definitely referred to as a type of World Emperor:

178

Leaven of hope: new leadership

And thow, Consience, in kynges court and sholdest neuer come thennes,
And Grace, that thow gredest so of, gyour of all clerkes,
And Peres with his newe plouh and also his olde
Emperour of al þe world þat men all were cristene.   (xxi. 424–27)

The vicar goes on immediately to juxtapose this to the corrupt state of the present papacy (lines 428ff.) while showing in the process that he sets little store by theories of papal dominion (line 443).[63] These attitudes are entirely consistent with Langland's views on *regnum* and *sacerdotium* as we know them from other passages in the poem. Unlike Joachim himself, but like some of his later disciples, Langland seems to look more to David the *king* than to David the *"pastor"* for spiritual leadership.[64] This, as we have said, is consistent with the Marsilian line which Langland seems to follow, but it makes the figure of Piers even more complex to read than he already seems – if that is possible.

As far as the apocalyptic side of Langland's conflation of pope and emperor figures in Piers is concerned, there is precedent in medieval religious prophecy for such a mixture. In some prophecies like, for example, those of John of Rupescissa, the two figures help one another to carry out the *renovatio*, but in other prophecies the traditional characteristics of the two leaders are interchanged or interchangeable. Interestingly, the best-known medieval prophecies in the angelic-pope tradition began as emperor prophecies, the *Vaticinia de summis pontificibus*. Existing in over fifty manuscripts, this is a series of illustrated predictions of future popes. Scholars have believed, until recently, they were composed by a group of Joachite Franciscan Spirituals under the leadership of Angelo of Clareno in 1304, during the interregnum between the death of the Spirituals' enemy, Pope Boniface VIII, and the election of Benedict XI (McGinn, *Visions*, p. 188).[65] Whoever originated the *Vaticinia*, however, had come in contact with the Byzantine prophecies known as "The Oracles of Leo the Wise," which portrayed a series of present and future emperors.[66] The form was easily adaptable to predictions of papal leadership. One of the figures in "The Oracles of Leo the Wise," a hermit-emperor, was especially amenable to transformation into an angelic pope. In the *Vaticinia* he becomes a hermit, who lives on a peasant's diet of herbs, and will be called forth from his seclusion to take up the papal throne.[67] Still another pope in the series, like a harvesting angel, wields a sickle and promises to restore poverty, obedience, chastity and temperance, and to destroy hypocrisy.[68] Some of the popes are conquering figures or are associated with kings in some way.[69] Certainly, a convention of these prophecies, as in other Franciscan-influenced prophecies with their strong idealizations of poverty, is the election of a holy pauper or peasant as a pope or emperor figure.[70]

By the 1340s the *Vaticinia* had run their course (that is, they had run out of popes) and so a new set of fifteen was developed which ended – unlike the old set – with Antichrist in the papal chair (McGinn, *Visions*, p. 189). In the new set a more conventional eschatology has taken over from the optimistic Joachite hope for the Church's End under an angelic pope. Remarking on this switch in eschatological views Marjorie Reeves has said,

Perhaps this is the reason why, in the second half of the fourteenth century, the two sets were
put together, making thirty in all, with the second series placed first. This meant that the
figure of Antichrist became less menacing in the middle of the Sequence and that it
culminated in the clear angelic portraits of the first series. By the time number fifteen (i.e.
'Antichrist') was reached in actuality it could be interpreted as Urban VI and associated with
the Schism.   (Reeves, "Some Popular Prophecies," p. 119)

This is the point in time during which Langland was writing the B-text (Urban VI
held the papal throne from 1378 to 1389) and the fact that the first series of
prophecies was added on after Antichrist to form a whole new prognosis of good
and bad popes would fit Langland's sense of apocalyptic periodization well.
However, in spite of the popularity of the *Vaticinia* in England, there is very little
concrete evidence at present for connecting it with *Piers Plowman* other than
general similarities in the expectation of an antipope, the idealization of eremitical
poverty in the figure of Peter, the belief in a coming pope or series of popes who
would reform the Church and some tenuous bits of symbolism.[71] Still, the
Vaticinia give us some sense of current apocalyptic mentalities with regard to the
papacy – obviously Langland was not the only writer who fantasized about a new
Peter drawn from the ranks of the humble and godly poor, who would carry those
ideals to the top of the Church hierarchy and see that they were followed by all
within his power.

More research on religious prophecy in England will have to be carried out
before we can know more certainly whether Burdach was correct in recognizing
the angelic-pope tradition as one of the motivating forces behind Piers.[72] He saw
the eremitical role which Piers takes on in the middle section of the poem as
relating to this radical, but widely known prophetic typology. Langland's view of
hermits and of the eremitical life is unfortunately not a topic which can be explored
here, but surely his great concern with distinguishing between true and false
hermits is just one facet of what was probably a lifelong fascination with the
eremitical ideal.[73] Langland obviously chose to exploit the mystique of eremitical
poverty, as so many evangelical writers did; however, I cannot help but feel that his
preoccupation with it is partly apocalyptic as well as evangelical – and this goes as
surely for his anti-eremiticism as for his (less recognized) pro-eremitical idealism.

At another point in *Piers Plowman* Langland hoped that the trials of the Christian
Church would be solved by a secular leader. The belief that the world would one
day be united under "one shepherd" is common in religious prophecy (John
10:16) and was likely to refer to either a king or a pope. For example, a prophecy
usually attributed to one "Frater Columbinus," which was frequently copied in
medieval England, predicts the conversion of all non-Christians after the death of
Antichrist and "Tunc erit unum ouile et unus pastor; et reliquie Israel soluere fient
et tunc . . . erit omnis pax et tranquillitas."[74] Langland uses this motif similarly in
his millennial prophecy of the general moral and spiritual reform which will be
ushered in by a new David:

> I, Consience, knowe this, for Kynde Wit me tauhte
> That resoun shal regne and reumes gouerne
> And riht as Agag hadde happe shal somme;

Leaven of hope: new leadership

Samuel shal sle hym and Sauel shal be yblamed
And Dauid shal be ydyademed and adaunte alle oure enemyes
And o cristene kyng kepe vs echone.   (*Piers Plowman*, III. 436–41)

The notion that David will "adaunte alle oure enemyes" seems to mean that this new leader is to be a secular as well as a spiritual force in the tradition of the "Last World Emperor," whose role in both vernacular and Latin prophecy is usually as a great conqueror or crusader. As one might expect, a number of kings and emperors in the Middle Ages were hailed as "new" Davids or "second" Davids,[75] but analogues to prophecies of a *coming, undesignated* new David are rarer. Langland's use of this theme fits more easily into the context of pseudo-Joachite apocalypticism than into any purely political prophecy or propaganda that I know of.[76]

In the traditional Augustinian periodization the time of King David was the zenith of world history, as we have seen. Joachim took up this notion and developed it in his periodization of seven dominant, ascendant kingdoms of the Old Testament and seven parallel kingdoms in the New Testament. The one bright spot in his Old Testament series is the fourth *regnum*, which is David's and which Joachim spells out as "Locus victorie: JERUSALEM: DAVID: PACIS VISIO" in one of his accompanying figures (Reeves and Hirsch-Reich, *Figurae*, p. 189). Parallel to this is the fourth *regnum* of the New Testament periodization, also a time of blessedness under Pope Silvester (*ibid.*, p. 190). For Joachim, of course, the time of Silvester was the happiest in the New Testament period, but both the original and the later Joachite periodizations reflect the view that there has been no such period of glory for the Church since. In fact, Joachim parallels his own generation with Jeremiah's, thus implying the expectation of an imminent second Babylonian exile (*ibid.*). However, he also expected a third "Jerusalem" in parallel with David's reign and Pope Silvester's time, and this was to occur after the Tribulation of the New Babylon and upon entry of God's people into the third *status* (*ibid.*, p. 191). He writes in the *Liber concordia* that at that time "tanta exultatio electorum erit in ecclesia quanta non fuit a diebus Constantini" (quoted *ibid.*).

David and Samuel are also paired together in another of Joachim's schemes, this time in one of the seven seals of the Old Testament. They occupy the position of the third seal in what is essentially a list of spiritual leaders from Joseph to Zorobabel, the latter being Joachim's type of what later came to be known as the angelic pope. In later Joachite thought the typology of David replacing Saul was used to support the expectation that the true sons of the Church would eventually take spiritual supremacy over the "carnal Church," just as the Roman Church had received it from the Synagogue (Bloomfield, "Joachim," pp. 300–01). The Joachite use of the typology of David was, then, largely spiritual or ecclesiastical rather than political; however, Langland's own "*pacis visio*" fits the Joachite pattern in that it predicts "the worste" before the best (*Piers Plowman*, III. 477ff.), and speaks specifically, though not exclusively, of clerical reform (III. 465ff.). This prophecy of Langland's contains two more common apocalyptic motifs in the overcoming of avarice (Mede) and the conversion of the Jews. Many apocalyptic thinkers focused on avarice as the main evil of the times and looked forward to its demise, as we shall see below (p. 185). The conversion of the Jews is a particularly appropriate apocalyptic concern in a Davidic prophecy; in fact, Langland treats the whole passage in an Old Testament messianic vein, promising that the "Iewes shal wene in her wit and wexen so glade / That here kyng be ycome fro þe court of heuene, / That ilk Moises or Messie" (III. 454–56). Langland's concern in this prophecy and throughout the poem with the conversion of all non-Christian peoples is reminiscent of the great emphasis placed upon such missions by the Franciscan Spirituals, many of whom were inspired by Joachite apocalypticism to hope for such a thing (see Daniel, *Franciscan Concept*). Similarly, Langland shows little interest in militaristic crusading, which would be odd for a writer drawing upon political "Last World Emperor" prophecies. It would seem that although his views were "pro-*regnum*" on the question of the division of temporal powers between secular and clerical authorities, spiritual reform was the dominant force behind his apocalypticism and religious prophecies were his main sources.

Perhaps the most widely known prophecy of a reforming David occurs in the *Vade mecum in tribulatione* of John of Rupescissa, whose prophetic ideology we will consider in greater detail at the end of this section. John speaks of a "David futurus, de quo prophetat Ezechial cap. 34" (*Vade mecum*, p. 502). Ezechiel 34 does indeed describe a utopian period, following upon the chastisement of the negligent shepherds of Israel, under the leadership of David: "And I will set up one shepherd over them: and he shall feed them, even my servant David . . . and he shall be their shepherd" (verse 23). John's account of this reforming David, who as yet only prepares the way for Christ's Second Coming, fits Langland's sense of events in the Passus III prophecy very well, and given the wide circulation of the *Vade mecum* in England, there is a good possibility of Langland's having encountered it.

Another prophecy which mentions a "novus David" was known in the fourteenth century largely through its inclusion in Arnold (or Arnau) of Villanova's *Tractatus de mysterio cimbalorum ecclesiae*, written before the end of the year 1301. The short prophecy itself, usually called by its incipit, "Ve mundo in centum annis" ("Woe to the world in one hundred years"), is largely a political prophecy (Lerner, *Powers*, p. 40, p. 6); however, there are a number of interesting religious motifs of the Joachite type scattered throughout. Arnold of Villanova (1238–1311) was an important Joachite writer, whose *Tractatus de tempore de adventu antichristi* provoked something of an international academic controversy when he presented the first part of it to the theologians of Paris in 1299 (Daniel, *Franciscan Concept*, p. 92). English scholastics took part in this debate over whether or not the coming of Antichrist could be predicted and some of the surviving treatises show that both Arnold's writings and other Joachite works were known in England at this time.[77]

As so often in apocalyptic prophecy Arnold attributes the revelation of "Ve mundo" to a very devout but almost illiterate man ("virum fere illiteratum").[78] This attribution, coupled with the remark made part way through the prophecy that "the nest of Aristotle" will be wasted away and made void,[79] establishes the twin features of veneration of simplicity and hatred of scholasticism so often found in Joachite prophecy. The prophecy begins by predicting the continued loss of cities in the Holy Land until a new David comes to repair the ark of Syon. Other typical apocalyptic events such as the return of the Greek Church to obedience and the chastisement of the clergy are woven into a tissue of obscure political prophecy that ends with a prediction concerning the sorting out of the sons of Jerusalem from the sons of Babylon.

Other prophecies reflect concern for renewal through their periodization of past and future history. A number of prophetic works known to have circulated in England espouse detailed non-traditional programs of future events and reforms as the main structural device of their apocalypticism. As we have seen, Langland shows enough fragmentary evidence of a non-traditional apocalyptic program of his own to make it worth giving some space here to consideration of the kind of thing with which he could have come in contact. One such is the *De semine scripturarum*, which was quite popular in England, where it was cited by writers like Roger Bacon and John Wyclif, and found its way into a handful of English chronicles and medieval library catalogues.[80] It is based on the unlikely notion that clues to the meaning of history may be found in the letters of the three alphabets of the three languages used on the Cross, Hebrew, Greek and Latin. Each letter is allotted one century and any century can be understood by examining the characteristics of each letter. Most of the prophecy is concerned with H to Z (or the Incarnation to the End of the World) of the Latin alphabet. Here the author surveys the history of the Church and the Roman Empire and the development of the Church is conceived, not surprisingly, as a succession of chastisements and renewals. During K to L, Christ liberated the Church from persecutions and during M from heresy. In the time of Q, simony had begun to penetrate the Church and by the time of X (that is, the century from 1215 to 1315) the author declares the Church to be thoroughly corrupt. At this time Christ will drive out the unchaste and mercenary clergy, as he did the money-changers from the temple.[81] The reformed Church will attract the "Gentiles" into it and all the peoples of the world will be received into the Church in the time of Y, the three arms of Y symbolizing Europe, Africa and Asia. Also under X, the Holy Land, which had been lost to the Saracens during V, is returned to Christian hands, but there will be more suffering, particularly among the clergy, from the effects of war, plundering and general turbulence during the X period.[82] In view of the fact that the writer is (on the basis of internal evidence) probably writing in about the year 1205, it is not surprising that he details his starkest prophecies, no doubt as warnings to clerics, for the X (1215–1315) and Y (1315–1415) periods. During the last period, Z, the author expects Antichrist to come – that is, some time after 1415. The traditional eschatological events are still a comforting two centuries or more away. Church reform, therefore, is the overwhelming concern of the writer, a reform which he believes will bring about the conversions of the Jews and Pagans.

Even though the *De semine* was not Joachite in origin, it certainly shares many concerns with that tradition and it was popularly attributed to Joachim himself. It differs, however, in placing the coming of Antichrist at the End of the World, following the traditional eschatology. As Marjorie Reeves has said, this work was no doubt of particular interest to fourteenth-century readers since it prophesied the

End of the World soon after 1400. By the fifteenth century it must have looked far less interesting. Reeves cites a disgruntled comment about Joachim of Fiore by the fifteenth-century chronicler John Capgrave, based partly on the condemnation of his views on the Trinity and partly on the all-too-evident fact that the world had not yet ended, as "Joachim" had predicted in the *De semine*:

1152. In this tyme was abbot Joachim in Calabir, that wrote many thingis upon the Apocalypse: but he erred in many thingis; first in a mater concernyng the Holy Trynyte. For the Cherch hath determined his opinion fals . . . This same abbot mad also a othir book "De Seminibus Literarum" where be gret craft he drove oute the 3ear in whech the day of dome schuld falle. But he failed foule and erred in his counting.

(In Reeves, *Influence*, p. 70)

The popularity of the *De semine* in England *before* the fifteenth century, however, is impressive. It holds the honor of being one of the few Latin prophecies to have been cited extensively in a Middle English text, a reformist tract called *The Last Age of the Church*, which was edited in 1840 by J. H. Todd, who believed it to have been written by Wyclif. In his Preface Todd exclaims over the influence of so much Joachism (which he calls the "prophetical Speculations of the Beguines, circulated under the Name of the famous Abbot Joachim") hitherto unnoticed in scholarly discussions of Wyclif (Todd edition, pp. xi–xii). In fact the *Last Age* is rare among such tracts (and indeed among Middle English works in general) for its heavy use not just of the *De semine* (which the author usually refers to as "þe seedis of profetis") but also of *De oneribus prophetarum* (which he refers to as Joachim's book "of þe chargis of profetis") and probably the *Vaticinia de summis pontificibus* (which he calls "þe seyingis of popes"). All are attributed to Joachim and his name occurs throughout the little tract, alongside other less frequently cited prophetic authorities like Bede, the Sibyl and Merlin.

The tract is mainly concerned with the abomination of simony and is anxious to show that clerical tribulation is at hand. It begins with a rather dramatic opening based on a reworking of the devil's temptation of Christ (Matthew 4:9). Now it is the "grete prestis sitting in derkenessis" who are easy prey for him "þat openly crieþ al þis I wille 3eue 3if if þou auaunce me" (Todd edition, p. xxiii). The author goes on to complain of the reservation of "fatte beneficis" and other forms of clerical income, and then cites Joachim and St. Bernard as authorities for the interpretation of Psalm 90:5–6 ("his truth shall compass thee with a shield: thou shalt not be afraid of the terror of the night. Of the arrow that flieth in the day, of the business that walketh about in the dark: of invasion, or of the noonday devil") as referring to the four tribulations of history.[83] The author summarizes the first two tribulations (the martyrdoms and heresies of the early Church, respectively) and then continues:

Chaffare walkynge in derkenessis is þe pryui heresie of symonyans / bi resoun of whiche þe þridde tribulacioun schal entre into Cristis Chirche / . . . in þe tyme of þe hundrid 3eer of .x. lettre / whos ende we ben / as I wele preue / & þis myscheif schal be so heuy þat wel schal be to þat man of holy Chirche þat þane schal no3t be on lyue. (Todd edition, p. xxv)

Leaven of hope: new leadership

The notion that the present age was characterized by rampant avarice and simony is very common in reformist thought, espoused by writers as influential as St. Bernard and St. Bonaventure.[84] The *Last Age* description of the third tribulation as "chaffare walkynge in derkenessis" and similar descriptions throughout (for example, "marchaundise walkynge in derkenessis," Todd edition, pp. xxix and xxxi) are reminiscent both of the common prophetic motif of the clerical *mercenarius* and of Langland's own foreboding comment in the Prologue of *Piers Plowman*, spoken of the mendicants in particular:

> Mony of þise maistres of mendenant freres
> Here moneye and marchandise marchen togyderes.
> Ac sith charite hath be chapman and chief to shryue lordes
> Mony ferlyes han falle in a fewe ȝeres,
> And but holi chirche and charite choppe adoun suche shryuars
> The most meschief on molde mounteth vp faste.   (Prol. 60–65)

What Langland only alludes to in the Prologue the anonymous author spells out clearly. Citing various lines from the Joachite prophecy "Gallorum levitas" (quoted above, p. 177) he concludes:

Þei pat treten þes verse of Sibille / alle þat I haue seen / acorden in þis þat seculer powr of þe Hooly Goost elispirid / & þat deþ / veniaunce of swerd / myscheifs vnknowe bifore / bi whiche men þes daies schule be ponyschid / schulen falle for synne of prestis. Men schal falle on hem / & caste hem out of her fatte beneficis / and þei schule seye / he cam in to his benefice by his kynrede / þes bi couenant maad bifore / he for his seruyse / & þes for moneye / cam into Goddis Chirche.   (Todd edition, pp. xxxiii–xxxiv)

Like Langland, he promises a "beating" for the clergy, and promises it in Middle English, too. The fact that the tract is in the vernacular is important evidence for this study because it provides another instance of a vernacular writer using prophetic sources to support what have been usually explained as (or with reference to) Wycliffite views.[85] The author of the *Last Age* says that he is writing in 1356 and if so this is much too early for a vernacular Wycliffite treatise. It is instructive that all the main tenets of this tract (disendowment, clerical avarice, and so forth) which cause it to be listed among Wycliffite treatises even by modern scholars[86] can just as easily be derived – as the author so often tells us – from the Joachite works he is drawing upon. The *Last Age* contains much of the kind of material which, when it occurs in *Piers Plowman*, scholars have almost always used Wyclif to illuminate. I would argue rather that both Langland and other reformist writers, like the Wycliffites, were drawing upon the same sources. Fortunately for us the *Last Age* author was not reluctant to name a few of his sources.

The author of the *Last Age* then proceeds with a detailed description of the alphabetical periodization of the *De semine* (Todd edition, pp. xxvi–xxviii) and then sets out to prove that the third tribulation will be manifested in the hundredth year of the letter X (which he later proves to be the current period). His reasons are rather ingenious:

I preue it bi two resouns / þe firste is þis. Petir þe Apostle þe whiche was in þe tyme of .i. lettre / myȝte not vttirly distrie Symoun Magus / but bi helpe of Poul / þe whiche was þe þritteneþ Apostil. So / if .x. lettre be þe þritteneþe fro .i. lettre / in þe tyme of .x. lettre Crist schal clanse his Chirche fro marchaundise walkynge in derkenessis. Þe secunde resoun is suche. Ȝit cam noȝt þat tribulacion þat schal be in Goddis Chirche bi cause of chaffare walkynge in derkenesses / & þat þat is prophesied schal come.

(Todd edition, pp. xxviii–xxix)

No one could argue with this logic. Clearly the third tribulation will be a purgation of simony and in this the author has captured the reformist apocalyptic mentality precisely. He ends with the assertion that the fourth tribulation, "bi þe deuel of mydday þat is Antecrist" (*ibid.*, p. xxx) will follow upon the third tribulation of X and this also, by an odd leap of logic, proves the imminence of the third tribulation.

Citing other authorities, he then shows that pestilences and other tribulations will be the punishment for "defaute of prestis" (this must have been especially pertinent in 1356 so soon after the Black Death, which had itself raised apocalyptic expectations, swept England). He then indulges in a bit of prodigy or portent prophecy, which is often a feature of popular apocalypticism, by showing that his authorities say that when this tribulation is nigh "men schulle wante teeþ" and by reminding his audience that since the first pestilence "comynly" all children "ben such þat wanten eiȝte grete teeþ" (Todd edition, pp. xxxii–xxxiii)! This is no doubt the type of "ferly" that Langland alludes to in the Prologue to *Piers Plowman* (line 63).

As Reeves notes (*Influence*, p. 83), there is no trace here of genuine Joachite expectations of renewal, although there is the promise of the cleansing of God's Church; however, the little tract is fascinating as evidence of the availability of a fairly wide range of prophetic sources to a mid-fourteenth-century English writer. The anonymous reformist certainly had concerns similar to Langland's for what he saw as the rampant growth of simony in the Church and the need for clerical disendowment. We no longer need to turn to Wyclif to explain the presence of such ideas in a fourteenth-century English writer, and this, to me, is an important point. It will be some time yet before we can sort out the complex relationship between Langland's and Wyclif's works, but from an apocalyptic and reformist standpoint the relationship seems to be one of independent contemporaries drawing almost simultaneously upon the same sources.[87] When we know more about currents of reformist and apocalyptic thought coming into and moving through fourteenth-century England we will be better able to solve this problem.

We will turn now to consider a key phase of many apocalyptic renewal programs, including Langland's – that is, the prediction of a return to a first state of purity. We have seen that a great many prophecies speak in general terms of clerical chastisement and reform but very few give specific details about what exactly this might mean. Many refer vaguely to some kind of process of clerical humbling, usually by tribulation and disendowment, but few outside of the odd theorist like Joachim ever go much further in their post-reform descriptions. Langland is unusual among writers and retailers of short prophecy in the specific nature of his concern with the kind of reforms which he foresees. While evidence for many aspects of his apocalypticism is scrappy, this concern places him among the more original and sophisticated prophetic thinkers who attempt to translate prophetic dreams into specific "demands" of the future. His disendowment prophecy in Passus v asks two things of the future: that the possessioners be reduced to their pristine state (*"ad pristinum statum ire"*) and that the friars be given a "fyndynge" from Constantine's coffers. Throughout the poem he idealizes the past Church at the expense of the present one and voluntary poverty at the expense of the contemporary clerical manner of living.[88]

There is a group of prophecies which do speak specifically about the aims of clerical reforms and many of these also use the phrase *ad pristinum statum* (*ire*), or a close version of it, to describe their belief that the only acceptable path forward for the clergy is backwards, to the simplicity of the *ecclesia primitiva* and adherence to the apostolic ideal. The *ad pristinum statum* motif[89] seems to have been particularly popular in the fourteenth century (we know, for example, that it was used by Bridget of Sweden, Cola di Rienzo and John of Rupescissa), but it was also used by twelfth-century prophetic writers, notably Gerhoh of Reichersberg and Hildegard of Bingen.[90] Obviously the concept of repristination need not always be linked with later Joachite prophecy – in fact, there is something of an irony here because Joachim himself believed in a historical progress of religious life. However, there can be little doubt that by the fourteenth century pseudo-Joachite and Joachite-influenced prophecies were the main carriers of repristination ideology, largely because of the Franciscan impetus behind so many of these works.

Guy Bourquin has pointed out that the phrase *ad pristinum statum* (*ire*) occurs often in the legends of St. Francis (Bourquin, *Etudes*, p. 716), and it certainly occurs in Franciscan Joachite prophecy. The most important example, as far as Langland is concerned, of Franciscan Joachite prophecy of repristination in England is to be found in the writings of John of Rupescissa, which deserve separate consideration below because of their complexity. A number of short prophecies in wide circulation in England also mention this motif.

Bloomfield (*Apocalypse*, p. 215, n. 64) notes two prophecies which make use of the *ad pristinum statum* motif – in fact, however, the two are slightly different versions of the same short "Last Emperor" brand of prophecy. The first, beginning "Externis populis dominabitur aquila fortis," was spuriously attributed to Grosseteste[91] and ends with part of the second prophecy (beginning "Ter tria lustra tenent cum semi tempora sexti"), recorded, among other places, in English manuscripts, with a commentary in the *Eulogium historiarum*.[92] Both prophecies share five lines in common and it is these five lines (beginning "En vagus in primo perdit . . .") which speak of a king reducing the clergy to their pristine state.[93] In the first prophecy the five lines are tacked onto the end of a "Last World Emperor" prophecy in which the king, under whom faith will thrive, conquers Jerusalem and becomes emperor of all the world, having begun as a poor wanderer. After he has reduced the clergy "ad statum primum," he will also renew the holy places, which the *Eulogium* commentator interprets as a return of the Holy Land from pagan to Christian hands (*Eulogium*, Haydon edition, vol. i, p. 419), before rejecting all earthly things and, in the words of the commentator, "in locis sanctissimis finem faciet felicem" (the typical "Last World Emperor" motif of the king's peaceful death in the Holy Land).

Yet another extremely popular English political prophecy (beginning "Anglia transmittet leopardum") ends with a similar five-line section which sounds like a variation on the Joachite *ad pristinum statum* theme. It speaks of the return of the Church to its first "liberty," the grinding of the altars of Babylon and the recovery of Jerusalem by a "Last Emperor" figure, who will then turn over the *imperium mundi* to a hermit, reflecting the usual concerns with Church reform, holy leadership and poverty (*Eulogium*, Haydon edition, vol. 1, p. 420).

Although Langland's apocalyptic reformism is not entirely backward-looking, there is a strong vein of yearning for past glory in his thought. In this he is similar to one of the most influential of the Franciscan Joachite prophets of repristination, John of Rupescissa, who, like most Franciscan Spirituals, yearned for a return to the rigorist simplicity of the days of St. Francis for his own order and a return to the first apostolic principles for the clergy in general.

John of Rupescissa (1310–65) has been described by Bernard McGinn as a "weathervane" of apocalyptic trends of the later Middle Ages (*Visions*, p. 231) and as such it is perhaps not surprising that many of his ideas are strikingly similar to Langland's. John's incorporation of the Black Death into a rather spectacular and somewhat eclectic periodization of future history probably first boosted his popularity to the level it maintained throughout the Middle Ages.[94] As Robert Lerner has pointed out, John was one of the first medieval writers to espouse literal millenarianism.[95] In the *Liber secretorum eventum*[96] he predicted that Antichrist would reign for three and one half years before 1370, but that by 1415 a millennium of peace and justice would begin, during which men would beat their swords into plowshares. This would last until 2370 (a date which still seems far away!), when the arrival of Gog and Magog would herald the End of the World.

As was mentioned in chapter 3, above, John was heavily influenced in his visions by both Hildegard and Robert of Uzès. He cites Robert's visions "comme témoinages mystiques," as Bignami-Odier says, of his forecasts of papal poverty and a coming angelic pope (*Roquetaillade*, p. 194). John also knew Gebeno's *Pentachronon* well and makes frequent reference to Hildegard on the corruption of the world and as an authority on the End Time (*Roquetaillade*, pp. 193–94). John's predictions of the disendowment of the clergy in his *Vade mecum* also bear the mark of Hildegard's thought on this subject, as we will see.

Not only was John familiar with these visionaries, but his writings can be seen as something of a clearing-house for medieval prophecy in general.[97] There seems to be scarcely a prophetic text or writer with which he has not had contact and one is tempted to say that it may have been partly through John's works that the tenets of European prophecy came to be more widely known in England in the fourteenth century. His knowledge of Joachite and Franciscan Spiritualist writings is especially impressive. John was himself a Franciscan with strong Spiritualist leanings and he seems to have written many of his prophetic works from various convent-prisons including the Papal prison at Avignon. It is not clear whether his prophetic activity caused his grueling imprisonments, but he seems to have been

Leaven of hope: new leadership

free to write prophecies from prison and was at least once commanded to do so by a cardinal. There is every possibility that his attitudes towards apostolic poverty, like those of many Franciscans with Spiritualist sympathies, caused his imprisonment. Whatever the case may be, the writings of John of Rupescissa are a fascinating chronicle of the thoughts of an apocalyptic Franciscan, zealous for Church reform and filled with the sense of an urgent need for change and repentance.

It is this mentality which he shares with Langland. To the best of my knowledge, Konrad Burdach is the only commentator on *Piers Plowman* to have noticed the resemblance, calling Rupescissa a "forerunner" of Langland.[98] Bloomfield (*Apocalypse*, pp. 92–93 and 94) also mentioned John in the context of his discussion of mid-fourteenth-century forecasts of the date of the coming of Antichrist. There is, however, no detailed scholarly discussion of John's ideas in relation to Langland's that I know of: what is offered here is only a beginning to such a study, as only the *Vade mecum in tribulatione*, which circulated most widely in England, will be considered, for reasons of space.

John entered the Minorite Order in 1322, having studied at the University of Toulouse, where he seems to have acquired, like many apocalyptic thinkers, a hatred of pagan philosophy, as well as a deep admiration for the works of the Franciscan Joachite Peter John Olivi (Reeves, *Influence*, p. 225). He read prophecies avidly and had visions himself, but, like Joachim of Fiore, says that he is no prophet but one who has unworthily received an understanding of the spirit of prophetic things of the Scriptures (*Vade mecum*, p. 496). The *Vade mecum* is divided into "intentiones" ("concepts" or, perhaps, "teachings"), as if to reinforce this idea of prophecy as inspired exegesis. He gives as his main purpose in writing down these prophecies the hope that others will be forewarned of the tribulations and be able to prepare themselves for what is ahead.

In the first "*intentio*" of the *Vade mecum*, John says that the tribulations to follow are just a stage in a plan which will bring the whole world "under one shepherd and one sheepfold" (pp. 497–98). In order that this may be accomplished, all clergy must return to the way of life established by Christ and his apostles as the only hope of salvaging this accursed generation (p. 498). Without such reform, it is impossible that the infidels will turn to the faith of Christ and John asks how the clergy can preach the humility and poverty of Christ with their great retinues and displays of worldliness. For him the return to apostolic life, as described by Christ in Matthew 10, is a purification process to which the clergy will be reduced: "cum flagellis durissimis, viz. infra A. D. M. CCC. LXX. praelibatum" (*Vade mecum*, p. 498). The first Antichrist he calls the Eastern Antichrist ("orientalis antichristus") and predicts that plagues and disasters will come in his wake. Like Langland in the final scenes of *Piers Plowman*, he foresees that these plagues will purge the world of the hardened reprobates ("reprobi indurati") and will help "ad unitatem fidei catholicae reducendam."

In "intentione septima" he foresees that the Church will be despoiled of its temporalities:

Intentio septima est intelligere modum denudandi Ecclesiam universam ab omnibus temporalibus rebus: indignabitur siquidem mundus ante annum Domini M. CCC. LXV. contra fastum divitiarum, temporalem gloriam mundanae superbiae clericorum, & tyrannici ac

189

laici populi subito & insperate consurgent & auferent ab eis dominia temporalia, regna, ducatus, comitatus, redditus, civitates & castra, & ipsos relinquent in puris & nudis Evangelicis declaratis. (p. 500)

This passage is very reminiscent of Hildegard's treatment of the same theme, especially John's comment "nec ipsis quibuscunque excommunicationibus aut bellicosis insultibus poterint obviare." Like Hildegard, John also uses the typical apocalyptic "false brethren" charge, here brought against all backsliding and hypocritical clergy: "quoniam Sathanas jam seduxit corda multorum hypocritarum incedentium in habitu humilitatis, in specie sanctitatis, in effigie poenitentiae, in fictione zeli ficti & falsi" (*Vade mecum*, p. 500). John then predicts violent treatment of the hypocrite clergy at the hands of the people:

ad extremum cognita eorum nequitia ipsi delebuntur & destituentur ac trucidabuntur per populos seculares: postquam autem videbunt principes Ecclesiae nullo modo de paupertate se posse resurgere, dabit illis *afflictio intellectum*, ut culpas suas humiliter recognoscant & disponant redire ad modum vivendi *Christi* & Apostolorum sanctorum, & convertet Deus corda iratorum contra illos Principum & populorum ad pacem, & ordinabuntur duntaxat qui tribulantur eis, videlicet competenter necessaria vitae. (p. 500)

This passage contains a number of now familiar ideas. First, John predicts, as Hildegard did, that the arrogant clergy will be slow to grasp that the despoliation is a real and permanent condition. Secondly, he suggests that the clergy will be made wiser by their chastisement and turn back to the apostolic life and thirdly, that the princes and the people will be the agents of the despoliation, much as Langland's prophecy in Passus v does. In fact, two further passages in the *Vade mecum* on the removing of temporalities from the Church add details of the participation of a reforming king and barons which we find in *Piers Plowman*. Finally, there is the usual reformist reference to the provision of the necessities of life.

Rupescissa follows the prophetic tradition of assigning the role of "reparator mundi" to two great leaders, "unum summum Pontificem" and an "Imperator sanctissimus." In "intentione duodecima" he speaks of the various reforms which the holy pope will make. Christ will beat the avaricious clergy with "funiculis pauperculis," literally, a scourge made of "little cords of the poor" or humble friars (McGinn, *Visions*, p. 232), and expell them from the temple just as he did the money-changers. Clearly, the presence of a few pure friars, tenaciously holding to the life of evangelical poverty, will eventually bring about their triumph over the corrupt and avaricious in John's view. We have already seen the pressure that the existence of the friars placed upon the *possessionati* in the anti-mendicant controversies, and this is in a sense what is being reflected here.[99] The reforms of this angelic pope are detailed at length, and include harsh measures to deal with simony, homosexuality and papal patronage. In spite of the doom and gloom of so much of John's message, his view of history is powerfully melioristic in true Joachite style. John's emperor, a king of great sanctity and humility, will execute the commands of the pope, conquer the Saracens, end the Greek schism and convert the Tartars.

John then moves on to consider the afflictions of the mendicants themselves. He says that they will suffer all the aforesaid tribulations of the clergy and more. The sins of the friars are the cause of all the coming tribulations, as predicted by St. Francis at his death (*Vade mecum*, p. 503). It is on account of the friars' transgressions of their rule that God allows them to be impugned by preachers, a clear reference to the anti-mendicant attacks ("quoniam propter peccatum transgressionis Regulae permisit Deus scandalum impugnationis Evangelicae paupertatis per praedicatores contra fratres minores"). As St. Francis predicted, the hearts of the people will be set against the friars ("cor populi contra eos") until the friars shall be forced to flee to the desert. Like most reformist prophets, John constantly returns to the idea that those who have faithfully kept to the apostolic life will be saved "Foelix qui in diebus illis ab obedientia & fide pauperis illius apostatice non discedet" (*Vade mecum*, p. 502). The future of the mendicants depends upon the angelic pope, who, after the tribulations, he hopes, will take an interest in helping restore the order. We might expect the friars to be so central in the writings of a Franciscan, but their centrality in *Piers Plowman* is surprising, until one realizes the key role they played in apocalyptic reformist thought. Perhaps, too, for Langland, as for John and other reformist thinkers, those who had vowed the life closest to that of Christ were most responsible in transgressing and most crucial to the "renovatio mundi" as the leaven in the bread or the salt of the earth.

There is much more in Rupescissa's *Vade mecum* which is of interest as an apocalyptic program, but it is not directly relevant here. Like Langland, he has a millenarian vision of the time when men shall beat their swords into plowshares and when the Holy Ghost shall pour God's Spirit upon the world. John also works, like Langland, with the uneasy partnership between desire for reform and apocalyptic vision. With something of a sense of humor he writes,

si autem non eveniant flagella gravia inferius describenda, hoc erat hoc quod ego quaero, videlicet, ut sententia durissima egressa, in forma fulguris & ignis, a facie *Antiqui dierum* & ab *ira Agni sedentis super thronum*, per poenitentiam revocetur, sicut *Ninive*, & ego confusus & iratus remaneam sicut *Jonas*.   (*Vade mecum*, p. 497)

He advises that, in preparing for the tribulations ahead, the reader pray earnestly for reform, for, at the very least, those who "sigh and mourn for all the abominations" (Ezechiel 9:4) will be passed over (as will those who have kept to the evangelical life). In Langland too, there is an "elect," made up of the fools for Christ and God's "priue disciples" (*Piers Plowman*, XXII. 61 and IX. 118), those few who have kept the faith and, especially in the case of the latter, have been faithful in the *ascesis* of apostolic poverty.

A JOACHITE PERSPECTIVE ON *PIERS PLOWMAN*

Having considered a number of medieval prophecies of Church reform we can now go back to some of the apocalyptic passages in *Piers Plowman* with some sense of their larger context. Obviously the Joachite prophecies do not tell us everything we would like to know about Langland's apocalypticism, but they do point up some of his main concerns.

Reformist apocalypticism and *Piers Plowman*

Four areas of interest emerge from placing *Piers Plowman* in the context of these prophecies. First of all, it becomes easier to understand Langland's perpetual concern with the distinction between true and false apostles against such a background. Secondly – and this is related to the first theme – there is the sense of crisis of leadership which emerges in various forms throughout the poem. Thirdly, we have Langland's fascination with eremiticism, evangelical poverty and the repristination of the clergy. And finally, in such a context it becomes easier to understand what type of apocalyptic program Langland imagined the future to hold.

Let us begin with the first of these notions. Konrad Burdach's remark (*Dichter*, p. 329) that the whole of *Piers Plowman* is concerned with the condemnation of false prophets has a corollary, and that is that it must also be concerned with the seeking out of true ones. He pointed to an important passage in Zacharias 13 in which, after promising to "take away the false prophets and the unclean spirit out of the earth," the Lord prophesies:

> And it shall come to pass in that day that the prophets shall be confounded, every one by his own vision, when he shall prophesy: neither shall they be clad with a garment of sackcloth, to deceive. But he shall say: I am no prophet. I am a husbandman: for Adam is my example from my youth. And they shall say to him: What are these wounds in the midst of thy hands? And he shall say: with these I was wounded in the house of them that loved me. Awake, O sword, against my shepherd and against the man that cleaveth to me, saith the Lord of hosts. Strike the shepherd, and the sheep shall be scattered. And I will turn my hand to the little ones. (13:4–7)

These verses go a long way toward encompassing the complex triangular arrangement between Piers, "Peter" and Christ in *Piers Plowman*, as well as the apocalyptic ties which bind them together. The notion of the plowman as a *true* prophet, scourge of the false spiritual leaders, a man with no intellectual or spiritual pretensions, a man who has looked only to Adam, the most human of men, as a model – this notion comes very close to capturing the spirit both of *Piers Plowman* and of much medieval apocalyptic writing. These works convey a sense of desperation for simplicity and honesty in both clerical and political leadership, and a sense of defiance toward the "establishment" which does not seem to answer these needs. The impetus in much apocalyptic writing is to seek both answers and leadership from outside the circles of the learned and the powerful. The attacks on superfluous possessions and on learning are just two symptoms of this mentality and both Langland's Christ and his Piers fit this concern with evangelical poverty and simplicity.[100]

The notion that only a leader of the utmost humility and simplicity – a leader like Piers – can bring about the needed or expected reforms is one of the key tenets of Joachite apocalypticism, especially as it was espoused by rigorist Franciscans. Burdach, Donaldson and Bourquin have all shown Langland's acquaintance with and sympathy for the early Franciscan literature and especially the ideology of poverty, simplicity and anti-intellectualism which it fostered. In the thirteenth century even moderate Franciscans saw themselves as fulfilling Joachim's prophecy of a group of coming spiritual men to help mankind make the *transitus* into the next age. No less a figure than Bonaventure espoused the view that in the present age God was sending men of voluntary mendicancy to fulfill such a role through the destruction of avarice.[101] However, by the fourteenth century it was no longer possible to maintain such a glorious view of the Franciscan mission. It is an irony of history that those who had been hailed as the true prophets came to be seen as the false ones. By Langland's time the *modus vivendi* of voluntary mendicancy was seen to have destroyed more saints than it had made, but the ideology itself was not dead.

Langland seems to have supplied his own version of holy mendicants in his "lunatik lollar" figures (IX. 109–18). Donaldson has shown the precise connection between these lunatic mendicants and the *joculatores domini* of St. Francis ("merye-mouthed men, munstrals of heuene, / And godes boys, bourdyors," lines 126–27), but he was unable to shed much light on their ability to prophesy (line 114). The missing link may well be the Joachite side of a Franciscan Joachite image.[102] We noted that the other prominent holy fools in the poem are those few who resist Antichrist (XXII. 58–68) and this surely is something of a clue. While both sets of fools are indebted to St. Paul's "fools for Christ," the complexity of these particular holy lunatics is somewhat greater than the Pauline concept. Langland clearly associates the lunatic mendicants with Christ's own disciples (IX. 119–25), with the *joculatores domini*, with the few fools who hold out against Antichrist and finally with the dreamer himself, as we saw earlier. The one thing that all these figures have in common is their ability to prophesy, in both senses of the word (and this includes the dreamer). In Joachite terms, the faithful remnant of true apostles who hold to the apostolic life against all the onslaughts of Antichrist is made up of those who will keep the ideals of Christianity alive until the dawn of the renewal. Such holy men are the focal point for Langland's concern about the crisis of leadership, apostolic poverty and the leaven of reform – they are the key figures in his apocalyptic grammar.

The only ambiguous figure in this list of holy mendicants is the dreamer himself and he is perhaps at the center of the poem's concern to sort out the true from the false prophets. When the poem opens Will has donned the guise of a hermit and with the most dubious of motives sets out to lead an eremitical life. The itinerant mendicancy he chooses may be seen as part of the eremitical ideal or he may be seen as an allegorical embodiment of *vagatio*, in monastic literature a common metaphor for spiritual instability.[103] Will's own motives are the main problem. He starts out as a false hermit mostly because he seems to believe that there are short-cuts to spiritual experience: that is, he believes that one can just simply go out and "hear wonders" (Prol. 4). Obviously, an awareness of the "mony ferlyes" that "han falle in a fewe ʒeres" (Prol. 63) is what has triggered this interest and this could be read as a legitimate desire to search for the meaning of present events by reading the signs of the times and their place in Salvation History.[104] However, there are no short-cuts to spiritual wisdom and this is something that Will does not seem to know when he sets out.

On the positive side, however, Will is not a false hermit in that he does increasingly take on the way of life of the holy ascetic in the course of his wandering, as we have seen. He has a very strong sense, right from the beginning of the poem, that the false hermits are false because they will not endure the hardships of the ascetic road and in the autobiographical passage of Passus v he makes sure that the reader distinguishes the dreamer from this type of hermit. Such hermits do, unlike the dreamer and the lunatic lollers, carry bags, and worry about tomorrow; they do not, if they can help it, walk, "wollewaerd and watshoed" (xx. 1); they do, unlike the dreamer, salute the rich in the middle of the street because they know which side their bread is buttered on.[105] And they do not, as Will does, refuse the temptations of Nede. Will may have begun his eremitical life for the wrong reasons, but this does not preclude his endeavor from bearing good fruit in the end. Like the other mendicants in the poem who suffer the apostolic way of life – whether willingly, or like the lunatic lollars, of necessity – the dreamer is capable of visions and of prophesying "of þe peple, pleyinge, as it were." I think we must concede Will a place, if a humble one, among the fools for Christ with a prophetic vocation.

Let us look now at the apocalyptic side of Langland's sense of leadership crisis. As R. H. Robbins has shown,[106] there was a good deal of the spirit of both political and religious dissent about in fourteenth-century England and there was plenty of potential for radical, even subversive, interpretation of apocalyptic ideology. Notions like the rise of a world emperor or pope from the class of the itinerant poor, or the stripping away of all clerical possessions except the bare necessities of life, are undeniably radical. Such ideas were motivated by the desire for a vigorous spirituality which was felt to be lacking in present leadership and a desire to make a statement about what really mattered in the apostolate: that is, the spirit and not the flesh in which it is clothed. These subversive apocalyptic fantasies may simply be symbolic gestures, but it is important to remember that symbols have their own power.

Implicit in Will's query as to how he can save his soul (I. 80) is the question, "Who can show me the way?", as Contemplation's comment (VII. 307–08) suggests. The motif of the search for a trustworthy model or leader repeats itself again and again throughout the poem, in the pilgrims' need to know the way to Truth, in Will's search for Dowell and in Conscience's ultimate search for Piers. The need is, above all, for a leader of great sanctity through whom the Church can be re-spiritualized and restored.

The prophecies we have been discussing spring out of this same desire for renewal and re-sanctification through a leader of great holiness. What they express in their generalized and impersonal form, Langland tries to bring to life at a much more local level. We do not know much about the king he expected, but we do have an extensive portrait of Piers to give us some insight into the kind of leadership he admired. We have already noted the radical elements in Piers' leadership; here I would like to note the reformist aspects. In "setting the world to work," he tries desperately to sort out as many social problems as he can, for example in his advice to the knight (VIII. 35ff.), in his attempt to deal with the Wasters and the lazy (VIII. 119ff.) and in the pardon sent to him from Truth which attempts to set out the duties and failings of the various groups of people and

Leaven of hope: new leadership

inspire them to turn toward perfection of life in their own "estate": "Alle þe peple hadde pardon ynow þat parfitliche lyuede" (IX. 43). The case of the merchants is a good example:

> Marchauntes in þe margine hadde many 3eres,
> Ac no *pena et a culpa* no Treuthe wolde hem graunte
> For they holde nat here haliday as holi chirch hem hoteth,
> And for they swere by here soule and god mote hem helpe
> A3en clene consience for couetyse of wynnynge. (IX. 22–26)

However, Truth promises them salvation "vnder his secrete seal" if they will give of their profits to charity. With this promise of salvation Langland actually pauses to give us a glimpse of the joy of the merchants:

> "And y shal sende 3ow mysulue seynt Mihel myn angel
> That no deuel shal 3ow dere ne despeyre in 3oure deynge
> And sethe sende 3oure soules þer y mysulue dwelle
> And abyde þer in my blisse, body and soule for euere."
> Tho were marchauntes mury; many wopen for ioye
> And preyde for Peres the plouhman þat purchased hem þis bulles.
> (IX. 37–42)

Such glimpses of communal enthusiasm testify not only to Langland's deep faith in the power of the Church's message to elicit real happiness, but also to his belief that the crying need of his day was for good leadership. It is as if the reprobate merchants were not really reprobate at all, but needed only the simplicity and sincerity of Piers' pardon to set forth their role in society, thereby releasing a great burden of anxiety about how they could achieve this mysterious thing called "salvation," no doubt made all the more mysterious for most people by the literacy barrier. We have seen that this impetus toward spiritual leadership goes back to Joachim's own spiritual utopianism.

Piers is a figure of reassurance and renewal as a guide toward salvation right from the beginning. His ability to cleanse and to purify is metaphorically expressed in his ploughing, "My plouh pote shal by my pyk-staff and pyche a-to þe rotes / And helpe my coltur to kerue and clanse þe forwes" (VIII. 64–65), and his reassurance of the path to salvation in his harvesting:

> And alle þat helpen me erye or elles to wedy
> Shal haue leue by oure lord to go and glene aftur me
> And maken hym merye þer-myde, maugrey ho bigruchen hit.
> (VIII. 66–68)

There are certainly apocalyptic overtones here in the imagery of pruning and harvesting. Without attempting a complete critical reappraisal of the role of Piers in the poem, I have suggested, following Burdach, that our understanding of that complex problem can be partly enriched by setting Piers against a background of the reform heroes of medieval prophecy. After a brief discussion of medieval prophetic writers such as John of Rupescissa and Cola di Rienzo, Burdach suggests that Piers Plowman might also be seen in the role of a "mystical Reformer of the future."[107] He mentions a list of reforms which Piers, like other apocalyptic reformers, champions in the poem, among which is his leadership "toward a state of freedom from all needs" ("der Bedürfnislosigkeit heraufführen"). He then goes on to say that Piers embodies two very different characteristics: a "possessionless and poor" aspect and a "busy, work-a-day" aspect in his role as ploughman.[108] There is a tension between these two themes of possessionlessness and earning a living throughout the poem. In Piers they represent two models of perfection: in the *Visio*, the model of the hard worker who labors for the good of his society and, in the *Vita*, the model of evangelical poverty which Christ expected of his disciples. In (pseudo-) Joachite terms clerical leadership progresses historically from an emphasis on the first, to an emphasis on the second (Joachim's disciples having literalized what was for the abbot himself primarily metaphorical).

Although it occurs in both texts, Piers' transition from one model of perfection to the other is explicitly announced in the B-text; he vows to give up the life of labor for the life of holy "carelessness" in B. VII, and in doing so he is in effect passing to a higher state of perfection:

> "I shal cessen of my sowyng," quod Piers, "& swynke noȝt so harde,
> Ne aboute my [bilyue] so bisy be na moore;
> Of preieres and of penaunce my plouȝ shal ben herafter,
> And wepen whan I shoulde [werche] þouȝ whete breed me faille."
>
> (B. VII. 122–25)

He then quotes one of the verses most cherished by evangelical enthusiasts:

> "And but if luc lye he lereþ vs [anoþer]
> By foweles [þat are] noȝt bisy aboute þe [bely joye];
> Ne *soliciti sitis* he seiþ in þe gospel . . .
> Haue þei no gerner to go to but god fynt hem alle."
>
> (B. VII. 129–31, 135)

This is the manner of life of "godes priue disciples" and of all those who, from St. Anthony to St. Francis, have followed the commandment: "Si vis perfectus esse, vade, vende quae habes . . . et veni, sequere me" (Matthew 19:21). Piers' brief appearances throughout the *Vita* portray him as an embodiment of this evangelical poverty. Once we are told that he looks like Patience himself:

> And there cam Pacience as a pore thyng and preyede mete pur charite,
> Ilyk Peres the ploghman, as he a palmere were,
> Crauede and cryede, for Cristes loue of heuene,
> A meles mete for a pore man, or moneye, yf they hadde.   (XV. 33–36)

As we have seen, medieval writers of prophecy expected of their reforming heroes, even the secular ones, a high degree of sanctity, and this usually meant a state of apostolic poverty. Piers is much like any one of these reforming heroes. Like the men of Joachim's first order of "viri spirituales," Piers epitomizes the apostolic life, serving mankind and yet wanting nothing of the world ("de rebus mundanis nihil cupient"). Like Joachim's Peter and John, Piers passes from the "ecclesie laborantium . . . prius desudantum in vita activa" of Peter to the "ecclesie quiescentium . . . postea exultantum in vita contemplativa" of Joachim's John, perhaps suggesting the historical progression which more radical disciples had imposed on the abbot's subtle distinction.[109] Like some of the holy popes of the *Vaticinia de summis pontificibus* and other prophecies, he is a leader drawn from the ranks of the patient and godly poor. Nearly all the prophecies of reform give some suggestion of the poverty and humility of the reforming hero, whether he comes from poverty to take up the position or, by renunciation, goes to a state of poverty. Piers is not out of place among reforming apocalyptic leaders and this is precisely the role the "lewed vicory" gives him (xxi. 425–30).

The third theme which the comparison with medieval prophecies brings out is the expectation of progression through return to a pristine state, a paradox which is characteristic of Joachite thought. The prophecy in Passus v tries to deal with this problem. The possessioners are to be beaten for the breaking of their rule (especially, here, their vow to poverty) and the means by which they have been able to break it, that is, their temporalities, are to be taken away from them, "*ad pristinum statum ire*" (v. 171–72). As Bourquin points out (*Etudes*, p. 698), the whole idea of aspiring to perfection, of perpetually searching for Dowell, Dobet and finally Dobest, is part of a concern to return to this pristine state, to the life of Christ himself. However, while this concern is evident throughout the poem and while he holds the ideal of perfect poverty in the highest esteem, Langland is also driven to forego it in his perpetual search for practical reforms. In the second part of the prophecy Langland proposes that the friars be provided with a living, although this nearly turns the previous reform of the possessioners on its head: Constantine, who caused so much trouble for the older orders, is now to be "cook and couerour" (line 175) of the *friars'* churches. Of course, the keynote here is moderation as Langland no doubt intends that the friars will be given the necessities and no more, but in so doing he has taken away the fraternal ideal of absolute poverty.

Since we know that in other places Langland looked upon the ideal of evangelical poverty as the highest form of perfection, his desire to give the friars a "fyndynge" must spring from a recognition of the inability of most men to keep such a vow in day-to-day life. In chapter 4 we looked at the views and charges of the friars' critics regarding abuses of their rule, and noted that, while real abuses no doubt existed, these were in many cases exaggerated. A side of the mendicant story which has not often been stressed is the well-documented evidence that the friars were in fact often quite needy. M. W. Sheehan has shown, in his dissertation "Franciscan Poverty in England (1348–1538)," that the daily quest for alms did not produce enough to make ends meet and that the friars were rarely free from debt (pp. 319–20). There is also evidence of a slow, steady erosion of alms (*ibid.*, p. 321). Sheehan concludes that the friars could not be supported by alms alone in medieval England and that their need was in many cases very real.[110] Langland's representation of "Nede" as a friar was obviously quite apt. In such a situation, as Sheehan shows, abuses were bound to develop. In the harsh light of the everyday world, among everyday men Nede is more common than Patience, and flattery is more practical than the *pater-noster* as a means to an end. In an earlier passus Patience had told Actyf,

197

"Lo, here lyflode ynow, yf oure beleue be trewe . . .
Quodcumque pecieritis in nomine meo dabitur enim vobis. Et alibi: Non in solo pane viuit homo."
"Hastow," quod Actyf, "ay such mete with the?"
"ȝe," quod Pacience, and oute of his poke hente
A pece of þe *pater-noster* and profred hit to vs all.
And y lystnede and lokede what lyflode hit were
And thenne was hit *fiat voluntas tua* þat sholde fynde vs alle.
"Haue, Actyf," quod Pacience, "and eet this when þe hungreth
Or when thow claumest for colde or clingest for eny drouthe . . ."

(xv. 238, 245a–52)

This passage contains one of a handful of instances in which the perspective shifts back suddenly to Will (lines 249–50); visionary convention suggests that this is because Langland wants to point up the response of the ordinary man here. The reader participates in his incredulity. What Patience offers as a "fyndynge" is truly the life of evangelical poverty, as starkly depicted as any rigorist Franciscan would have described it (lines 254–61). Placed beside Nede's comments, Patience's mode of livelihood can only be described as that of a fool.

However, alongside this idealism Langland also gives us Conscience's response to Nede's "realism"; it is a double-layered one in which neither the real needs of life nor the ideals of evangelical poverty are disclaimed. As we have seen, Conscience offers the friars a "fyndynge," but it is a conditional one (xxii. 243–53). Like Patience, Conscience promises all the necessities of life "yf oure beleue be trewe" (xv. 238). The friars must stay within Unity, harbor no envious feelings (xxii. 246) and live by their rule (line 247). Finally, they must "leue logyk" and learn to love.[111] Under these conditions they will lack for nothing. If, however, the friars can make these reforms, Conscience promises them a 'fyndynge": "Y wol be ȝoure borwh . . . ȝe shal nothyng lakke." Conscience's words suggest two things: one is a promise of provision for physical necessities, as is implied in the prophecy when "Constantyn shal be here cook and couerour of here churches," but his words are also strongly reminiscent of Christ's question to his disciples: "When I sent you without purse and scrip and shoes, did you want anything? But they said: Nothing" (Luke 22:35). While Langland seems to feel that most friars may require a "fyndynge" to keep them on the straight and narrow, he obviously could not deny the possibility of evangelical poverty to all, even with Antichrist knocking at the gates. Therefore Conscience's words work on two levels, one for the vast numbers of "apprentices" and one for the precious few "masters." As Langland is constantly trying to show, some will do well and some will do better, and some may even, against all odds, do best.

We turn finally to the question of Langland's eschatology. At the end of the reformer-king prophecy, Langland writes, "Ac ar þat kyng come, as cronicles me tolde, / Clerkes and holy churche shal be clothed newe" (v. 178–79). We have seen that this fragmentary process of scheduling occurs in the earlier prophecy (iii. 477) as well, and that Langland seems to have a penchant for apocalyptic programming.[112] In all cases where this pattern occurs, what is being described is a period of renewal in the future *after* a battle with the forces of "Caym" (B. x. 334). There is also the promise at the end of the poem of reforms that Piers will carry out, which implies the same pattern of renewal after tribulation. Furthermore, the image of "a knok vppon here crounes" in the disendowment prophecy may be seen as a sign of *permanent* renewal after Antichrist, since Langland continues "and incurable þe wounde." This obviously stems from the *"plaga insanabili"* of the quotation from Isaias 14:5–6 (*"Contriuit dominus baculum impiorum, virgam dominancium, plaga insanabili,"* v. 177). There is, however, another biblical quotation which had a great significance in Joachite prophecy that uses the same image. The beast with seven heads receives a mortal wound in Apocalypse 13:3 which is then cured: "And I saw one of his heads as it were slain to death; and his death's wound was healed. And all the earth was in admiration after the beast." Many Joachites interpreted this blow to the head of the beast as having been dealt by St. Francis with his doctrine of apostolic poverty. Langland's point that the wound is incurable may suggest that this time the return to apostolic poverty will be permanent.

The final passus of the poem describes the onslaught of Antichrist's forces, culminating in Conscience's search for Piers. As we have seen, various critics have puzzled over the problem of reconciling a battle with Antichrist, which in traditional eschatology would imply that the End of the World was at hand, and Conscience's expectation that Piers will return to destroy pride and solve the crisis of the friars.[113] In the apocalyptic programs of Joachite writings, and in many of the prophecies which they influenced, there is always an age of reform before the Last Judgment and after Antichrist. In looking for writers who, like Langland, foresee a spiritual *renovatio*, we can cast the net even more widely to include some of the prophecies which espouse what Robert Lerner has called post-Antichrist chiliasm.[114] This group consists mainly of exegetical writers whose apocalyptic theories were derived from speculations about the period for "refreshment of the saints" after the tribulations of Antichrist.[115] Pre-Antichrist chiliasm is, as Lerner says, the most popular variety and is the kind most often found in vernacular works and prophecies.[116] Langland's sense of the events of the End places him among the group of exegetical thinkers who espoused a fairly self-conscious post-Antichrist chiliasm – a factor which, I think, sheds a little more light on Langland's intellectual background. Whether in the end we decide that Langland's is a Joachite-influenced eschatology or not, we know at least that the problem is more complicated than the traditional eschatology allows for.

Obviously, it is impossible to say for certain that Langland was influenced by a Joachite tradition of prophecy. What we can say, though, is that there are several elements in *Piers Plowman* which are characteristic (although not always *exclusively* characteristic) of Joachite-influenced prophecy: the promise of reform after Antichrist, the belief in a necessary return *ad pristinum statum* and the expectation of a leader of great simplicity and sanctity are some of the aspects which we have looked at in some detail. To these may be added various other themes from *Piers Plowman*, such as the descent of the Holy Spirit and his distribution of gifts to strengthen Holy Church against Antichrist:

> "For y wol dele today and deuyde grace
> To alle kyne creatures þat can his fyue wittes,
> Tresor to lyue by to here lyues ende
> And wepne to fihte with þat wol neuere fayle.

For Auntecrist and hise al the world shal greue
And acombre þe, Consience, bote yf Crist the helpe.
And false profetes fele, flateres and glosares,
Shal come and be curatours ouer kynges and erles.
And thenne shal pryde be pope and prince of holy chirche,
Coueytise and vnkyndenesse cardynales hym to lede." (XXI. 215–24)

Predicting the onslaught of an antipope, as well as pseudo-apostles, Grace here lays stress upon the Holy Spirit, which will unify Unity against the enemy, upon gifts that are as important now as in the first century.[117] There is also the centrality of the friars in Langland's concern for reform, his suspicion of contemporary scholastic philosophy (or at least, its abuse) and his use of various images or *tableaux* which are common in apocalyptic prophecy (such as the scenes of mass devotion he portrays in Passus VII and Passus XXI).

As the passage above prophesies, Langland sees the imminent apocalyptic crisis largely as a clerical one: the false prophets will be "curatours" over kings and earls while an antichrist figure, Pride, will rule the papal throne. This, for Langland, is the crisis developing even now in the Church and his vision at the end of the poem tries to capture the force of the onslaught of the false apostles. However, as we have seen, this is not the End of the World for Langland. Although we do not know everything we would like to know about his apocalyptic expectations, we know enough to align them with some of the radical and ultimately optimistic reformist prophets of his day. In Langland's apocalyptic grammar Piers, and perhaps the various "fools for Christ" figures of the poem, reappear again and again as the leaven of hope for a better age.

6

Conclusions

This study has attempted to consider the extent to which Langland may be seen to reflect attitudes typical of what Robert Lerner has recently called the medieval European apocalyptic mentality (Lerner, "Black Death"). We have looked at some of the works which reflect this mentality and which were available in fourteenth-century England in our study of the Hildegardian visionary tradition, the eschatological propaganda of the anti-mendicant writers and the non-visionary prophetic tradition of the Joachite thinkers. When supplemented by some knowledge of the formal and stylistic features of the early apocalypses of the Christian tradition, this body of material can begin to provide answers to some questions which have troubled critics of *Piers Plowman* for years. Whether it be the problem of Langland's "non-medieval" allegorical style or his troublesome beginning of a new pilgrimage after the coming of Antichrist or his seemingly odd obsession with the reform of the fraternal orders, an awareness of medieval religious apocalypticism has helped to illuminate some of the poem's supposed idiosyncrasies. This should suggest to us that it is not Langland who is "non-medieval" or idiosyncratic in his symbolism or inconsistent in his allegory, as so many critics have charged – it is we who do not know enough about the conventions and models he was working with. Some day, I hope that we will know much more than we do now about the reformist apocalypticism which lies behind the poem. Scholarship could further illuminate every facet of apocalypticism touched on here. With so many questions still unanswered, one can only hope that it does.

It should be apparent by now that reformist apocalypticism, as I have described it, is motivated by the dual concerns of a felt need for social and spiritual renewal. To this end, writers try to place the current events and problems of their times within the larger framework of crisis and resolution in Salvation History. And I have argued that the same is true of Langland's concerns with the clerical and fraternal problems of his day: apocalypticism provided him with a framework in which he could understand the role of seemingly catastrophic developments in the course of history. Reformist apocalypticism was so comforting for medieval thinkers not simply because it promised *renovatio*, but because it gave meaning to the ills of the present, and meaningless suffering is, as modern existentialism has taught us, the hardest of all types of suffering to bear. This brand of apocalypticism must have been particularly appealing to Langland because of the spiritual richness of its symbolism (compare, for example, the cardboard symbolism of contemporary political prophecy).

As we have seen, apocalyptic works deal in the perpetual conflict between true and false apostles, and the literary ones often attempt to do this by analogy to the narrator's own internal spiritual conflict – here we move from the social concerns of the apocalyptic form to the spiritual ones. We saw that in an apocalypse like *The Shepherd of Hermas*, the visions which the narrator experiences soon begin to be a reflection of his own spiritual state, and visionary conventions, even simple ones like the distinction between waking and sleeping, often denote spiritual condition in medieval religious visions. The question of the visionary's credibility as a prophet comes to rest upon his credentials for the position, and among these medieval audiences came to expect a portrait of a social outsider who had rejected all worldly comforts and concerns.

By the sixteenth century, as P. V. Brady has shown,[1] the ambiguous *propheta* figure – poorly clad, mad or mentally distracted, wandering, denunciatory – had become a stock figure in chronicles and broadsheets, a figure who needed no interpretation for contemporary readers and whose appearances were included among the other news of wonders, portents and signs of doom which filled the pages of such popular writings. The fact that such "newer prophets," as they were called in sixteenth-century Germany, were regarded by some as true spokesmen of God and by others as pseudo-prophets and forerunners of Antichrist, and that this stock figure was even open to parody,[2] suggests that the ambiguity of the medieval tradition upon which Langland and his reformist predecessors were drawing lived to attain the status of a convention in Reformation Europe. By this time Protestant reformers like Robert Crowley were reading *Piers Plowman* as an apocalypse and the poem was enjoying a "brief vogue" among like-minded readers.[3]

This study has explored a wide range of prophetic thought in an attempt to inform readers of the choices available to a fourteenth-century English writer with a taste for religious prophecy. The most important question, however, is not so much which precise bit of apocalyptic prophecy Langland used as why he would have used apocalyptic prophecy in a poem so vitally concerned with the present. I hope that by now the answer to this question is clear: Langland used fragments of the apocalyptic tradition precisely because he did not believe that the End of the World was at hand, but rather because he believed that Providence was likely to leave mankind to reap the whirlwind it had sown for itself. The apocalypticism established Langland's sense of urgency and indignation; if his readers were disturbed by the eschatological signs and allusions or implications in his portrayal of current events, so much the better, he must have felt. The relationship between a passionate concern for present world problems and an elusive sense of apocalyptic crisis has been much discussed by scholars of that other great religious visionary of the Middle Ages, Dante. In a recent article on Canto XIX of the *Inferno*, R. K. Emmerson and R. B. Herzman comment on the relationship between the political and apocalyptic levels of the allegory in Dante:

Conclusions

Dante emphasizes both the contemporary and the apocalyptic, the simoniac popes and Antichrist. To put the matter specifically into the critical vocabulary most often associated with the *Commedia*, the language of fourfold interpretation: in this canto Dante emphasizes the anagogical level in order to heighten the impact of the allegorical.[4]

Langland too sometimes emphasizes the "anagogic" or apocalyptic in order to heighten the impact of the "allegorical" or contemporary. The role of the indignant prophet is, after all, to paint a vision for the visionless of where the road *now* leads and juxtapose it with a vision of where it might.

Notes

1 From "The Marriage of Heaven and Hell," plate 12, *Blake: Complete Writings*, ed. Geoffrey Keynes (London, 1966), p. 153.

2 All references to *Piers Plowman* are from the C-text, edited by Derek Pearsall (*Piers Plowman by William Langland. An Edition of the C-Text* [London, 1978]), unless otherwise indicated. (The List of Abbreviations and Select Bibliography contain bibliographical details of works frequently cited or of most importance for this study; other citations appear in the notes only.) References to the B-text will be preceded by "B" and will be taken from the edition of George Kane and E. T. Donaldson, *Piers Plowman: The B Version* (London, 1975; revised 1988). The A-text of *Piers Plowman* has been edited by George Kane (*Piers Plowman: The A Version* [London, 1960; revised 1988]). A. G. Rigg and Charlotte Brewer have recently edited a version of the poem which they believe predates the A-text, *Piers Plowman: The Z-Version* (Toronto, 1983); however, this thesis has not gained wide acceptance and it is not, in any case, relevant to this study. The use of the C-text should no longer require defense; it forms the basis of this study because it is only in the poem's final version that Langland's spiritual concerns receive their fullest expression.

3 The political prophecies of the later Middle Ages are distinguished by a stereotyped use of animal symbolism to represent the kings, noblemen or countries of various factions and they are usually written in the vernacular. Some of these prophecies have a popular or folklorish quality (see J. Murray, *The Romance and Prophecies of Thomas of Erceldoune*, EETS no. 61 [London, 1875]). Close study of the vernacular political prophecies reveals few of the parallels which editors of *Piers Plowman* have frequently suggested in their notes on the prophetic passages, nor does comparison with the "John of Bridlington" prophecies, outside of a few allusions to current events such as any contemporary writers might share. A few parallels with political prophecy will be noticed below; however, one might have expected more from what was, judging from the number of English manuscripts in which they survive, a popular genre. On political prophecy in England see O'Sullivan', "Treatment of Political Themes," and see Caroline D. Eckhardt, *The Prophetia Merlini of Geoffrey of Monmouth* (Cambridge, Mass., 1982). On the "John of Bridlington" prophecies see Michael Curley, "The Cloak of Anonymity and *The Prophecy of John of Bridlington*," *Modern Philology*, 77 (1979–80), pp. 361–69. For a recent discussion of parallels with *Piers Plowman* see A. V. Globe, "Apocalyptic Themes in the Sibylline Oracles, the Revelation, Langland, Spenser and Marvell," unpublished University of Toronto Ph.D. thesis, 1970.

4 For a different point of view see Emmerson, *Antichrist*, and Adams, "Need" and "Versions". My disagreement with Emmerson and Adams is discussed in greater detail below. On my use of the term "popular," see note 17 below, this chapter.

5 See B. McGinn in "Apocalypticism in the Middle Ages: An Historiographical Sketch,"

Medieval Studies, 37 (1975), pp. 253–54. For a useful discussion of the difference between an apocalypse and apocalyptic eschatology, see McGinn, "Early Apocalypticism," p. 3. The apocalypse as genre will be discussed in chapter 3, below.

6 For a concise discussion of millenarianism/chiliasm, as the terms apply to medieval writers, see Lerner, "Black Death." Biblical citations in this study, unless otherwise indicated, refer to the Vulgate version, *Biblia sacra, Vulgatae editionis* (London, n.d.). Translated biblical quotations, unless otherwise indicated, are from *The Holy Bible: Douay Version* (London, 1956).See note 13 below, this chapter, for the practice followed with respect to other translated quotations.

7 The definitions in this paragraph are drawn from the *Oxford English Dictionary*. The role of the medieval visionary is defined and discussed in greater detail in Chapters 2 and 3, below, especially pp. 56–57; the medieval understanding of the prophet and prohecy in Chapter 3, pp. 112–15.

8 See Reeves, "Development," p. 41, and McGinn, "Early Apocalypticism," p. 28 and *passim*.

9 There seems to be no consensus among scholars as to what the "new" apocalypticism of the later Middle Ages should be called. I have used the term "new" to distinguish it from the more established, popular eschatology (described in more detail below; my use of the term "popular" is discussed in note 17, below, this chapter). Robert Lerner has recently written an article in which he suggests that what I have called the "old" and "new" apocalyptic theories might be distinguished from each other as "pre-" and "post-Antichrist chiliasm" (see Lerner, "Black Death," pp. 541ff.), according to whether any given writer foresaw better times to come *before* or *after* the reign of Antichrist. Although this is a very useful distinction, as an index of apocalyptic optimism it creates some problems of application. (Lerner himself has shown [see "Refreshment," p. 119] that there are problems with over-emphasizing the optimism of the post-Antichrist period.) I prefer to emphasize the distinction between the old Augustinian historical pessimism and the optimism of "new" apocalyptic theories, the optimism of the latter differing from the former in its new emphasis on spiritual and clerical renewal.

10 *The Study of the Bible in the Middle Ages* (Notre Dame, 1964; repr. of the Oxford, 1952 edition), pp. 291–92.

11 Rauh makes this point about Hildegard of Bingen (*Antichrist*, pp. 512–13).

12 On dualism, or the cosmic struggle between good and evil in pre-medieval apocalyptic writings, see McGinn, "Early Apocalypticism," pp. 11–12.

13 Cited in R. W. Southern, "Aspects of the European Tradition of Historical Writing: 3. History as Prophecy," Presidential Address to the Royal Historical Association, *Transactions of the Royal Historical Association*, 5th series, no. 22 (1972), pp. 172–73, from the introduction to Bacon's *Opus maius*, ed. A. Gasquet, *English Historical Review*, 12 (1897), pp. 514–15. I have quoted from translations of Latin sources throughout this study where reliable published translations exist, supplying references to the Latin edition in such cases. Where reliable translations do not exist, the Latin text is given. Rudimentary translations of these passages can be found in my doctoral thesis, but space limitations prevent their inclusion here.

14 See, for example, Aers, *Creative Imagination*, pp. 67ff. When one considers that Hildegard of Bingen corresponded with the great figures of her day, both political and ecclesiastical, that Bridget of Sweden threatened popes, and that Joachim of Fiore advised both kings and popes on apocalypticism, it must be seen as a serious concern in the medieval world.

15 See Emmerson, *Antichrist*, p. 49, on the influence of the *Tiburtine Oracle* and the *Pseudo-Methodius Revelations* "in the expansion and transformation of the Antichrist tradition to include legends such as Gog and Magog and the reign of the Last World Emperor . . .

Antichrist became . . . a central figure around whom many other legends and expectations could be organized." The *Tibertine Oracle* and the *Pseudo-Methodius* have been edited by Ernst Sackur, *Sibyllinische Texte und Forschungen* (Halle, 1898). On these texts see Emmerson, *Antichrist*, pp. 48–49 and *passim*; McGinn, *Visions*, pp. 43–50 and 70–76; Rauh, *Antichrist*, pp. 145–52. These texts were vastly popular in the Middle Ages; the *Pseudo-Methodius* was translated into Middle English (ed. Charlotte D'Evelyn in *Proceedings of the Modern Languages Association*, 33 (1918), pp. 135–203).

16 The Sibylline literature is responsible for much of the accretion of the Last World Emperor legend (see note 15, above) to standard eschatology, a legend which introduces a note of meliorism foreign to Augustinian thought in the concept of a reign of peace which, however, ends with the coming of Antichrist.

17 The *Cursor Mundi*, ed. in 5 vols. Richard Morris, EETS nos. 57, 59, 62, 66, and 68 (London, 1874–78) (see vol. 4, EETS no. 66, lines 21,847ff. for the eschatological section); *The Pricke of Conscience*, ed. Richard Morris (London, 1865), pp. 110–27: and see the discussion of these works in Emmerson, *Antichrist*, pp. 160–62. Accounts of the End Times like these two invariably draw upon the Sibylline literature and the famous *Libellus de Antichristo* by Adso of Montier-en-Der (also edited by Sackur, in the volume cited in note 15 above), as well as biblical sources. This eschatology, which I call "popular," simply because it was widely read and copied in vernacular sources, Robert Adams calls "learned" in a recent essay on *Piers Plowman* (Adams, "Versions", at the same time as he calls Joachite prophecy (which was available almost exclusively in Latin in the Middle Ages) "popular." Adams' reason for his terminology is not clear, and it runs counter to the use of the term both in this study and in the scholarship of recent historians. See, for example, Lerner's explicit discussion of the problem in "Black Death," p. 544.

18 For the ideas gathered below see Töpfer, *Reich*, p. 47; McGinn, *Visions*, p. 95; Czarski, "Prophecies," pp. 19–21; and Lerner, "Refreshment," pp. 110–12.

19 See, for example, Bischoff, "Eschatology," p. 50.

20 See Bischoff's discussion of Rupert of Deutz, Anselm of Havelberg and Eberwin of Steinfeld, *ibid.*; see also McGinn, *Visions*, chs. 12–14.

21 See Gerhart Ladner, *The Idea of Reform* (New York, Evanston, and London, rev. ed. 1967), pp. 224–25 and pp. 232–38; the ages of history are set out in *De civitate Dei*, XXII, 30, Corpus Christianorum, Ser. Lat. 48, pp. 865ff.; the six ages of man can be found in *De Genesi contra Manichaeos*, I, 23, 39, *PL* 34, cols. 190ff.

22 Although this passage will be discussed in greater detail in chapter 5 of this study, it should be noted here that in a recent article Adams, "Versions," has advanced the view that the new David Langland speaks of is Christ in His Second Coming. This interpretation has the odd effect of making Christ the "cristene Kyng" of the prediction (III. 441) – i.e., a follower of Himself. And, more importantly, it makes Christ the ruler of a utopian Kingdom *here on earth*, a view which would require much more explanation than Adams gives.

23 See note 3 above, particularly the thesis by Victor Globe, and the notes of various editors on the prophetic passages, e.g. Pearsall's note to Prol. lines 62–65 and VIII. 343ff.; Schmidt, *B-Text*, notes to III. 325 and VI. 320.

24 See J. J. Jusserand, *Piers Plowman: A Contribution to the History of English Mysticism* (London, 1894); Burdach (*Dichter*) and Bloomfield (*Apocalypse*) have been the two most important proponents of this view, but various other critics have taken up the question of Langland's Joachism: see Frank, *Scheme*, p. 17, n. 4; Henry W. Wells, "The Philosophy of *Piers Plowman*", in Vasta, *Interpretations*, p. 129. For a fuller discussion of this, and the other previous scholarship which can only be briefly mentioned here and in Chapter 5, see Kerby-Fulton, "Voice," pp. 41–71.

25 See Bloomfield, *Apocalypse*, and Bourquin, *Etudes*; and for a negative view see especially

W. Erzgräber, *Piers Plowman* (Heidelberg, 1957), pp. 72–76 and Adams, "Versions."
26 See note 24 above, and on specific passages as follows: (1) on the Tree of Charity, see Bloomfield, *"Piers Plowman* and the Three Grades of Chastity," *Anglia*, 76 (1958), pp. 227–53, Dronke, *"Arbor,"* and Reeves and Hirsch-Reich, *Figurae*, pp. 312–14; (2) on the Burning of "Book," see R. E. Kaske, "The Speech of 'Book' in *Piers Plowman*," *Anglia*, 77 (1959), pp. 117–44 and Reeves and Hirsch-Reich, *Figurae*, p. 314, but see R. L. Hoffman's refutation "The Burning of the 'Bake' in *Piers Plowman*" in *Modern Language Quarterly*, 25 (1964), pp. 57–65. Adams has recently put forward evidence that the rubrics (*Visio, Vita*, etc.) may not be authorial, at least with regard to the B-text. The rubrics are certainly part of the C-text tradition, and if nothing else, provide us with a contemporary response to the problem of the poem's structure and the nature of its dreams. They are used here as part of this tradition, and for convenience of reference. Adams' article "The Reliability of the Rubrics in the B-text" appears in *Medium Aevum*, 54:2 (1985), pp. 208–31.
27 Emmerson ("The Prophetic") tries to distinguish between the two in an interesting, but ultimately strained reading, concluding that the *Visio* is prophetic while the *Vita* is apocalyptic. As I have suggested above, this (essentially biblical) distinction is not as clear in medieval writers, and Emmerson's reading, though attractive, is gained at the expense of an over-rigid application. See Kerby-Fulton, "Voice," pp. 62–64.
28 As Marjorie Reeves has pointed out, a thinker like Joachim is "radical" (meaning "of the root, fundamental, thorough") but not "revolutionary" (which suggests an overturning, or violent overthrow of the current system); see Reeves, "Originality," p. 294. This distinction is useful for understanding other medieval reformist apocalyptic thinkers, including Langland. For a recent essay in which Langland is treated, rather anachronistically, as a revolutionary, see Aers, *Creative Imagination*, pp. 64ff.
29 See also Adams, "Versions," Szittya, *Antifraternal Tradition*, and Emmerson, "The Prophetic."
30 See especially Woolf ("Qualities") whose views, among others, are discussed at length in chapter 3; also A. C. Spearing, in his *Medieval Dream Poetry* (Cambridge, 1976); Hieatt, *Realism*; Dronke, *"Arbor,"* and Michael Klein, "The Apocalyptic Configuration in Literature: A Study of Fragmentation and Contradiction in *Piers Plowman*," unpublished University of Sussex D.Phil. thesis, 1973.
31 For a more detailed analysis of the two medieval visionaries, Bridget of Sweden and Robert of Uzès, discussed in Chapter 3, see Kerby-Fulton, "Voice," chapter 2. With the help of a Social Sciences and Humanities Research Council of Canada Fellowship I am currently undertaking further study of the Hildegardian visionary tradition.
32 "Apocalypticism in the Middle Ages: An Historiographical Sketch," *Medieval Studies*, 37 (1975), p. 252. McGinn's own excellent but only recently published book *Visions of the End* is perhaps the closest thing to a guidebook to the field.
33 See Reeves, *Influence*, pp. 165–66, 184–85 and 398–99. See Salimbene's *Chronicle*, ed. O. Holder-Egger, *MGH SS*, vol. XXXII (1905–13), pp. 238ff.
34 See the discussion of Gebeno's *Pentachronon* on pp. 29–30 below.
35 The writer of *The Last Age of the Church*, discussed in chapter 5 of this study, pp. 184–86, similarly prophesies clerical chastisement.
36 I define a "user" (as opposed to an author of such prophecies) as a writer who cites apocalyptic prophecy in a chronicle, sermon or other work. Whether Langland is an author or simply a user (or adapter) of such material in his prophetic passages is an interesting but, as yet, unanswerable question.
37 Lerner suggests that this type of prophecy was the province of theologians (see "Black Death," pp. 539–40 and p. 544) rather than popular writers.
38 See Adams, "Versions," for a discussion of these passages in the B-text, although Adams reaches very different conclusions than I do in this study.

39 Cf. the following passage from a fourteenth-century Latin prophecy, edited and translated by Martha Fleming from Yale University MS Marston 225, in which, upon the anointing of a holy Last World Emperor figure, "ecstasy, fear and trembling will lay hold of the people. Afterward, striking their breasts, with tears running down their cheeks, and lifting their hands to the sky, they will say: 'So be it Lord, since you have given us that man, he pleases us'" (Fleming, "Sibylla" (pp. 135–36).

40 On vernacular prophecy which circulated as folklore, see Murray (note 3, above), who cites a similar *impossibilia* prophecy to Reason's, p. xviii. Compare also the anonymous *Winner and Waster*, ed. I. Gollancz (London, 1930), lines 13ff.

41 See Pearsall's note on this passage, in his edition of the C-text.

42 See for example the use of Saturn in the "Tripoli Prophecy" (Lerner, *Powers*).

43 "The Spheres and Planets," ed. F. J. Furnivall in *The Book of Quinte Essence*, EETS no. 16 (London, 1866), p. 26.

44 See for example the prophetic passages involving windstorms in Fleming, "Sibylla," p. 134 and p. 160, or in the "Toledo Letter" (Lerner, *Powers*, p. 191). On the tree (often the Tree of Life) as a common motif in visions and apocalypses, see Rüegg, *Jenseit vorstellungen*, pp. 100–08. In the *Apocalypse of Paul (New Testament Apocrypha*, vol. II, ed. E. Hennecke and W. Schneemelcher [Philadelphia, 1965]) for example, which was very popular in the Middle Ages, Paul enters a garden which contains the Tree of Life and is greeted there by the patriarchs. Langland may have had this type of vision in mind when he wrote his Tree of Charity passage.

45 As, for example, John of Rupescissa (see Chapter 5, pp. 188–91). For a discussion of the dangers of writing political prophecy in medieval Britain see Eckhardt, *Prophetia Merlini*, pp. 30ff. (cited in note 3, above).

46 See W. Heist, *The Fifteen Signs Before Doomsday* (Detroit, 1952), pp. 28, 93–94 and 189–90.

47 Although Langland really never overtly discusses prophecy, there are a few places in the poem where he speaks of prophecy approvingly, for example, in XXI. 242–44, where he places the vocation of the prophet among those needful for society, classing it as a gift from the Holy Spirit. Similarly, the lunatic lollars who, for Langland, lead the most "perfect" of Christian lives, are graced with the gift of prophecy and he elsewhere portrays prophets as the most stoical sufferers of patient poverty (XII. 197–202).

48 An awkward and dislikeable term, used by historians of the reform period; see Bischoff, "Eschatology," p. 46 (quoted below, p. 21).

49 See Bloomfield's index to his *Apocalypse*, p. 250, for a listing of his many discussions of this topic. For a brief survey of the history of the concept up to and including the Franciscans, see Duane V. Lapsanski, *Evangelical Perfection: An Historical Examination of the Concept in Early Franciscan Sources* (St. Bonaventure, N.Y., 1977).

50 Among visionaries see for example Elizabeth of Schönau's treatise *Liber Viarum Dei*, ed. Roth, *Visionen*, pp. 88–122, and see Holdsworth, "Visions," p. 152; among apocalyptic writers the concept was especially a concern of Franciscan Joachites. It was, of course, of interest to many other non-apocalyptic writers. Hildegard of Bingen takes the clergy to task in a long passage in her *Scivias* (II, 5, 27: 870–31: 1023) for not living up to their obligations: "Tu enim es uelut incipiens et non quasi perficiens, quia bonum tangis in inceptione, sed illo te non pascis in perfectione, ut uentus qui os hominis percutit et non sicut esca quae in uentrem eius uadit."

51 See Kerby-Fulton, "First Dawn," for Hildegard. Joachim's future *ordo eremitarum* is different in many respects, but the impetus is similar (see pp. 165–67, below).

52 The following is not intended as a definitive listing of extant manuscripts (either copied or owned in England) containing Hildegard's works, but it is intended to give a sense of the availability of her prophecy in medieval England: British Library MSS Royal 8 C VII, Arundel, 337, Cotton Vitellius DIII, Add. 15418 and MS Harley 1725; Oxford,

Merton College MS L. 2.9; Oxford, Bodleian Library MS Digby 98 and MS Hatton 56 (s. c. 4062); Cambridge University Library MS Ii. vi. 11 and MS Dd. xi. 78; Cambridge, Trinity College Library MS 366; Cambridge, Corpus Christi College MS 107, MS 288 and MS 404; Cambridge, St. John's College MS 27. Pseudo-Hildegardian material occurs in Exeter Chapter Library MS 3625; Dublin, Trinity College MS 516 and MS 517; Oxford, Bodleian Library MS Bodley 158 (s. c. 1997) and MS Bodley 623 (s. c. 2157); Lambeth Palace Library MS 357; British Library, MS Cotton Domitian IX. References to Hildegard in medieval English library catalogues are also frequent: see the references in the medieval catalogues of Christ Church Priory and in St. Augustine's Abbey, Canterbury (discussed below, pp. 23–24, and in note 61 below, this chapter); in *Catalogues of the Library of Durham Cathedral*, Surtees Society, 7 (London, 1938), p. 43; in the *Catalogue of the Library of Syon Monastery*, ed. M. Bateson (Cambridge, 1898), p. 227; and in the library of the York Austins (discussed below, p. 24, and notes 63, 64, below, this chapter) no. 271.

53 Bloomfield outlines some of the problems of this approach (*Apocalypse*, p. 118); see notes 24 and 26 above. See also R. E. Kaske, "The Speech of 'Book' in *Piers Plowman*, *Anglia*, 77 (1959), 117–44, and Frank, *Scheme*, p. 17, n. 4.

54 See the various appendices in Reeves, *Influence*, and *passim*.

55 See Bloomfield, *Apocalypse*, Appendix A and Bloomfield and Reeves, "Penetration."

56 See Lerner, *Powers, passim* and appendices.

57 See Bignami-Odier, *Roquetaillade*, appendix of extant manuscripts of John of Rupescissa.

58 In a paper entitled "Langland's Reading: Some Evidence from Manuscripts of English Provenance Containing Religious Prophecies," delivered at the 1988 Medieval Congress at Western Michigan University, I discuss seven fourteenth-century manuscripts in order to draw some conclusions about the manuscript context in which prophecies are most likely to appear; much more, however, could be done in this area. The paper is to be published in a memorial volume for Judson Boyce Allen, edited by Charlotte Morse, Penelope R. Doob and M. C. Woods (Medieval Institute Publications, Western Michigan University).

59 See, for example, Cambridge, Corpus Christi College MS 404 or the British Library copy of *Super Esaiam* (Venice, 1517). See Lerner, *Powers*, for a fascinating study of the temptation to revise a prophecy to which many scribes succumbed.

60 *The Ancient Libraries of Canterbury and Dover*, ed. M. R. James, (Cambridge, 1903).

61 See p. 292 and, for Christ Church Priory, p. 118.

62 See for example Oxford, Bodleian Library MS Hatton 56 (s. c. 4062) in which there is a prophecy beginning "Of wonders that shull fall after our day" (fol. 9^v) or Bodleian Library MS Douce 88 (s. c. 21662) in which a copy of the pseudo-Joachite "Pope Prophecies" is grouped with material on monsters and portents.

63 "The Catalogue of the Library of the Augustinian Friars at York," *Fasciculus J. W. Clark Dicatus* (Cambridge, 1909).

64 This last item is most likely to be, coming as it does in the company of William of St. Amour, the pseudo-Hildegardian prophecy "Insurgent gentes," discussed in chapter 4 of this study.

65 The list of John Erghome's own prophetic books appears on pp. 53–54, no. 361. Some others are entered in Erghome's hand, however (see pp. 5–6).

66 As, for example, Cambridge, Corpus Christi College MS 138, which contains Pseudo-Joachite prophecies and a work by John of Rupescissa along with a variety of historical and political pieces. Similarly, Lincoln's Inn Hall MS 73 and Cambridge, Trinity College MS 740 are copies of the *Eulogium historiarum* with texts of John of Rupescissa's *Vade mecum* inserted in the middle (see N. R. Ker, *Medieval Manuscripts in British Libraries* [London, 1969], vol. 1, p. 127). Yet another type of historically oriented

manuscript which carries prophetic material is well represented by Cambridge, Corpus Christi College MS 288, which contains a number of works relating to the Tartars along with a prophecy of Hildegard's and some theological material. On the threat of the Tartars as a focal point for apocalyptic thought, especially in the thirteenth century (which is when this manuscript dates from) see Lerner, *Powers*.

67 See for example MS Phillips 3119, now Oxford, Bodleian Library MS Lat. Misc. c. 75 (described in A. G. Little, ed., *Fratrus Thomae vulgo dicti de Eccleston Tractatus de adventu Fratrum minorum in Angliam* [Manchester, 1915], pp. xiv and ff.) or Dublin, Trinity College MS 514 (which also contains some historical works).

68 For prophecies in the midst of anti-clerical and/or anti-mendicant texts see Oxford, Bodleian Library MS Digby 98 or MS Bodley 158 (s. c. 1997). Goliardic material occurs with a number of prophecies in MS Bodley 233 (s. c. 2188).

69 Theological works are a very common context for apocalyptic reformist prophecy: see for example Oxford, Bodleian Library MS Bodley 397 (s. c. 2228) which contains a pseudo-Joachite prophecy along with some other pieces relating to Salvation History. See also Dublin, Trinity College MS 347, which contains largely theological works, a geographical tract, and some Joachite prophecies, or Dublin, Trinity College MS 517, which contains a prophecy of Hildegard's amidst several texts of clerical interest.

70 E.g. Oxford, Bodleian Library MS Arch. Selden B. 8 (s. c. 3338).

71 On Henry of Kirkstede see R. H. Rouse, "Bostonus Buriensis and the author of the *Catalogus Scriptorium Ecclesiae*," *Speculum*, 41 (1966), pp. 471–99, and on Cambridge, Corpus Christi College MS 404 itself see especially the insightful commentary in Lerner's *Powers*, chapter 5. For listings of manuscripts partly or largely given over to Joachite texts, see notes 54–57 above.

72 My guess, however, is that if Langland had ever got hold of anything as comprehensive as Kirkstede's anthology we would see more evidence of it in *Piers Plowman*. Other interesting anthologies of popular Latin religious prophecy include Oxford, Bodleian Library MS Hatton 56 (s. c. 4062) and Dublin, Trinity College MS 516. Although these manuscripts contain political prophecies as well, they show a definite interest in prophecy of Church reform.

73 Some of these citations will be mentioned in the chapters that follow. Marjorie Reeves has noted citations of Joachim, Joachite, or related prophetic material in English medieval chronicles in: Galfridus le Baker of Swynebroke (*Influence*, p. 83); Roger of Wendover (*Influence*, pp. 45–46 and 65, n. 1); Ralph of Coggeshall (*Influence*, pp. 12–14 and *passim*); J. Capgrave (*Influence*, p. 70); the *Eulogium historiarum* (*Influence*, pp. 73–74); Matthew Paris (*Influence*, pp. 49, 62 and *passim*), Peter of Langtoft (*Influence*, p. 50, n. 3 and p. 312, n. 1); Luke Wadding (*Influence*, pp. 105 and 239–41); Walter of Coventry (*Influence*, p. 312, no. 1); Henry Herford (*Influence*, p. 65, n. 1 and p. 170) and Roger of Howden (*Influence*, pp. 7–10 and *passim*). See also Lerner, *Powers*, and M. Haeusler, *Das Ende der Geschichte in der Mittelalterlichen Weltchronistik* (Cologne, 1980) for treatments of a number of English chronicles with prophetic content, including some not listed above.

74 A number of these citations by English writers will be mentioned in the following chapters. See also Reeves, *Influence*, and Bloomfield, *Apocalypse*.

2 THE VISIONARY PROPHECY OF HILDEGARD OF BINGEN IN RELATION TO *PIERS PLOWMAN*

1 On Hildegard's life see Schrader, "Hildegarde," col. 506; Dronke, *Women Writers*, pp. 144–83; the *Vita Sanctae Hildegardis*, written by Gottfried of St. Disibod and Dieter of Echternach, was edited by Migne in *PL* 197, cols. 91–130. Dronke's bibliographical entry on Hildegard (*ibid.*, pp. 326–27) gives further references.

2 McGinn, *Visions*, p. 95, and see pp. 94–102 and accompanying notes for introductory and preliminary bibliographical material on these writers.

3 After the Middle Ages Hildegard also exerted an influence on reformation polemics (see Reeves, *Influence*). See Schrader, "Hildegarde," col. 519 for a brief treatment of Hildegard's later influence. As well as citations in contemporary sources, both medieval and modern library catalogues testify to the availability of her prophetic works in England. See above, chapter 1, pp. 22–24, especially note 52, and see Kerby-Fulton, "Antimendicant Propaganda."

4 Quoted in McDonnell, *Beguines*, p. 282, from *MGH SS*, XVI, 90. See Roth, *Visionen*, pp. LX–LXXXVI, for further references to mentions of these two visionaries in contemporary chronicles.

5 On Hildegard's correspondence see Führkötter's edition of her *Briefwechsel*; Schrader and Führkötter, *Echtheit*; Dronke, *Women Writers*, pp. 183ff.; Czarski, "Prophecies," chapter 3. For more general comments see Schrader, "Hildegarde," col. 513 and Paul Franche, *Sainte Hildegarde*, 3rd ed. (Paris, 1903), pp. 111ff.

6 See, for example, Ep. LII, col. 269, from Werner of Kircheim and Ep. CXLIV, col. 380, from a Cistercian prior.

7 See Dronke, *Women Writers*, p. 190, on Hazzecha of Krauftal. It seems that Dronke was unaware that other abbesses had written to Hildegard about the same problem (see, for example, Ep. C, col. 321 and Ep. CI, col. 322) and that he jumped too swiftly to the conclusion that the unidentified letter was Hazzecha's.

8 See Dronke, *Women Writers*, p. 149, and Schrader, *"Hildegarde,"* col. 514, on Hildegard's contacts with scholars. The monks of Villers sent thirty-eight questions to her on various mysteries such as the problem of what type of bodies the angels who appeared to Abraham had or what type of fire burned in the burning bush Moses saw. See McDonnell, *Beguines*, p. 288.

9 See Dronke, *Women Writers*, pp. 163ff.

10 "Ego autem timida et paupercula per duos annos valde fatigata sum, ut coram magistris et doctoribus ac caeteris sapientibus in quibusdam majoribus locis ubi mansio illorum est, vivente voce ista proferrem. *Sed quia Ecclesia divisa erat*, vocem hanc interim subtraxi" (Ep. XLVIII col. 253B). This remark, which ends the letter and is not an interpolation, suggests that the schism was a powerfully disillusioning force in Hildegard's life. On these preaching tours see Dronke, *Women Writers*, p. 164; Führkötter's *Briefwechsel*; and see also Schrader, "Hildegarde," cols. 506 and 508.

11 McGinn, *Visions*, p. 91. Although Hildegard's apocalyptic thought is unquestionably original, some sources and analogues may be traced. See Liebeschütz, *Weltbild*, pp. 136ff. and 146ff., and Czarski, "Prophecies."

12 On Hildegard's competence in Latin see below, pp. 68–69 and notes 106 and 107, below, this chapter, and p. 218. On the whole question of her "collaborators" see Schrader and Führkötter, *Echtheit*, pp. 180ff.; Dronke, *Women Writers*, p. 307, n. 11; Schrader, "Hildegarde," col. 518, and A. Derolez, "The Genesis of Hildegard of Bingen's *Liber divinorum operum*," *Litterae Textuales. Essays presented to G. I. Lieftinck*, 2 vols. (Amsterdam, 1972), vol. II, pp. 23–33.

13 "Dream-Poems," in *Medieval Literature: Chaucer and the Alliterative Tradition, Pelican Guide to English Literature*, vol. I, pt. 1, ed. B. Ford (Harmondsworth, 1982), p. 241.

14 J. B. Allen, *The Ethical Poetic of the Later Middle Ages* (Toronto, 1982).

15 "Popularizations" here, however, refers to texts written, in most cases, in Latin rather than the vernacular, thus qualifying the word somewhat. There is no full printed edition of the *Pentachronon*, but there is a partial text in Pitra's *Analecta* giving incipits and explicits and references to *PL*. This is the text used here. Schrader and Führkötter have studied the problem of the genuineness of various works in the Hildegard canon in *Die Echtheit des Schrifttums der heiligen Hildegard von Bingen*, which deals primarily with

the disputed sphere of Hildegard's writings, the correspondence, the greatest problem being the large number of letters contained uniquely in the unreliable Riesen Codex (Hs. 2 in the Wiesbaden Landesbibliothek), in which the redactor sought to magnify the abbess's reputation by tinkering with addressees or interpolating and recombining material from different letters (Schrader and Führkötter, *Echtheit*, p. 59). For discussion of the textual problems in English see Czarski, "Prophecies," p. 101 and *passim*, or Kerby-Fulton, "Voice," pp. 80–83. The letters printed in *PL* 197 are edited from the Riesen Codex and for this reason most Hildegard scholars prefer to quote from a manuscript; however, since Gebeno used the Riesen Codex to make his extracts there is every reason to quote the *PL* text here.

16 Indications are that the number of extracts varies in different manuscripts of the compilation and that some have Gebeno's commentary while others do not. See Hauréau, *Histoire*, p. 619, and *Bibliothèque Nationale catalogue général des manuscrits latins* (Paris, 1966), vol. v, description of MS 3222, p. 187.

17 Hildegard's other works remained virtually unknown until the nineteenth century. Czarski has pointed out that while only four manuscripts of the *Liber divinorum operum* and ten of *Scivias* survive, there are according to Pitra "innumerable" manuscripts of the *Pentachronon* in European libraries (*Analecta*, p. 483, n. 1). No listing of all the manuscripts has been made, although Schrader and Führkötter suggested in a note in *Echtheit* (p. 8) that A. Borst was editing the compilation for *MGH* (I have found no trace of this edition). The editing of this work would be a difficult task, not only because of the number of manuscripts (for example, there are at least eleven in the Bibliothèque Nationale alone), but also because of the variations between manuscripts.

18 Pitra, *Analecta*, p. 484, n. 1; Hauréau, *Histoire*, pp. 616–17; Bloomfield and Reeves, "Penetration," pp. 789–90; Czarski, "Prophecies," pp. 216ff. Bloomfield and Reeves see Joachite influence in the *Pentachronon* but by their own admission the discussion of Joachim's doctrine seems to have been limited to his prophecy of the birth of Antichrist (see "Penetration," p. 790). This reading is perhaps an example of the recent tendency to overstress Joachim's influence.

19 "Igitur ad confutandos et convincendos hujusmodi pseudo-prophetas, libellum hunc compilavi; *maxime autem propter correctionem et emendationem claustralium et cleri eum descripsi*, quia juxta prophetiam beatae virginis, gravissimi schismatis laqueus et confusionis in fine illius primi temporis super omnem clerum et ordinem ecclesiasticum extenderetur, ita ut de patria et locis suis expellantur, ubi Dei clementiam ad misericordiam ardore sacrae devotionis studeant revocare" (in Pitra, *Analecta*, p. 284; emphasis mine).

20 In the years between the completion of *Scivias* (1151) and the completion of the *Liber divinorum operum* (1174) Hildegard saw renewed conflict between papacy and empire, and she witnessed the papal schism created by Emperor Frederick in 1159. She condemned the corruption of Pope Anastasius IV (1153–54), as well as that of her local archibishop and papal legates. Her many preaching tours and visits to other monasteries also brought her into contact with a wide range of people and, one imagines, standards of observance. Her vast correspondence is witness to her ceaseless attempts to urge reform and castigate corruption. See Czarski, "Prophecies," p. 123ff., and Schrader, "Hildegarde," col. 508. (The quotation in the title of this section comes from Leff, *Heresy*, p. 32.)

21 See note 50 to chapter 1, above.

22 "Et quoniam isti recto foederi patrum suorum non adhaerent, idcirco semper noui et rudes in magna instabilitate hac et illac secundum uoluntatem suam uagantur" (ii, 5, 28: 954–57). See also Leclercq *et al., Spiritualité*, pp. 223–24, on Hildegard's animus against *vagatio*.

23 See for example Dronke, *Women Writers*, on Hildegard's letter to Tengswindis, pp. 165ff., and see *Piers Plowman*, v. 61ff., for example.

24 "Vnde ne exspiratio Spiritus sancti quae in antiquis patribus operabantur per superbam inflationem euacuetur, uolo ut fideli homini cum humilitate sufficiat quod sibi a praedecessoribus suis institutum est, ne si plus inaniter uoluerit quam humiliter quaerere debuerat, postea tepefactus inde recedens ex hoc ruborem confusionis accipiat, ut in euangelio scriptum est" (II, 5, 30: 978–83).

25 *Scivias*, II, 11; 75ff. The vision is translated by McGinn (*Visions*), with some notes and commentary, pp. 100–02. McGinn used the *PL* edition of *Scivias*, but there are no significant variants with the new edition by Führkötter and Carlevaris in the passage quoted below.

26 On the blurring of images in visionary writing, see Hieatt, *passim*. For an illuminating analysis of this passage, see Newman, *Sister of Wisdom*, pp. 243–45.

27 See Czarski, "Prophecies," ch. 2 (on *Scivias*) and see also Töpfer, *Reich*, p. 37, where he suggests that the later *Liber divinorum operum* alters the emphasis in *Scivias* on inner change towards an outer revolution in Church reform.

28 See below, note 34, this chapter.

29 For a different point of view see Aers, *Creative Imagination*, pp. 68ff.

30 *Confessio amantis*, Ed. G. C. Macaulay (Oxford, 1904), vol. I, Book 2, lines 3056–62.

31 Pearsall, in the Introduction to his edition of the C-text, p. 16.

32 I have emended "sanat" to "sonat" (col. 1013B) in order to make sense of this line.

33 See Töpfer, *Reich*, p. 35. Compare for example the prediction of Gerhoh of Reichersberg (who as a canon was a member of one of the new orders) that the reform would come through a change of heart (Czarski, "Prophecies," p. 199, n. 179).

34 A similar situation surrounds Langland's disendowment prophecies. On the resentment of both the English nobility and the friars against the wealth of the possessioners in the period shortly before 1370 and subsequent calls for disendowment, see David Knowles, *The Religious Orders in England* (Cambridge, 1955), vol. II, pp. 67–68. (For a more detailed discussion of this problem see chapter 5 of this study, pp. 175–77.) It should be noted, however, that Langland chose to cast his own treatment of the topic into an apocalyptic and prophetic form. This would be, of course, because the traditional discussions of the subject had often been characterized by apocalyptic influence.

35 Hildegard's sympathy with those excluded from the power bases of the medieval church may well derive from that fact that she, as a woman, was herself excluded from certain kinds of involvement. While it would be wrong to attribute modern feminist ideals to Hildegard, there can be little doubt that she managed to do some things which were very unconventional for a woman of her day (for example, her preaching tours and her move from Disibodenberg to Rupertsberg, on which see Dronke, *Women Writers*, pp. 150–53). On these problems see Newman, *Sister of Wisdom*.

36 See Dronke, *Women Writers*, p. 165, and also Hildegard's letter to the Cistercians (in Pitra, *Analecta*, pp. 335–36) for examples of this comic or "low-life" style applied to figures of evil.

37 I.e. because it contains one of the Reisen Codex interpolations (the section from the opening of the extract to "alia et pejora venient" (*PL* 197, col. 249C) is part of the first interpolation). For further details see Schrader and Führkötter, *Echtheit*, pp. 94–95 and 169–70. Schrader and Führkötter argue that the interpolations, although they cannot be proven genuine, "do bear the stamp of Hildegard's style" (p. 170). The letter can be dated about 1169. See Czarski, "Prophecies," pp. 194–95, no. 125.

38 The other letter is printed in Pitra, *Analecta*, pp. 347–51.

39 For the notion of a "grammar of apocalyptic imagery" see Frye, *Anatomy*, p. 141, and chapter 3 below, p. 96.

40 See P. Szittya's article "Antifraternal Tradition," especially p. 313, on the friars as eschatological symbols in *Piers Plowman*. Szittya's argument is that they function in the poem in the same way as they do in Langland's source, William of St. Amour: that is, as apocalyptic symbols. By a further coincidence of history, the friars played exactly the same role in fourteenth-century England (in encouraging the nobility to move towards a disendowment of the possessioners) as Hildegard predicted that the pseudo-prophets would play.

41 See for example Leff, *Heresy*, vol. 1, pp. 13ff., and J. Russell, *Dissent and Reform in the Early Middle Ages* (Berkeley and Los Angeles, 1965), ch. 2. Elizabeth of Schönau in a revealing letter to Hildegard seems disposed to admire them (see Eckenstein, *Woman under Monasticism*, p. 281). Eckenstein comments on the exchange: "Considering that nothing is known of these early dissenters except what their opponents have preserved, these remarks are interesting as showing that though Hildegard treated the Cathari with unhesitating contempt Elizabeth was perplexed about them." The full text of the discussion can be read in Elizabeth's *Liber viarum dei*, ed. in Roth, *Visionen*, p. 104.

42 See Hauréau, *Histoire*, p. 619; and Rauh, *Antichrist*, p. 510, where he points out that Hildegard's works are also reassuring because they set no dates.

43 See Hildegard's letter to the clergy of Trier, Ep. XLIX, especially col. 256C and the letter to Conrad, Ep. XXVI, cols. 185C–186A especially. On the heightened level of spirituality see the remark, "Tunc aurora justitiae et novissima vestra, meliora prioribus erunt," col. 251D in the letter to the clergy of Cologne, Ep. XLVIII, and *Liber divinorum operum* col. 1022D, discussed below in the section "Chronicling the future," pp. 48–50. For a more detailed discussion of Hildegard's post-reform ideology see Kerby-Fulton, "Voice," pp. 120ff., and also Kerby-Fulton, "First Dawn."

44 See Kerby-Fulton, "First Dawn," on Hildegard and eremiticism; see *Piers Plowman*, XVII. 1–15, for Langland's idealism.

45 Hildegard here plays on the monastic term *conversus*. She often has a key word or concept which gives a kind of unity to a particular letter. In this letter she plays on *convertere*. In Ep. XLIX she uses a theme of expulsion as the unifying idea and plays on *expellere* and its various synonyms.

46 In many cases we know very little about Hildegard's correspondents – often we do not even know if the surviving letter to Hildegard is genuinely from the correspondent named or whether it is spurious. Most of the letters to Hildegard that survive are from the Riesen Codex and therefore are always under the shadow of suspicion. In some cases it is possible to see a direct relationship between the tone of the correspondent's letter and Hildegard's response. See for example Ep. VI, cols. 157–8, where skepticism in the correspondent breeds hostility from Hildegard, and Ep. XLIX, cols. 253–58, where humility breeds a reciprocal humility, but much more work would have to be done on both the textual problems of the letters (what has been done has often ignored the correspondents' letters in favour of concentrating on establishing the genuineness of Hildegard's responses) and habits of medieval letter-writing.

47 "Sed tamen vidi quod plurimos timoratos, puros et simplices sacerdotes in adversitate ista sibi Deus observabit, velut Eliae respondit, ubi dicebat, quod dereliquisset sibi in Israel septem milia virorum, quorum genus non sunt incurvata ante Baal (III Reg. XIX). Nunc autem inexstinguibilis ignis Spiritus sancti, ut in meliorem partem convertamini, vobis infundat" (Ep. LII, col. 271B–D).

48 Compare XVII. 225ff. with *Liber divinorum operum*, cols. 1018D–1019A.

49 Although there may be some irony intended in the line that follows the reformer-king prophecy in the B-text: "'Thanne is dowel and dobet', quod I, '*dominus* and knyʒthode?'" (B. x. 336).

50 See *Piers Plowman*, XVII. 228.

51 *Piers Plowman*, v. 172; B. x. 327–28.
52 See Liebeschütz, *Weltbild*, pp. 121, 126–27 and 139.
53 The pattern (often including Abel as well) is used in many places. See for example *Prooemium vitae s. Disibodi*, pp. 53ff., and Ep. xlviii, col. 245. Her periodization of Old Testament history follows a pattern which dates back to Origen and was made popular in the Middle Ages by Jerome and Gregory (Czarski, "Prophecies," pp. 13–14 and 108, n. 66). It may be worth noting here, in view of Langland's use of the Abraham–Moses–Good Samaritan/Christ typology, that Hildegard too singles out Abraham and Moses for special treatment: "Sed et Abraham et Moyses, quasi duo planetae incarnationis Filii erant, quemadmodum et planetae velut flamma ignis sunt" (*Prooemium*, p. 353). Hildegard's treatment of the two figures is rather different in emphasis from Langland's. Hildegard emphasizes Abraham's obedience to God in his institution of circumcision, which, she asserts rather graphically, "wounded the neck of the old serpent" (*ibid.*). For Hildegard, circumcision was a prefiguration of the vows of chastity of the Christian priesthood; for Langland it seems to be a kind of blood sacrifice (xvii. 252ff.). Both Langland and Hildegard also focus on the visit of "the Trinity" to Abraham (xviii. 240ff. and *Prooemium*, p. 353). Hildegard remembers Moses for his giving of the Law, his obedience through mortification of the flesh and his offering of animal sacrifices which in her view prefigure Christ's own sacrifice (*ibid.*), while for Langland he is mainly a law-giver (xix. 1ff.).
54 See for example *Piers Plowman*, xvii. 194–203, the passage which introduces Langland's second disendowment prophecy.
55 "Vt enim praedictum est, in sex diebus perfecit Deus opera sua. Quinque dies quinque numeri saeculi sunt; in sexto noua miracula in terris propalata sunt, uelut in sexta die primus homo formatus est. Sed nunc sextus numerus finitus est usque ad septimum numerum, in quo nunc cursus mundi uelut in septima die requiei positus est" (*Scivias*, iii, 11, 23; 445–55). Czarski ("Prophecies") does not seem to have noticed this passage and refers throughout to Hildegard's own time as the sixth age. Töpfer, however (*Reich*, p. 38), mentions this odd departure in Hildegard's thought from the traditional Augustinian theory, but does not speculate on the reason for it. I am grateful to Dyan Elliott for sharing with me her unpublished paper, "Prophecy and Permissible Knowledge in Hildegard of Bingen's *Scivias*," which first directed my attention to this passage and to the one in note 56, below, this chapter.
56 *Scivias*, iii, 11, 18; 385–90. See the section "Visionary Self-Image," in this chapter, on Hildegard's self-image as prophet. On Hildegard's concept of achieving a deeper and more direct understanding of divine truth see Töpfer, *Reich*, p. 37.
57 See Töpfer, *Reich*, p. 34. There is some possibility that Langland's reference to female domination in the foreboding prophecy at the end of B. vi (line 328) is related to Hildegard's age of feminine debility. The latter was a widely known concept from her works, e.g. its inclusion in Vincent of Beauvais's *Speculum historiale* (Book 32, ch. 107). Hildegard derived no hope from either the empire or the papacy and scholars have remarked on this point in their attempts to explain why she expects no Last Emperor or "angelic-pope" figures, so much a part of apocalyptic thought elsewhere. See Töpfer, *Reich*, p. 34; Liebeschütz, *Weltbild*, pp. 149–50. Hildegard incorporated many of the motifs of earlier apocalyptic thought into her works, drawing on Sibylline literature and Pseudo-Methodius extensively in some instances (see Czarski, "Prophecies," and Liebeschütz, *Weltbild*, especially pp. 147ff.) but consistently rejecting any messianic leader. A comparison with her sources makes this absence much more noteworthy. However, in her letter to the clergy of Trier she speaks briefly of a wise, reforming warrior (Ep. xlix, col. 257a). She uses the same image in the letter to Conrad, although there it is really just an image: "just like a warrior [*vir praeliator*] raising a banner against the time of error" (Ep. xxvi, col. 186a, my translation). See Kerby-Fulton, "Voice," pp.

140ff., for further details. However, if Hildegard has any expectation of coming leadership, it would be perhaps fairer to say, as Töpfer suggests (*Reich*, p. 40), that it is prophets she expects to fulfil this role: "And then strong men will arise and prophesy . . ." (Ep. XLIX, col. 257A, my translation).

58 This notion was popularized for the later Middle Ages by Adso of Montier-en-Der's *Libellus de Antichristo*. See J. Wright's translation in *The Play of Antichrist* (Toronto, 1967), p. 106, translated from the edition of E. Sackur, *Sibyllinische Texte und Forschungen* (Halle, 1898).

59 See Töpfer, *Reich*, p. 41 and Rauh, *Antichrist*, p. 512. Czarski has pointed out ("Prophecies," p. 167) that during the twelfth century many monasteries came to be controlled by the papacy rather than by the local bishops and that this process promoted lack of discipline. Hildegard's concern about the deterioration of monastic discipline probably led her to frown on such centralized papal control. He also points to other reasons for her disgust with the papacy by the time of the writing of the *Liber divinorum operum* (*ibid.*).

60 See Lerner, "Refreshment." Hildegard is in fact more interested in (i.e. she lavishes more attention and detail upon) the imminent cycle of clerical chastisement and renewal she foresaw for her own age.

61 From his *Epistola quedam consolatorice*, *Historische Jahrbuch*, 30 (1909), p. 306, cited in Bloomfield, *Apocalypse*, p. 206.

62 See Lerner, "Medieval Prophecy," pp. 9 and 12.

63 The building of "Unity" is similar to Hildegard's view of the history of the Church as the building of the New Jerusalem (the architectural motif is very common in Hildegard to describe this process; see Schrader, "Hildegarde," col. 510, and Rauh, *Antichrist*, p. 496).

64 See chapter 3 below, pp. 127–29.

65 Piers' role in this scene will be discussed further in chapter 5, as will the "angelic-pope" tradition in medieval prophecy.

66 See the recent work by Emmerson (*Antichrist* and "The Prophetic") and by Adams ("Versions"); see also Aers, *Creative Imagination*, p. 77. The views of these critics are discussed in chapter 1 of this book, pp. 9–11.

67 See Reeves, "Originality," but see also Lerner, "Refreshment," and see chapter 5, below.

68 This program and its sources are discussed in the Introduction, p. 7, above.

69 The passage occurs in his commentary on the Apocalypse of St. John (*PL* 196, cols. 686ff.), and is discussed by Dronke in *Women Writers*, p. 146.

70 See Töpfer, *Reich*, p. 39; Rauh, *Antichrist*, pp. 478–79.

71 See Dronke, *Women Writers*, pp. 145ff. Medieval views of the visionary experience will be discussed in greater detail in chapter 3, below.

72 *Fearful Symmetry* (Princeton, 1947), p. 8.

73 See Ep. XLVIII, col. 252B.

74 Some of the characteristics of dream experience exploited by medieval literary writers and discussed below are outlined in Hieatt, *Realism*.

75 Dronke makes no attempt to distinguish mystics from visionaries (see "Arbor," p. 233, for example) or apocalyptic from non-apocalyptic writers (even though he is dealing with a good deal of apocalyptic literature in the article).

76 See Hieatt, *Realism*, and Piehler, *Visionary Landscape*, especially.

77 See especially Russell, *Method*. An attempt to develop a literary theory of medieval apocalyptic writing (something we are still a long way from being able to do) would probably conclude that this use of typology is the medieval descendant of the dependence on myth found in biblical apocalyptic literature (see Russell, *ibid.*, pp. 122ff.).

78 See Heschel, *Prophets*, vol. II.

79 Schrader has summarized these last features very well in her description of Hildegard's use of symbolism: "C'est au symbole que la vision d'Hildegarde emprunte son cachet particulier. Il est un élément essentiel de ses visions. En cela, elle adopte la forme d'expression écrite propre à son siècle. Dans la façon intuitive, prénotionnelle, de voir ce qui existe, subsiste encore ce monde imaginatif qui s'efforce de s'exprimer dans un symbolisme plus marqué" ("Hildegarde," col. 517).

80 See for example the collection of visions in Lambeth Palace Library MS 51 (described by M. R. James and C. Jenkins, *A Descriptive Catalogue of the Manuscripts in the Lambeth Palace Library* (Cambridge, 1930–32), pp. 71ff.). Interestingly, the collection includes Elizabeth of Schönau (p.81) but not Hildegard. Elizabeth's visions fit the edificatory mold much better than do Hildegard's, although the existence of a manuscript of Hildegard's correspondence like the Berlin Manuscript (Preussische Staatsbibliothek MS Lat. qu. 674) suggests that there were attempts to *make* her works fill this kind of role (see Schrader and Führkötter, *Echtheit*).

81 This formula usually signals an attempt at interpretation or clarification, or, more simply, the heart of the message itself. In this prophecy it does in fact act as a summary.

82 Other examples are B. x. 334–35 and C. v. 178–79. Note also the prophecy at the end of C. VIII. This is assuming, of course, that Langland composed or adapted the prophecies himself rather than simply copying them from elsewhere, something we cannot know for certain.

83 "The twelfth century regarded the discovery of the *homo interior* or *seipsum*, as the discovery within oneself of human nature made in the image of God – an *imago Dei* that is the same for all human beings . . . The development of the self was toward God" (Caroline Walker Bynum, *Jesus as Mother: Studies in the Spirituality of the High Middle Ages* [Berkeley, 1982], p. 87).

84 See Pearsall's note to line 126, in his edition of the C-text.

85 Most recently, Adams ("Versions") and Emmerson, *Antichrist* and "The Prophetic."

86 The letter is printed in Pitra, *Analecta*, p. 349, and occurs in the *Pentachronon*, and the relevant passage runs from "Nam viginti . . ." to "populos deludere coepit." See the discussion in Kerby-Fulton, "Voice," pp. 195ff.

87 *Liber divinorum operum*, col. 1005D. Langland uses typology in his prophecy in III. 436–41 in a similar, if more restrictive, fashion.

88 Roth's suggestion that the letter may have originally been written to Elizabeth of Schönau is noteworthy in this context (*Visionen*, p. xxviii).

89 See Rauh, *Antichrist*, p. 481.

90 Quoted in Dronke, *Women Writers*, p. 168 [Latin text, p. 252].

91 Scholars of apocalyptic history have not generally recognized some of the striking parallels between Hildegard's and Joachim's thought, for example between Hildegard's idealization of the eremitical life in the age of renewal and Joachim's "ordo eremitarum"; between Hildegard's age of prophetic outpouring and Joachim's *status* of the Holy Spirit; or between Hildegard's prophet-leaders and Joachim's "viri spirituales" (but see Töpfer, *Reich*, p. 40). On Hildegard's side these motifs are not highly developed, but they are consistent and can be attested to in more than one of her prophecies. Marjorie Reeves does a very brief comparison in her "Originality," p. 286; and see Kerby-Fulton, "First Dawn." A full study of the two writers would reveal some striking resemblances.

92 *Man's Unconquerable Mind* (London, 1939), p. 109. On this passage see George Economou, "Self-consciousness of Poetic Activity in Dante and Langland," in *Vernacular Poetics in the Middle Ages*, ed. Lois Ebin, Studies in Medieval Culture, 16 (Kalamazoo, 1984).

93 Donaldson, *Piers Plowman*, p. 220. For a fuller discussion of critical views, see Economou, "Self-consciousness," pp. 188ff.

94 On Hildegard's self-assurance see Schrader, "Hildegarde," col. 517 and col. 511, where Schrader discusses the *Liber divinorum operum*, in which Hildegard asserts that the Holy Spirit inspires her like St. John before her. This may be the source of Gebeno's comparison of Hildegard with St. John.

95 On the modesty topos see E. R. Curtius, *European Literature and the Latin Middle Ages*, trans. W. R. Trask (London, 1953), pp. 83–85.

96 See S. S. Hussey, "Langland's Reading of Alliterative Poetry," *Modern Language Review*, 60 (1965), pp. 167ff.

97 Frequently, however, he does switch into the second person and address the reader in the voice of admonition and warning associated with the preacher's or prophet's stance. Through this voice, which is so different from the voice of the dreamer, Langland arrogates a certain authority to himself not unlike Hildegard's.

98 As, for example, in the visions of Elizabeth of Schönau or Bridget of Sweden (see Chapter 3). See also Holdsworth, "Visions."

99 For an understanding of some of Hildegard's attitudes toward knowledge in *Scivias* I am grateful, once again, to Dyan Elliott for allowing me to read her unpublished paper, "Prophecy and Permissible Knowledge in Hildegard of Bingen's *Scivias*." On Hildegard's anti-intellectualism see also Leclercq *et al.*, *Spiritualité*, p. 222.

100 As Donaldson has shown, Recklessness cannot be written off as a totally misguided character; some of his "teachings" on poverty, for example, are echoed by more sober authorities elsewhere in the poem (see Donaldson, *Piers Plowman*, pp. 171ff.).

101 The context of this statement must be remembered before it is taken too literally: the audience includes Cergy and the overwhelming friar, and the comment is therefore aimed at the very learned. Langland is presumably not recommending illiteracy nor condemning a moderate pursuit of learning or any learning wisely used. Hildegard writes very similar advice in a letter to the Cistercians (upon their inquiry to her as to whether anything displeases God in their order), urging them to leave vain intellectual pursuits and take up "their sweet mother," Love (in Pitra, *Analecta*, p. 334).

102 See Pearsall's note on this passage in his edition of the C-text, and see especially J. S. Wittig's article, "Piers Plowman B ix–xii: Elements in the Design of an Inward Journey," *Traditio*, 28 (1972), pp. 211–80.

103 On Hildegard's (and later Joachim's) opposition to scholasticism see Töpfer, *Reich*, pp. 39 and 42. Both preferred the traditional allegorical-typological approach to the Bible. Chenu, summarizing Rupert of Deutz (1076–1129) on the new approach of scholasticism, writes: "The simple words of the shepherds and fishermen who were Christ's companions were worth far more than all the discussions of philosophers . . . Theology is nourished by faith, he felt, and not by 'reasoning' in the manner of the schoolmasters, the *scholares*" (Chenu, *Nature, Man and Society*, p. 272). This attitude is also common among the Middle English mysics. See Richard Rolle of Hampole, *Incendium Amoris*, chs. 5 and 33; see also *The Cloud of Unknowing*, ed. Hodgson, chs. 6 and 7. Julian of Norwich, *A Revelation of Love* (ed. M. Glasscoe [Exeter, 1976]), ch. 2, stresses her own simplicity and unlearnedness much as Hildegard does.

104 Töpfer, *Reich*, p. 40; Chenu, *Nature, Man and Society*, chs. 7 and 8.

105 Scholarship has shown that she was indebted to more than the Bible and her visions for some of her ideas; however, see Dronke, "*Problemata*," and Liebeschütz, *Weltbild*, pp. 156ff., on some of her sources.

106 See further the quotation from her *Vita* in Schrader and Führkötter, *Echtheit*, p. 182, where she claims not to know "cases, tenses and genders" of Latin. On Hildegard's ideal of knowledge without teaching, see Töpfer, *Reich*, p. 38.

107 On Hildegard's learning and the problem of female authority, see Barbara Newman's excellent recent study, *Sister of Wisdom*.

108 On Hildegard's evangelical ideal of the unlearned but inspired preacher see Töpfer, *Reich*, pp. 39–40.
109 This was first suggested by Mabel Day, "The Revisions of *Piers Plowman*," *Modern Language Review*, 23 (1928); see Economou, "Self-consciousness," especially p. 197, n. 24.
110 In a recent article Wendy Scase similarly argues that this passage "looks like a response to criticism" of earlier writing, but there is no reason to assume, as she suggests, that this criticism could *only* be in response to advance circulation of material on false hermits from C. ix. The A- and B-texts are full of passages on false hermits, none of which would have pleased the "lewede ermytes" of London, e.g. A. Prol. 50–54 (B. Prol. 53–57). See W. Scase, "Two Piers Plowman C-text Interpolations: Evidence of a Second Textual Tradition," *Notes and Queries*, Dec. 1987, pp. 456–63.
111 In the autobiographical excerpt from her *Vita*, edited and translated by Dronke, *Women Writers*, p. 145 [Latin text, p. 232].
112 Guibert was born in the mid-1060s and died sometime during the 1120s. The Latin text is edited by Georges Bourgin as *Guibert de Nogent: Histoire de sa vie* (Paris, 1907); it has been translated by J. F. Benton as *Self and Society in Medieval France: The Memoirs of Abbot Guibert of Nogent* (New York, 1970). See also Benton, "Consciousness."
113 See Saward, *Fools*.
114 "Explanatio symboli S. Athanasii," cited in Bernard Scholz, "Hildegard von Bingen on the Nature of Woman," *American Benedictine Review*, 31 (1980), p. 381 from *PL* 197, col. 1078B. Obviously, it was easier for a woman to plead naivety than for a man – a fact which, paradoxically, would give women more literary freedom. Hildegard's insistence on her childlikeness is reminiscent of Chaucer's Prioress's comparison of herself to a "child of twelf month oold, or lesse, / That kan unnethes any word expresse" in the Prologue to "The Prioress's Tale" (lines 484–85, F. R. Robinson, ed., *The Works of Geoffrey Chaucer*, 2nd ed. [Boston, 1961]).
115 On Hildegard's toughness and energy as an administrator and in other areas, see Schrader, "Hildegarde," col. 507. See also Dronke, *Women Writers*, pp. 200–01.
116 See Dronke, *Women Writers*, pp. 180ff.
117 See for example xx. 1–5; xviii. 179–81; xi. 103–04; or B. xv. 1–11. The last of these is perhaps clearest of all.
118 On this question of insecurity in Hildegard see Barbara Newman's illuminating article, "Divine Power Made Perfect in Weakness: St. Hildegard on the Frail Sex," in *Peace Weavers*, ed. J. A. Nichols and L. T. Shank (Kalamazoo, 1987), pp. 106–09.
119 "Langland's Characterization of Will in the B-text," *Dutch Quarterly Review*, 11 (1981), pp. 60–61.

3 *PIERS PLOWMAN* AND THE MEDIEVAL VISIONARY TRADITION

1 Gordon Leff delineates the Southern tradition in a chance remark that St. Catherine of Siena "was in the spiritual tradition of intense fervour and visionary denunciation of ecclesiastical abuses associated with Conrad of Offida (1237–1306), John of Parma (1209–88), Jacopone da Todi (1228–1306), Angelo of Clareno (1247–1337) and Angela of Foligno (1248–1309)" (*Heresy*, p. 32). On these visionaries see also Pou y Marti, *Visionarios*. Robert of Uzès is considered among Northern visionaries here, in contrast with the Southern Italian writers with whom he has less in common in terms of the influences on and dissemination of his work.
2 Eugene Rice, "Jacques Lefèvre d'Etaples and the Medieval Christian Mystics," *Florilegium Historiale: Essays Presented to Wallace K. Ferguson*, ed. J. Rowe and W.

Stockdale (Toronto, 1971), p. 91. Lefèvre's edition was published by Henri Estienne and Jean de Brie, in Paris, May 30, 1513.

3 Lefèvre also published the *Visio Wettini*, but under the wrong name, calling it *Libellus de visione Uguentini monachi*. See Rice, "Jacques Lefèvre d'Etaples," p. 113. The *Visio Wettini* was a fairly well-known medieval "other-world" vision; see Fritzsche, "Lateinische Visionen," pp. 337ff. The sixth work was by Mechthild of Hackenborn (1242–99), whose visions are more of the mystical variety.

4 Cited Rice, "Jacques Lefèvre d'Etaples," p. 92, from Lefèvre, fol. i^r.

5 Dronke has noted a number of instances where the influence of *Hermas* is evident (see *Women Writers*, pp. 161 and 169).

6 On John, see chapter 5 below, and on the influence of Hildegard and Robert on his writings, see Bignami-Odier, *Roquetaillade*, pp. 193–94 especially. In this study I will deal only with John's *Vade mecum in tribulatione*, which is not a visionary work, but it was the main work through which John was known in England. However, even this work is suggestive of his visionary style. See, for example, passages like the one on the rejuvenation of the Franciscan order (*Vade mecum*, p. 503) or (p. 502) where he speaks graphically of the chastisement of the clergy.

7 See Knowles, *Tradition*, pp. 9ff.

8 On Mechthild, Jacopone and Ramon Lull in relation to Langland see Dronke, "*Arbor*." Ubertino's *Arbor vite crucifixie Jesu* shows the visionary tendency toward "stream of consciousness" style. See Philip Martin Caliendo, "Ubertino da Casale: A Re-evaluation of the Eschatology in the Fifth Book of His *Arbor Vite Crucifixe Jesu*," unpublished Ph.D. thesis, Rutgers University, 1979.

9 See *The Book of Margery Kempe*, ed. H. E. Allen, pp. 276–77, n. 39/24, and George M. Tuma, *The Fourteenth Century English Mystics* (Salzburg, 1977), pp. 89 and 170–73. If there is any tradition of religious visions native to England it is to be found in the (usually brief) visions recorded by recluses and monks. See Holdsworth, "Visions," and also Holdsworth, "Christina."

10 Robert of Uzès uses the terms *visio* and *revelatio* interchangeably.

11 This prophecy, in all its variations and versions, is the subject of Lerner's *The Powers of Prophecy*, the first thorough modern study of any of the shorter religious prophecies. Lerner translates the prophecy on p. 16.

12 Joachim of Fiore, who was not a visionary prophet, records instances of a type of mystical vision in which an image appears to him which helps him solve or understand an exegetical problem. See Reeves, "*Arbores*," p. 128. On medieval meditation and the "associative stream of thought" which accompanied it see Jill Mann, "Eating and Drinking in *Piers Plowman*," *Essays and Studies*, 32 (1979), p. 36, n. 2, for references. On the role of images in the creative problem-solving process see Heschel, *Prophets*, vol. ii, pp. 161ff., "Accounts of Inspiration."

13 "The Genre of Palestinian Jewish Apocalypses," in Hellholm, *Apocalypticism*, p. 456.

14 Sanders gives lists of characteristics by Klaus Koch and P. Vielhauer especially (Hellholm, *Apocalypticism*, p. 448) and discusses the categories recently proposed by John Collins (*Apocalypse: The Morphology of a Genre* [Missoula, 1979], pp. 451–2).

15 On Crowley, see note 43 below, this chapter. On Bloomfield's discussion, see the conclusion of this section, pp. 95–96.

16 On the important distinction between apocalypses and apocalypticism, see McGinn, "Early Apocalypticism," p. 3.

17 Copies of *Esdras* (and commentaries upon it) and *Hermas* are quite common in English collections. Prophecies and popular prognostics were sometimes attributed to "Esdras." See, for example, Oxford, Bodleian Library MS Ashmole 788 or Cambridge, Magdalene College MS Pepys 2125.

18 On (1) see Hayes, *Introduction*, p. 365, and McGinn, "Early Apocalypticism," p. 5; on (2) see Russell, *Method* p. 165; on (5) see Farrer, *Rebirth*, p. 36, and R. H. Charles, *The*

Book of Enoch (London, 1966), p. x (discussed below). (3) and (4) are given brief but insightful attention in Joly's edition of *Hermas, Le Pasteur*, pp. 11–12, and in J. C. H. Lebram, "The Piety of Jewish Apocalypticists," in Hellholm, *Apocalypticism*, pp. 200–05.

19 Charles, *Book of Enoch*, p. x.
20 Michael Stone, *Scriptures, Sects and Visions. A Profile of Judaism from Ezra to the Jewish Revolts* (Philadelphia, 1980), pp. 41–42.
21 "The Apocalyptic Literature," in *The Interpreter's One Volume Commentary on the Bible*, ed. C. Laymon (Nashville, 1971), p. 1108.
22 All quotations from *The Apocalypse of Esdras* are cited from the King James translation in *The Holy Bible and Apocrypha* (Oxford, n.d.) along with page references to Klijn's edition for readers wishing to follow the Latin text. Any Latin inserted into the text in square brackets is from Klijn. (And see note 25, below, this chapter.)
23 Chapters 1–2 were added in the second century and 15–16 in the third century, putting a Christian beginning and ending on what was originally a Jewish apocalypse. (These segments were known as v Ezra and vi Ezra respectively in the Vulgate tradition; see Klijn's, edition p. 9.) The final editing of the whole work would have been done around AD 120.
24 Robert C. Dentan, "The Second Book of Esdras" (in Layman, *Interpreter's Commentary*, p. 521), and see Lebram, "Piety," pp. 199ff.
25 I Esdras and II Esdras are the canonical Ezra and Nehemiah of the Protestant Bible. III Esdras (which is I Esdras for Protestants) is an historical work. *The Apocalypse of Esdras* or Vulgate IV Esra is the II Esdras of the Protestant apocrypha (because I am quoting the King James version I have referred to it throughout as II *Esdras*, not IV Esra, as it is in the Vulgate tradition). To avoid confusion with the protagonist "Esdras," I have italicized *Esdras* when using it as a short title for the work. On the Latin manuscripts of the apocalypse see Dentan, "The Second Book," pp. 521–22, and Klijn's edition, pp. 13–19.
26 "Esdras" is, of course, a pseudonym. The apocalypse has been fathered on this venerable figure of earlier Jewish history.
27 See, for example, A. C. Spearing's comment in *Medieval Dream Poetry* (Cambridge, 1976), p. 20, that the visionary in Alanus de Insulis' *De planctu naturae* is "the forerunner of many medieval dreamers who fall below the level of their dreams."
28 See the discussion of *The Shepherd of Hermas* below, and Apocalypse 5: 1–5.
29 Taylor's, translation, vol. I, pp. 10–11. See Joly's edition, pp. 12–16, and Reiling, *Hermas*, p. 160 and *passim*, on the question of authorship and problems presented by textual incongruities. Joly summarizes the arguments for and against autobiographical authenticity. All quotations from *The Shepherd of Hermas* here are taken from the translation by Taylor. Unfortunately, there is no modern edition of the Latin text of *Hermas* as it was known to the Middle Ages, although there is the Latin "Vulgate" text in *PG* 2, cols. 891–1012, to which I have provided references in parentheses. Latin texts of *Hermas* in medieval manuscripts can differ widely. See Dronke, "*Arbor*," p. 221, no. 26.
30 See K. D. MacMillan, "The Shepherd of Hermas: Apocalypse or Allegory?", *Princeton Theological Review*, 9 (1911), p. 87, and, more recently, Joly's edition, p. 13.
31 On the manuscripts see C. H. Turner, "*The Shepherd of Hermas* and the Problem of His Text," *Journal of Theological Studies*, 21 (1920), p. 205, and Dronke, "*Arbor*," p. 221.
32 See Bloomfield, *Apocalypse*, pp. 9–10.
33 See Benton, "Consciousness," p. 172.
34 See Reiling, *Hermas*, pp. 164–65. In view of these characteristics, I cannot agree with Bloomfield's contention (*Apocalypse*, p. 9) that the spiritual quest is foreign to the apocalypse form.

35 Difficulty, at least, came to be expected of prophetic writing during the Middle Ages, as we saw in Gebeno of Eberbach's defense of Hildegard's difficult style as a testimony to her divine inspiration.

36 See Mearns' Introduction to his edition of *The Vision of Tundale*, p. 19.

37 Although the Shepherd phrases this in a general way, the reference is unmistakeably to Hermas, who had been mixed up with worldly affairs earlier in his life.

38 See, for example, Taylor, vol. i, pp. 84–85: Vision iii, ch. vi; *PG* 2, cols. 903–04, or Taylor, vol. i, pp. 89–90: Vision iii, ch. viii; *PG* 2, cols. 905–06, or Taylor, vol. i, p. 103: Vision iv, ch. iii; *PG* 2, cols. 911–12.

39 Hermas asks the Shepherd the same question, with regard to true and false prophets or teachers, in Taylor, vol. i, p. 151: Mandate xi; but *PG* 2: Mandate xii, ch. i, cols. 945–46. On this theme in *Hermas* see Reiling, *Hermas*.

40 See Rüegg, *Jenseitvorstellungen*; Fritzsche, *Lateinische Visionen*, pp. 337ff; and Dinzelbacher, *Vision*.

41 On the vision of the tree in *Hermas*, see Dronke, "*Arbor*." In *The Vision of Tundale* there is also a tree which Tundale, now purified and repentant, is shown when he reaches Heaven. The tree, like the one in *Piers Plowman* (and, to some extent, in *Hermas*) is a tree of perfection; men and women who have given themselves wholeheartedly to clerical vocations or who have been benefactors of the clergy, shelter beneath its branches (*Tundale*, ed. Mearns, lines 2040–68). In *Tundale* as well, the vision is something of a climactic point. The tree also figures in the apocalypse of *Esdras* (ii, 2:12–13; ii, 8:52) and, of course, in the Apocalypse of St. John (22:1–2).

42 "The Role of the Dreamer," in *Piers Plowman: Critical Approaches*, ed. S. S. Hussey (London, 1969), pp. 200–01.

43 The frequency with which the prophecies are noted in the margins of manuscripts of the poem provides some contemporary evidence of this (I would like to thank Derek Pearsall for pointing this out to me). Crowley's edition of *Piers Plowman* was first published in 1550 (STC 19906). On Crowley see John N. King, "Robert Crowley's Editions of *Piers Plowman*: A Tudor Apocalypse," *Modern Philology*, 1976, pp. 342–52. On its manuscript context see Middleton, "Audience."

44 Bloomfield, *Apocalypse*, p. 10. Bloomfield cites Father H. Musurillo, "History and Symbol: A Study of Form in Early Christian Literature," *Theological Studies*, xvii (1957), p. 366.

45 Robert has received little attention from modern scholars. See Bignami-Odier, "Robert," p. 260, n. 7, for a bibliography.

46 *Ibid.*, p. 264, and Reeves, *Influence*, pp. 167–68.

47 Bignami-Odier, "Robert," p. 259, and Bignami-Odier, *Roquetaillade*, p. 193.

48 Many of the visions involve Robert's concern over the choice of the right order. Interestingly, this is a common motif in clerical visions and no doubt reflects the great controversies of the later Middle Ages about the various routes to salvation or paths of monastic perfection on offer. See Holdsworth, "Visions," p. 152.

49 It is recorded that when Robert made his profession each priest of the order was commanded to celebrate a Mass of the Holy Spirit, and each convent a Mass of the Virgin on Robert's behalf. See Bignami-Odier, "Robert," p. 262.

50 The passage is quoted in Bignami-Odier, "Robert," pp. 263–64. Henry seems to have had the wrong information about the date of Robert's death.

51 See Bignami-Odier, "Robert," pp. 269–70, and G. Mollat, "Jean de Cardaillac: prélat réformateur du clergé au XIVᵉ siècle," *Revue d'histoire ecclésiastique*, 48 (1953), pp. 74–121.

52 See Reeves, *Influence*, pp. 235, 255, 442 and 495.

53 See Bignami-Odier, "Robert," p. 271 and James, "Catalogue," p. 53. John Bale also owned a copy of Robert's works (see Reeves, "History and Eschatology," p. 106), and

there is a hitherto unnoticed extract in Cambridge, Gonville and Caius College MS 249, fol. 183ᵛ.

54 On this problem see Lerner, *Powers*, pp. 6–7. John Tortsch, the fifteenth-century compiler of Bridget's prophecies, makes a plea to future scribes to copy the compilation as a single work and not to embed it in a large manuscript. Obviously medieval writers were quite aware of the problem. See Montag, *Werk*, p. 252.

55 Vision 13, ed. Bignami-Odier, "Robert," p. 279; trans. McGinn, *Visions*, p. 193.

56 A vision setting which includes family members is thought by Dinzelbacher (see below, p. 118) to be one of the markers of "real" visions; see below, chapter 4.

57 Vision 18 and Vision 34 especially. For a more detailed discussion, see Kerby-Fulton, "Voice," pp. 221ff.

58 Robert also imitates Hildegard's description of seeing her visions in a cloud; see Vision 7 (Bignami-Odier, "Robert," p. 276), for example. Bridget also imitates this mode of seeing; see, for example, her *Revelationes extravagantes*, ch. 47, p. 162, in the edition by L. Hollman, *Den Heliga Birgittas Reuelaciones Extrauagantes* (Uppsala, 1956).

59 The *Liber sermonum Domini* is a more outwardly directed prophetic work than the *Liber visionum*. See p. 118, below, on Dinzelbacher's view that religious visions are generally of great autobiographical import and are perhaps more introspective in nature.

60 On the Saccantes, see Bignami-Odier, "Robert," p. 282, n. 37, and see R. W. Emery, "The Friars of the Sack," *Speculum*, 18 (1943), pp. 323–34. The order was suppressed in 1274.

61 Marjorie Reeves notes that the Saccantes were the target of pseudo-Joachite prophecy (*Influence*, p. 168, no. 6).

62 The image is used throughout *Hermas*, but especially in Similitude ix. The vision also owes something to Ezechiel 47:1–12.

63 Mme Bignami-Odier sees in this image and in the columns themselves an allusion to the Colonna Cardinals who supported Celestine V and were deposed by Boniface VIII ("Robert," pp. 287, n. 55, and 281, n. 33). If so, the suggestion that the golden fruit represents the good clergy is still correct, although more specifically defined.

64 The tower of the opening vision of *Piers Plowman* may belong to this tradition begun by *The Shepherd of Hermas* and carried through the allegories of the visionary reform writers like Hildegard and Robert, although the image is simple enough that it may not need scholarly explanation.

65 All references below to Book 1 of the *Revelations* are from *Sancta Birgitta Revelationes*, vol. 1, ed. Carl-Gustav Undhagen (Stockholm, 1977). References to other books of the *Revelations* are to Gonzales Durante's edition (Antwerp, 1611), from which abbreviations are silently expanded here.

66 Alphonse's role was much like that of Guibert of Gembloux's role in Hildegard's life. Lagorio gives a preliminary list of medieval visionaries' secretaries, "Women Mystics," pp. 74–75. Alphonse's *Epistola solitarii* is also printed in Gonzales Durante's Antwerp, 1611 edition of the *Revelations*, pp. 579–90.

67 For a concise summary of her messages to the popes see Colledge, "*Epistola*," pp. 37–38.

68 See Walter Ullmann, *A Short History of the Papacy in the Middle Ages* (London, 1972), p. 291, for a brief assessment of the pressures on Urban to return to Rome. Ullmann mentions Catherine of Siena, but not Bridget.

69 William de Guellesis and Adam Easton: see Johnston's *Syon Abbey: A Short History of the English Birgettines* (Eccles, 1964), pp. 3ff. See also James A. Schmidtke, "'Saving' by Faint Praise: St. Birgitta of Sweden, Adam Easton and Medieval Antifeminism," *American Benedictine Review*, 32 (1982), pp. 149–61. On Easton and knowledge of Bridget in the Norwich area, see *The Book of Margery Kempe*, ed. Allen, pp. 280–81.

70 Johnston, *Syon Abbey*, p. 5.
71 Book VIII was added after Bridget's death, probably between 1380 and 1391. On this book and the various other editing projects of Bridget's secretary, Alphonse, see Ellis, "*Flores*," p. 164, and Colledge, "*Epistola*." Jorgenson records that when the process of canonization began in 1377 the *Revelations* still consisted of only seven books (*St. Bridget*, vol. I, p. 301).
72 See Ellis, "*Flores*," p. 173, where the discussion includes a list of English manuscripts in which the passage is found; see also Colledge, "*Epistola*," p. 32.
73 Lerner, *Powers*, p. 89. The *Onus mundi* can be found in Ulrich Montag, ed., *Das Werk der heiligen Birgitta von Schweden in oberdeutscher Überlieferung* (Munich, 1968).
74 Montag's edition (*Werk*) has made this task a little easier by using quotation marks for direct quotes.
75 Both these earlier prophets, he claims, predicted that the goods of the clergy would be taken away and that the clergy would be reduced to a life of poverty. In his discussion of this prophecy in the pseudo-Joachite *Super Jeremiam*, he fastens on the notion that the clergy will be expelled from region to region and will enter the heremetical life. He asserts that Hildegard also predicted this (indeed, the actual wording of the Latin is Hildegard's), thereby showing how easily Hildegardian and Joachite ideas could be associated and reconciled. As we have seen, Hildegard's post-reform ideology was in no way as explicitly stated as one could hope and Tortsch's reading of her prophecies shows both careful study and the cumulative effect of being associated with Joachite prophecies in the intervening centuries. It is no doubt on the basis of the Hildegardian and Joachite predictions that Tortsch claims (in his discussion of Bridget's *Revelations* IV, 49) that the clergy will lose their possessions *at the hands of the laity*. This last detail is nowhere to be found in *Revelations* IV, 49 (where it is simply threatened that unregenerate clergy will lose their prebends) and provides a good example of Tortsch's sophisticated reworking of Bridget.
76 Bridget may have been influenced by Joachite and Franciscan sources, but much in her thinking is attributable to non-Joachite prophecies like those of Hildegard. On possible Joachite influences see Jorgenson, *St. Bridget*, vol. II, pp. 22ff.
77 See, for example, *Piers Plowman*, XXII. 247ff.
78 See Matthew 22:16, Mark 12:14, Jude 16 and 1 Peter 1:17.
79 This is hardly surprising: the agricultural metaphor immediately brings to mind the parable of the sower interpreted in Matthew 13:37–43 (see especially verses 39 and 40). See also Apocalypse 14:14.
80 On Jerome's notion of the refreshment of the saints, see Lerner, "Refreshment."
81 R. B. Dobson, ed. *The Peasants' Revolt of 1381* (London, 1970), p. 381. The same image is also found in a common Latin proverb. See H. Walther, *Proverbia sententiaeque latinitatis medii aevi* (Göttingen, 1963–66), no. 28109.
82 Dobson, *Peasants' Revolt*, p. 381.
83 On some of the biblical apocalyptic associations and images in the poem see S. A. Barney, "The Plowshare of the Tongue: The Progress of a Symbol from the Bible to *Piers Plowman*," *Medieval Studies*, 35 (1973), pp. 261–93.
84 The notion of the three ages of the world in Bridget's *Revelations* VI, 67 and the belief in a coming chastisement and reform could be pointed to as showing Joachite influence, but Bridget's heavy emphasis on various reforming leaders is more a mark of general reading of reformist religious prophecy than of genuine Joachite texts.
85 R. M. Ellis, ed., *The Liber Celestis of St. Bridget of Sweden*, vol. I, EETS no. 291 (Oxford, 1987); Book VII, ch. 21, p. 485.
86 See Jorgenson, *St. Bridget*, II, pp. 232ff. and vol. I, p. 302 on the woodcuts in the Lübeck edition.

87 Bloomfield, *Apocalypse*, Appendix III, p. 172.
88 See Osmund Lewry's review of Torrell in *Medium Aevum*, 49 (1980), p. 130.
89 Synave and Benoit, *Commentary*, Explanatory Note 15 (to Q. 171, a. 5. c). On the distinction between a prophet as a direct spokesman of the divine and as the reporter of divine revelations in the early Church, see Reiling, *Hermas*, pp. 163–68. Reiling judges Hermas to be the latter.
90 In support of his suggestions about medieval attitudes toward prophetic style, Minnis refers the reader to his article "Discussions of 'Authorial Role' and 'Literary Form' in Late-Medieval Scriptural Exegesis," *Beiträge zur Geschichte der deutschen Sprache und Literatur*, 99 (1977), pp. 37–65, but it would be nice to see further exploration of this important suggestion.
91 In Synave and Benoit, *Commentary*, Explanatory Note 10 (to Q. 171, a. 3. c).
92 See also Kane, *Evidence*, p. 57. John Burrow has recently questioned Kane's emphasis on the fictional aspect of autobiographical elements in medieval poetry, suggesting that critics have been too quick to dismiss the possibility of autobiographical realism in many instances, as mentioned in the section entitled "Visionary Self-Image" in chapter 2 above.
93 But see Burrow, "Autobiographical Poetry," on Hoccleve.
94 On authorial intention in autobiography, see Burrow, *ibid.*
95 I am following Warren Ginnsberg's analysis, pp. 86–88, in *The Cast of Character* (Toronto, 1983).
96 John Alford makes a similar point about autobiographical aspects of Rolle's writings in his "Biblical '*Imitatio*' in the Writings of Richard Rolle," *English Literary History*, 40 (1973), p. 10.
97 On other possible reasons for the conventionalization see Holdsworth, "Visions," pp. 149–50.
98 Summarized from Dinzelbacher, *Vision*, pp. 65–77.
99 Bignami-Odier, "Robert," Vision 36, p. 287; Vision 10, p. 278; Vision 34, p. 286, Vision 17, p. 281, respectively.
100 *Ibid.*, Vision 13, p. 279, trans. McGinn, *Visions*, p. 193.
101 On Hildegard's mode of receiving visions and her apparent disapproval of the ecstatic experiences described by Elizabeth of Schönau, see K. Kerby-Fulton and D. Elliott, "Self-Image and the Visionary Role," *Vox Benedictina*, 2 (1985), pp. 204–23.
102 Dinzelbacher deals with prophetic vision on pp. 84 and 182 of *Vision*.
103 See Russell, *Method*, p. 118.
104 For evidence of some interchange between the two types of vision during the twelfth to fifteenth centuries, see Dinzelbacher, *Vision*, pp. 70–72.
105 Le Goff, "Dreams," p. 349. Julian of Norwich records one vision which was diabolically inspired and comments, "This oggley shewing was made slepyng, and so was non other" (*A Revelation of Love*, ed. Marion Glasscoe [Exeter, 1976], ch. 66, p. 82).
106 See Thomas D. Hill, "'Half-waking, Half-sleeping': A Tropological Motif in a Middle English Lyric and Its European Context," *Review of English Studies*, 29 (1978), pp. 50–56.
107 See Mearns' edition of *The Vision of Tundale*, p. 18, for a list of examples.
108 Notably, Jean Gerson, Henry of Langenstein and Adam Easton; see Colledge, "*Epistola*," pp. 45, 21 and 42ff., respectively.
109 Translated by Jorgenson, *St. Bridget*, vol. II, p. 141, from Master Matthias' Preface to the *Revelations*.
110 See Colledge, "*Epistola*," p. 45, and Synave and Benoit, *Commentary*, p. 63.
111 See Colledge, "*Epistola*," p. 39, where he gives the example of John of Jenzenstein, who both inveighed against the "modern multiplicity of prophets" and yet sent Pope

Urban an account of a dream he had had which forecast victory for Urban in the outcome of the papal schism. Colledge points out that Urban actively collected prophecies favorable to his cause.

112 See Chenu, *Nature, Man and Society*, p. 243 and *passim*; Leyser, *Hermits*; and P. V. Brady, "The Ambiguous 'Newer Prophet': A Sixteenth-Century Stock Figure," *Modern Language Review*, 62 (1967), pp. 672–79.

113 See R. M. Clay, *The Hermits and Anchorites of England* (London, 1914), pp. 155ff. Unfortunately, there is still no convenient, recent study of prophets in medieval England.

114 See Hieatt, *Realism*, p. 25; Harvey, *Inward Wits*, p. 49; R. Arbesmann, "Fasting and Prophecy in Pagan and Christian Antiquity," *Traditio*, 7 (1949–51), pp. 1–72.

115 Arbesmann, "Fasting," p. 31.

116 This attitude is echoed in *The Cloud of Unknowing*, where the author promises that God will provide either the material goods or the patience one needs to lead a life of divine dependence (ed. Hodgson, ch. 23).

117 *The Revelations of Mechthild of Magdeburg*, trans. L. Menzies (London, 1953), pp. 217–18. Mechthild knew Hildegard's visions, and probably knew Joachim's writings in some form (*ibid.*, p. xxvii).

118 "The Concept of Mysticism: An Analysis of a Letter Written by Hildegard of Bingen," *Review of Religion*, 12 (1948), p. 283.

119 E. Salter and D. Pearsall, *Piers Plowman* (London, 1967), p. 6.

120 "Concept of Mysticism," p. 281.

121 *The Allegory of Love* (Oxford, 1936), p. 160. Lewis is speaking of Langland.

4 LEAVEN OF MALICE: FALSE APOSTLES IN THE ANTI-MENDICANT APOCALYPTICISM OF LATER MEDIEVAL ENGLAND

1 Taylor edition, vol. I, p. 151: Mandate XI; but *PG* 2: Mandate XII, ch. i, cols. 945–46.

2 On the literature of these controversies about apostolic perfection see Bloomfield *Apocalypse*, chs. 2 and 3; Chenu, *Nature, Man and Society*, chs. 5 and 6; Pantin, "Origins"; K. J. Thompson, "The Development of the Theory of Evangelical Poverty in the Fourteenth Century," unpublished University of London M. Phil. thesis, 1976; McGinn, *Visions*, pp. 126ff. Holdsworth noticed that these concerns were frequently expressed in visions (see his "Visions," p. 152).

3 See Constable, "Renaissance," pp. 62–65, and Czarski, "Prophecies," pp. 20ff. See also Bischoff, "Eschatology," especially p. 68, where he coins the term "ecclesiastical chiliasm."

4 For references to the many optimistic prophecies of the new fraternal orders see Reeves, *Influence* (for the Franciscan, Dominican and Augustinian orders in particular). Not all of these by any means came from within the ranks of the fraternal orders themselves.

5 A good example of this can be seen in Lerner's recent study of the many versions of the Tripoli prophecy, some of which were pro-mendicant (Lerner, *Powers*, p. 16), anti-mendicant (p. 43), or neutral (pp. 106–7).

6 Adams ("Need," p. 298, n. 50) suggests that Langland's knowledge of the literature of the mendicant controversies was profoundly detailed. The intensity of fourteenth-century English interest in these conflicts is astonishing and many English manuscripts survive which contain a variety of documents and treatises of the Paris controversies (see Szittya, "Antifraternal Tradition," p. 288, and Szittya, *Antifraternal Tradition*, chapter 2).

7 For a list of English anti-mendicant literature see Szittya, "Antifraternal Tradition," p. 287, and pp. 291ff. on the apocalyptic elements of antifraternalism. See also Szittya, *Antifraternal Tradition*.

8 Szittya argues this cogently in his "Antifraternal Tradition," pp. 288ff.

9 I am using the term "ecclesiology" in the sense of a philosophy or doctrine of ecclesiastical manner of life and organization. See Gordon Leff, "The Apostolic Ideal in Later Medieval Ecclesiology," *Journal of Theological Studies*, n.s., 18 (1967), pp. 52–82.

10 On apocalyptic tensions (Joachite and otherwise) at this time see Reeves, *Influence*, pp. 53ff. One of the most obvious indicators of these tensions was the outbreak of the Flagellant movement. See Reeves, *ibid.*, pp. 54ff.

11 For the account that follows, see Reeves, *Influence*, pp. 59ff., and Szittya, *Antifraternal Tradition*, pp. 15ff.

12 University of Cornell, 1971. See also his "The Friar as False Apostle: Antifraternal Exegesis and the Summoner's Tale," *Studies in Philology*, 71 (1974), pp. 19–46, and Szittya, "*Sedens*."

13 Szittya, "Antifraternal Tradition," pp. 292–93. The one exception to this statement seems to be William's direct naming of the *Eternal Gospel* (*De periculis*, p. 27). This technique of exegetical cover was no doubt for reasons of self-defense. William knew that he was likely to incur papal censure since he was directly attacking the rights and privileges the friars had obtained by a series of papal decrees (see McDonnell, *Beguines*, p. 458).

14 The fullest treatment of this theme is in William's popular sermon *De Pharisaeo et Publicano* (delivered in 1256), but the *De periculis* contains similar charges (see *De periculis*, pp. 35ff., Signs [of pseudo-apostles] nos. 25, 28 and 30, for example). The *De Pharisaeo et Publicano* is printed in E. Brown, ed., vol. II (Appendix) to O. Gratius, *Fasciculus rerum expetendarum* (London, 1690) pp. 43–47, and this set of charges is discussed extensively in Szittya, "Antifraternal Tradition," pp. 294ff.

15 See *De periculis*, pp. 31ff. and Signs nos. 9 and 13 among others. See also Szittya, "Antifraternal Tradition," pp. 304ff.

16 See *De periculis*, pp. 19–23, especially, and Signs nos. 1, 2, 22, 23 and 38. See also Szittya, "Antifraternal Tradition," pp. 304ff.

17 See *De periculis*, pp. 23–24 (beginning of chapter 4) and p. 34. Jannes and Mambres were thought to be Pharaoh's magicians (Exodus 7:11–13).

18 See especially Williams, "Relations."

19 Adams, "Need," expresses a similar view: see p. 289, n. 28.

20 See especially Adams' and Szittya's studies cited in the Select bibliography for the most recent views.

21 Donaldson (*Piers Plowmann*, pp. 205ff.) has shown that Langland was probably a clerk in minor orders, at the level of either acolyte or *tonsuratus*, but unable to earn a livelihood from the Church because he was married. I do not mean to imply that William's views were universally accepted, but that they could not help but give pause to an anti-mendicant sympathizer in the position in which Langland portrays himself.

22 " . . . illi qui de mendicitate vivere volunt, fiunt adulatores & detrectores & mendaces & fures & a justicia declinantes" (*De periculis*, p. 32).

23 See Leff, *Heresy*, pp. 88ff., and Leff, *Paris*, pp. 262ff.

24 In St. Bonaventure, *Opera omnia*, vol. V (Quaracchi, 1891), pp. 125–65; see Douie, "Conflict," pp. 10–11.

25 St. Thomas Aquinas, *Opera omnia*, vol. XVII (Venice, 1593), pp. 127–60.

26 Pamela Gradon has shown a connection between Langland's portrait of Nede and *Exiit*; see Gradon, "Dissent," p. 203. On the *Apologium pauperum* see Leff, *Heresy*, pp. 84–98; it is edited in Bonaventure's *Opera omnia*, vol. VIII (Quaracchi, 1898), pp. 233–330.

27 Two discussions of this aspect of Franciscan spirituality which are very helpful in this context are E. R. Daniel, "Spirituality and Poverty: Angelo da Clareno and Ubertino da Casale," *Medievalia et Humanistica*, 4 (1973), pp. 89–98; and Gordon Leff, "The Franciscan Concept of Man," in *Prophecy and Millenarianism: Essays in Honour of Marjorie Reeves*, ed. Ann Williams (Harlow, Essex, 1980). As Bourquin notes (*Etudes*, p. 698), Langland's Patience begs for "A meles mete for a pore man, or moneye, yf they hadde" (xv. 36) and is represented as a "palmere," "Ilyk Peres the ploghman" (xv. 34). Patience's discourse throughout this section centers largely on the spiritual efficacy of poverty. See, for example, xvi. 47ff. Langland's sympathy with the ideology of poverty need not, of course, have come entirely from Franciscan sources, but his familiarity with the literature of the mendicant controversies makes this an obvious source among possible ones. Maguire has suggested that Langland's familiarity with Franciscan thought may well stem from his education, given the vast influence of the friars in monastic, grammar and cathedral schools, as well as at the universities (see Maguire, "Franciscan Elements," pp. 34ff.).

28 Reason begins his query by asking, "Can thow seruen . . . or syngen in a churche"? (v. 12). Donaldson has suggested (*Piers Plowman*, p. 206) that this may be (slight) evidence that Langland was an acolyte rather than a *tonsuratus*.

29 See especially v. 89ff. Conscience is very suspicious of what seems to be Will's own freelance attempt at living a life of evangelical poverty. He voices here the "establishment" view of such would-be religious or semi-religious practitioners. The medieval Church was extremely suspicious of groups or individuals who did not fit into a traditionally recognized role or order. Even the friars, with official recognition and papal sanction, encountered suspicion. See Leff, *Heresy*, pp. 15ff., McDonnell, *Beguines*, and Leff, *Heresy*, pp. 21ff. on the troubles which Beguine groups encountered in this regard.

30 If we knew more about the ideals and practices of the eremitical life in fourteenth-century England, we could perhaps shed further light on this passage.

31 See Szittya, "Antifraternal Tradition," p. 312, and Szittya, *Antifraternal Tradition*, pp. 265ff. Szittya explores only the negative side of Will's associations with various wanderers in the poem.

32 *De periculis*, p. 34. He is alluding to II Timothy 3:7.

33 These arguments are reviewed in Adams, "Need," especially pp. 275ff. See also Szittya, *Antifraternal Tradition*, pp. 267ff.

34 Gradon, "Dissent," p. 203. Gradon is actually extrapolating from Adams' view of Nede; see Adams, "Need," p. 299.

35 Gordon Leff summarizes *Exiit qui seminat* (ed. J. Sbaralea, *Bullarium Franciscanum*, vol. III [Rome, 1765]) as follows: "In particular it sought to justify absolute poverty by the example of Christ's life, which he had shown by word and deed to be the path of perfection. Here *Exiit* drew upon St. Bonaventure. Firstly, it employed his argument of Christ's condescension to the imperfect, to rebut the argument of Judas's bag. Secondly, it invoked the same distinction between necessity and legal right to distinguish between use and possession. Extreme necessity knew no law, and its fulfilment required no other justification than that . . . For *Exiit*, like St. Bonaventure, simple use amounted to purely natural demands for sustaining life . . . Superfluity, in any form, was condemned as derogating from poverty; and in no circumstances was provision to be made for the future" (*Heresy*, pp. 98–100). See note 26, above, this chapter.

36 See especially the section of the poem in which Patience tutors Activa-Vita on patient poverty (xv. 233ff.). Will seems to merge with this character in many ways (see Pearsall's note to xv. 194 in his edition of the C-text).

37 Langland rehearses some of these tales in Passus XVII. 1ff.

38 See, for example, the comment in *The Cloud of Unknowing*, ed. Hodgson, ch. 23, p. 57, lines 3–16.

39 Hence the common critical comment that Nede offers bad advice to Will but good advice to Conscience. See Adams, "Need," p. 279: "If Need is such a charlatan, why does he offer Conscience such astute advice about the motives of the friars?"

40 See, for example, the fourteenth-century Paris, Bibliothèque Nationale MS Lat. 3183, of English provenance, which contains polemics of William of St. Amour and Uhtred of Boldon as well as Aquinas, Bonaventure and Pecham. Phillips MS 3119, now Oxford, Bodleian Library MS Lat. Misc. c. 75 (of probable English provenance and dating in various parts from the thirteenth to the fifteenth century) contains works by William, Gerard of Abbeville and other anti-mendicant writers as well as defenses by Pecham, Roger Conway, Bonaventure and others. It also contains a number of pseudo-Joachite prophecies including the anti-mendicant one discussed below ("Insurgent gentes"), which usually travels under Hildegard's name. See the description of Phillips MS 3119 in A. G. Little, *Fratris Thomae vulgo dicti de Eccleston tractatus* (Manchester, 1951), pp. xivff. Other interesting collections of pro- and anti-mendicant writings can be found in Oxford, Bodleian Library MS Digby 113; Cambridge, Corpus Christi College MS 103; and Oxford, Balliol College MS 149.

41 See Leff, *Heresy*, pp. 51ff.

42 FitzRalph is a more helpful figure than Wyclif to study as background to Langland's anti-mendicant thought partly because he is slightly earlier than Langland and because he is entirely orthodox in his views (on the problems of comparing Langland and Wyclif, see Gradon, "Dissent," and on the possibility of Langland knowing FitzRalph's sermons see T. P. Dolan, "*Passus* in FitzRalph and Langland," *English Language Notes*, XXIII [1985], pp. 5–7). On FitzRalph see especially Walsh, *FitzRalph*, and Szittya, *Antifraternal Tradition*, ch. 3, among the studies cited below. FitzRalph's most widely known work, the *Defensio curatorum* is printed in Melchior Goldast, *Monarchia s. romani imperii*, vol. II (Hanover, 1614; repr. Graz, 1960). The Middle English translation cited here is from *John Trevisa dialogus*, ed. A. J. Perry, EETS no. 167 (Oxford, 1925).

43 On the sermon-diaries see A. Gwynn's article in *Proceedings of the Royal Irish Academy*, 44 (1937–38), and Walsh's discussion, cited below.

44 See especially Williams, "Relations," and Szittya, "Antifraternal Tradition."

45 Walsh, "Archibishop FitzRalph," p. 227, and *FitzRalph*, Appendix, pp. 469ff.

46 Walsh, "Archbishop FitzRalph," p. 240; Szittya, *Antifraternal Tradition*, pp. 126ff.

47 Note the incident which Walsh records ("Archbishop FitzRalph," p. 240) in which a member of Oxford University came to the attention of the chancellor because he was advocating disendowment of the clergy and abolition of offerings to the friars. See also the "Lollard Disendowment Bill" among the Wycliffite writings edited by Hudson, *Selections*, pp. 203ff. See Knowles, *Religious Orders*, vol. II. pp. 67ff. on the role of the mendicants in agitating for disendowment of the possessioners.

48 See Mildred E. Marcett, *Uhtred de Boldon, Friar William Jordan and Piers Plowman* (New York, 1938), pp. 63ff., where she assumes that because Langland uses the phrase "*Periculum est in falsis fratribus*" (XV. 76a) and refers to the gluttonous friar as a "iurdan" (chamber pot) at XV. 92 he is alluding to Uhtred of Boldon's *Contra querelas fratrum*, which was written against the Dominican William Jordan. The "*Periculum*" phrase comes from II Corinthians 11:26 and occurs in most anti-mendicant literature in the tradition of William of St. Amour. "Iurdan" may or may not refer to Jordan (note that it is one of the alliterative rhyme words and may have been chosen for its colorfulness and convenience), but Langland would not have agreed with much in Uhtred's polemics, particularly his views on royal and papal power and on disendowment. See Marcett, *Uhtred*, pp. 19ff., and Knowles, *Religious Orders*, vol. II, p. 66, on Uhtred's

views. Mother Catherine Maguire has also commented on ideological similarities between Langland and the Franciscans on issues such as disendowment (see Maguire, "Franciscan Elements," pp. 17-18).

49 See Walsh, "Archbishop FitzRalph," pp. 236-37, and Williams, "Relations," p. 25. FitzRalph's strictures against the friars' right to hear confession were based on a literalist reading of the 1215 Lateran Council's canon *Omnis utriusque sexus*, which required annual confession to one's parish priest. At the time of the Lateran Council the friars were not formally constituted and so it is obvious why the decree is silent on the question of confession to a friar (Williams, "Relations," p. 26). FitzRalph's position on burial in any place other than the parish church cemetery (for example in a fraternal cemetery) was ludicrously severe: he argued that burial outside of the parish church cemetery could lead to eternal damnation! See Walsh, *FitzRalph*, p. 364.

50 This may be a reflection of the fact that Langland was not himself a secular priest, although many members of the secular clergy were not opposed to fraternal work in the pastoral field: see Williams, "Relations," p. 93.

51 See Dawson, "William," p. 234, n. 22.

52 My interpretation of Langland's apocalypticism and its relationship with his anti-mendicant sources differs widely from that of Szittya, *Antifraternal Tradition*, who follows the lead of Emmerson and Adams on Langland's eschatology (see above, chapter 1, pp. 10-11).

53 This periodization is based on traditional exegetical interpretation of the four horses of the Apocalypse. See Szittya, *Antifraternal Tradition*, p. 33, and Emmerson, *Antichrist*, pp. 64ff. The persecution of the early martyrs is represented by the red horse, the Arian and other heretical groups by the black.

54 This was one of the most popular Joachite texts. See Reeves, *Influence*, p. 62, and see chapter 5, below, pp. 172-73.

55 This was a standard interpretation. In the twelfth century Anselm of Havelberg, Honorius of Autun, Otto of Freising and Gerhoh of Reichersberg all believed that the regular clergy were the agency which held back Antichrist. Adso of Montier-en-Der assigned the role to the Roman Empire and its heirs in his influential treatise on Antichrist (see McGinn, *Visions*, p. 86, and Emmerson, *Antichrist*, pp. 38-39). This view was also widely held throughout the Middle Ages.

56 See Szittya, "Antifraternal Tradition," p. 292; Leff, *Paris*, p. 261.

57 Neither FitzRalph nor the anti-mendicant authors quoted in the *Omne bonum* chose to dwell on the eschatological issues, as Szittya, *Antifraternal Tradition*, has shown.

58 Ed. W. W. Skeat, EETS no. 30 (London, 1867). See also the Wycliffite tract "De blasphema contra fratres" in Arnold, ed., *Select English Works*, vol. III, p. 413. Szittya, *Antifraternal Tradition*, cites instances in Matthew Paris (p. 104) and in the genuine works of Wyclif (pp. 173-4); and see also p. 220, n. 103.

59 I have discussed this problem at greater length in Kerby-Fulton, "Antimendicant Propaganda." William of St. Amour knew Hildegard's Cologne prophecy (see Szittya, *Antifraternal Tradition*, p. 59).

60 On the use of Hildegard by William of St. Amour see Szittya, *Antifraternal Tradition*, p. 59, and Pecham's response to this (or another) citation (see *Tractatus tres de paupertate*, ed. Kingsford, Little and Tocco, p. 18). Pecham seems to have realized that Hildegard's prophecy need not necessarily refer to the friars; see his *Tractatus pauperis* (*ibid.*, p. 64). He uses various ruses to cast doubt on her writings, including some predictable anti-feminism (*ibid.*, p. 76). He ends by asserting "Credo autem donec aliud mihi innotescat, prophetiam Hildegardis ex dyaboli astutia processisse" (*ibid.*).

61 See Dufeil, *Guillaume*, p. 342, n. 181; Szittya, *Antifraternal Tradition*, pp. 220-21. Szittya is incorrect in his assertion that Wimbledon was citing "Insurgent gentes." See Knight's note to line 841ff. in 'her edition of *Wimbledon's Sermon*.

62 See Szittya, "*Sedens*," p. 31.
63 There are transcriptions of the text in A. G. Little and R. Easterling, *The Franciscans and Dominicans of Exeter* (Exeter, 1927), pp. 60–61, and Johann Albert Fabricius, *Bibliotheca latina mediae et infimae aetatis* (Florence, 1858), pp. 243–44. The section quoted below is based on Little and Easterling's text but the first line as quoted here comes from Fabricius' text, which reads "peccata" (as manuscripts usually do) rather than "pecuniam(?)," as Little and Easterling give.
64 The prophecy occurs in a number of manuscripts of English provenance, for example London, Lambeth Palace Library MS 357; Phillips MS 3119 (now Oxford, Bodleian Library MS Lat. Misc. c. 75); Oxford, Bodleian Library MS Bodley 158; Exeter Chapter Library MS 3625; and Dublin, Trinity College MS 516 and MS 517. Szittya, *Antifraternal Tradition*, p. 220, attests to its popularity with Middle English writers, and suggests that Gower knew it because he cites Osee 4:8 (on which the opening line of the prophecy is based) with reference to the friars in the *Vox clamantis* (*ibid.*). It seems very likely that Langland would have known it given its popularity with his contemporaries.
65 In Little and Easterling, *Franciscans*, p. 61.
66 Conscience voices the traditional view of the secular propagandists when he hesitates over Contrition's request to allow the friar-physician to come in, "'We haen no nede,' quod Consience; 'y woet no bettere leche / Then person oper parsche prest, penytauncer or bischope'" (xxII. 318–19), but he relents and the friar is given permission to enter. There may be a play here on the word "nede": the friars are an incarnation of need for Langland and the spiritual advantage which the parish priest has over the friar is that the former is not plagued by need.
67 Burdach, *Dichter*, p. 329. This notion will be discussed further in chapter 5, below.

5 LEAVEN OF HOPE: NEW LEADERSHIP AND JOACHITE APOCALYPTICISM

1 See Lerner, "Refreshment," and Reeves, "Originality," for some recent attempts to delineate the extent of Joachim's influence.
2 On Joachism in Northern Europe and Britain see Bloomfield and Reeves, "Penetration." On Britain in particular, see Reeves, *Influence*, pp. 6–7, 12–14, 37, 42–43 and 45–48; Bloomfield, *Apocalypse*, Appendix 1; B. Smalley, "Flaccianus *De visionibus Sibyllae*," in *Mélanges offerts à Etienne Gilson*, Etudes de philosophie médiévale, hors série (Toronto and Paris, 1959), pp. 547–62, and her "John Russell, O.F.M.," *RTAM*, 22 (1956), pp. 277–320; Reeves, "Protestant Thought"; S. Medcalf and M. Reeves, "The Ideal, the Real and the Quest for Perfection," in *The Later Middle Ages*, ed. S. Medcalf (London, 1981), pp. 95ff.
3 Smalley, "Flaccianus," p. 552. On the Continent Joachism had become an ideological justification for the convictions of a number of extremist and heretical groups and individuals, the most famous of which were probably the Franciscan Spirituals and the heretical Fraticelli. On the Spirituals see Daniel, *Franciscan Concept*; Reeves, *Influence*; McGinn, *Apocalyptic Spirituality*, ch. 4; Leff, *Heresy*, ch. 2; Bloomfield, *Apocalypse*, pp. 95ff. and 205. On the Fraticelli see Leff, *Heresy*, ch. 3; C. T. Berkhout and J. B. Russell, *Medieval Heresies: A Bibliography* (Toronto, 1981), pp. 77–84; D. Douie, *The Nature and Effect of the Heresy of the Fraticelli* (Manchester, 1932); McGinn, *Visions*, ch. 28. Joachim's views on the Trinity were condemned in 1215 and this affected his reputation very early on. See Reeves, *Influence*, pp. 28ff., and Bloomfield and Reeves, 'Penetration," pp. 773ff.
4 However, it should be added that a genuine Joachite expectation of a coming "age" of the Holy Spirit is missing from the apocalypticism of many writers, Continental as well as English, who came in contact with Joachism. See Reeves, "Originality," and

Notes to pages 163–65

Reeves, *Influence*. See note 16 below, this chapter, on the use of "age" as a translation of Joachim's "status."

5 See Bloomfield, p. 95 and *passim*; Daniel, *Franciscan Concept*, ch. 5, *passim*. Bourquin (*Etudes*, p. 725) argues that even though, as Bloomfield says, the English Franciscans were largely untouched by the Spiritualist movement, the literature it produced was widespread. John Fleming makes a similar point in his "Antifraternalism."

6 There seems to have been relatively little interest in Joachism among the Lollards. Wyclif himself did not think much of (non-biblical) religious prophecy; see his *De vaticinia seu prophetia* in *Opera minora*, ed. Johann Loserth (London, 1913). See Bloomfield, *Apocalypse*, p. 226, for a list of Wyclif's references to Joachim, and Leff, *Heresy*, vol. II, p. 587, on Lollard apocalypticism.

7 The English were known in the Middle Ages to be avid collectors of obscure prophecy, usually of the political type (see Holder-Egger, "Italienische Prophetieen," p. 119). Some of the shorter pseudo-Joachite prophecies would certainly cater to this taste for "dark" prognostications and this no doubt partly accounts for their popularity.

8 On which see Bloomfield, *Apocalypse*, Appendix 1; Reeves, *Influence*; and Bignami-Odier, *Roquetaillade*.

9 See Bloomfield, *Apocalypse*, ch. 3; Pantin, "Origins"; Reeves, *Influence*, pt. 2.

10 Bloomfield, *Apocalypse*, ch. 3; Bloomfield, "*Piers Plowman* and the Three Grades of Chastity," *Anglia*, 76 (1958), pp. 227–53; Reeves, *Influence*, pp. 37ff.; Reeves and Hirsch-Reich, *Figurae*; Reeves, "Joachim's Disciples."

11 Surviving copies of *Super Jeremiam* seem to be scarce in England: there is one in British Library MS Add. 11439 and a fragment in British Library Royal 8. F. XVI. Wimbledon cited the work in his famous sermon (along with Hildegard's *Scivias*) as witness to the imminent End of the World (see Reeves, *Influence*, p. 82). By contrast copies of *Super Esaiam* are more plentiful (see Bloomfield, *Apocalypse*, Appendix 1), and *De oneribus* turns up in handful of medieval English productions and citations (see Bloomfield, *Apocalypse*, Appendix 1; Reeves, *Influence*, p. 82; and see below, pp. 184–86, on *The Last Age of the Church* and note 55, this chapter). Numerous commentaries in both medieval and modern catalogues are simply referred to as "*Super Jeremiam*" or "*Super Esaiam*" and without more information it is impossible to know for sure how many copies of these works were in circulation in England.

12 Kermode, *The Sense of An Ending* (Oxford, 1966), p. 8. On Joachim's life see McGinn, *Apocalyptic Spirituality*, pp. 97ff., and Reeves, *Influence*, pp. 3ff.

13 McGinn, *Apocalyptic Spirituality*, p. 98. Joachim met with Richard I when he was in Messina on the Third Crusade. Both Roger Hoveden and the so-called Benedict of Peterborough record the interview. In fact, English chroniclers of the twelfth century provide some of the most important information we have on Joachim's life. See Reeves, *Influence*, pp. 9–10, and on Ralph of Coggeshall's account of Joachim see p. 12.

14 Joachim believed that there would be more than one antichrist and that reform would *follow* (not precede) the worst onslaught of Antichrist. One of the fascinating things about Langland's apocalypticism is that this distinction – whether he picked it up from Joachim or not – was not lost on him and that he persisted in espousing the non-traditional view.

15 Joachim's *Liber de concordia novi ac veteris testamenti*, Books I–IV (which I will refer to as the *Liber concordia*), is now available in a modern critical edition by E. Randolph Daniel, *Transactions of the American Philosophical Society*, vol. 73, pt. 8, 1983. The entire *Liber concordia* (Venice, 1519), as well as the *Expositio in Apocalypsim* (Venice, 1527) and the *Psalterium decem chordarum* (Venice, 1527) are available in reprints (Frankfurt-am-Main, 1964). The *Liber figurarum*, now generally believed to be genuine, was edited by L. Tondelli, M. Reeves and B. Hirsch-Reich (rev. ed., 2 vols., Turin, 1954). The *Tractatus super quatuor Evangelia* was edited by E. Buonaiuti, Fonti per la storia d'Italia, 67

232

(Rome, 1930). On Joachim's many systems of concords and historical patterns see Reeves, *Prophetic Future*, ch. 1; Reeves, *Influence*, pp. 16–27; Reeves and Hirsch-Reich, *Figurae*; Reeves, "Seven Seals"; Daniel, "Double Procession"; McGinn, *Visions*, ch. 17; McGinn, *Apocalyptic Spirituality*, pp. 102ff. On his famous Trinitarian scheme see below, note 16, this chapter. Closely related to his pattern of the three *status* was his pattern of the two dispensations (see especially Reeves, *Influence*, pp. 19ff., but see also Daniel, "Double Procession"). In his Augustinian-based pattern of the seven ages (*etates*) of world history Joachim divided the sixth or present age (*etas*) into seven subdivisions (*tempora*) based on the seven seal-openings of the Apocalypse (see Reeves, *Prophetic Future*, pp. 8–10). The sixth age would end in the great tribulations of Antichrist, but this would be followed by the "sabbath" of the seventh seal, symbolized by the "silence in heaven about the space of half an hour" (Apocalypse 8:1). Joachim thus diverged from the traditional Augustinian view in his conviction that the "sabbath" or seventh age would be a time of renewal *on earth* and not in heaven.

16 On Joachim's Trinitarian scheme of history see Reeves, *Prophetic Future*, p. 13 (for a concise account), and Daniel, "Double Procession," as well as the sources cited in the note above. Joachim actually uses the term for "state" or "condition" (*status*) rather than *etas* ("age") in describing his Trinitarian view of history. Unlike later Joachites he does not talk of an *Age* of the Holy Ghost, but rather of a "state" of spirituality arrived at in the "ordo eremitarum" or "monachorum." See Reeves, *Prophetic Future*, p. 8. Because my study deals mainly with non-genuine Joachite writings I have used the term "age" throughout, although in quotation marks with reference to Joachim himself.

17 On Joachim's idealization of eremiticism see Reeves, "Joachimist Expectations," p. 113; Pantin, "Origins," p. 191; and Bloomfield, *Apocalypse*, p. 70. This kind of idealization of the eremitical life is evident in Hildegard as well. (See chapter 2, above.)

18 See *Expositio in Apocalypsim*, fol. 5^r-v, and see Dronke's comment on this passage in "*Arbor*," p. 217. Dronke has suggested that the affinity between Joachim and Langland is closest in their treatments of *liberum arbitrium*.

19 Frank, *Scheme*, pp. 17–18, n. 4. Henry W. Wells also compares Langland's triune system to Joachim's and suggests that "Dobest" stretches from the Ascension to a time beyond the poet's own, but with reservations ("The Philosophy of Piers Plowman," in Vasta, ed., *Interpretations*, p. 129). Unfortunately, Wells does not seem to realize that the condemnation of Joachim's academic views on the Trinity (written against those of Peter Lombard) has very little relevance here. In any case, Joachim's ideas would have reached most English readers in a less academic form. However, Wells is (probably unknowingly) very close to a Joachite reading when he says, "The gist of this article is that Langland's three lives are not vocational callings but mental states." Lynne Hunt Levy, in an unpublished thesis on "*Piers Plowman* and the Concept of Poverty" (University of Oklahoma, 1976), suggests (in rather more strident terms than I have below) that the poem can be looked at as an unfinished Joachite view of the world's history, with the last chapter, that is, the *renovatio* of the third *status*, left unwritten.

20 On Joachim's notion of a *transitus* see Reeves, "Joachimist Expectations," pp. 111–12, and see "Two Poems," ed. Reeves and Fleming, p. 19. The basis for this notion in Joachim's typology is in the Israelites' crossing of the Jordan into the Promised Land.

21 At VIII. 92ff. Piers makes a will before passing on to "penaunces and pilgrimages" and, although it is never directly stated that he leaves his wife and family, both this passage and an earlier passage at the end of Passus VII imply that it is impossible to move on to an eremitical (or contemplative) life without rejecting the "ordo conjugatorum." At VII. 299ff. "Actif," a married man, excuses himself from the pilgrimage because "a Kitte so cleueth on me" while "Contemplacioun" vows to follow Piers anywhere and suffer any tribulation.

233

22 Joachim saw a mixture of the clerical and eremitical or monastic modes of life as the characteristic of spiritual leadership in the second *status*.

23 See Joachim's explanation in the *Liber figurarum*, ed. Tondelli *et al.*, Table xiv, trans. McGinn, *Apocalyptic Spirituality*, pp. 138–39.

24 The *transitus* into the seventh time, of course, corresponds with the *transitus* into the third *status*, so the one reading does not preclude the other.

25 Presented in one of Joachim's annotated figures, the seven oratories contain: (1) a kind of transformed, monasticized papacy ruled by a "Spiritual Father"; (2) Contemplatives; (3) Holy Doctors; (4) Manual Laborers; (5) Weak and Elderly Brothers; (6) Secular Clergy; (7) The Laity; in the *Liber figurarum*, ed. Tondelli, *et al.*, Table xii, trans. McGinn, *Apocalyptic Spirituality*, pp. 142ff.

26 Trans. in McGinn, *Visions*, p. 140, from the *Expositio in Apocalypsim*, "Epistola prologalis" (unnumbered folio) (see note 15, above, this chapter).

27 The Cistercians seem to have regarded him as a deserter when he founded his new order. See Reeves, *Influence*, p. 3.

28 Joachim did, however, have a great deal of sympathy for this notion. Bloomfield quotes two passages from the *Liber concordia* (Venice, 1519) to this effect: "Necesse quippe est, ut succedat similitudo vera apostolice vite, in qua non acquirebatur possessio terrene hereditatis, sed vendebatur potius . . ." *Liber concordia* 4.39, fol. 59ᵛ (see also 4.25); "Reformari statum ecclesie in eum gradum et similitudinem, in quo fuit tempore apostolorum," *Liber concordia* 5.86 fol. 114ʳ ("Joachim," p. 297, n. 215).

29 See Joachim's two letters translated in McGinn, *Apocalyptic Spirituality*, pp. 113ff. from the edition in J. Bignami-Odier, "Notes sur deux manuscrits de la Bibliothèque du Vatican," *Mélanges d'archéologie et de l'histoire*, 54 (1937), pp. 220–23.

30 In Joachim's typology this reforming pope would be a figure of Zorobabel, who arose at the end of the Old Dispensation to rebuild the Church. See Reeves, *Prophetic Future*, p. 14.

31 There may even be, in the B-text, a tenuous association between Piers' tearing of the pardon and Moses' breaking of the tablets in Exodus 32:19.

32 See, for example, the Joachite prophecy of a "third David" discussed by Reeves, *Influence*, p. 492. Reeves gives several examples of this phenomenon in Joachite disciples throughout *Influence*.

33 Schmidt, *B-text*, p. 313. For Bennett's comments on the passage see J. A. W. Bennett, ed., *Piers Plowman: The Prologue and Passus I–VII* (Oxford, 1972), note to Passus iii, lines 323–27.

34 In the *Liber concordia* Joachim writes, "Igitur prout ego arbitror in anno vel in tempore quo venturi sunt, sicut tenet ecclesia, Enoch et Helias, eligendi sunt 12 viri similes patriarcharum et apostolorum et ad predicandum Iudeis: et erunt preclarissima monasteria similis 12 tribuum et 12 ecclesiarum" (Reeves and Hisch-Reich, *Figurae*, p. 15, from the edition of Venice, 1519, fol. 57ᵛ). These twelve would, then, be elected to preach to the Jews. The very popular fourteenth-century prophet Telesphorus of Cosenza follows Joachim in expecting twelve spiritual men and the angelic pope to purify the Church and bring it *in statum paupertatis* (see Reeves, *Influence*, p. 423).

35 See xvii. 297. The concern for conversion of non-Christians is well illustrated in a similarly obscure prophecy on which Joachim wrote a commentary, and which appears in five chronicles, all British (see McGinn, "Joachim").

36 As Bloomfield says ("Joachim," p. 303), pseudo-Joachim works seem to have been especially popular in England in the 1350s and 1360s. See above, note 11, this chapter, and Reeves, *Influence*, p. 82. On the origins of these works, see note 42, below, this chapter. Marjorie Reeves has suggested (in a private communication) that the popularity of the *De oneribus* in England may have been owing to the Thomas à Becket prophecy it contains.

37 All these works follow Joachim in seeing the German emperors as enemies of the Church. See McGinn, *Visions*, p. 127, and Reeves, *Influence*, p. 57.
38 On this passage in the preface to *Super Jeremiam* see Reeves, *Influence*, p. 397. I have used the version of this passage cited by Vincent of Beauvais in the *Speculum historiale*, p. 1324, which is the form in which it would have been most widely transmitted in England, I believe. In a recent article ("The Development of the 'Pseudo-Joachim' Commentary 'Super Hieremiam': New Manuscript Evidence") Robert Moynihan has argued that Joachim himself may have had a hand in the composition of the *Super Jeremiam* (*Mélanges de l'Ecole Française de Rome. Moyen Age, Temps Modernes*, 98 [1986], pp. 109–42).
39 On Vincent's treatment of his source see Martin Haeusler, *Das Ende der Geschichte in der mittelalterlichen Weltchronistik* (Cologne, 1980), pp. 79ff.
40 The recurrent motif of Peter casting off his clothing before plunging into the sea is an oddly inverted allusion to John 21:7, as, for example, in the following: "Ac per hoc quia Petri nauicula periclitabitur conteri: necesse erat vt nudus pastor abiectis rerum temporalium sarcinis occurrat furentibus imperu*ius* fluctibus aduentum saluatoris" (*Super Esaiam*, fol. 58ᵛ). (I have used a microfilm of the Venice, 1517 edition in the British Library, for this and all citations below.)
41 *The Bush Garden: Essays on the Canadian Imagination* (Toronto, 1971), p. 225.
42 On the Franciscan Spirituals see above, note 3, this chapter. Other groups, some heretical, were attracted to these early Joachite works for similar reasons (see Reeves, *Influence*). Scholars have disagreed about whether *Super Jeremiam* and *Super Esaiam* originated in Franciscan Spiritualist circles or from early followers of Joachim in the Cistercian or Florensian orders. See Reeves, "Joachim's Disciples," and Reeves, *Influence*, pp. 157ff. The classic study of these works is still Friderich, "Kritische Untersuchung" (of which I have used section C, "Kirche und Papstthum nach den beiden Commentaren und nach den ächten Schriften Joachim's," pp. 454–76) and see the article by R. Moynihan mentioned in note 38 above, this chapter.
43 *De Oneribus* (Holder-Egger, "Italienischen Prophetieen," p. 185). The motif appears in John of Rupescissa (see Lerner, "Black Death," p. 541) and even in the vernacular tract, *The Last Age of the Church* (Todd, ed., *Last Age*, pp. xxxi–xxxii).
44 See John 10:12–13.
45 *Confessio amantis*, ed. G. C. Macaulay (Oxford, 1904), vol. II, lines 3056–62.
46 There is a translation of the "Donation of Constantine" in B. Tierney, *The Crisis of Church and State* (Englewood Cliffs, N.J., 1964), p. 143, for the details of Constantine's supposed subjection.
47 Olivi's works were known to some extent in England. Bloomfield lists some manuscripts of his works, *Apocalypse*, pp. 227–28, n. 13 (to which should be added Cambridge, Corpus Christi College MS 321 and Oxford, New College MS 49), although his non-apocalyptic works seem to have been more common.
48 See Marsilius' *Defensor pacis*, ed. R. Scholz (Hanover, 1932), vol. II, chs. 11–14. See especially Olsen, "*Ecclesia Primitiva*," for a history of the idea of the *ecclesia primitiva* in medieval thought. The era of the primitive Church was usually regarded as the pre-Constantine period, although opinions on this differed (see Olsen, *ibid.*, pp. 81 and 84). Olsen traces the first distrust of the post-Constantine Church to St. Bernard (*ibid.*, pp. 82ff.).
49 The one exception to this (of prophetic works easily available in England) is the Hildegard material on disendowment. This would not, however, have provided a source on the Donation. Strong condemnation of the Donation of Constantine, as Bloomfield says ("Joachim," p. 305), is characteristic of Joachite writings from the time of *Super Jeremiam* onwards.

50 H. S. Offler, ed., *Guillelmi de Ockham Opera Politica*, vol. I (Manchester, 1974), Introduction, pp. 22off. See especially ch. 8.

51 VII, 4, cited in Arthur McGrade, *The Political Thought of William Ockham* (Cambridge, 1974), p. 87, from the *Opera politica*, ed. H. Offler and R. Snape (Manchester, 1940), vol. I, pp. 176–77.

52 See, for example, criticism of the Donation of Constantine in Wyclif's *De civili dominio*, ed. J. Loserth (London, 1885–1904), vol. II, pp. 195–96; vol. III, 215–18, and *De ecclesia*, Book xvi, ed. Loserth (London, 1886); and Gradon, "Dissent." For a summary of Wycliff's position on disendowment see *Fasciculi Zizaniorum*, ed. W. W. Shirley, Rolls Series, 5 (London, 1858), pp. 248–49.

53 See V. Galbraith, "Articles Laid before the Parliament of 1371," *English Historical Review*, 34 (1919), pp. 579–82.

54 Translated by Gradon, "Dissent," p. 187, from Galbraith, "Articles," p. 582.

55 Ed. Holder-Egger "Italienische Prophetieen." See note 11 above, this chapter, on the circulation of Joachite works in England. John Erghome owned a copy (see Reeves, *Influence*, p. 255) and the Englishman Henry of Harclay knew the work (*ibid.*, p. 320). A fourteenth-century copy of it survives with some other Joachite texts in British Library MS Royal 8. F. xvi and there are two so far unnoticed copies in British Library MS Sloane 156 and MS Cotton Tiberius B. v, and extracts in Cambridge University Library MS Gg. iv. 25 and Gonville and Caius College MS 249. It was cited extensively by the author of *The Last Age of the Church* (on which see below, pp. 184–86). An English preacher, who may have been Archbishop Stratford, quoted *De oneribus* in a sermon given during the 1340s and now preserved in Hereford Cathedral MS P. 5. XII (fol. 104^{r-v}) on which see Owst, *Literature and Pulpit*, p. 130; Reeves, *Influence*, p. 82; and Holder-Egger, "Italienische Prophetieen," p. 148.

56 Isaias 14:4–6; Holder-Egger, "Italienische Prophetieen," pp. 172–73. The image of the incurable (Isaias 14:4–6) or curable (Apocalypse 13:3) wound is a recurrent theme in Joachite works. See McGinn, *Apocalyptic Spirituality*, p. 137, "Commentary," translated from *Liber figurarum*, ed. Tondelli *et al.*, Table XIV.

57 See Holder-Egger, "Italienische Prophetieen," pp. 119–20, for references to the prophecy in a number of English chronicles. See also Reeves, *Influence*, p. 526, and references.

58 On "Corruent nobiles" see Reeves, *Influence*, pp. 50–51 (including a lengthy list of British manuscripts which contain this piece).

59 Trans. McGinn, *Visions*, p. 190, from J. S. Brewer, ed., *Fr. Rogeri Bacon opera quaedam hactenus inedita* (Rolls Series, 15), p. 86.

60 Trans. McGinn, *Visions*, pp. 190–91, from Brewer, *Bacon opera*, p. 402. On Bacon's view of the angelic pope see Daniel, "Roger Bacon."

61 On this aspect of the new "viri spirituales" see Reeves, "Joachimist Expectations."

62 On the "angelic pope" see McGinn, *Visions*, ch. 22; Reeves, *Influence*, pt. 4; Reeves, "Some Popular Prophecies"; McGinn, "Joachim" (McGinn argues here that Joachim and Gerhoh of Reichersberg were the creators of the *pastor angelicus*; see p. 127); McGinn, "Angel Pope"; H. Grundmann, "Die Papstprophetien des Mittelalters," *Archiv für Kulturgeschichte*, 19 (1929), pp. 77–139; Daniel, "Roger Bacon." On the Last World Emperor figure see Reeves, "Joachimist Influences"; Alexander, "Diffusion"; O'Sullivan, "Treatment of Political Themes"; Reeves, *Influence*; McGinn, *Visions*, chs. 7 and 30 especially.

63 In XXI. 426–27 he is not advocating a theory of papal dominion, although the lines (in isolation) could be read as such.

64 See Reeves, *Influence*, p. 304.

65 Robert Lerner challenges this view in an article to appear in *Fälschungen im Mittelalter*, 5

(Hanover, 1988), in which he proposes an English origin for the *Vaticinia*. I am most grateful to Prof. Lerner for sending me a pre-publication copy of this article.

66 On the "Oracles of Leo the Wise" see C. Mango, "The Legend of Leo the Wise," *Recueil des travaux de l'Académie Serbe des Sciences*, 65/*Institut d'études Byzantines*, 6 (1960), pp. 59–93.

67 I have used the fourteenth-century English copy of the *Vaticinia* in Cambridge, Corpus Christi College MS 404, fols. 88ʳ–95ʳ, and concluding on fol. 41. The holy-hermit pope appears on fol. 92ᵛ in this manuscript (where he is identified as Benedict XII in Henry of Kirkestede's hand). I would like to thank the Fellows of Corpus Christi College for providing me with a microfilm of the manuscript. For a translation of the caption accompanying this illustration see McGinn, *Visions*, p. 195, no. XI.

68 Fol. 89ᵛ (identified by Kirkestede as Nicholas IV); no. V, p. 194, in McGinn, *Visions*.

69 E.g. 89ᵛ (the latter is identified as Boniface VIII by Kirkestede).

70 See the prophecies edited in Fleming, "Sibylla," pp. 129–131 and 158, for the same motif. On the relation of the harvesting angel to Piers see Bourquin, *Études*, p. 730.

71 For example, the papal figure who follows the holy pope with the sickle in the *Vaticinia* is interesting in that it represents an evil pope (usually Boniface VIII) and there are two heads in the illustration beside it (Reeves, "Some Popular Prophecies," p. 110), originally monks' heads in the "Oracles of Leo the Wise" at least (Mango, "Legend," p. 65). Langland's obscure prophecy at B. VI. 327–28 refers to "two monkes heddes" and also alludes to the moon being "amys" (a common symbol of trouble in the Church in Joachite prophecy). On the motif of a woman having the "maistrie," see Martha Fleming's edition of *Sibylla: De Imperatore*, p. xxxiii, Bignami-Odier, *Roquetaillade*, p. 224, and Bloomfield, *Apocalypse*, p. 212. The Whore of Babylon is a key figure in some Joachite prophecies, and often represents the carnal Church.

72 See Burdach, *Dichter*, pp. 326–51.

73 Praise of the Desert Fathers and the rhetoric of a "new Egypt" was common in monastic reformist literature; see Constable, "Renaissance," p. 58, and Little, *Poverty*.

74 British Library Cotton MS Cleopatra C x, fol. 157ᵛ. I am currently working on an edition based on the English manuscripts of the Colombinus prophecy with the help of E. Randolph Daniel.

75 See "The Prophecies of John of Bridlington," pp. 148, 174 and 167, Reeves, *Influence*, p. 341, and E. W. Kantorowicz, *The King's Two Bodies* (Princeton, 1957), p. 81.

76 See Reeves, *Influence*, p. 365, for a discussion of a sixteenth-century prophecy applied to Charles V in which he was to be "the Pastor, like David, to gather all sheep into one fold." Joachite prophecies of great secular leaders began to flourish in the "second generation" of Joachite works, particularly with the blending of the old French political motif of the return of Charlemagne with Joachite expectations; see Reeves, *Influence*, pp. 320ff. Robert Adams has recently argued that the king Langland expects in this prophecy is Christ in his second coming, but it is difficult to see how "O cristene king" could mean Jesus *himself* (see Adams, "Versions," pp. 211ff.). Once again Langland's use of David in a prophetic passage suggests that Langland had a *prophetic* model in mind, not merely an exegetical one.

77 See F. Pelster, "Die Quaestio Heinrichs von Harclay über die zweite Ankunft Christi und die Erwartung des baldigen Weltendes zu Anfang des XIV. Jahrhunderts," *Archivio italiano per la storia della pieta*, 1 (1951), pp. 25–82. Morton Bloomfield discusses the English participants in this debate (Henry of Harclay, Hugh of Newcastle, John Eshenden and Wyclif) in Bloomfield, *Apocalypse*, p. 231. See also Reeves, *Influence*, pp. 315–17. Arnold's medical works survive in great numbers in England (see, for example, the *Index to Manuscripts in the British Library*, vol. I, pp. 156–57) and, like the alchemical works of John of Rupescissa, they often carry an apocalyptic as well as a

scientific message (see Daniel, *Franciscan Concept*, p. 93). A copy of the *De mysterio* can be found in the fourteenth-century English MS Phillips 3119 (now Oxford, Bodleian Library MS Lat. Misc. c. 75) and the medieval library at Merton College contained a number of his works, some of which were apocalyptic. See F. M. Powicke, *Medieval Books in Merton* (Oxford, 1931), pp. 140 and 257. John Bale owned a copy of the *De mysterio* as well, see Reeves, "History and Eschatology," p. 105. There is an allusion to one of Arnold's works in Chaucer's "Canon Yeoman's Tale" (lines 1428–32): see F. R. Robinson, *The Works of Chaucer*, 2nd ed. (Boston, 1961), p. 762, n. to line 1428.

78 The text of "Ve mundo" used here is Pou y Marti's, in *Visionarios*, pp. 54–55. See Lerner, *Powers*, p. 40.

79 "Nidus etiam Aristotilis contabescens euacuabitur."

80 As Bloomfield says, the *De semine* had a "strong English following" ("Joachim," p. 303, n. 236). Bacon cited it (see Daniel, "Roger Bacon"); Galfridus le Baker of Swynebroke explains in his *Chroniculum* the theory of world ages according to the *De semine* and explains how many years are left (ed. E. M. Thompson [Oxford, 1889], pp. 157 and 173–74; see Reeves, *Influence*, p. 83); Wyclif cites it in the *Trialogus* (see Bloomfield, "Joachim," p. 303, n. 236) and it is used extensively in *The Last Age of the Church* (see below, pp. 184–86). Henry of Harclay cited the *De semine* in his *Quaestio* (see Reeves, *Influence*, p. 316); finally, John Capgrave had come across it (Reeves, *Influence*, p. 70, and see below, p. 184). On this prophecy see Daniel, "Roger Bacon," and Töpfer, *Reich*, pp. 45ff. There is no printed edition; the text I have used is Cambridge, Corpus Christi College MS 404, fols. 43ᵛ–64ᵛ.

81 This figural reading of the money-changers also occurs in the Joachite *Oraculum Cyrilli* (see McGinn, *Visions*, p. 192). There is a handful of medieval English copies of the *Oraculum* still extant (in Cambridge, Corpus Christi College MS 404; MS Phillips 3119 [now Bodleian Library Oxford, MS Lat. Misc. c. 75] and Cambridge, Gonville and Caius College MS 388/608).

82 In Cambridge, Corpus Christi College MS 404, X begins fol. 58ᵛ; Y at 61ᵛ; and Z at 62ᵛ.

83 He is referring to Bernard's thirty-third sermon on the Canticles. See Todd edition, p. xxiv. Adams also cites this Bernardian interpretation in his discussion of the eschatological aspects of Nede (see Adams, "Need," p. 297). See also McGinn, "Saint Bernard." The author appears to link "Joachim" (i.e., references in pseudo-Joachim prophecy to the clerical *mercenarius*) with "the business that walketh about in the dark."

84 For Bonaventure's view see the reference in note 101, below, this chapter; Dr. Reeves has also reminded me (in a private communication) of the importance of this notion in Dante.

85 As we have seen there are references to (Pseudo-)Joachim in Gower and Wimbledon, and references to Hildegard in Wimbledon and to Pseudo-Hildegard in anti-mendicant Middle English writers. Scholars at a loss to explain radical reformist features in Middle English writers often use Wyclif to fill in such gaps.

86 See the *Manual of the Writings in Middle English*, vol. ii, ed. J. Burke-Severs (Hamden, 1950), no. 92, p. 376.

87 Gradon suggests a similar view in her "Dissent."

88 Langland's use of these concepts is very similar to that of the historicist thinkers described in Leff, "Apostolic Ideal," as discussed above, pp. 174–75.

89 See Bischoff, "Eschatology," pp. 48–49. As Derek Pearsall has pointed out in his note to v. 171 in his edition of the C-text, the concept was also used in discussions of penance.

90 There are several examples of *ad pristinum statum* European prophecies. See Reeves, *Influence*, p. 423, for its use by Telesphorus of Cosenza; see Lerner, "Refreshment," p. 114, for Gerhoh of Reichersberg's use of it; for its use in a Franciscan Spiritualist commentary on "Ve mundo" see Reeves, *Influence*, p. 418; for its use in an anonymous

fourteenth-century diary see Reeves, *ibid.*; for its use by Cola di Rienzo see Reeves, *ibid.*, p. 421; for Hildegard see *Liber divinorum operum*, col. 1005; for Bridget see the discussion on pp. 106–07, above.

91 The first prophecy is from a fifteenth-century manuscript (Oxford, Bodleian Library MS Digby 196, fol. 28), and is printed in *The Writings of Robert Grosseteste, Bishop of Lincoln 1235–1253*, ed. S. Harrison Thomson (Cambridge, 1940), p. 260.

92 Ed. Frank S. Haydon, Rolls Series, 9 (London, 1858), vol. 1, pp. 417ff. I have quoted only the lines of the prophecy, omitting the prose glosses.

93 The relevant lines (from the "Grossteste" version) read: "Orbem subvertit reliquo clerumque reducet. / In statum pristini seviens renovet loca sancta." The prophecy occurs in a number of manuscripts (see Bloomfield, *Apocalypse*, p. 215, n. 65).

94 On John's popularity see Lerner, "Black Death," esp. p. 543, n. 20, and Bignami-Odier, *Roquetaillade*, pp. 209ff. and Appendix II, pp. 235ff., for lists of manuscripts of John's works, a number of which are English. John was well known in England, where he was cited by chroniclers such as Henry of Herford (see Bignami-Odier, *Roquetaillade*, pp. 221ff.) and Froissart (*ibid.*, pp. 219ff.). There is a possibility that Wyclif knew Froissart's account (*ibid.*, p. 215). Bignami-Odier's *Roquetaillade* is still the only major study of John of Rupescissa. See also Lynn Thorndike, *History of Magic and Experimental Science* (Columbia, 1934), vol. III, pp. 349–51; Reeves, *Influence*, pp. 225–28, 323–24, 416–17; E. F. Jacob, "John of Roquetaillade," *Bulletin of the John Rylands Library*, 39 (1956), pp. 75–96. Manuscripts of the *Vade mecum* are plentiful in England (at least ten that I am aware of) and there is a fifteenth-century English translation of an extract extant in British Library MS Add. 24663, fol. 11ʳ⁻ᵛ. There is no modern edition of the *Vade mecum*; I have used the text in Brown, ed., Appendix to Gratius, *Fasciculus*, and all references below are to this edition. pp. 496–508.

95 That is, a belief in one thousand years of peace and prosperity (see Lerner, "Black Death," p. 542).

96 On this work see Bignami-Odier, *Roquetaillade*, pp. 113ff. The *Liber* is a series of thirty revelations concerning secular and ecclesiastical politics, coming tribulations, Antichrist and the renewal of the Church under a saintly pope, all topics which John discusses in his other works, although not always as lucidly as here.

97 Mme Bignami-Odier has done an excellent job of tracking down John's many different prophetic sources. See *Roquetaillade, passim*, but especially the listings of sources at the end of each chapter.

98 "Auch das prophetische Reformprogramm des unglücklichen Minoriten Johannes de Rupescissa muss man trotz seiner franzosenfreundlichen Tendenz als Vorläufer jener Gedanken Langlands heranziehen" (Burdach, *Dichter*, p. 329).

99 Similarly, the thirteenth-century Joachite *Prophécies de Merlin* contain reference to "la grand colee que la relegion saint Benoit recevra" (ed. Lucy A. Paton [London, 1927], vol. II, p. 189), which is very close to the wording of Langland's disendowment prophecy in Passus v. The French prophecy also implies that the poverty of the friars is the stick with which the *possessionati* will be beaten.

100 For Piers' simplicity or anti-intellectualism see xv. 129ff.; for Christ's see xx. 405–06. On anti-intellectualism and anti-scholasticism in Joachite prophecy, see Friderich, "Kritische Untersuchung," pp. 462ff.

101 *Collationes in Hexaemeron* (Quaracchi, 1891, vol. v, pp. 408–09). See Reeves, *Prophetic Future*, p. 37. See Burdach, *Dichter*, ch. 5, pt. 5, especially pp. 273ff.; Bourquin, *Etudes*, pp. 693ff.; Donaldson, *Piers Plowman*, pp. 146–7 and *passim*.

102 There are a number of sources that Langland could have turned to for his typology of the holy fool (see Saward, *Fools*, ch. 4 on the eremitical tradition of "foolery," ch. 5 on the Cistercian tradition and ch. 6 on the Franciscan and thirteenth-century tradition) and see also Doob, *Nebuchadnezzar's Children*, pp. 160ff. (and on medieval madness

generally). The fact that Langland's fools are explicitly said to *prophesy*, however, suggests to me a Joachite source. Donaldson's discussion of the lunatic lollars (as having been derived from the Franciscan *joculatores domini*) starts on p. 146 of his *Piers Plowman*.

103 See Little, *Poverty*, p. 73, and Bloomfield, *Apocalypse*, p. 70. The relationship between a life of wandering evangelical poverty and madness probably stems largely from the Pauline "fools for Christ" theme and what seems to be an almost superstitious medieval awe of imbecility or lunacy. For evidence from social history on the treatment of fools see the *Records of Early English Drama: Newcastle* (Toronto, 1982), pp. xxxix and xxxii.

104 Bloomfield suggests that the "wonders" he seeks are prophetic revelations (*Apocalypse*, pp. 69–70). Certainly a number of manuscripts which contain material on portents, miracles, monsters and travel lore also contain prophecies. See, for example, Oxford, Bodleian Library MS Douce 88 (s. c. 21662) or Dublin, Trinity College MS S 347. Anne Middleton has recently shown that *Piers Plowman* itself is frequently found in just this type of manuscript context (see Middleton, "Audience," pp. 104ff.).

105 Compare this aspect of the dreamer's life with Rolle's comment that the man who has truly given himself up to God "non respiciet personam hominis, ideo a pluribus stultus uel rusticus reputatur" (Rolle, *Incendium amoris*, p. 238).

106 "Dissent in Middle English Literature: The Spirit of (13)76," *Medievalia et Humanistica*, n.s. 9 (1979), pp. 25–51.

107 "*Piers Plowman* spielt also die Rolle des mystischen Reformators der Zukunft, der eine die Endzeit einleitende Ära des Friedens, der Gerechtigkeit, der Bedürfnislosigkeit heraufführen, das Weltregiment wie die Kirche von den Sünden der Falschheit und des Hochmuts, von der Sorge der Gewinnsucht erlösen . . ." However, he cautions, "Woher Langland im Einzelnen die Anregung zu diesem Teil seiner Konzeption empfangen hat, bleibt ebenso noch zu ermitteln, wie die Abhängigkeit Wiclefs von der reformatorischen Bewegung Italiens und Frankreichs, für die so vieles spricht, noch genauer nachgewiesen werden muss" (Burdach, *Dichter*, p. 326).

108 "Jener Reformator der Menschheit *Piers Plowman* trägt nun aber sehr besondere Züge. Er verkörpert eine doppelte ideals Forderung: einerseits die Besitzlosigkeit und Armut, anderseits die schaffende menschliche Arbeit in ihrer ursprünglichen, naturlichsten und notwendigsten Form, in der Form des Ackerbaues" (*ibid.*).

109 *Liber concordia* (Venice, 1519), fol. 92ᵛ; see Reeves, *Influence*, pp. 395–96, and Reeves and Hirsch-Reich, *Figurae*, p. 246.

110 M. W. Sheehan, unpublished Oxford D.Phil. thesis, 1975, p. 328. Sheehan discusses some startling evidence of English fraternal want.

111 A number of prophetic writers were strongly anti-scholastic. The Franciscan Joachite Peter John Olivi saw the pursuit of pagan philosophy as a major sign that Antichrist was active in the world (see Leff, *Heresy*, p. 127).

112 The use of the formula "Ac ar . . ." is a convention for the setting out of such programs, which were always oriented around the idea of "signs" of the approach of the end of time. For a discussion of the use of this formula in *Les Prophécies de Merlin*, see A number of prophetic writers were strongly anti-scholastic. The Franciscan Joachite

113 See the discussion above in the Introduction to this study (chapter 1) and in chapter 4.

114 Lerner argues that "numerous twelfth-century writers independently expressed varieties of post-Antichrist chiliasm" ("Black Death," pp. 539–40). The notion, however, only reached its full flowering with Joachim of Fiore, as Lerner says (see note 115 below, this chapter).

115 Exegetes expected this period of "rest" after the last battle with Antichrist and before the Last Judgment to last for forty or forty-five days, as Lerner has shown. This arose originally from some awkward exegetical calculations by St. Jerome (based on the

Book of Daniel) and continued through the writings of Bede, Haimo of Auxerre, Adso, the *Glossa ordinaria* and many standard compendia. The forty- or forty-five-day period was referred to variously as a period of rest, of penance for those who had been misled by Antichrist, of conversion of the infidels and, in the *Glossa ordinaria*, of "refreshment of the saints" ("refrigerium sanctorum"). Sometimes the period was lengthened but usually it retained its forty-five-day limit. Therefore even though a reference to a prolonged age of reform or renewal after Antichrist in the later Middle Ages is usually a reflection of Joachite influence, it is necessary to qualify this by remembering that there was something of an independent, though less developed, tradition of "rest for the saints" after Antichrist. See Lerner, "Refreshment."

116 "As opposed to post-Antichrist chiliasm, the pre-Antichrist variety had virtually no biblical underpinning and, therefore, was seldom espoused openly by theologians. Nonetheless, it appears to have been more 'popular' than the post-Antichrist form, in the sense both of having been expressed more frequently and of having had wider currency among nonliterate classes" ("Black Death," p. 544). As was mentioned in the Introduction to this study, this type of apocalyptic program usually included a Last World Emperor and all the elements of the traditional eschatology, including a good deal of folklore concerning the life of Antichrist. In this light, I cannot agree with Robert Adams' definitions of "learned" and "popular" in his study "Some Versions of Apocalypse." See note 17, chapter 1, above.

117 See West and Zimdars-Swartz, *Joachim*, p. 26, on Joachim's association of the unifying of the body of the Church with the gifts of the Spirit.

6 CONCLUSIONS

1 In "The Ambiguous 'Newer Prophet': A Sixteenth-Century Stock Figure," *Modern Language Review*, 62 (1967), pp. 672–79.
2 *Ibid.*
3 See John N. King, *English Reformation Literature* (Princeton, 1982), p. 339.
4 R. K. Emmerson and R. B. Herzman, "Antichrist, Simon Magus, and Dante's 'Inferno' XIX," *Traditio*, 36 (1980), pp. 373–98.

Select bibliography

This select bibliography gives bibliographical details for works most frequently cited and/or of most significance to the argument in this study. Full bibliographical details for other works cited can be found in the Notes, pp. 204–41.

PRIMARY SOURCES

The Apocalypse of Esdras [Vulgate: IV Esra; Protestant apocrypha: II Esdras]. English translation: in/from *The Holy Bible and Apocrypha* (Oxford, n.d.). Latin original: *Der lateinische Text der Apokalypse des Esra*, ed. A. F. J. Klijn (Berlin, 1983)

Bridget of Sweden, St. *Revelationum S. Birgitte*, ed. Gonzales Durante (Antwerp, 1611)

The Revelations of St. Birgitta, ed. William Patterson Cumming, EETS, no. 178 (London, 1929)

Sancta Birgitta Revelationes, vol. 1, ed. Carl-Gustav Undhagen (Stockholm, 1977)

Das Werk der heiligen Birgitta von Schweden in oberdeutscher Überlieferung, ed. Ulrich Montag (Munich, 1968)

The Cloud of Unknowing, ed. Phyllis Hodgson, EETS no. 128 (London, 1974)

Elizabeth of Schönau, St. *Die Visionen der hl. Elisabeth*, ed. F. E. W. Roth (Brunn, 1884)

Eulogium historiarum, ed. Frank S. Haydon, 3 vols., Rolls Series, 9 (London, 1858–63)

FitzRalph, Richard. *Defensio curatorum*, in Melchior Goldast, *Monarchia s. romani imperii*, vol. II (Hanover, 1614; repr. Graz, 1960); Middle English translation in *John Trevisa dialogus*, ed. A. J. Perry, EETS no. 167 (Oxford, 1925)

Hildegard of Bingen. [*Scivias.*] *Hildegardis Scivias*, ed. Adelgundis Führkötter and Angela Carlevaris, Corpus Christianorum Continuatio Medievalis 43–43A (Turnhout, 1978)

Liber divinorum simplicis hominis, PL 197, cols. 741–1038

[Epistles.] *PL* 197

Hildegard von Bingen Briefwechsel, ed. Adelgundis Führkötter (Salzburg, 1965)

Analecta sanctae Hildegardis opera spicilegio solesme parata. Analecta sacra, ed. Johannes Baptista Pitra, vol. VIII (Montecassino, 1882)

Prooemium vitae s. Disibodi, in *Analecta sanctae Hildegardis opera*, ed. Pitra, pp. 352–57

Pentachronon. Speculum futurorum temporum sive Pentachronon [a selection of excerpts from Hildegard's works compiled by Gebeno of Eberbach], semi-edited in *Analecta sanctae Hildegardis opera*, ed. Pitra, pp. 483–88

Translations and editions of autobiographical passages and letters by Hildegard can be found in P. Dronke, *Women Writers of the Middle Ages* (Cambridge, 1984)

"Insurgent gentes." In A. G. Little and R. Easterling, *The Franciscans and Dominicans of Exeter* (Exeter, 1927), pp. 60–61; also to be found in Johann Albert Fabricius, *Biblioteca latina mediae et infimae aetatis* (Florence, 1858), pp. 243–44

Joachim of Fiore. [*Liber concordia.*] *Liber de concordia novi ac veteris testamenti*, Books I–IV, ed. E. Randolph Daniel, Transactions of the American Philosophical Society, 73 (Philadelphia, 1983)

[*Liber figurarum.*] *Il libro delle figure dell'abbate Gioachino da Fiore*, ed. Leone Tondelli,

Select bibliography

Marjorie Reeves and Beatrice Hirsch-Reich, rev. ed., 2 vols. (Turin, 1954)
Tractatus super quatuor evangelia, ed. E. Buonaiutti, Fonti per la storia d'Italia, 67 (Rome, 1930)
Two Poems attributed to Joachim of Fiore, ed. M. Reeves and John V. Fleming (Princeton, 1978)
English translations of works by Joachim can be found in B. McGinn, trans. and ed., *Apocalyptic Spirituality* (New York, 1979)
Pseudonymous works:
De oneribus prophetarum, in O. Holder-Egger, "Italianische Prophetieen des 13. Jahrhunderts," pt. 3, *Neues Archiv der Gesellschaft für altere deutsche Geschichtskunde*, 33 (1908), pp. 96–187
Super Esaiam (Venice, 1517)
Super Jeremiam (Venice, 1516)
Vaticinia de summis pontificibus, Cambridge, Corpus Christi College MS 404, fols. 88ʳ–95ʳ, concluding on fol. 41
John of Bridlington (pseudonym). "The Prophecies of John of Bridlington," in *Political Songs and Poems*, ed. T. Wright, vol. 1, Rolls Series, 14 (London, 1859), pp. 123–215
John of Pecham. *Tractatus tres de paupertate*, ed. C. L. Kingsford, A. G. Little and F. Tocco (Aberdeen, 1910)
John of Rupecissa. *Vade mecum in tribulatione*, in E. Brown, ed., vol. II (Appendix) to O. Gratius, *Fasciculus rerum expedentarum* (London, 1690)
Kempe, Margery. *The Book of Margery Kempe*, ed. H. E. Allen, EETS no. 212 (London, 1940)
Langland, William. *Piers Plowman: the B Version*, ed. George Kane and E. T. Donaldson (London, 1975; rev. ed. London, 1988)
Piers Plowman by William Langland. An Edition of the C-Text, ed. Derek Pearsall (London, 1978)
The Vision of Piers Plowman, the B-Text, ed. A. V. C. Schmidt (London, 1978)
The Last Age of the Church, ed. J. H. Todd (Dublin, 1840)
Pierce the Ploughman's Crede, ed. W. W. Skeat, EETS no. 30 (London, 1867)
Robert of Uzès. *Liber visionum*, in Jeanne Bignami-Odier, "Les Visions de Robert d'Uzès, O.P. (d. 1296)," *Archivum Fratrum Praedicatorum*, 25 (1955), pp. 258–310
Rolle, Richard, of Hampole. *The Incendium Amoris of Richard Rolle of Hampole*, ed. M. Deansley (Manchester, 1915)
De semine scripturarum. Cambridge, Corpus Christi College MS 404, fols. 43ᵛ–64ᵛ
[*The Shepherd of Hermas*.] *Hermas, le pasteur*, ed. Robert Joly, Sources chrétiennes, 53 (Paris, 1958)
Sancti Hermae pastor, PG 2, cols. 891–1011
The Shepherd of Hermas, trans. C. Taylor, 2 vols. (London, 1903)
"Sibylla: De Imperatore, an edition from MS Yale University Marston 225," [ed.] Martha Hitchcock Fleming, unpublished Ph.D dissertation, Boston University Graduate School, 1975
Tortsch, John. *Onus mundi* (1433), in Ulrich Montag, ed., *Das Werk der heiligen Birgitta von Schweden in oberdeutscher Uberlieferung* (Munich, 1968)
Vincent of Beauvais. *Speculum historiale*, in *Speculum quadruplex sive speculum maius*, vol. IV (Douai, 1624; repr. Graz. 1964–65)
The Vision of Tundale, ed. R. Mearns (Heidelberg, 1985)
William of St. Amour. *De periculis novissimi temporis*, in E. Brown, ed., vol. II (Appendix) to O. Gratius, *Fasciculus rerum expedentarum* (London, 1690)
Wimbledon's Sermon, ed. I. K. Knight (Pittsburgh, 1967)
Wycliffite writings: *Select English Works of John Wyclif* [now thought to be by his followers], ed. T. Arnold, 3 vols. (Oxford, 1869–71)
Selections from English Wycliffite Writings, ed. Anne Hudson (Cambridge, 1978)

Select bibliography

SECONDARY SOURCES

Adams, Robert. "The Nature of Need in *Piers Plowman* XX," *Traditio*, 34 (1978), pp. 273–301

"Some Versions of Apocalypse: Learned and Popular Eschatology in *Piers Plowman*," in *The Popular Literature of Medieval England*, ed. T. Heffernan, Tennessee Studies in Literature, 28 (Knoxville, 1985), pp. 194–236

Aers, David. *Chaucer, Langland and the Creative Imagination* (London, 1980)

Alexander, P. J. "The Diffusion of Byzantine Apocalypses," in *Prophecy and Millenarianism: Essays in Honour of Marjorie Reeves* (Burnt Hill, 1980), pp. 56–106

Benton, John F. "Consciousness of Self and Perceptions of Individuality," in *Renaissance and Renewal in the Twelfth Century*, ed. Robert L. Benson and Giles Constable (Cambridge, Mass., 1982), pp. 263–98

Bignami-Odier, Jeanne. *Etudes sur Jean de Roquetaillade (Johannes de Rupescissa)* (Paris, 1952)

Bischoff, Guntram G. "Early Premonstratensian Eschatology: The Apocalyptic Myth," in *The Spirituality of Western Christendom*, ed. E. Rozanne Elder (Kalamazoo, 1976)

Bloomfield, M. W. "Joachim of Flora: A Critical Survey of his Canon, Teachings, Sources, Biography, and Influence," *Traditio*, 13 (1957), pp. 249–311

Piers Plowman as a Fourteenth Century Apocalypse (New Brunswick, N.J., 1961)

and M. Reeves. "The Penetration of Joachism into Northern Europe," *Speculum*, 29 (1954), pp. 772–93

Bourquin, Guy. *Piers Plowman: Etudes sur la genèse littéraire des trois versions*, 2 vols. (Paris, 1970)

Burdach, Konrad. *Der Dichter des Ackermann aus Böhmen und seine Zeit*, in vol. III of his *Vom Mittelalter zur Reformation*, pt. 2 (Berlin, 1926–32)

Burrow, J. A. "Autobiographical Poetry in the Middle Ages: The Case of Hoccleve," Sir Israel Gollancz Memorial Lecture, *Proceedings of the British Academy*, 68 (1982), pp. 389–412

Chenu, M.-D. *Nature, Man and Society in the Twelfth Century*, ed. and trans. Jerome Taylor and Lester K. Little (Chicago, 1968; first published Paris, 1957)

Colledge, E. "*Epistola solitarii ad reges*: Alphonse of Pecha as Organizer of Birgittine and Urbanist Propaganda," *Medieval Studies*, 18 (1956), pp. 19–49

Constable, Giles. "Renaissance and Reform in Religious Life: Concepts and Realities," in *Renaissance and Renewal in the Twelfth Century*, ed. Robert L. Benson and Giles Constable (Cambridge, Mass., 1982), pp. 37–67

Czarski, Charles. "The Prophecies of St. Hildegard of Bingen," unpublished doctoral dissertation, University of Kentucky, 1982

Daly, Lowrie J. "Wyclif's Political Theory: A Century of Study," *Medievalia et Humanistica*, 4 (1973), pp. 177–87

Daniel, E. R. "Roger Bacon and the *De Seminibus Scripturarum*," *Medieval Studies*, 34 (1972), pp. 462–67

The Franciscan Concept of Mission in the High Middle Ages (Lexington, Ky, 1975)

"The Double Procession of the Holy Spirit in Joachim of Fiore's Understanding of History," *Speculum*, 55 (1980), pp. 469–85

Dawson, James Doyne. "William of St. Amour and the Apostolic Tradition," *Medieval Studies*, 40 (1978), pp. 223–38

Dinzelbacher, Peter. *Vision und Vision-literatur im Mittelalter* (Stuttgart, 1981)

Donaldson, E. T. *Piers Plowman: The C-Text and its Poet* (New Haven, 1949)

Doob, Penelope. *Nebuchadnezzar's Children: Conventions of Madness in Middle English Literature* (New Haven, 1974)

Douie, D. L. "The Conflict between the Seculars and Mendicants at the University of Paris in the Thirteenth Century," Aquinas Society Paper 23 (London, 1954)

Select bibliography

Dronke, Peter. *The Medieval Lyric*, 2nd ed. (London, 1978)
"*Arbor Caritatis*," in *Medieval Studies for J. A. W. Bennett*, ed. P. L. Heyworth (Oxford, 1981), pp. 207–53
"*Problemata Hildegardiana*," *Mittellateinisches Jahrbuch*, 16 (1981), pp. 97–131
Women Writers of the Middle Ages (Cambridge, 1984)
Dufeil, M.-M. *Guillaume de Saint-Amour et la polémique universitaire parisienne (1250–1259)* (Paris, 1972)
Eckenstein, Lina. *Woman under Monasticism* (New York, 1963; repr. from the 1896 ed.)
Ellis, R. "'*Flores ad fabricandum . . . Coronam*': An Investigation into the Uses of the *Revelations* of St. Bridget of Sweden in Fifteenth-Century England," *Medium Aevum*, 52 (1983), pp. 163–86
Emmerson, R. K. *Antichrist in the Middle Ages: A Study of Medieval Apocalypticism, Art and Literature* (Manchester, 1981)
"The Prophetic, the Apocalyptic, and the Study of Medieval Literature," in *Poetic Prophecy in Western Literature*, ed. J. Wojcik and Raymond-Jean Frontain (London and Toronto, 1984), pp. 40–54
Farrer, Austin. *A Rebirth of Images* (Boston, 1963)
Fleming, John. "The Antifraternalism of the Summoner's Tale." *Journal of English and Germanic Philology*, 65 (1966), pp. 688–700
Frank, R. W. "The Conclusion of *Piers Plowman*," *Journal of English and Germanic Philology*, 49 (1950), pp. 309–16
Piers Plowman and the Scheme of Salvation (New Haven, 1957)
Friderich, K. "Kritishe Untersuchung der dem Abt Joachim von Floris zugeschreiben Commentare zu Jesajas und Jeremias," *Zeitschrift für Wissenschaftliche Theologie*, 2 (1859), pp. 449–514
Fritzsche, C. "Die Lateinische Visionen des Mittelalters bis zur Mitte des 12. Jahrhunderts," *Romanische Forschungen*, 2 (1886), pp. 247–79, and 3 (1887), pp. 337–69
Frye, Northrop. *Anatomy of Criticism* (Princeton, 1957)
Gradon, Pamela. "Langland and the Ideology of Dissent," Sir Israel Gollancz Memorial Lecture, *Proceedings of the British Academy*, 66 (1980), pp. 179–205
Harvey, E. Ruth. *The Inward Wits: Psychological Theory in the Middle Ages and the Renaissance* (London, 1975)
Hauréau, B., ed. *Histoire littéraire de la France*, vol. xxx (Paris, 1888)
Hayes, John H. *An Introduction to Old Testament Study* (Nashville, 1979)
Hellholm, David, ed. *Apocalypticism in the Mediterranean World and the Near East* (Tübingen, 1983)
Heschel, Abraham. *The Prophets*, vol. ii (New York, 1962)
Hieatt, Constance B. *The Realism of Dream Visions: The Poetic Exploration of the Dream Experience in Chaucer and his Contemporaries* (The Hague, 1967)
Holdsworth, C. J. "Visions and Visionaries in the Middle Ages," *History*, 48 (1963), pp. 141–53
"Christina of Markyate," in *Medieval Women*, ed. D. Baker (Oxford, 1978), pp. 185–204
James, M. R., ed. "The Catalogue of the Library of the Augustinian Friars at York," in *Fasciculus J. W. Clark Dicatus* (Cambridge, 1909), pp. 2–96
Jorgenson, Johannes. *St. Bridget of Sweden*, 2 vols., trans. Ingeborg Lund (London, 1954)
Kane, George. "The Autobiographical Fallacy in Chaucer and Langland Studies," Chambers Memorial Lecture, University College, London (London, 1965)
Piers Plowman: The Evidence for Authorship (London, 1965)
Kerby-Fulton, Kathryn. "The Voice of Honest Indignation: A Study of Reformist Apocalypticism in Relation to *Piers Plowman*," unpublished D.Phil. thesis, University of York (UK), 1986
"Hildegard of Bingen and Antimendicant Propaganda," *Traditio*, 43 (1987), pp. 386–99

Select bibliography

"A Return to 'the First Dawn of Justice': Hildegard's Visions of Clerical Reform and the Eremitical Life," forthcoming in *American Benedictine Review*, Dec. 1989 volume

Knowles, David. *The Religious Orders in England*, vol. II (Cambridge, 1955)

The English Mystical Tradition (New York, 1961)

Lagorio, V. "The Continental Women Mystics of the Middle Ages: An Assessment," in *The Roots of the Modern Christian Tradition*, ed. E. Rozanne Elder (Kalamazoo, 1984)

Leclercq, Jean, F. Vandenbroucke and L. Bouyer, *La Spiritualité du moyen âge* (Aubier, 1961)

Lee, H. "*Scrutamini Scripturas*: Joachimist Themes and *Figurae* in the Early Religious Writing of Arnold of Villanova," *Journal of the Warburg and Courtauld Institutes*, 37 (1974), pp. 33–56

Leff, Gordon. "The Apostolic Ideal in Later Medieval Ecclesiology," *Journal of Theological Studies*, n.s. 18 (1967), pp. 52–82

Heresy in the Later Middle Ages, 2 vols. (Manchester, 1967)

Paris and Oxford Universities in the Thirteenth and Fourteenth Centuries (New York, 1968)

Le Goff, Jacques. "Dreams in the Culture and Collective Psychology of the Medieval West," in his *Time, Work and Culture in the Middle Ages*, trans. Arthur Goldhammer (Chicago, 1980), pp. 201–04; first published as "Les rêves dans la culture et la psychologie collective de L'Occident médiéval," *Scolies* 1 (1971), pp. 123–30

Lerner, Robert. "Medieval Prophecy and Religious Dissent," *Past and Present*, 70 (1976), pp. 3–24

"Refreshment of the Saints: The Time after Antichrist as a Station for Earthly Progress in Medieval Thought," *Traditio*, 32 (1976), pp. 97–144

"The Black Death and Western European Eschatological Mentalities," *American Historical Review*, 86 (1981), pp. 533–52

The Powers of Prophecy: The Cedar of Lebanon Vision from the Mongol Onslaught to the Dawn of the Enlightenment (Berkeley, Calif., 1983)

Leyser, Henrietta. *Hermits and the New Monasticism: A Study of Religious Communities in Western Europe 1000–1150* (London, 1984)

Liebeschütz, H. *Das allegorische Weltbild der heiligen Hildegard von Bingen* (Darmstadt, 1964)

Little, L. K. *Religious Poverty and the Profit Economy in Medieval Europe* (Ithaca, N.Y., 1978)

Maguire, Mother Catherine Elizabeth. "Franciscan Elements in the Thought of *Piers Plowman*," unpublished Ph.D. thesis, Fordham University, 1949

McDonnell, Ernest W. *The Beguines and Beghards in Medieval Culture* (New York, 1954)

McGinn, Bernard. "Joachim and the Sibyl," *Cîteaux*, 24 (1973), pp. 97–138

"Saint Bernard and Eschatology," in *Bernard of Clairvaux: Studies presented to Dom Jean Leclercq* (Washington, 1973), pp. 161–85

"Angel Pope and Papal Antichrist," *Church History*, 47 (1978), pp. 155–73

Visions of the End: Apocalyptic Traditions in the Middle Ages (New York, 1979)

"Early Apocalypticism: The Ongoing Debate," in *The Apocalypse in English Renaissance Thought and Literature*, ed. C. A. Patrides and J. Wittreich (Ithaca, N.Y. and New York, 1984), pp. 2–39

trans. and ed., *Apocalyptic Spirituality* (New York, 1979)

Middleton, Anne. "The Audience of *Piers Plowman*," in *Middle English Alliterative Poetry and its Literary Background*, ed. D. Lawton (Cambridge, 1982), pp. 101–54

Miller, Robert P. *Chaucer: Sources and Backgrounds* (New York, 1977)

Minnis, A. "Langland's Ymaginatif and Late-Medieval Theories of Imagination," in *Comparative Criticism: A Yearbook*, ed. E. S. Shaffer (Cambridge, 1981), pp. 71–103

Newman, Barbara. *Sister of Wisdom: St. Hildegard's Theology of the Feminine* (Berkeley, 1987)

Olsen, Glen. "The Idea of the *Ecclesia Primitiva* in the Writings of the Twelfth-Century Canonists," *Traditio*, 25 (1969), pp. 61–86

O'Sullivan, Margaret Mary. "The Treatment of Political Themes in Late Middle English

Select bibliography

Verse, with special reference to MS Cotton Rolls ii. 23," unpublished Ph.D. dissertation, Queen Mary College, University of London, 1972

Owst, G. R. *Preaching in Medieval England* (Cambridge, 1926)
Literature and Pulpit in Medieval England (Oxford, 1961)

Palmer, William. "The Intellectual Background of *Piers Plowman*, with particular reference to the English and Latin Writings of John Wyclif," 2 vols., unpublished doctoral thesis, University of Kansas, 1957

Pantin, W. A. "Some Medieval English Treatises on the Origins of Monasticism," in *Medieval Studies presented to Rose Graham*, ed. Veronica Ruffer and A. J. Taylor (Oxford, 1950), pp. 189–215

Patrides, C. A. and J. Wittreich, eds. *The Apocalypse in English Renaissance Thought and Literature* (Ithaca, N.Y. and New York, 1984)

Piehler, Paul. *The Visionary Landscape: A Study in Medieval Allegory* (Montreal, 1971)

Pou y Marti, José M. *Visionarios, Beguinos y Fraticelos Catalanes* (Vich, 1930)

Rauh, Horst D. *Das Bild des Antichrist*, Beiträge zur Geschichte der Philosophie und Theologie des Mittelalters, n.s. 9 (Munster, 1979)

Reeves, Marjorie. "The Abbot Joachim's Disciples and the Cistercian Order," *Sophia*, 19 (1951), pp. 355–71
"The Seven Seals in the Writings of Joachim of Fiore," *RTAM*, 22 (1954), pp. 211–31
"The *Arbores* of Joachim of Fiore," in *Studies in Italian History presented to Miss E. M. Jamison*, Papers of the British School at Rome, 24 (1956), pp. 124–36
"Joachimist Expectations in the Order of Augustinian Hermits," *RTAM*, 25 (1958), pp. 111–41
The Influence of Prophecy in the Later Middle Ages: A Study of Joachimism (Oxford, 1969)
"Some Popular Prophecies from the Fourteenth to the Seventeenth Centuries," in *Studies in Church History*, vol. 8: *Popular Belief and Practice*, ed. G. J. Cuming and D. Baker (Cambridge, 1972), pp. 107–34
"History and Eschatology: Medieval and Early Protestant Thought in some English and Scottish Writings," *Medievalia et Humanistica*, n.s. 4 (1973). pp. 99–123
"Joachimist Influences on the Idea of a Last World Emperor," in *Joachim of Fiore in Christian Thought*, ed. Delno West, vol. II (New York, 1975), pp. 511–58
Joachim of Fiore and the Prophetic Future (London, 1976)
"The Originality and Influence of Joachim of Fiore," *Traditio*, 36 (1980), pp. 269–316
"The Development of Apocalyptic Thought: Medieval Attitudes," in *The Apocalypse in English Renaissance Thought and Literature*, eds. C. A. Patrides and J. Wittreich (Ithaca, N.Y. and New York, 1984), pp. 40–73
and Beatrice Hirsch-Reich, *The Figurae of Joachim of Fiore* (Oxford, 1972)

Reiling, J. *Hermas and Christian Prophecy: A Study of the Eleventh Mandate* (Leiden, 1973)

Roth, F. E. W., ed. *Die Visionen der hl. Elisabeth* (Brunn, 1884)

Rüegg, A. *Die Jenseitvorstellungen vor Dante* (Einsiedeln, 1945)

Russell, D. S. *The Method and Message of Jewish Apocalyptic 200 B.C.–A.D. 100* (London, 1964)

Saward, John. *Perfect Fools* (Oxford, 1980)

Schrader, Marianna. "Hildegarde de Bingen," *Dictionnaire de spiritualité*, vol. VII, cols. 505–21
and Adelgundis Führkötter, *Die Echtheit des Schrifttums der heiligen Hildegard von Bingen* (Cologne and Graz, 1956)

Southern, R. W. *Western Society and the Church in the Middle Ages* (Harmondsworth, 1970)

Spitzer, Leo. "Note on the Poetic and the Empirical 'I' in Medieval Authors," *Traditio*, 4 (1946), pp. 414–22

Steele, Francesca Maria. *The Life and Visions of St. Hildegard* (London, 1914)

Select bibliography

Synave, Paul and P. Benoit, *A Commentary on the Summa Theologica II–II, Questions 171–178* (New York, 1961)

Szittya, Penn. "'Caimes Kynde': The Friars and the Exegetical Origins of Medieval Antifraternalism," unpublished doctoral thesis, Cornell University, 1971

"The Antifraternal Tradition in Middle English Literature," *Speculum*, 52 (1977), pp. 287–313

"*Sedens Super Flumina*: A Fourteenth-Century Poem against the Friars," *Medieval Studies*, 41 (1979), pp. 30–43

The Antifraternal Tradition in Medieval Literature (Princeton, 1986)

Thomson, K. J. "The Development of the Theory of Evangelical Poverty in the Fourteenth Century," unpublished M.Phil. thesis, Birkbeck College, University of London, 1976

Töpfer, B. *Das kommende Reich des Friedens* (Berlin, 1964)

Torrell, Jean-Pierre. *Théorie de la prophétie et philosophie de la connaissance aux environs de 1230: la contribution d'Hugue de Saint-Cher (Ms. Douai 434, Question 481)* (Louvain, 1977)

van der Linde, Antonius. *Handscriften den königlichen Landesbibliothek in Wiesbaden* (Wiesbaden, 1877)

Vasta, Edward, ed. *Interpretations of Piers Plowman* (Notre Dame, 1968)

Walsh, Katherine. "Archbishop FitzRalph and the Friars at the Papal Court in Avignon, 1357–60," *Traditio*, 31 (1975), pp. 223–45

A Fourteenth-Century Scholar and Primate: Richard FitzRalph in Oxford, Avignon and Armagh (Oxford, 1981)

West, Delno, ed. *Joachim of Fiore in Christian Thought*, 2 vols. (New York, 1975)

and Sandra Zimdars-Swartz, *Joachim of Fiore: A Study in Spiritual Perception and History* (Bloomington, 1983)

Williams, Arnold. "Relations between the Mendicant Friars and the Secular Clergy in England in the Later Fourteenth Century," *Annuale Mediaevale*, 1 (1960), pp. 22–95

Woolf, Rosemary. "Some Non-Medieval Qualities of *Piers Plowman*," *Essays in Criticism*, 12 (1962), pp. 111–25

General index

Due to space limitations, the names of modern scholars have not been included. See the Select bibliography for a partial listing; others occur in the notes.

Abraham 45, 215
Adam 45, 46, 192
Adso of Montier-en-Der
    Libellus de antichristo 206, 216, 230, 241
Alanus de Insulis
    . *De planctu naturae* 221
Alphonse of Jaen, author of *Epistola solitarii*
    103, 124–25, 223–24
Anastasius IV, Pope 47, 212; Hildegard's letter
    to 59–60
Angela of Foligno 219
Angelo of Clareno 179, 219, 228
"Anglia transmittet leopardum" 188
Anselm of Havelberg 26, 206, 230
Anthony, St. 20, 124
Antichrist 2, 4, 7, 10, 11, 23, 30, 32, 33, 46–50,
    52–56, 101, 102, 110, 137, 148–49, 155,
    156, 158, 170, 171, 173, 174, 177, 178,
    179, 180, 183, 188–89, 193, 199, 201, 202,
    205, 206, 212, 230, 232, 233, 239, 240–41
anti-clericalism 24, 36, 210
anti-intellectualism 5, 18, 20, 66–69, 66–73, 97,
    101, 110–11, 166, 182, 189, 192, 218, 239,
    240
anti-mendicant apocalypticism 11, 15, 22,
    153–61
anti-mendicantism 9, 11, 12, 15, 18, 22, 24, 31,
    39, 110, 133–61, 163, 164, 175, 190, 191,
    201, 210, 214, 226–31
anti-papalism 5, 174, 177, 179, 216
antipope 200
apocalypse 3; genre of 2, 12, 13, 17, 56, 79–81,
    85–96, 164, 201, 205, 220; *see also* John,
    St.
Apocalypse of Paul, The 208
Apocalypsis Goliae 95
"apocalyptic grammar" 39, 96, 102, 170, 193,
    213

apocalyptic program 2, 4, 156, 183, 184–86; *see
    also* Hildegard of Bingen; Langland,
    William; Joachim of Fiore; Bridget of
    Sweden, St.; William of St. Amour
apocalyptic visionary tradition 2, 19, 76–111, 216
apocalypticism 1–10, 12–16, 18, 19, 22, 133,
    201, 205, 207
Arnold of Villanova 182–83, 237–38
    Tractatus de mysterio cimbalorum ecclesiae 182,
    238
    Tractatus de tempore de adventu antichristi 182
Augustine of Hippo, St. 117, 121, 124, 141,
    206; influence 4, 71; on revelation 4, 113;
    Augustinian eschatology 4, 7, 42–43, 47,
    48, 205, 206, 215, 233; "World Week" 8,
    24, 46, 50, 155, 181, 206, 233
autobiography, monastic 71, 74, 87

Bacon, Roger 6, 178, 183, 205, 236, 238
Bale, John, Reformation antiquarian 104, 157,
    222, 238
Ball, John, rebel leader 100, 108–09, 224
Bede, St. 184, 241
beggars (or "lollars") 21, 123–29, 193, 208
begging, issue of 135, 138, 141–49, 193, 228
Beguines 184, 228
Benedict, St. 166
Benedict XI, Pope 179
Benedict XII, Pope 237
Benedict of Peterborough, chronicler 232
Bernard of Clairvaux, St. 21, 29, 184, 185, 238;
    pseudo-Bernard 68
Blake, William 1, 56, 64, 204
Boethius 36
Bonaventure, St. 143, 146, 185, 193, 227, 228,
    229, 238, 239
    Apologium pauperum 143, 146, 227
    Collationes in Hexaemeron 239
Boniface VIII, Pope 98, 179, 223, 237
Bridget of Sweden, St. 12, 13, 77, 96–97,
    102–11, 113, 124–25, 187, 205, 207, 218,
    239; apocalyptic program 108–10; Joachite
    influence 224
    Revelationes 103–11, 223–24
    Revelationes extravagantes 223

249

General index

Brinton, Bishop Thomas 176
Bunyan, John, author of *The Pilgrim's Progress*
85, 96

Cain 51, 52, 54, 198
Capgrave, John, chronicler 184, 210, 238
Cathars 39
Catherine of Siena, St. 219, 223
"Cedar of Lebanon" vision 78; *see also* "Tripoli
Prophecy"
Celestine V, Pope 98, 223
Charlemagne 237
Chaucer, Geoffrey 12, 13, 15, 64, 77, 115, 116,
119, 123, 139, 219, 238
chiliasm 3, 11, 15, 41, 48, 168, 205;
ecclesiastical 226; pre-Antichrist 199, 205,
241; post-Antichrist 50; "refreshment of
the saints" 49, 199, 240–41; *see also*
millenarianism
Christ Church Priory, Canterbury, medieval
library catalogue of 209
Christina of Markyate 121, 131
Clement IV, Pope 178
Clement VI, Pope 103, 151
clerical chastisement 2, 3, 4, 10, 15, 20, 21, 22,
30, 31, 33, 35, 59, 97, 100, 101, 105, 162,
164, 170–71, 173, 177, 183, 190, 220, 224;
see also visionary literature
clerical reform 2, 3, 4, 6, 7, 9, 10, 11, 15, 17,
19, 20, 21, 22, 31–45, 99–100, 102, 103,
106, 107, 142, 149, 150–53, 163, 164, 165,
168, 169–70, 179, 183, 188–89, 191, 199,
210, 234, 237, 239; *see also* visionary
literature
Cloud of Unknowing, The 218, 226, 229
Cola di Rienzo 187, 195, 239
Columbinus, prophecy attributed to 180–81,
237
confessions, friars' rights to hear 152–53,
159–60, 181, 187, 229
Conrad of Offida 219
Constantine the Great, Roman Emperor, 181,
187; Donation of 150, 173, 174–77, 235,
236
Conway, Roger 229
"Corruent nobiles" 236
Crowley, Robert, Reformation editor of *Piers
Plowman* 79, 95, 202, 220, 241
Crusades 7, 232
Cursor mundi 7, 206

Daniel 114, 156
Dante 86, 92, 102, 120, 175, 202–03, 238, 241
David 8, 16, 51, 168, 179; a "new David"
180–83, 206, 234, 237
De semine scripturarum 24, 164, 183–84, 238
Desert Fathers 20, 21, 41, 147, 168, 237

disendowment of the clergy 22, 33, 37–41,
43–44, 150–53, 162, 164, 172, 173–77,
185–87, 188, 189–90, 213, 214, 215, 224,
229, 236, 239; *see also* clerical chastisement;
clerical reform
Dominican order 97, 100, 134, 136
Dunbar, William 135
Durham Cathedral, medieval library catalogue
of 209

Easton, Adam 223, 225
Eberwin of Steinfeld 42, 206
ecclesia primitiva 20, 162, 169, 175, 187, 235
ecclesiology 135–36, 137, 140–49, 154, 227
Echenden, John 237
Edward III, King of England 175
Eli and his sons 172–73
Elijah 7, 44, 55, 166, 234
Elizabeth of Schönau 26, 56, 76, 210, 214, 217,
218, 225
Liber viarum Dei 208, 214
England, religious prophecy in 6, 13, 22, 23,
24, 25, 162–64, 172, 175–76, 177, 180,
182, 183, 186, 188–89, 208–09, 210, 224,
226, 231, 232, 234, 237, 239; *see also*
prophecy, Latin religious, dissemination
of
Enoch 7, 55, 234
eremiticism 180, 188, 192–94, 219, 228, 233–41
passim; *see also* poverty; Desert Fathers
Erghome, John 24, 96
eschatology 3, 15, 16, 17, 18, 22; alternative 4,
7, 9, 183, 205 (*see also* apocalyptic
program; Salvation History; reformist
apocalypticism); traditional 3, 7, 8, 9, 10,
15, 16, 48, 49, 54, 55, 154–55, 160, 179,
199, 205, 206; *see also* Augustine of Hippo,
St., Augustinian eschatology
Esdras, Apoaclypse of 77, 79, 80, 81–84, 85–96
passim, 114, 131, 220, 221
Eulogium historiarum 187–88, 209, 210
Exiit qui seminat 143, 146, 227, 228
"Externis populis dominabitur aquila fortis"
187–88
Ezekiel 1

false apostles 21, 22; *see also* pseudo-prophets
"Fifteen signs before Doomsday" 7, 55, 208
FitzRalph, Archbishop Ralph 15, 140, 150–53,
160, 229–30
Defensio curatorum 152, 229
Flagellant movement 227
Florensian order 164, 235
fool, concept of the 193, 196, 202, 208; "fools
for Christ" 21, 54, 72–75, 111, 129, 173,
191, 193–94, 200, 239, 240

General index

Francis, St. 147, 148, 149; *Rule* of 110–11, 151–52, 191
Franciscan order 10, 14, 19, 20, 21, 22, 111, 134, 135–36, 151, 162, 176, 189
Franciscan Spirituals 16, 107, 111, 146, 151, 163, 173, 175, 179, 182, 188–89, 228, 231–32, 235; *see also* Joachism; Langland, William
Franciscanism 10, 175, 176, 192–93, 224, 228, 239
Fraticelli 163, 176, 231; *see also* Franciscan Spirituals; heresy
Frederick I, Holy Roman Emperor 212

Galfridus le Baker of Swynebroke 210, 238
"Gallorum levitas" 177, 185
Gebeno of Eberbach, compiler of the *Pentachronon* 14, 28–31, 31–56 *passim*, 61, 105, 188, 207, 211–12, 217, 218, 222
Gerard of Abbeville 150, 229
Gerard of Borgo San Donnino 136
Gerhoh of Reichersberg 26, 187, 213, 230, 236, 238
Gerson, Jean 125, 225
Gog and Magog 7, 55, 188, 205
Goliardic literature 24, 210; *see also Apocalypsis Goliae*
Good Samaritan, the 215
Gower, John 35, 139, 174, 231, 235, 238
Greek schism 177, 178, 183, 190
Gregory the Great, Pope 121, 124, 154, 215
Gregory VII, Pope 47
Gregory X, Pope 178
Gregory XI, Pope 107, 125
Gui, Bernard, Dominican inquisitor 97
Guibert of Gembloux 56, 223
Guibert of Nogent 71, 219

Haimo of Auxerre 241
heathen 105, 171, 183, 187, 190; conversion of 48, 50, 55, 171, 178, 180, 182, 190, 234; *see also* Crusades
Henry IV, Holy Roman Emperor 8, 47
Henry of Harclay 236, 237, 238, 239
Henry of Hassia 50
Henry of Herford, chronicler 97, 210, 222
Henry of Kirkstede, medieval librarian at Bury St. Edmunds 25, 210, 237
Henry of Langenstein 225
heresy 7, 22, 31, 39–41, 98, 100, 154, 163, 175, 184, 214, 223, 230, 231; *see also* Wyclif, John; Waldensians; Cathars
Hermes 85, 114; *see also Shepherd of Hermes, The*
Hildegard of Bingen 12, 19, 20, 21, 22, 23, 24, 25, 26–75, 76, 81, 85, 86, 98, 102, 104, 119, 121, 130, 134, 158, 165, 173, 174, 187, 188, 205, 207, 208, 210–19; and

Joachim of Fiore 212, 217, 224, 233;
apocalyptic program 20, 42, 43, 44, 45–56, 61, 62, 165, 211, 215, 216; and clerical reform 5, 20, 31–45, 59, 212, 213;
influence 2, 9, 12, 22, 24, 25, 26–27, 156, 176, 188, 190, 208–09, 211, 220, 223, 229, 230, 232, 238; visionary style 56–64, 211, 213, 217, 222, 226; visionary self-image 65–66, 68–74, 217, 218, 225; *Vita* of 29, 74, 210, 218, 219; *see also* Gebeno of Eberbach, compiler of the *Pentachronon*; Guibert of Gembloux
Scivias 27, 31, 32, 46, 47, 56, 69, 101, 208, 212, 213, 214, 218, 232
Liber vitae meritorum 27
Liber divinorum operum 27, 29, 35, 36–39, 45, 47–50, 212, 213, 214, 216, 217, 218, 239
Prooemium vitae s. Disibodi 21, 45–46, 61–63, 215
letters 211, 212, 213, 214; letters to Cistercians 213, 218, to Cistercians of Eberbach 42–43, 214, to clergy of Cologne 31, 39–41, 157, 214, 230, to clergy of Trier 214, 215, exchange with Elizabeth of Schönau 214, with Hazzecha of Krauftal 211, to King Conrad 214, 215, to Pope Anastasius 59–60, to Tengswindis 213, to Werner of Kircheim 43, 211
Hildegardian visionary tradition 2, 76–77, 96–111, 201; *see also* apocalyptic visionary tradition; Hildegard of Bingen, influence; visionary literature; visionary reformist writers
Hoccleve, Thomas 104
Honorius of Autun 230
Hugh of St. Cher 113–14
Hugh of St. Victor 124
Hundred Years War 104

Investiture Controversy 8
"Insurgent gentes" 156–58, 209, 229, 230–31, 238
Isaiah 1, 114

Jacopone da Todi 77, 219, 220
Jean de Cardaillac 222
Jerome, St. 108, 109, 119, 121, 124, 240
Jews 7, 105, 109, 172, 181–82, 183; conversion of 47, 55, 172
Joachim of Fiore 3, 5, 14, 19, 20, 21, 22, 23, 24, 26, 28, 29, 30, 44, 98, 104, 108, 109, 134, 135, 163–72, 174–200 *passim*, 205, 207, 210, 212, 218, 220, 232–41; influence 2, 9, 10, 14, 19, 22, 24, 136, 162–64, 172–200, 212, 231; apocalyptic program 165–71; third *status* 48, 63, 136, 162, 165–71, 172, 173, 208, 232, 233, 234

251

General index

Liber figurarum 167, 168, 181, 232, 233, 236
Liber concordia 24, 167, 170, 181, 232, 233, 234, 240
Expositio in Apocalypsim 24, 232, 233
Psalterium decem chordarum 232
Tractatus super quatuor Evangelia 169, 232
"Testamentary Letter" 168
letters 233
Joachism 2, 16, 19, 22, 23, 134, 136, 162–200, 209, 210, 224, 227, 229, 232, 240; dissemination of 210, 232, 235, 236–37, 239; Franciscan 19, 22, 107, 136, 154, 155, 174, 179, 187, 191, 193, 208 (*see also* Franciscan Spirituals); *De oneribus prophetarum* 24, 164, 172, 174, 177, 184, 232, 234, 235, 236; *Oraculum Cyrilli* 238; *Super Esaiam* 24, 163, 164, 172, 174, 209, 232, 235; *Super Jeremiam* 155, 172–73, 224, 232, 235; *see also Vaticinia de summis pontificibus*
John, St., author of the Apocalypse 29, 73, 80, 81, 88, 95, 96, 169–70, 216, 218, 222
"John of Bridlington" commentary 98; prophecies 204, 237
John of Jenzenstein 225–26
John of Paris 175
John of Parma 134, 136, 219
John of Rupescissa 23, 24, 76, 97, 98, 102, 104, 110, 163, 172, 179, 182, 187–91, 195, 208, 209, 235, 238, 239
Vade mecum in tribulatione 164, 182, 188–91, 209, 220, 239
Liber secretorum eventum 188, 239
Judas 142, 145, 228
Julian of Norwich 218, 225

Kempe, Margery 220, 223

Langland, William: allegorical style 57–58, 60–61, 63–64, 84, 92–96, 109, 129–131, 149, 201; apocalyptic program 22, 45–48, 50–56, 154, 161, 172, 174, 183, 192, 198–200; question of autobiographical reference 1, 64–66, 69–73, 116–29, 140, 141, 142, 144–49, 194, 217, 218–19, 225, 227, 228, 230; as visionary 1, 12, 13, 28, 57; *see also Piers Plowman*; visionaries, self-image of
Last Age of the Church, The 184–86, 207, 232, 235, 236
"Last World Emperor" 10, 55, 178–82, 187–90, 194, 206, 208, 215, 236, 238, 241
Lavenham, Richard, Carmelite theologian 104
leadership, crisis of 5, 9, 16, 102, 192, 193, 194; new leadership 162, 164, 165–72, 178, 194–96, 215–16, 234; secular leadership 16, 21, 24, 178–82, 194, 234, 237; *see also*

"viri spirituales"; *papa angelicus*; pseudo-prophets; "Last World Emperor"
Lefèvre d'Etaples, Jacques, sixteenth-century editor of visionary writings 76, 101, 219–20
Lollards 105, 229, 232; *see also* Wyclif, John; Wycliffite writings
Lull, Ramon 77, 220

Macrobius, commentary on the *Somnium Scipionis* 121
manual labor 143, 145, 150, 153
Marsilius of Padua 175, 179, 235
Mechthild of Hackenborn 220
Mechthild of Magdeburg 77, 129–31, 220, 226
mendicancy, *see* begging, issue of
Merlin 24, 178, 184, 204, 208, 239, 240
Merton College, Oxford, medieval library of 238
millenarianism 3, 15, 31, 33, 48, 188, 191, 205
Milton, John 102
Moses 45, 56, 168, 170, 215, 234
Muratori Fragment 85, 95

Nicholas III, Pope 146
Nicholas IV, Pope 237
Omnis utriusque sexus 230
Nicholas of Lyra 124

Ockham, William 175, 236
Olivi, Peter John 174, 189, 235, 240
"Oracles of Leo the Wise," The 179, 237
Origen 85, 215
Otto of Freising 230

papa angelicus (angelic pope) 54, 98, 170, 177–80, 190, 194, 215, 216, 234, 236–37, 239, 240
papal schism, in prophetic thought 180, 211, 212
Paris, Matthew 137, 210, 230
Pateshull, Peter, anti-mendicant propagandist 157
Paul, St. 141, 143, 170, 186; *see also* references to the Epistles of Paul in the Index of biblical citations, below
Paul the Hermit, St. 20
Pearl poet 64, 77, 86, 120
Pecham, John 229, 230
"perfection," medieval concept of 19, 20, 21, 31, 33, 60, 133, 139, 152, 162, 195, 196, 197, 208, 222, 226, 228
Peter, St. 98, 99, 156, 169–70, 173, 178, 180, 235; "ship of Peter" 171, 177, 192
Peter of Langtoft, chronicler 210
Pierce the Ploughman's Crede 12, 156
Piers Plowman 1, 204; and anti-mendicantism 11, 12, 134–61, 226–31; apocalypticism in

252

General index

vagatio 32, 147, 166, 170, 193–94, 202, 187, 212, 228, 240; *see also* beggars; anti-mendicantism; Langland, William, question of autobiographical reference
Vaticinia de summis pontificibus 24, 164, 179–80, 184, 197, 236–37
"Ve mundo in centum annis" 182–83, 238, 239
Vincent of Beauvais 8–9, 24, 30, 173, 215, 235
Vincent Ferrer, St. 98
"viri spirituales" 134, 136, 138, 172, 196–97, 234, 236; *see also* leadership, crisis of, new leadership visionaries 19; role of 1, 3, 57, 75, 79–83, 202; self-image of 1, 12, 64–75, 85–91, 217, 221–22, 225; *vis imaginativa*, role of 112–15, 121–23; *see also* Joachim of Fiore
Visio Wettini 220; *see also* poverty; "perfection," medieval concept of
visionary literature 12, 16, 22, 77–78, 112–32, 217, 220; conventions of 2, 12, 22, 27, 28, 57–64, 69, 78, 79, 99, 101, 102, 202, 208, 213, 223, 225; in *Piers Plowman* 12, 16, 22, 91–94, 115–32, 198 (*see also* clerical chastisement; clerical reform); style in 29, 32, 35, 56–64, 77, 220; allegory in 56–64, 79–81, 83–84, 85, 92–95, 98–99, 101, 107, 116, 129–31, 149; *see also* Langland, William, allegorical style

visionary reformist writers 22, 26, 27, 66, 77–78, 97, 219
vita apostolica 2, 16, 19, 20, 34, 41, 73, 99, 135, 139, 140–49, 150, 162, 189, 191, 198–99

Wadding, Luke, chronicler 210
Waldensians 175
Walter of Coventry, chronicler 210
wandering, *see vagatio*
William of St. Amour 22, 24, *135–49, 153–61, 209, 214, 227–31*; apocalyptic program *137, 153–56*; influence of *135, 156*
De periculis 227–31
De Pharisaeo at Publicano 227
Wimbledon, Thomas 17, 230, 232, 238
Winner and Waster 208
Wyclif, John 15, 100, 175, 176, 183, 184, 185, 186, 229, 230, 232, 236, 237, 238, 239
De vaticinia seu prophetia 232
De civili dominio 236
De ecclesia 236
Trialogus 238
Wycliffite writings 54, 163, 185, 229, 230

York, Austin Friary, medieval library catalogue of 24, 209

Zacchaeus 142
Zorobabel 234

Index of biblical citations

Biblical citations, unless otherwise indicated, refer to the Vulgate version, *Biblia sacra, Vulgatae editionis* (London, n.d.). Translated biblical quotations, unless otherwise indicated, are from *The Holy Bible: Douay Version* (London, 1956).

Index of manuscripts

Berlin, Preussische Staatsbibliothek MS Lat.
  qu. 674, *217*
Cambridge
  Corpus Christi College MS 107, *209*; MS
    138, *209*; MS 288, *209*, *210*; MS 321, *235*;
    MS 404, *25*, *209*, *210*, *237*, *238*
  Gonville and Caius College MS 249, *223*,
    236; MS 388/608, *238*
  Magdalene College MS Pepys 2125, *220*
  St. John's College MS 27, *209*
  Trinity College Library MS 366, *209*; MS
    740, *209*
  University Library MS Dd. xi. 78, *209*; MS
    Gg. iv. 25, *236*; MS Ii. vi. 11, *209*
Dublin, Trinity College MS 347, *210*, *240*; MS
    514, *210*; MS 516, *209*, *210*, *231*; MS 517,
    209, *210*, *231*
Exeter, Chapter Library MS 3625, *209*, *231*
Hereford, Cathedral MS P. 5. XII, *236*
London
  British Library
    MS Add. 11439, *232*
    MS Add. 15418, *208*
    MS Add. 24663, *239*
    MS Arundel 337, *208*
    MS Claudius B I, *110*
    MS Cotton Cleopatra C X, *237*
    MS Cotton Domitian IX, *209*
    MS Cotton Tiberius B V, *236*
    MS Cotton Vitellius D III, *208*
    MS Harley 1725, *208*

    MS Royal 8. C. VII, *208*
    MS Royal 8. F. XVI, *232*, *236*
    MS Sloane 156, *236*
  Lambeth Palace Library
    MS 51, *217*; MS 357, *209*, *231*
  Lincoln's Inn Hall MS 73, *209*
New Haven, Yale University MS Marston 225,
    208
Oxford
  Balliol College MS 149, *229*
  Bodleian Library
    MS Arch. Selden B. 8 (S. C. 3338), *210*
    MS Ashmole 788, *220*
    MS Bodley 158 (S. C. 1997), *209*, *210*, *231*
    MS Bodley 233 (S. C. 2188), *210*
    MS Bodley 397 (S. C. 2228), *210*
    MS Bodley 623 (S. C. 2157), *209*
    MS Digby 98, *209*, *210*
    MS Digby 113, *229*
    MS Digby 196, *239*
    MS Douce 88 (S. C. 21662), *24*, *209*, *240*
    MS Hatton 56 (S. C. 4062), *209*, *210*
    MS Lat. Misc. C. 75 (previously MS
      Phillips 3119), *210*, *229*, *231*, *238*
  Merton College MS L. 2. 9, *208–09*
  New College MS 49, *235*
Paris, Bibliothèque Nationale MS Lat. 3183,
    229; MS 3222, *212*
Wiesbaden, Landesbibliothek Hs. 2 (Riesen
    Codex), *212*, *213*